THE RIGHTEOUS
GENTILES
OF THE
HOLOCAUST

THE RIGHTEOUS
GENTILES
OF THE
HOLOCAUST

A Christian Interpretation

David P. Gushee

FORTRESS PRESS   Minneapolis

THE RIGHTEOUS GENTILES OF THE HOLOCAUST

Portions of chapter 5 are based on the author's previously published article "Many Paths to Righteousness: An Assessment of Research on Why Righteous Gentiles Helped Jews" in *Holocaust and Genocide Studies*, fall 1993. Reprinted by permission of the publisher: Oxford University Press, 200 Madison Avenue, New York, NY 10016.

Chapter 6 contains much of the information summarized in the author's article "A Certain Kind of Faith: Christian Rescuers of Jews during the Holocaust" in *The Holocaust: The Uses and Abuses of Knowledge*, Marcia Littell, editor, Lewiston, N.Y.: Edwin Mellen Press, 1994.

Scripture passages from the Holy Bible, New International Version, are copyright © 1973, 1978, 1984 by the International Bible Society. Used by permission of Zondervan Bible Publishers.

Cover design: Cheryl Watson/Graphiculture

Cover photo: Close-up of Dieuwke Hofstede, who, with her husband, Philip, hid Henny Kalkstein and another Jewish girl during the Holocaust. The photograph is reprinted courtesy of the United States Holocaust Memorial Museum and the Hidden Children Foundation/ADL.

Library of Congress Cataloging-in-Publication Data

Gushee, David P., 1962-
    The righteous Gentiles of the Holocaust : a Christian interpretation / by David P. Gushee.
      p.   cm.
    Includes bibliographical references.
    ISBN 0-8006-2902-7 (alk. paper) : ISBN 0-8006-2838-1 (pbk.) :
    1. Holocaust (Christian theology) 2. Righteous Gentiles in the Holocaust. 3. Christian ethics—History—20th century.
4. Christianity and other religions—Judaism. 5. Judaism—Relations—Christianity. I. Title.
    BT93.G87 1994
    231.7'6—dc20
                               94-29881
                                     CIP

The paper used in this publication meets the minimum requirements of American National Standard for Information Sciences—Permanence of Paper for Printed Library Materials, ANSI Z329.48-1984. ∞™

Manufactured in the U.S.A.

98   97   96   95   94   1   2   3   4   5   6   7   8   9   10

*To my wife, Jeanie, and my children, Holly, David, and Marie—
and in memory of all the Jewish men, women, and children
who died at the hands of unrighteous Gentiles*

On July 18, 1994, after this book had been completed,
but before it was printed, Jeanie and I experienced
the stillbirth of our fourth child.

In memory of Elizabeth Mary Gushee,
safe in the arms of God.

Contents

Preface   xi

1. **Christian Ethics and the Righteous Gentiles**
   Dimensions of a Needed Encounter   1

2. **The Holocaust**
   The Destruction of European Jewry   19

3. **European Gentiles**
   In the Moral Crucible   45

4. **The Righteous Gentiles**
   Partners in Resistance   69

5. **Many Paths to Righteousness**
   Why Rescuers Helped Jews   91

6. **Compelled by Faith**
   Religious Motivations for Rescue   117

7. **The Quest for Righteousness**
   Implications of the Righteous Gentiles
   for the Church   149

Notes   177

Bibliography   229

Index of Biblical References   249

Index of Modern Authors   251

Index of Rescuers   257

Preface

This project was born at approximately 11:30 A.M. on March 5, 1990. I was in Nashville to present a paper at the annual meeting of the Scholars' Conference on the Holocaust and the Churches. At 11:30, Lawrence Baron, professor of history at San Diego State University, offered a discussion of Europeans who had rescued Jews during the Holocaust. He called his paper "The Moral Minority: Psycho-Social Research on the Righteous Gentiles." I was enthralled by his description of these people, many of them associated with a Christian church and some of them quite devout, who had risked their lives to save Jews while Hitler and his minions were annihilating European Jewry. His presentation offered a bewildering and exciting new angle of vision on a historical catastrophe that had haunted me for a number of years. Indeed, I attended the conference in order to present a paper on Christian responsibility for the Holocaust and the ways in which our theology needed to be reconsidered because of its role in contributing to that disaster.

Toward the end of his talk, Baron raised a question that affected me deeply. He said, as I remember it (with apologies to Lawrence Baron if I've got it wrong), "Where are the Christian scholars in the study of the Righteous Gentiles? You would think they would want to study their own heroes, at least. But perhaps their few heroes remind them too much of their many nonheroes." At that moment, my project on the Righteous Gentiles of the Holocaust was born. For four years I have been responding to that call.

There are both appropriate and inappropriate reasons for Christian silence about the rescuers. Much of the inappropriate silence simply reflects the complacent nonresponse to the Holocaust that characterizes too large a portion of the Christian church. In my experience of North American church life—in particular, its more conservative regions—the Holocaust has very little place in Christian reflection and has had little or no effect on the shape of Christian theology, worship, biblical interpretation, or moral instruction and practice. Christian faith and life go on almost as if this catastrophe of both Jewish and Christian history had never occurred. To shatter this indefensible silence is one of the purposes of this study.

The far more appropriate reason for Christian silence about the Righteous Gentiles has been the need for Christians to confess and confront their guilt for the Holocaust rather than to celebrate their handful of heroes. Some Christians are silent about the rescuers not because they do not care about the Holocaust but precisely because they understand just how deep Christian guilt for the Holocaust runs. Eva Fleischner, one of the few Christians who has undertaken Righteous Gentile research, has written: "It has always seemed fitting to me that this remembering [of the rescuers] be done by Jews rather than Christians. We Christians have so much to account for vis-à-vis Judaism that is not good, not heroic. . . . It is not for us, I had always felt, to speak of the light."[1] But Fleischner, a veteran of Holocaust studies, has proceeded with her work on the rescuers because Jewish researchers have asked her to help them understand why Christian rescuers acted as they did. I think that Lawrence Baron was issuing the same kind of invitation to Christian scholars at the Holocaust conference. The Christian's temptation in a study of the rescuers is to slip into a misguided triumphalism about Christian goodness—as if swarms of Christian rescuers could be found all over Europe, or as if the rescuers' deeds somehow exonerate Christianity. Neither is true. This danger is one reason why only Christians who are well aware of Christian wrongdoing during the Holocaust should attempt to address this subject. This is the path I have taken to arrive at a study of the Righteous Gentiles of the Holocaust. I have sought earnestly to avoid Christian triumphalism and self-congratulation here. My readers will know whether I have succeeded.

Those who write about any aspect of the Holocaust face an extremely difficult task. I agree with Irving Greenberg, who wrote: "No statement, theological or otherwise, should be made that would not be credible in the presence of burning children."[2] But how does one write in the company of those flames, of those screams? An attempt to communicate something of the pathos of the Holocaust easily turns to bathos. Likewise, an attempt to write "objective history" easily slides into a dispassion about Jewish suffering and death that risks objectifying the Holocaust's victims for a second time. It may well be that other forms of communication, such as poetry, the novel, painting, and sculpture are better suited to the subject than is historical or analytical writing. Over time I have grown more and more daunted by the difficulty, perhaps the impossibility, of writing adequately about this terrible human tragedy.

The best that I can do is to try to treat Jewish suffering in the Holocaust with the respect it demands. This has meant writing with passion and a minimum of academic jargon, with a clear, blunt style that reaches not for pedantic impressiveness but for straightforward moral conviction and integrity. My goal in writing about the Holocaust is not to impress the reader with subtlety and cleverness, but instead to challenge her or him—you, in fact—to moral change through encounter with these events. In particular, I write as a Christian ethicist and minister to fellow Christians. I write to help us learn from both the worst and the best in our history. It is my hope and prayer that this encounter with both the unrighteous and the Righteous Gentiles of the Holocaust will help Christians conduct themselves better today and in the future than most of our forebears did during that terrible European tragedy.

❖

Many people contributed to the writing of this book. Over these four years I have learned that major writing projects are not the result of any one individual's work but instead require the help and support of numerous people—to whom I am most grateful. My thanks go to the doctoral dissertation committee that originally supervised the development of this work: Larry Rasmussen and Beverly Harrison, Christian ethicists who teach at Union Theological Seminary, New York; Ruth Zerner, a historian at Herbert Lehman College in the Bronx; and Rabbi Irving Greenberg, president of the National Jewish Center for Learning and Leadership. I am deeply in their debt for their conversation, ideas, and support, and for the push toward excellence. (Of course, these conversation partners and all others whose names appear here are not responsible for any errors or limits that this work may possess.)

I also thank other members of the Holocaust studies community for the same good gifts. Franklin and Marcie Littell, leading lights in the annual Scholars' Conference on the Holocaust, talked with me about my work several times, while graciously initiating me into this rich interfaith and international scholarly community. Eva Fogelman, Stanlee Stahl, and Diana Stein of the Jewish Foundation for Christian Rescuers/ADL offered invaluable help and fresh information, as did Mordecai Paldiel, director of the Department for the Righteous at Yad Vashem, Israel's Holocaust memorial and research center. I also very much appreciated the kindness of the organizers of the 1991 Hidden Child Conference in New York, who allowed me to witness that extraordinary event—and the openness of the survivors of the Holocaust, at that event and others, who were willing to speak with me about their terrible experiences. Though this project offers a survey and interpretation of the Righteous Gentile phenomenon rather than new primary research on rescuers or survivors, the study has been deeply enriched by the conversations that have happened along the way.

Lynn Rothstein, an administrator at Union Theological Seminary, provided valuable research leads for the social psychological materials considered in chapter 5. I also would like to express my appreciation to Stockton State University in Pomona, New Jersey, for granting me access to their collection of oral testimonies of Holocaust survivors. As well, I would like to thank the library staffs of Duke Divinity School, Union Theological Seminary, Columbia University, and Gratz College (Philadelphia) for their cooperation and help—and Rich Mattis of the Whole Works Bookshop at Eastern Baptist Theological Seminary, who helped me keep up with the flood of new books relevant to this study. Thanks also go to that seminary's students, and now my students at Southern Baptist Theological Seminary, who have heard more about the Righteous Gentiles in my Christian ethics classes than they probably wanted to hear. I feel a special gratitude to my former coworkers at Evangelicals for Social Action, who shared my life and struggles throughout the arduous dissertation-writing years and provided crucial community and support.

Nevlynn Johnson, one of my students at Southern Seminary, compiled the indexes. I appreciate his work on this arduous task.

I offer my thanks to Marshall Johnson, Julie Odland, and their colleagues at Fortress Press for a first-class job every step of the way. It is not every author who is so satisfied with his or her publisher.

I especially would like to thank Dr. and Mrs. W. Vance Grant, Jr., my in-laws, who provided financial assistance during the long years of graduate study and dissertation writing. Thanks also go to Mrs. Grant for her careful and skilled reading of the entire manuscript and many valuable suggestions, as well as her words of support. I thank my children, Holly, David, and Marie, for their patience with their busy and sometimes distracted daddy, and for their invaluable help in keeping me normal and balanced while dealing with a most painful subject. Finally and above all, I thank my wife and life-partner, Jeanie, whose love, support, and patience were so crucial to the successful completion of this project.

1

Christian Ethics and the Righteous Gentiles

❖

Dimensions of a Needed Encounter

Prologue: A Day in Nesvizh

The Jews of Nesvizh, a small town under German control in what had been eastern Poland,[1] were scheduled to be destroyed on July 21, 1942. On July 17, leaders of the Nesvizh Jewish community learned that numerous Jews had been massacred in Horodzei, only eight miles away. Sensing that they were next, and remembering the terrible day in October 1941 when the great majority of their community had been murdered, the Jews of Nesvizh made plans to offer armed resistance when the German forces arrived.

On the morning of July 21, an *Einsatzgruppe* (mobile killing squad unit) appeared at the gate of the Nesvizh Jewish ghetto. As was customary, the German commander told the head of the Jewish community to arrange an immediate "selection." All but a small number of skilled artisans would be taken from the village; the people knew that those taken would face immediate execution. Prepared to fight rather than die quietly, the Jews standing at the gate announced their refusal to comply with the German order. According to Shalom Cholawski, the Nesvizh Jew who led the armed resistance that day:

> The Germans opened fire. The fighting unit in the synagogue responded with a surprise volley of machine-gun fire. The Germans crashed through the ghetto gate. The Jews drew their knives and irons. They reached for their pile of stones. . . . The Germans increased their firing. A battle began between Jews with steel weapons and Germans and police with guns.[2]

Soon the dead and dying filled the streets. As previously planned, Jews set fire to their homes to provide cover for any who might be able to flee. The inferno spread rapidly toward the center of town as the Nesvizh ghetto exploded in chaos.

Neighbors arrived on the scene. "A horde of local peasants . . . swarmed into the ghetto, plundering before all was devoured by fire. The madness of their pillaging and the fury of the Germans to kill matched the frenzy of every Jew, man, woman, child, to flee from the burning ghetto."

Cholawski and two other resistance fighters waited in an attic for a chance to escape from the ghetto. From there "we could see crowds of non-Jews with arms full of clothes and goods, wildly jumping and jeering whenever a Jew was shot." Finally, Cholawski and his friends seized an opening, racing through the alleys of the ghetto and then out into the grain fields, in search of refuge in the forest just beyond. Escape from the ghetto did not guarantee safety for the Nesvizh Jews, however:

> Once outside, some were beaten by zealous peasants. Others were killed in flight. Small groups succeeded in reaching the forest. I saw Simcha Rozen carrying his small son wrapped in a pillow. As Simcha ran, he passed the bundle to a Christian woman standing near the gate and then continued running towards the woods.[3]

A Century of Mass Murder

Ours has been a century drenched in an unprecedented tide of human blood. People have always killed each other, and war, unfortunately, is no stranger. But, as Michael Marrus has written, "The twentieth century has seen a quantum leap in the numbers of people who fell victim to such man-made catastrophes as war and revolution, numbing those who assemble previously unheard-of statistics of the dead."[4] This century's roll call of mass death begins with World War I, which cost between ten and fifteen million lives in five years.[5] Perhaps one-third of the dead were civilians, including the nearly one million Armenians who lost their lives at the hands of the Turkish government between 1915 and 1917, in the first genocide of the twentieth century.[6]

"The war to end all wars" turned out to be the first rather than the last mass killing of our age. To the east was the Soviet regime, born in terror and murder, while the subsequent periods of annihilation flowed together in a great ocean of blood and tears. The Russian Civil War (1918–1922) consumed over a million lives.[7] Almost fifteen million people died as a result of Stalin's campaign against the Russian and Ukrainian peasantry, which culminated in the 1932–1933 terror-famine.[8] In sheer numbers, this constitutes the worst mass killing of the twentieth century. At least three million (and perhaps far more) Soviet citizens were executed or died in prison camps during the Great Terror of 1936 to 1938.[9]

In this study I will focus on events that occurred during the next great cataclysm, World War II (1939–1945), in which between fifty and fifty-five million people died.[10] The dead included twenty million Soviets, fifteen million Chinese, five million Germans, between two and three million non-Jewish Poles, nearly one million Gypsies, and as we will see, approximately six million European Jews—one-third of the estimated eighteen million civilian victims of the war.[11] The mass killing did not end in 1945, despite the horrific flash of atomic bombs over Hiroshima and Nagasaki. Two years later, approximately 800,000 people died after the partition of the Indian subcontinent, and between two and three million Bengalis perished in the same region when Bangladesh seceded in 1971. Between 1967 and 1970 some two million people died in Nigeria during the Biafra war, and at least one million were massacred by Pol Pot's Khmer Rouge regime in Cambodia during its genocidal campaign in the 1970s. To date, our century has produced thirteen wars that each have taken over one million lives, at least forty wars that have cost 100,000 or more lives, and over 100,000,000 wartime and genocide fatalities altogether.[12]

The threat of mass death is still very much with us. Until recently, the world lived under the fear that a climactic Soviet-American nuclear war would leave billions dead and the planet itself unable to sustain life. Thankfully, the political conflict that spawned those fears finally has eased. It should not be forgotten, however, that tens of thousands of nuclear weapons remain in existence, and more and more states continue to try to join the nuclear club. The demise of the Soviet Union and the end of the Cold War have sparked great hope. Yet even these welcome developments may offer a reprieve rather than an acquittal. Throughout human history we have proven ourselves morally capable of murdering as many people as our technology enables us to kill. Technology now enables us to obliterate human existence and destroy the ecosystem upon which all life depends. The future can no longer responsibly be assumed; instead it must be chosen, day after day.[13] Our ability to "choose life, so that [we] and [our] children might live" (Deut. 30:19) remains in doubt. Learning how to choose life—despite having the capacity to choose not only death but mass death—is the profound moral challenge facing humanity at the end of our century of mass murder.

The Holocaust

In the Western world, the genocidal assault on the Jews of Europe during World War II looms starkly as the central paradigmatic event of our century of mass death. The story remains unthinkable, no matter how many times it is told—that on the basis of an extraordinarily hate-filled anti-Semitic ideology, the National Socialist regime of Germany beginning in 1941 planned and executed a program in which it murdered nearly every Jewish man, woman, and child it could find for the duration of the war.[14] The horrible frenzy of violence that followed across the continent of Europe was organized under the pretense of legality by a vast network of skillful government bureaucracies, implemented with the most modern technology available, carried out by thousands of Germans assisted by numerous non-Germans, and witnessed in relative silence by most other Europeans and by the rest of the world.

The Nazis were extraordinarily committed to their task and achieved considerable "success." Approximately six million Jews were murdered in one way or another—amounting to two out of every three Jews in Europe and one out of every three Jews in the world. The killers took the lives of an estimated 1.25 million Jewish children who, as the future of the Jewish people, were considered especially important to annihilate. Nazi crimes permanently altered the landscape of Jewish existence, not only destroying what had been the historic center of Jewish culture but also forcing those Jews who survived to rethink their history, their politics, their faith, and their future, all while grieving enormous losses. Despite (or in tandem with) its unique elements and its particularity vis-à-vis the Jewish people, the murder of the Jews has come to symbolize more broadly the blood-stained course of this century, the perilous nature of the human condition in our time, the human capacity for evil, and the "choosing death" which may be our destiny if we do not change course. This historic catastrophe is now called "the Holocaust."[15]

The Bystanders and the Boundaries of Moral Obligation

Holocaust researchers have settled on three main categories with which to label the participants in this horrific tragedy: perpetrators, victims, and bystanders.[16] Enormous attention rightly has been paid both to the German perpetrators and their Jewish victims. Others on the scene have received somewhat less notice. Yet the deaths of six million and the survival of one million Jews in Nazi Europe cannot be understood without reference to the conduct of a host of those who "stood nearby"—and, though there were other bystanders,[17] clearly the most important ones were the local European non-Jews.

The success of the "Final Solution to the Jewish Question" depended to an important degree on the cooperation, or at least the passivity, of the non-Jewish populations under Nazi rule.[18] That regime's Promethean endeavor required the definition, identification, expropriation, and concentration of every one of the approximately seven million Jews who by 1941 lived with and among the 300,000,000 non-Jews under German domination. Nazi officials needed local cooperation in these essential preliminary stages of the Final Solution. Moreover, the Nazis required a European population that on the whole would not offer significant resistance to the harsh measures taken against the Jews once they had been plucked out from among them. Because the Nazis were busy fighting a global war and administering nearly the whole of Europe, they did not commit large numbers of people to their annihilation machinery. They needed both locals to supplement their personnel and the noninterference of the European masses, who vastly outnumbered both their forces and the Jewish victims.[19]

To win this cooperation and passivity, the Nazis threatened death to those who helped Jews and offered rewards to those who harmed them. This "carrot and stick" approach, however, was only one dimension of a comprehensive, ideologically rooted attack on the various ties that had linked Jews with their Gentile neighbors. Nazi officials, beginning in Germany itself in the 1930s, sought to destroy the complex web of relationships that existed between Jews and Gentiles—as friends, schoolmates, colleagues, neighbors, fellow citizens, and, most fundamentally, fellow human beings—and used the full power of the state to accomplish this goal. They wanted Europeans not to protest the working out of an ideology antithetical to the best of their religious, moral, and political heritage—an ideology in which the very idea of the unity and equality of the human race was completely effaced.[20] Instead, they wanted non-Jews to believe that they were vastly superior to Jews in worth and dignity. They wanted non-Jews to view Jews as subhuman bacilli, as worthless and dangerous parasites whose destruction would be no loss but instead an "ethnic cleansing" of the European body politic from infection. At the least, they wanted non-Jews not to stand in the way of their conquerors as they acted against Jews on the basis of this palpably hateful ideology.

Most Nazis did not lack a code of honor or the ability to treat some people with care and solicitude. In that code of honor, however, such humane conduct was restricted to fellow members of the "master race." All others, especially Jews, were considered subhuman creatures whom one might rob, humiliate, and murder without scruple. Numerous students of the Holocaust and of human behavior generally have noted this unfortunate tendency to establish "boundaries of moral obligation."[21] Daily, people act with care and compassion on behalf of their mates, children, dear friends, and other loved ones, even at great risk or sacrifice to themselves. Most people consider themselves morally obliged to extend care within this circle of people. Usually, however, they place many other human beings, such as strangers, enemies, and members of different ethnic and national groups, outside that circle of concern. They see these "others" as less important or as completely beyond the realm of moral obligation. The Nazis epitomized the devastating consequences of this tendency at its worst. Those outside the boundaries ultimately were seen not merely as less important but as unworthy of life. The Nazis asked Europeans to excise Jews from the ranks of those worthy of their human care and concern— to construe the boundaries of their moral obligation in a way that excluded Jews.

At the same time, Jews pleaded for inclusion within those sacred boundaries. Under siege, they called on precisely those ties that previously had bound them to Gentiles. Especially once the killing began in earnest, at least occasional help from Gentiles was usually indispensable for Jewish survival.[22] Thus, many (but not all) Jews begged their one-time friends, neighbors, colleagues, and schoolmates for help. They asked their fellow Danes, Poles, Rumanians, and Bulgarians to defend them as fellow citizens. They appealed to precisely those ties of fellow-humanity that in the best of Western thought—Jewish, Christian, and secular—link every human being with every other one.[23] They called on the human kindness, compassion, and moral decency of both Gentile friends and strangers. They asked for help in streets and woods, in offices and government buildings; they banged on the doors of homes and churches. They asked their neighbors to help them live.

On a day-to-day basis, then, the Holocaust was a triangular affair involving German perpetrators, their intended Jewish victims, and local non-Jewish bystanders. These bystanders, most of them self-identified Christians,[24] were forced by the situation and by the other participants to decide how to relate to both perpetrators and victims during the life-and-death struggle that was the Holocaust. They had to make this fundamental decision while facing the grim and often all-consuming struggles that afflicted every European during the war. It was an intense moral crucible, a testing of European civilization and of the principles, character, courage, and conduct of millions of individuals. It was a trial by fire.

A stark continuum of choices offered itself to these bystanders, as it does to all bystanders to harmdoing. They could *add harm*, helping the killers destroy those considered unworthy of life. They could *prevent harm*, helping the designated victims resist destruction. Or they could *do nothing*, remaining "neutral." How did the European Gentiles fare? By all accounts, most chose to do nothing. Unfortunately, when power is unequal, doing nothing aids the more powerful; thus neutrality eased the task of the Nazi murderers.[25] There was no such thing as harmless noninvolvement. A fairly small but dangerous minority (not so small in some places) seized the opportunity to help the killers destroy the hated Jews. These bystanders-turned-perpetrators contributed significantly to Jewish suffering and the ultimate death toll.[26] Finally, a different small minority stood in solidarity with the Jews and refused to allow them to be treated as outside the boundaries of moral obligation. Resisting the "Final Solution," these bystanders-turned-rescuers helped Jews survive the Holocaust. This latter group is the focus of my study.

Perpetrators, victims, and bystanders all appear in Shalom Cholawski's remarkable account of that July 1942 day in Nesvizh. The perpetrators are represented by the dreaded *Einsatzgruppen,* the mobile killing squads that shot to death an estimated one and a half million Polish, Baltic, and western Soviet Jews during the German invasion and occupation of the Soviet Union, beginning in June 1941. Those struggling-not-to-be-victims are there as the residents of the Nesvizh Jewish ghetto—planning, praying, defying, fighting, dying, and fleeing death. The bystanders are present as well and participating in the scene. They appear as the non-Jewish onlookers who "jump and jeer" when a Jew is shot; as looters who swoop down on the Nesvizh ghetto to plunder Jewish homes; as peasants who "zealously" beat Jews as they flee into the forest; and as a "Christian woman" handed a Jewish baby . . .

What did the "Christian woman" do with Simcha Rozen's baby? Our narrator does not report her actions, for he flees without knowing the boy's fate. Did she have a chance to hide him—and would she have considered him worth trying to save? Did she choose to remain uninvolved, leaving him on the ground and to his fate, there on the outskirts of Nesvizh? Or did she, perhaps, laughingly hand him to a German soldier and watch him grab the "subhuman Jew-vermin" baby by the legs and smash his head against a wall? (This was a technique commonly employed by German soldiers when executing "dangerous Jewish racial criminals" of that age.) We will never know what she did. But we do know that Simcha Rozen's baby boy likely did not survive that day in Nesvizh. He certainly did not survive it unless the anonymous "Christian woman" took some action to help him. Her dilemma is representative of the situation faced by millions of Europeans during the Holocaust. The "Christian woman" stands frozen in narrative time, mute. We can know something of the choices she faced; we cannot know the outcome.

The Righteous Gentiles of the Holocaust

The Holocaust, like the other mass killings of our century, primarily consisted of a series of acts of violence, deprivation, sadism, and murder. The

Jewish community's corporate response to the Holocaust, emerging over the past fifty years, fully reflects the horrific nature of the events. However, with growing intensity in recent years, space has been made in Jewish reflection on the Holocaust for a glimpse of the better side of human conduct. This has occurred through recognition of those non-Jews who were neither perpetrators nor passive bystanders but instead risked their lives to save Jews. These rescuers are known in Jewish life today as the "Righteous Gentiles of the Holocaust" and "Christian rescuers." Most Jews consider them heroes.

In 1953, Israel established Yad Vashem, "The Holocaust Martyrs' and Heroes' Remembrance Authority." Yad Vashem was founded in order to provide an appropriate "place and name" (the translation of the Hebrew terms *Yad Vashem*) for the victims of the Holocaust and to serve as a central location for ongoing research on the European catastrophe. Remarkably, given the extent of Jewish victimization at the hands of non-Jews and the nearness of the catastrophe at that time, the law establishing Yad Vashem mandated remembrance of that tiny minority of "high-minded righteous who risked their lives to save Jews." Reaching deep into Jewish tradition, Yad Vashem designated them by the Hebrew term *hasidei ummot ha-olam*. The phrase means "the righteous ones among the nations of the world," commonly shortened to "Righteous Gentiles" of the Holocaust.[27]

Undoubtedly the most attractive feature of Yad Vashem is the collection of several thousand evergreen carob trees that lines the short stretch of road one walks to reach the main Holocaust memorial hall in the Jerusalem hills. This area is known as the "Garden of the Righteous." Each tree in the garden is planted in recognition of a Gentile who helped Jews survive the Holocaust; whenever possible the planting has been done by the rescuer himself or herself. A plaque with the name of the honored rescuer is placed at the base of each tree. Israel takes recognition and verification of rescuers quite seriously. Holocaust survivors generally begin the procedure by submitting the names of those who helped them during the war. A distinguished committee of Israelis, mainly made up of Holocaust survivors and always headed by a supreme court judge, reviews all such nominations for Righteous Gentile status. The committee examines as much evidence as can be amassed—primarily interviews with the survivors, but including evidence offered in testimonies before Israeli consulates in Europe and materials in foreign historical institutions if necessary and relevant. Essentially, Gentiles qualify as *hasidei ummot ha-olam* if their deeds can be verified, if they aided Jews without imposing monetary compensation as a condition of rescue, and if they knowingly risked their lives.[28]

For thirty years those named Righteous Gentiles have been flown to Jerusalem for a glorious tree-planting ceremony in their honor. (Today, because the Garden of the Righteous is completely full of trees, the plaques are placed on a wall in the memorial building.)[29] Rescuers also receive a medallion, inscribed with the name of the recipient and an inscription in Hebrew and French that reads: "In gratitude from the Jewish people. Whosoever saves a single life, saves the entire universe."[30] Yad Vashem's "Department for the Righteous Among the Nations" manages rescuer research and commemoration. By now, according to Mordecai Paldiel, director of the department, eleven thousand Gentiles have been verified as rescuers, while evidence on other candidates continues to be submitted. The exact number of rescuers will never be known; estimates range from 50,000 to 500,000.[31] Paldiel, perhaps the person in the best position to know, now suggests that 100,000 is a conservative estimate of the number of Gentiles who aided Jews during the Holocaust, and that there may have been as many as 250,000. He believes that these Righteous Gentiles helped to save up to 250,000 Jewish lives.[32]

In the U.S. Jewish community, celebration and study of the Righteous Gentiles has accelerated dramatically in the past decade. A September 1984 conference sponsored by the U.S. Holocaust Memorial Council, called "Faith in Humankind: Rescuers of Jews During the Holocaust," brought together rescuers, survivors, and a number of scholars and theologians to discuss the rescuers.[33] In 1987, California rabbi Harold Schulweis, who has been a tireless advocate of rescuer recognition since 1962,[34] established what is now called the Jewish Foundation for Christian Rescuers (JFCR/ADL). The group seeks to honor the rescuers by supporting aggressive research into the identification of more Righteous Gentiles, offering financial assistance to those who are needy, and sponsoring rescuer-related educational events and materials. Now a project of the Anti-Defamation League, the Foundation directly aids over 1,200 aging rescuers in twenty-four countries on an annual aid budget of $575,000.[35] Rescuer conferences now occur nearly every year, sponsored by the JFCR/ADL and other groups. An emotional May 1991 conference in New York, bringing together Jewish children hidden during World War II and some of their rescuers, provided a major opportunity for the Righteous to be honored. This extraordinary event received considerable media attention.

Reflection on the rescuers now constitutes a growing part of the Holocaust literature. Hundreds of rescue stories have been compiled in various newspaper articles, magazines, journals, books, films, oral archives, and so on. New stories seem to appear as frequently as the daily newspaper. A small but significant body of social scientific research on the Righteous Gentiles also has developed, almost all of it done by Jewish social psychologists, sociologists, and historians. This research has begun to produce theories concerning patterns of socialization, personality, motivation, and beliefs among those who aided Jews, which I will explore in chapter 5. The practical and moral purpose of this work is often explicit. These scholars seek to "help the few become the many"—to expand the pool of compassionate and courageous people who will include the stranger and the victim within the boundaries of moral obligation.[36]

Not every Jewish person applauds the heightened attention given to the rescuers today. Some think it inappropriate to focus on goodness when evil so profoundly prevailed. As Mordecai Paldiel has said, "One may light a candle for goodness, but not too many candles."[37] The 6,000,000 dead far exceed the 250,000 saved, and the number of rescuers is dwarfed by the number of non-Jewish Europeans who could have helped but did not do so. Rescuers constituted a tiny minority, under one percent. When Jews think of Gentile behavior during the Holocaust they will never fail to think of the tens of thousands of Gentiles involved in murdering their people, and the tens of millions who did nothing to stop it. Any study of rescuers must retain this perspective with great care.

Even so, Jews both in Israel and the Diaspora appear very likely to incorporate the Righteous Gentiles permanently into their ongoing remembrance of the Holocaust.[38] They will do so, at the barest level, because they have concluded that Jews understand the history of that period incompletely if rescuers are not added to the perpetrators, victims, and bystanders who populate the desolate Holocaust landscape. But for most Jews the importance of the rescuers is felt most profoundly at the "hermeneutical" rather than the historical level. In other words, rescuers help Jews to find at least a shard of "usable" and morally constructive history in the shattering events that befell the Jewish people during World War II.[39]

Those most strongly advocating rescuer celebration tend to emphasize the themes of gratitude and hope. On one level, the Jewish community simply wants to offer its thanks to those it unabashedly calls "saviors" and heroes. Rescuer celebration is a heartfelt and probably unprecedented offering of thanks from one people to another. Yet rescuers are thanked not only for saving Jewish lives, but also for saving the possibility of Jewish hope. As its vast literature attests, the Holocaust has threatened to snuff out hope in either God or humanity; but the rescuers help some Jews retain a measure of faith in one, the other, or both. Schulweis writes, "[W]e know that even in the midst of that impenetrable darkness there were scattered sparks of sanctity."[40] Finding those sparks enables some Jews to live in the present without being overwhelmed by the grief and despair that the Holocaust engenders, and to send their children and grandchildren into the future with the requisite supply of hope.

The Vocation of Christian Ethics

We have pointed to the place of the Holocaust in our century of mass murder, the significant role of the bystanders in the Holocaust, and the moral importance for Jews of those who abandoned a bystander role to save Jewish lives. But we have yet to suggest why the discipline of Christian ethics should be interested. Why undertake a study in Christian ethics on the Righteous Gentiles of the Holocaust? An answer begins with a sketch of the task of our discipline.

Jewish theologian David Novak has written that "ethics primarily functions as the norm for humans-in-community," not for "rational self-legislating" individuals, nor for the elusive humanity-in-general.[41] This comment nicely illuminates my own sense of the vocation of Christian ethics and points to dimensions of this academic and ecclesial task that are relevant to this study. Fundamentally, Christian ethics has to do with the moral practice of that particular community of humans who bear Christian identity. The central task of Christian ethics is to help Christian faith-communities discern the nature of a way of life appropriate to a people who profess allegiance to Jesus Christ as Lord, and to contribute directly to the shaping of Christian communities that will live in faithfulness to such a way of life.

Christian ethics is thus a perennial vocation of the churches, under-taken by Christians (and not just professional Christian ethicists) on the basis of their commitment to being faithful to the God they have met in Jesus Christ and whom they believe responsible for their existence as faith-community. The ecclesial identity and vocation of Christian ethics does not imply an uncritical embrace of the historic or current moral practice of the churches. Quite the contrary—Christian ethics is and must always be a relentlessly critical discipline, rigorously examining Christian moral practice and bringing this moral practice into dialogue with an understanding of the normative content of a Christian way of life. Those doing Christian ethics ask, What does it mean to be Christian in this time and place? Are we being that kind of Christian people? Are we following Jesus in the way that authentic disciples must? The discipline clearly recognizes the pro-found gap that often exists between the normative shape of Christian character and conduct and the manner in which Christians actually live. It knows the taste of sorrow, self-recrimination, and repentance. Christian ethics is the church examining itself in the presence of its Lord, that it might serve that Lord more faithfully.

Yet not all people profess allegiance to Jesus Christ; and human beings gather together in any number of other communities. The discipline of Christian ethics (like the church itself) must construe its mission in a way that includes dialogue with other humans-in-community. This includes not only other faith-communities but also many other morally concerned communities and subcommunities. Christian ethicists encourage the churches to remember that communities other than our own have much to teach us about the struggle for moral goodness and human well-being. A horrendous gap exists between the way the world is and the way God intended it to be. Can the existence of that gap be any clearer than in the Holocaust? To recognize, grieve over, and try to close this chasm is fundamental to what it means to be human.[42] The Christian community seeks to close this gap, beginning in its own life and then moving well beyond its doors. Believing that it does so not under its own power but through the power of God, the church also trusts that the efforts of other communities toward the same end are not bereft of God's presence.

Moreover, Christian ethics calls the church to go beyond dialogue to service. Central to our task is a foundational normative conviction we must hold before the church: that fidelity to the "way" of Jesus Christ requires an expansive recognition of the worth, dignity, and basic rights of all human beings and groups, and requires the concrete practice of care on behalf of those who are threatened, vulnerable, or in need. Followers of Jesus must have no doubt about this—that no human being is beyond the boundaries of moral obligation. Christian ethics thus serves and undergirds the mission of the church in the world, at the same time participating in the broader human quest for a decent and dignified life for all people. Christian ethics encourages the churches to relate constructively to a range of efforts on behalf of human well-being, while recognizing that perhaps the best service the churches can offer in the quest for a better world is to nurture better churches and better Christians.[43] Nearly two billion people claim a Christian identity. Millions worship in Christian communities every week. The world has been made to wait too long for the churches to be faithful to the One they claim as Lord, and for the fruit of that fidelity.

Jesus taught his disciples to pray for the coming of God's kingdom and the doing of God's will on earth as it is in heaven (Matt. 6:10). In his teaching about this reign of God, Jesus described the righteousness, lovingkindness, and justice characteristic of a world in which God's will is indeed done. Christians believe that in his life and ministry Jesus embodied that will. Yet we live in the tension between this dream of the reign of God, a dream shared by Jews and Christians—of a time "when they shall not hurt or destroy on all my holy mountain" (Isa. 65:25)—and the hurtful and destructive realities of a world that defies God's rule. Jesus intended that his followers should be able to offer the quality of their lives as evidence that the inbreaking of the reign of God indeed has occurred. We are to be a sign to the world that one day all the earth shall enjoy the peace, justice, and wholeness that is the perennial dream of both humankind and the earth's Creator. Christian ethics seeks to nurture churches that can be such a sign.

Christian Ethics and the Holocaust

Much of the response that Christian ethics (and other Christian disciplines) has offered to the Holocaust has occurred in the context of an overall reaction to the mass killing and mass injustice of our age. At this level, Christian ethics has viewed the Holocaust as one terrible manifestation of our century's evils. It has been appropriate for the churches' ethicists and theologians to think of the Holocaust in this broader context. Christians need to reflect on such issues as the nature of modern warfare, religio-ethnic nationalism, genocide and mass murder, the use and abuse of political power, the question of God's involvement in history and the problem of evil, human responsibility for the human future, and so on. Here the Holocaust functions as a paradigm of a broader set of problems that raise profound theological and moral questions for the churches. These concerns have preoccupied Christian social ethics since World War II.

However, Christian ethics errs badly when it addresses the Holocaust solely or even primarily at this broad level. Such an approach too easily allows the churches to distance themselves from Christian involvement in this *particular* catastrophe. Unlike, for example, the slaughter in Bangladesh in 1971 or in Cambodia throughout the 1970s, this mass killing directly involves us. *The Holocaust is an event in the history of the Christian faith and the Christian church.* Both in its historical antecedents and in its wartime course, the annihilation of the European Jews was inextricably related to Christianity and the behavior of Christian people. Indeed, most students of the subject agree that the Holocaust was not merely an event in Christian history but in several critical ways a stunning Christian moral failure. For these reasons, careful consideration of this particular catastrophe falls naturally, even urgently, within the purview of Christian ethics in its critical reflection on Christian moral practice. Though considerable work has been done in some Christian circles to address the issues raised by Christian moral failure during the Holocaust,[44] many churches and many Christian thinkers have not dealt with the problem at all. Let us consider some of the dimensions of Christian involvement in the Holocaust, indicating their relevance to our study of the Righteous Gentiles.

First, since the Holocaust a number of scholars have addressed the history of Christian theological anti-Judaism and its relationship to European political and cultural anti-Semitism, including Nazi anti-Semitism.[45]

The history of anti-Judaism/anti-Semitism is not our subject here, and a thorough discussion of this matrix of complex issues would lead us astray. Suffice it to say that historians now recognize the importance of an anti-Semitism that long preceded Adolf Hitler and that was to a considerable degree rooted in Christian doctrine and church practice. Centuries ago, having pushed the Jews beyond the boundaries of moral obligation, this Christian anti-Semitism prepared the ground for the more radical Nazi Jew-hatred that produced the Holocaust. Moreover, during the Holocaust itself this legacy of contempt for Jews was a crucial impediment to appropriate Christian behavior in occupied Europe. When the Nazis set to work an-nihilating Jews, they found a deep reservoir of scorn for Jews on which to draw in seeking collaborators and in stifling action, or even sympathy, on behalf of their prey.

Recognizing the deadly consequences of this theological anti-Judaism (as well as modern anti-Semitism), a significant amount of Christian at-tention has gone toward understanding and, if possible, uprooting it from the contemporary theology and practice of the churches. Proposals have ranged from the most radical acts of theological revision to more modest changes in liturgy, theology, and biblical exegesis. The effort has been a major focus of post-Holocaust Jewish-Christian dialogue. This study of the rescuers assumes the existence of historic Christian anti-Semitism; indeed, at many points in what follows we will see evidence of this "legacy of hatred," as the evangelical historian David Rausch calls it, and witness its tragic consequences. To address fully the question of what the church must do about this poisoned legacy is beyond our purposes here. However, I believe that the discussion of religiously motivated Christian rescuers (chap-ter 6) does offer some clues about a way forward for the church on this crucial question. There we will meet individual Christians who overcame the heritage of Christian contempt for Jews, as well as particular faith communities in which respect rather than contempt for Jews was taught.

Second, a handful of Christian thinkers have found it impossible not to notice that most of the Holocaust's perpetrators were baptized Christians and had received Christian religious and moral instruction in their youth. If they were married, they had been married in a Christian church; if they had children, those children would have been baptized in a Christian church. Jewish memoirs record, with bitterness, that even at places like Auschwitz and Dachau, their jailers celebrated Christmas and Easter. Most perpetrators officially belonged to a Christian church body of one kind or another; some were even devout, and a few were ordained Christian min-isters. Certainly, Nazi ideology was fundamentally anti-Christian as well as anti-Jewish, and those who led the way in the murder of Jews were not acting on Christian theological grounds. This was not a medieval pogrom or the Crusades. But still, the church must do significant mental gymnastics not to count most of the perpetrators as "Christians" in some real sense, their moral failure a Christian moral failure, the Holocaust a Christian moral catastrophe. It is not Hindus or Buddhists or Muslims whose fingerprints can be found all over the Holocaust, nor did the Holocaust occur in lands in which those faiths historically have been dominant. Today's Christians must acknowledge what Jews have been saying all along. Jews were murdered by Christians, in the heart of historically Christian Europe.

Historians and a range of others have been interested in the mentality of the perpetrators. How do human beings become mass murderers? Though Christian participation in this research has been relatively slight, a host of studies have been undertaken along with a range of philosophical, moral, and theological reflections.[46] These studies have helped to illuminate the ways in which systemic evil sweeps many thoroughly average people into its service. Unfortunately, these studies have paid little attention to the local Christian collaborators who eagerly and voluntarily participated in killing Jews during the Holocaust. A close study of both German and indigenous perpetrators from a Christian perspective would be most valuable for Christian ethics. Though our subject here will be the rescuers, their perpetrator kinfolk will never be far from view, especially in the discussion of Gentile behavior in chapter 3. Understanding the perpetrators will help us to understand the full range of possibilities for Gentile behavior, only one of which was to rescue Jews.

Third, some of those examining Christian involvement in the Holocaust have examined the Christian bystanders. These were Christians who gained materially from Jewish distress, and Christians who "jumped and jeered" when Jews were shot. These were Christians who coldly turned Jews away when they were desperately looking for help, and Christians who had sparks of compassion but not enough courage to do anything about it. These were also church leaders at every level who did not participate in rescue and did not use their influence to lead their flocks to help their Jewish neighbors. Considerable attention has been focused on Pope Pius XII, seen by many as the "chief bystander" due to his considerable influence over an international church, his specific knowledge about what was happening to the Jews, and (despite the Vatican's significant private rescue efforts) his unwillingness to intervene publicly on their behalf.[47] But every church official at every level who had the opportunity to help Jews faced a test of Christian moral leadership, while every Christian with similar opportunity faced a test of Christian moral character. A thorough study of the behavior of the Christian bystanders would make a most helpful project in Christian ethics. Though ours is not such a study, a sketch of different types of bystanders and the motivations behind their (in)actions is included here (chapter 3), because it is profoundly relevant in a study of the rescuers.

Christian Ethics and the Righteous Gentiles

Not every Gentile fell short of the mark. Some counted Jews within the boundaries of moral obligation and risked their lives to save them. Some died in the attempt. These Gentiles recognized the evil nature of Nazi ideology and policy and by their actions exemplified the highest in moral values. Some analyzed the crisis in explicitly Christian categories and acted to help Jews on the basis of Christian commitments; some did not. Whatever their motivations, the rescuers should be seen by Christians as exemplars of worthy moral practice, people whose character and conduct can give us clues about both the nature of our moral obligations today and how to meet those obligations. We can and must learn from those Gentiles/Christians who did not pass the moral test presented by the murder of their Jewish neighbors. But perhaps we can learn even more from those who did pass that test, who found the moral resources to defy a poisoned cultural legacy, Nazi enticements and threats, and their own fears in order to save Jewish lives.

Earlier I discussed the prominent place of these Righteous Gentiles in Jewish memory and reflection. Yet these people, whom many Jews actually call "Christian rescuers," have no such place in Christian memory or reflection. Jews have not failed to notice this, as the preface indicated. These were people who acted in a way consistent with the highest of Christian values. For thirty years the Jewish community has been publicly honoring them as heroes who may have saved the honor of Christianity. Yet most Christians know nothing about them. Jews are right to wonder about our moral seriousness. Not only have large swaths of the Christian community ignored the Holocaust or learned nothing from it, but even our most impressive moral exemplars are better known in the Jewish community than in the churches. It is past time for a serious Christian encounter with the Righteous Gentiles of the Holocaust.

Aims of This Book

This book offers a survey of the phenomenon of the Righteous Gentiles of the Holocaust and an interpretation of their significance for Christian ethics and the church. To my knowledge, no Christian ethicist previously has attempted a full-length study of the rescuers. This project functions as an introductory, discipline-bridging encounter on two levels, attempting to introduce the Righteous Gentile phenomenon into ongoing conversation in the discipline of Christian ethics, and to introduce a Christian ethical perspective into the research and reflection on the Righteous Gentiles that occurs today in the discipline of Holocaust studies.

Having laid the groundwork in this introductory chapter, I will next offer a description of the course of the Holocaust. I will focus on how the Nazis progressively severed relationships between Jews and Gentiles and tried to place the Jews beyond the boundaries of moral obligation. In chapter 3 I will consider the full range of behavior of Europe's non-Jews during the Holocaust, from murder to rescue, thereby placing the conduct of the rescuers in appropriate context. In the next chapter I will offer a detailed description of the relief and rescue activities of the Righteous Gentiles throughout Europe during the war. Why did rescuers risk everything to help Jews? I will consider this question in chapter 5 through a critical review of the social scientific literature that explores the character and motivations of rescuers. In chapter 6 I will probe motivations further by describing the thinking of rescuers who acted on explicitly religious grounds, seeking to discover how their understanding and practice of the Christian faith differed from that of their nonrescuer Christian contemporaries. I will conclude with reflections on the significance of the Righteous Gentiles for Christian ethics and the church today.

Conclusion

Why undertake a study in Christian ethics on the Righteous Gentiles of the Holocaust? Why now, fifty years after these events? Why now, when the world demands our attention to other pressing problems, including the "ethnic cleansing" occurring in our own day? Because a "Christian woman" was handed Simcha Rozen's baby in Nesvizh on July 21, 1942. A child's life lay in her hands. Everything that had gone into shaping her character and conduct was called upon that day. If she was a typical non-Jewish resident of 1942 Europe, we can imagine that much of that character and conduct was shaped within the walls of a Christian home, in the streets of a Christian village, and in the sanctuary of a Christian church.

We study the Righteous Gentiles because we want to nurture the kind of people who would have tried to save that baby boy. We want to create communities of Christian people prepared to stand with victims rather than hide in facile neutrality or join in victimization. We return to the past to learn from our predecessors in the Christian faith, people who spent six years in an unimaginably intense moral crucible. Those who melted under this heat, and especially those who withstood it, have much to teach us. If we can learn something about the nature of a faithful Christian way of life, and about what may be done to nurture such moral quality in the lives of our own communities of faith, then our study will have been well worth the effort.

2

The Holocaust

❖

The Destruction of European Jewry

Though it is not necessary to rehearse in detail the deeply researched and horrifying history of the Holocaust, a discussion of the Righteous Gentiles must place these people and their deeds in appropriate historical context. Thus in this chapter I offer a brief account of the Holocaust, with special attention to two crucial dimensions of the tragedy relevant to our study. First, I will trace the several stages in the Nazi assault on the Jews, which at each step included progressively more intense efforts to sever ties between Jews and Gentiles and to place Jews beyond the perceived boundaries of moral obligation. Second, in this chapter and especially the next I will note those moments in this process in which Gentiles had the opportunity to help Jews, to harm them, or to remain bystanders. These encounters were a moral crucible in which Gentiles were tested, with Jewish lives hanging in the balance.

Nazi Anti-Semitism and Its Political Agenda

The Nazi party made its contempt for Jews known from its inception. The first party platform, drawn up in 1920, offered a conception of German citizenship that excluded Jews. Point 4 of the document laid out a specious syllogism for this racist redefinition of citizenship: (1) Only *Volksgenossen* (fellow members of the German community) can be citizens of Germany; (2) only a person with "German blood" can be a *Volksgenosse*; (3) no Jew is a person of German blood; ergo, no Jew may be a citizen.[1] Defining Jews as outside the boundaries of citizenship carried considerable freight; for in the modern era, as Helen Fein notes, the nation-state constitutes the most fundamental "perimeter of a compulsory universe of obligation—that circle of persons to whom obligations are owed, to whom the rules apply, whose injuries call for expiation by the community."[2] The Nazi platform called for the descent of German Jews to a status like that of other noncitizen "aliens." Like these other second-class residents in the German nation, the document asserted, German Jews should be prohibited from holding public office at any level.[3] Other provisions pointed to the expropriation of property for community purposes and the expulsion of post-1914 immigrants to Germany. Both measures were to be aimed specifically at the Jews.[4]

This first Nazi platform, however, offered only the merest hint of what was to come. A less varnished early statement of the spirit and program of Nazi anti-Semitism was offered by Adolf Hitler, future leader of the party and of the nation, in 1919. In a letter to a military superior, Hitler described Jewry as "definitely a race and not a religious community," an alien people within the German body politic. The mingling of this debased "race" with the German nation had caused the illness and decay—indeed, the "racial tuberculosis"—of Germany. Hitler argued that Jews lust voraciously for money and power and that they dominate and exploit the press. He prescribed a "rational anti-Semitism," leading to "systematic legal combating and removal of the rights of the Jew," rather than the emotional release offered by pogroms. This systematic program would lead first to the reduction of German Jews to the status of aliens, and finally "the removal [*Entfernung*] of the Jews altogether."[5]

In a speech the next year, Hitler argued that Jews must be removed from Germany, "not because we would begrudge them their existence . . . but because the existence of our own nation is a thousand times more important to us than that of an alien race."[6] For Hitler, this was a comparatively mild statement. Elsewhere he made clear his view that Jews were not only well beyond the boundaries of moral obligation, but also in fact not quite human. Hitler said, "The Jew is the creature of another god, the anti-man. . . . He is a creature outside nature and alien to nature." Borrowing the language of ancient theological anti-Judaism, Hitler and his propagandists sometimes called Jews "the children of Satan."[7] Except as enemies to be fought, Jews were of no interest or importance. By so radically disvaluing Jewish life, this demonic ideology carried within it the potential for murder.

The Purging of the German Jews, 1933–1939

The Nazis were not the only right-wing anti-Semitic party in Germany in the 1920s—nor were they the first in German history. Anti-Semitism had been a part of German cultural life for centuries and a significant dimension of right-wing German political and social thought since the late 1700s.[8] (The same is true of several other European countries. Modern anti-Semitism was never confined to Germany alone.)[9] But it required a peculiar confluence of forces in the late 1920s and early 1930s to create an opening for the ascension to power of a representative of the radical anti-Semitic right, Adolf Hitler. On January 30, 1933, after months of political crisis, Hitler was named chancellor of Germany. It was the worst mistake in German political history—and, given what Hitler had already revealed about himself and his hatred of the Jews, a colossal moral failure on the part of Germany's political leaders. Most historians agree that Hitler's anti-Semitic ideology was peripheral rather than central to his popular support.[10] But with his appointment to the chancellorship, he had the opportunity to turn this hatred of Jews from theory into political practice, using the full repertoire of resources available to a modern state.

For the first several months of his rule, Hitler primarily was occupied with consolidating his political power. With lightning quickness he accomplished the task by July 1933, in the process skillfully destroying Germany's weak parliamentary democracy. Thereafter free from democratic constraints, his regime set to work incorporating all aspects of German society into the new Nazi order. Germany's Jews, however, were to have no place in this new order. The Nazi regime instead isolated the Jews from the nation's social, cultural, and economic life over the next six years.[11] From 1933 to 1939, as Raul Hilberg writes, "the bureaucracy cut, link by link, the ties between the German and Jewish communities."[12] It did so with wide (but not universal) support and the cooperation of numerous elements in German society.

The regime's pattern was to employ a mix of street terror, propaganda, and administrative measures against German Jewry.[13] The terror at first was provided by the Nazi party's huge private political army, the SA. A brownshirted paramilitary unit primarily drawn from the disaffected and unemployed young, the SA dramatically aided Hitler's rise to, and consolidation of, power. Among their other activities, these Nazi stormtroopers harassed and murdered Jews before January 1933, with the terror accelerating after Hitler became chancellor. The actions of these hundreds of thousands of thugs did not always conform to the precise wishes of the powers in Berlin, who wanted centralized control over a more systematic anti-Jewish program. Their violence was channeled rather than prevented, however, for it was an essential instrument of Nazi power.

The first official anti-Jewish measure undertaken by the regime was a general boycott against Jewish commercial establishments; this represented a systematizing of the street terror already being undertaken against

Jews.[14] Intensive propaganda flooded the country in an effort to explain the need for the planned April 1, 1933, boycott and to garner wide support. The boycott was staffed by the SA (and its then-subsidiary unit, the SS), giving the stormtroopers an opportunity to vent their hatred against Jews in the disciplined way favored by Berlin. SA and SS guards were stationed in front of the homes of Jewish lawyers and doctors as well as at the entrances to Jewish commercial establishments, many of which were marked with the Jewish star and crude anti-Jewish messages. Germans were "encouraged" not to enter. Throughout Germany, Jews were arrested at their workplaces while others were beaten, harassed, and humiliated. Jewish lawyers were prevented from entering courts or were hauled out of them. One Jew was murdered. Due to overwhelmingly negative world reaction, the boycott was quickly terminated. But Jews, for the first time in the Hitler era, had been slapped down by a governmentally coordinated act of intimidation.

In the same period, the central government promulgated the first of what would ultimately amount to some four hundred anti-Jewish legal and administrative measures. An April 7, 1933, law removed most Jews from important posts in the German civil service. On April 22, a new law excluded Jewish physicians from the state health service. This law merely ratified the action taken by the professional association for physicians, now under the leadership of Nazis. Indeed, anti-Jewish administrative measures frequently emerged from grassroots public and private organizations rather than the Nazi government. Large swaths of German society, inspired by the anti-Semitism of their leaders, were turning on their Jewish neighbors.

Meanwhile, many Jewish academics were dismissed on the basis of the civil service law. Nazi students brutally harassed their remaining Jewish professors and fellow students, demanding their removal. An April 25 law partially ratified this sentiment by reducing the number of Jewish students allowed in higher education. On May 10, Nazi propaganda minister Joseph Goebbels organized book-burnings on the nation's campuses, with works by Jewish authors particularly targeted. The combination of laws, violence, propaganda, and administrative measures rapidly drove leading Jews out of the professions, government, culture, and public life, many of them fleeing Germany altogether.[15]

Throughout 1933, numerous Jews were incarcerated without charge in the new concentration camps, such as Dachau (outside Munich). According to Martin Gilbert, forty-five Jews were murdered in that first year of the Nazi era.[16] An incident in Dachau that April revealed the spirit of the new regime:

> We were going out as usual to work. All of a sudden the Jewish prisoners
> . . . were ordered to fall out of the ranks. Without even a word, some

Stormtroop men shot at them; they had not made any attempt to escape.
All were killed on the spot. . . . [After their burial] a meeting was called,
and a Stormtroop leader . . . told us that it was a good thing these four
Jewish sows were dead. They had been hostile elements who had no
right to live in Germany.[17]

Germany's Jews were shocked at the collapse of their place in German
life. Some recognized early that they were no longer welcome and no longer
safe in Germany; approximately thirty-five thousand of the 500,000 German
Jews emigrated in 1933. But *Daseinrecht* (the right to exist as Jews in Germany) was the official stance of the Jewish communal leadership, which
encouraged Jews to stay and to resist by fighting to preserve their citizenship
rights. The Jewish sense of identity and community solidarity actually
flourished under Nazi siege.[18]

No major anti-Jewish legislation was enacted during 1934, though
propaganda continued to vilify the Jews and numerous acts of violence
occurred. Those Jews scattered in villages rather than in the large cities
found themselves particularly vulnerable. In March 1934, the nineteen
Jewish families who lived in the village of Gunzenhausen tasted Nazi
terror:

A member of [Nazi propagandist] Julius Streicher's personal bodyguard,
Kurt Baer . . . ordered these Jews to be dragged from their homes and
from the cellars in which they had hidden. He himself dragged one
Jewish woman through the streets by her hair. Throughout the night,
the Jews were beaten, whipped, and cursed: and on the following
morning two Jews were found dead, a seventy-five-year-old man, Ro-
senfelder, his chest torn open with knife wounds, and a thirty-year-old
man, Rosenau, hung on a garden fence.[19]

Jews fled to the major cities, and their concentration in urban areas ultimately eased later annihilation efforts. Jewish existence in Germany was
becoming increasingly precarious.

In September 1935, after months of heightened propaganda, violence,
and numerous administrative measures against Jews, the Nuremberg Laws
were enacted. The "Reich Citizenship Law" stripped Jews of German citizenship and thus of the right to vote or hold public office (illusory rights
in a dictatorship, to be sure), declaring Jews mere "subjects" of the State.[20]
As promised in the 1920 Nazi party platform, the Jews—many of whose
families had lived in Germany for centuries—were now disenfranchised.
The "Law for the Protection of German Blood and German Honor" established race as the fundamental legal principle in German life and demanded
the segregation of Jews from the rest of the population. Earlier in 1935,
measures had been taken to prevent social contact between Jews and Gentiles, such as regulations prohibiting Jews from entering movie houses and

other recreational sites. The new law banned marriages and nonmarital sexual relations between Jews and Germans, calling them a violation of the purity of German "blood." Defined as inferior aliens, segregated from their fellow Germans in increasingly constricting ways, many deprived of the opportunity to earn a living, subject to random unpunished violence at any time, Jews were being forced out of German life. As British diplomat Eric Mills commented in 1935 of Nazi policy: "The Jew is to be eliminated and the state has no regard for the manner of his elimination."[21] Jewish morale slipped as the community became ever more financially impoverished and weakened by the losses to emigration.

Over the next three years, Jews continued to face measures that made life in Germany increasingly difficult. Jewish businesses were steadily transferred into the control of non-Jews, often at a fraction of their value. Jews throughout the economy were increasingly pressured out of their jobs. In 1938, the remaining Jewish doctors and lawyers were prohibited from working. All of these steps offered economic advantage to those Germans who filled the forced vacancies and ran the formerly Jewish businesses. Meanwhile, violence continued to simmer; Jews were placed under the control of the police, who merely implemented more restrictive regulations on Jewish life while offering no protection. These regulations included a restriction on the names of Jews. New laws in 1938 required Jews in certain cases to add to their given name the names Israel (males) and Sarah (females).[22]

Heightened violence during the spring and summer of 1938 made these measures seem tame. Hitler began his inexorable march toward war by annexing Austria in March 1938. The Nazi leadership long had planned more radical measures against the Jews when war came. Now economic czar Hermann Göring made plans for the total expropriation of Jewish possessions and the complete expulsion of Jews from German economic life. The treatment of Austria's 180,000 Jews after the *Anschluss* illustrated the shape of things to come. Anti-Jewish measures there were swift and radical, dramatically telescoping the process as it had occurred in Germany. Overnight, Austria's Jews were deprived of all civil rights, completely expropriated, segregated from other Austrians, physically abused and humiliated, and pushed toward immediate emigration. Nearly fifty thousand Austrian Jews left the country within six months.[23] These sensational measures contributed to a growing tide of violence in Germany itself during the summer of 1938. The Gestapo (the dreaded secret police) began to coerce Jews toward emigration, as well as to incarcerate many hundreds of Jews without charge for forced labor.

The infamous *Kristallnacht* of November 9–10, 1938, proved to be a watershed event, climaxing the increasing harassment, terror, and economic impoverishment of Jews during the preceding months and years.

Orchestrated by Nazi propaganda minister Joseph Goebbels, this nation-wide night of terror ostensibly marked a response to the assassination in Paris of a minor German embassy official by a young Polish Jew. That night, as Lucy Dawidowicz puts it, "the Jewish community of Germany went up in flames."[24] Stormtroopers burned down thousands of Jewish synagogues, businesses, and homes. Nearly one hundred Jews were murdered, with thousands of others tortured and beaten. Thirty thousand Jewish men (10 percent of all the Jews then in Germany) were incarcerated in Nazi concentration camps.[25] Francis Schott, then a twelve-year-old Jew from Solingen, has described that night:

> A jarring sound jolts us awake in the middle of the night. Glass and wood of the apartment door shatter. My little sister and I sit up in our beds, uncomprehending. The noise gets louder yet, things are breaking and gruff male voices can be heard. . . . Then they are gone. Ghastly silence. We open the bedroom doors. No one is hurt, but the psychic shock is staggering. . . . My father's Italian cello is nothing but splinters, the Bechstein piano smashed beyond repair. The Emil Nolde watercolors and Paul Klee drawings are on the floor, crushed. The china and crystal, my mother's heirlooms, are in the apartment corridor, in thousands of pieces.[26]

After Kristallnacht, Jewish communal existence in Germany was effectively at an end. The regime now codified the total elimination of Jews from the German economy and exclusion from German public life, with the aim of expelling them from Germany. The imposition of a one-billion-mark fine for "the hostile attitude of Jewry toward the German Volk and Reich" intensified the expropriation of the economic assets of German Jewry. By January 1939 "everything related to the Jewish question, it seemed, had been disposed of, except the Jews themselves."[27]

The remaining 300,000 German Jews faced a desperate race against time and circumstance. The German authorities pushed for emigration, and thousands of German Jews likewise sought desperately to leave. The purging of the Jews from Germany was set for completion; but, to the world's lasting shame, immigration quotas and requirements were tight all over the world in 1939.[28] Little room was found for German Jews within the boundaries of international moral obligation. Jews used whatever connections they could muster—Gentile or Jewish—to get some or all of their family out, especially the children. Many grief-stricken families were separated as Jewish children emigrated to Great Britain or Palestine, the majority never to see their parents again. Most Jews who wanted to leave, however, were trapped in the German Reich; over 200,000 were never able to escape. The invasion of Poland and the beginning of World War II on September 1, 1939, foreclosed most remaining opportunities for emigration.

Some two million Polish Jews[29] immediately joined the remaining "Reich Jews" (German, Austrian, and Czech) under Nazi control.

In retrospect, the best help that Germans could have offered their Jewish neighbors would have been to prevent Hitler's rise or to topple him from power while opportunity still existed. Failing to do so, Germans ended up living under a deeply entrenched totalitarian regime which vigorously sought to snuff out resistance of any kind, including action (or even public sympathy) on behalf of Jews. Non-Jewish Germans still encountered choices concerning their relations with Jews. They could still join in harming Jews, they could help Jews, or they could do nothing, and they faced these choices at every stage of the anti-Jewish program. But now their actions largely occurred on the margins of those powerful forces that conspired to crush European Jewry. Non-Jews in occupied Europe soon inherited the same situation. Broadly effective political resistance, by and large, had been made profoundly difficult. The alternative was courageous action on a small scale, most often the work of individuals and small groups boldly attempting to save one Jew or a handful of Jews at a time. Under these circumstances, the deck was stacked against the Jews. It was already too late to save most of them—but it was never too late to save some. At this level, local Gentile behavior made a profound difference.

Prelude to Annihilation: The Invasion and Conquest of Poland

Poland was the site of the heaviest concentration of Jews in Europe—a total of 3.3 million Jews lived within its 1939 boundaries. As the Nazi *Wehrmacht* swept eastward across Poland, Jews suffered all manner of humiliation, sadism, torture, and murder. "Terror enveloped the Jews. The Germans reenacted the Kristallnacht in every town and city they invaded and occupied."[30] Jewish possessions were confiscated, Jewish businesses expropriated, Jews rounded up for forced labor. Synagogues were burned down and other Jewish buildings converted into stables or even houses of prostitution. Local anti-Semitism was deliberately inflamed; the Germans organized pogroms, inviting Poles to join in humiliating, torturing, and murdering Jews.[31] A German or Pole "could do anything he wanted to a Jew."[32] This was a time of wanton terror rather than systematic extermination, as would happen after 1941; yet at least five thousand Jews were murdered in one hundred towns during the first two months of the war.[33] In more than one city, Jews were burned alive.

The sadism and humiliation often stand out as much as the killing in Jewish accounts of this early period. On the Day of Atonement, in Raciaz, the Nazis made all Jewish men shave off their beards. Then, in the words of Abraham Altus:

> Since the Nazis were drunk with spirits and liquor, they cruelly thrashed the old men, while some stood photographing these scenes of horror and hell. Between the beating and the photographing they made us dance and jump, and hit us with sticks and mistreated us.[34]

Another account, from Czestochowa:

> On a frosty night in January 1940, the police surrounded a densely populated Jewish area, shouting *Juden raus!* [Jews out!] Thousands of half-naked men and women were assembled in a large square and beaten to bleeding. Then they were kept standing for hours in the biting frost. Others—especially young girls—were taken into the synagogue . . . forced to undress, sexually shamed, and tortured.[35]

Jews had no way to predict exactly what the Germans would do when arriving in their town or village, but they knew to be terrorized by their presence. Many Jews stayed off the streets or found hiding places during the initial arrival of the Nazis. Some sought refuge with Gentile friends. Approximately 300,000 Polish Jews (along with tens of thousands of non-Jewish Poles) fled eastward, trying to escape Nazi terror by reaching the area of Soviet occupation. In the confusion characteristic of Nazi policy at this time, some Jews were murdered for attempting to reach the Soviet zone while others were murdered for being unwilling to go.

German racial policy in Poland

While the SS and army terrorized Poland's Jews, the Nazi leadership in Berlin struggled to improvise its overall occupation policy in the east. Set into motion in the fall of 1939, this policy ultimately amounted to an absurd attempt to reshuffle the entire population of Eastern Europe along the racial lines envisioned in Nazi ideology.[36] Initially, much of western and northern Poland was annexed and incorporated into an expanded German Reich. This area, like the rest of the Reich, was to be *Judenrein* (free of Jews). German settlers and certain Poles (seen by the Nazis as suitably Aryan-looking) were encouraged to live in these incorporated territories and participate in their racial "reclamation." Large numbers of "Aryan-type" Polish children were taken from their families and sent to these incorporated areas or to Germany proper. Some 500,000 "Aryans" ultimately resettled, while as many as one million Jews and non-Jewish Poles were forced to the east,[37] as always, accompanied by sadism, terror, and death. The population movements were immense and chaotic.

The remainder of German-controlled Poland was placed under a German civil administration called the *Generalgouvernement*. This was where the "racially undesirable elements"—Jews, Gypsies, and Poles—from the expanded German Reich were to be dumped: that is, those who were not killed or left to suffer in ghettos rather than shipped east. The Polish leadership elite—intelligentsia, clergy, and nobility—was targeted for annihilation by the *Einsatzgruppen* rather than deported. Hundreds of thousands of such Poles ultimately were killed.[38] The main thrust of Nazi policy toward the Jews in the Generalgouvernement was ghettoization, "for a better possibility of control and later possibility of deportation," according to a decree issued by SS second-in-command Reinhard Heydrich on September 21, 1939. Tens of thousands of Jews both from the annexed territories and from smaller towns in the Generalgouvernement were uprooted from their homes over the next year and a half and forced into already overcrowded ghettos in a few major cities which, significantly, had access to railroad lines. Jewish councils (*Jüdische Ältestenräte*, or *Judenräte*) were established and forced on penalty of death to cooperate with the *Einsatzgruppen* in carrying out these measures.

The uprooting of Jews from their ancient communities meant the beginning of a slow death for Polish Jewry. Driven from their homes and stripped of most or all of their possessions, Jews were deprived of the means necessary to survive. Some died of exposure during horrendous marches in the winter snow. Some died of hunger on cattle cars heading east, others of disease once they got there. The commander of the German army in the Lublin region complained that Jewish children often had frozen to death in the transport trains; others who survived the journey soon died of starvation.[39] Because population transfers and ghettos were seen as no more than interim measures, and particularly because Jewish life was seen as without value, "there was little planning and much confusion"[40] on the part of the Nazis. The result for the Jews was suffering and death.

The ghettos

The ghettos (including Warsaw, Lublin, Cracow, Kielce, and Czestochowa in the Generalgouvernement, Lodz in the incorporated area, and others added after the invasion of Soviet-controlled territory) constituted a unique and grim social order. Christopher Browning has argued that while some ghetto masters ("attritionists") sought merely to eliminate ghettoized Jews by starvation and disease, others ("productionists") preferred the enslavement of the ghetto population in a massive system of forced labor for the German Reich.[41] Most Jewish accounts of ghetto life record both terrible attrition and massive forced labor, with the same ultimate result—appalling mortality via the method of "natural death."[42]

Conditions in each ghetto varied, and historians are reluctant to generalize about the ghettos as a whole. Most accounts do, however, reveal certain shared characteristics. These included acute impoverishment, over-crowding (six or more people to a room, the streets full as well), starvation, rampant disease, noise, dirt, inadequate sanitation, forced labor (often by abduction), random confiscation of property, overwhelming exhaustion, daily humiliation, sadism, torture, and murder.[43] Death was everywhere. Jan Karski, a key courier for the Polish underground and a leader in efforts to get the Allied nations to act on behalf of the Jews,[44] recorded these impressions of his visit to the Warsaw ghetto in 1942:

> These were still living people, if you could call them such. For apart from their skin, eyes, and voice there was nothing human left in these palpitating figures. Everywhere there was hunger, misery, the atrocious stench of decomposing bodies, the pitiful moans of dying children, the desperate cries and gasps of a people struggling for life against impossible odds. . . . The entire population of the ghetto seemed to be living in the street. There was hardly a square yard of empty space. As we picked our way across the mud and rubble, the shadows of what had once been men or women flitted by us in pursuit of someone or something, their eyes blazing with some insane hunger or greed.[45]

Yet Jews resisted communal and individual annihilation by organizing for physical survival and for the maintenance of cultural life and morale. Usually completely barred from contact with the outside world, ghetto Jews developed or maintained a range of institutions from newspapers to synagogues to theaters, as well as schools, hospitals, relief agencies, and concert halls. As Warsaw Jew Chaim Kaplan put it, "Every dance is a protest against our oppressors."[46] Despite this resistance, the ghettos were designed to annihilate Polish Jewry, and Jewish efforts to resist death could slow but not stem the tide.

The ghettos occasionally presented the resourceful, the well-connected, or the desperate Jew with an opportunity to escape. To try to escape, and to fail, meant certain death—yet most recognized that to remain in the ghetto also meant near-certain death and certain misery. Some decided to take the chance, to resist the Nazis by finding a way out of the ghetto and trying their luck on the "Aryan side." Life or death depended on the reception received there at the hands of Gentiles. Interestingly, some Jews had the opportunity to escape but decided that this would mean a breaking of solidarity with their fellow Jews. One Jewish woman wrote at the time:

> [Escaping] seems to me like treason against my own people. Here, in the worst, most awful moments, I am after all among my own. Never have I felt myself so strongly a Jew, never was I so united with my brothers as now. Intellectually, I admit that hiding out among Aryans is perhaps the best, perhaps the only solution. Emotionally, I consider it desertion.[47]

The period from September 1939 to June 1941 marked a transitional stage from an earlier Nazi policy of forced emigration to what became the "Final Solution"—extermination. In these chaotic months tens of thousands of Jews in eastern Europe lost their lives by murder, starvation, disease, torture, suicide, forced labor (often little more than torture),[48] and in military service. The ghettos remained in existence after the initiation of the policy of extermination—but only until each was slated for "liquidation," a process largely undertaken during 1942 and 1943. During these long months, the net loss of Jews in the largest ghettos was such that Polish Jewry would have been wiped out within two or three decades.[49] But for the Nazis, this pace of "natural death" was not sufficient.

Mass Shootings in the Soviet Zone

The center of Hitler's foreign-policy vision since the 1920s had been the quest for expanded German *Lebensraum* ("living space") to the east. For Hitler this meant an inevitable confrontation with Russia, now under Communist rule. During World War II, Hitler's military efforts in Western Europe were essentially a means to an end—to free the full resources of his society for the apocalyptic final struggle for national existence between Germany and the USSR.[50] Planning for the war in the east had an entirely different character than for that in the west. This was to be a fearsome *Vernichtungskrieg* (war of destruction). Customary rules of war would not apply. Soviet prisoners of war, political officials, and intelligentsia would be annihilated without scruple.[51] One other mortal ideological enemy was targeted: the Jews. Hitler had imbibed a strand of anti-Semitism that described Communism as a Jewish invention. The apocalyptic final war against Soviet Communism meant an apocalyptic final war against the USSR's several million Jews.[52] Long ago having been defined as valueless, Jews were now considered dangerous military enemies as well. As such, they could be killed with impunity.

A decision to annihilate Soviet Jewry thus was part of the planning for the German invasion of the USSR.[53] Primarily placed in charge of killing the Jews were the *Einsatzgruppen*, now functioning as mobile SS killing squads which followed the Wehrmacht into Soviet-occupied territory (eastern Poland and the Baltic states) and the Soviet Union to murder Jews (as well as other "political/ideological" enemies). The *Einsatzgruppen* were encouraged to involve indigenous collaborators and local auxiliary police units in their efforts, and they received considerable help from ethnic Germans, Poles, Ukrainians, Latvians, Lithuanians, and Rumanians.[54] Cooperation from the army, even direct involvement in the mass killing, was broad.[55]

But the bulk of the job fell to these four groups of six hundred to a thousand men each, some three thousand in all.

The mass killings began on the first day of the invasion, June 22, 1941. During the first month, to note only a few of the major massacres, 5,200 Jews were slaughtered in Bialystok, 3,000 in Kovno, and 5,000 in Vilna. Lvov Jewry lost 3,000 victims, Brest-Litovsk 5,000, and Tarnopol 5,000.[56] Hundreds of Jewish communities were devastated. Jews were also vulnerable to attacks at the hands of the local populations. This was especially true after the retreat of the Russians and before the arrival of the Germans. In Kamien Koszyrski, in the Volhynia region,

> For several weeks, until the Germans' entry, we were without government. The local Ukrainians, joining up with brigands from neighboring villages, and led by a priest and one Dr. Babiecz roamed the city, shot into the houses, beat Jews on sight, and looted and pillaged at will.[57]

In July and August, as the German Army continued to sweep eastward across the Soviet Union, the massacres grew larger. In southern Ukraine, 12,000 Jews were killed at Kishinev and 14,000 in Kamenets-Podolsk. Further north, 11,000 Jews were killed in Pinsk and thousands in smaller Jewish settlements.[58] "Within five *weeks* of the German invasion . . . the number of Jews killed exceeded the total number killed in the previous eight *years* of Nazi rule."[59] September and October of 1941 witnessed two of the most infamous massacres of the war—the Babi Yar killings outside Kiev on September 29 and 30, in which 33,000 Jews lost their lives, and the brutal murders in Odessa, spearheaded by the Rumanians, in which as many as 48,000 Jews died.[60] Now entire Jewish communities—men, women, and children—were being massacred at one stroke.

Most *Einsatzgruppen* actions followed a similar script. Normally the commandos would enter a town and order the establishment of a Judenrat, demanding that it organize the appearance of all or a portion of the Jews at a central location—for example, the city square or a train depot—at a specified time within forty-eight hours. A ruse was customarily offered for this assembly, such as a registration, resettlement to a different area, or the selection of laborers. The order was sternly accompanied by threats. Afraid but often unsuspecting of their actual fate,[61] most of the requested Jews would assemble at the appointed time. Some would not do so, however, instead attempting to hide or barricade themselves in their homes, find other hiding places, flee into the forests, or seek shelter with Gentiles. The Nazis conducted intensive house-to-house searches to find and kill any such persons. Meanwhile, local Gentiles were warned of severe reprisals for giving aid to Jews, with commensurate rewards for turning fugitive Jews in. Such prizes included vodka, sugar, salt, cigarettes, and money.[62]

Those who appeared at the announced location would either be marched or driven to a spot several miles out of town, from which groups were steadily led to a ravine or ditch some distance away, where the shootings occurred. Sometimes Jews managed to flee during the march toward the ditches, but most did not yet comprehend what awaited them, and the Nazis made escape nearly impossible. The survivor Rivka Yosselevska has left this heartbreaking account of what happened next to a group of Byelorussian Jews during the first sweep of the *Einsatzgruppen*:

> We saw naked people lined up. But we were still hoping that this was only torture. . . . One could not leave the line, but I wished to see—what are they doing on the hillock? I turned my head and saw that some three or four rows were already killed—on the ground. . . . I also want to mention that my child said while we were lined up in the ghetto, "Mother, why did you make me wear the Shabbat dress, we are being taken to be shot." . . . We were driven up to the grave. . . . When it came to our turn, our father was beaten. We begged with my father to undress, but he would not undress, he wanted to keep his underclothes. He did not want to stand naked. Then they tore the clothing off the old man and he was shot. I saw it with my own eyes. And then they took my mother . . . and shot her too; and then there was my grandmother, my father's mother, standing there; she was eighty years old and she had two children in her arms. And then there was my father's sister. She also had children in her arms and she was shot on the spot with the babies in her arms. . . . And finally my turn came. . . . [The German] turned around and asked, "Whom shall I shoot first?" I did not answer. I felt him take the child from my arms. The child cried out and was shot immediately. And then he aimed at me. I heard a shot, but I continued to stand and then he turned my head again and he aimed the revolver at me, ordered me to watch, and then turned my head around and shot at me. Then I fell to the ground into the pit amongst the bodies; but I felt nothing.[63]

Rivka lost consciousness. On somehow regaining her senses, she managed to work her way to the top of the bodies.

> With my last strength I came up on top of the grave, and when I did I did not know the place, so many bodies were lying all over, dead people; I wanted to see the end of this stretch of dead bodies, but I could not. It was impossible. They were lying, all dying; suffering; not all of them dead, but in their last sufferings; naked; shot, but not dead. Children crying, "Mother," "Father"; I could not stand on my feet.

The Germans were gone. Around her were a few others who had climbed out of the grave. In the pit many were still alive, crying and screaming and struggling for life. Soon the Germans came back to kill any still alive. Rivka and three others managed to elude them. Finally, the Germans left. In grief,

> I was digging with my fingernails, trying to join the dead in that grave
> . . . but the grave would not open. I did not have enough strength. I
> cried out to my mother, to my father, "Why did they not kill me? What
> was my sin? I have no one to go to. I saw them all being killed. Why
> was I spared?"

After she had lain on the grave for three days and three nights, local
shepherds passed by and began throwing stones at her. She left, finally
managing to find a farmer who took pity on her. He helped guide her to
Jewish partisans in the forest, where she survived until the end of the war.
Like Rivka Yosselevska, most Jews who survived to tell of these shootings
did so because the shot did not kill them. Once the Germans and their
collaborators had left, they then staggered away, naked and bloody, in a
desperate search for help from someone in the vicinity, thereby presenting
a local Gentile with a momentous choice.[64]

In the case of larger Jewish communities, the *Einsatzgruppen* usually
destroyed the Jews in stages. The first step was often a terrible massacre
of a portion of the Jewish community. Sometimes parents were murdered,
leaving children orphaned; other times children were murdered, leaving
parents in unutterable grief. In Vilna, on August 31, 1941, the *Einsatzkom-
mandos* were accompanied by several hundred armed Lithuanians as they
swept into the Jewish section. Jews were confined to their homes, and after
dark the *Aktion* commenced, as the eyewitness Abba Kovner, later a leader
of the Jewish partisans in Vilna, reported:

> People were taken out of their flats, some carrying a few of their pos-
> sessions, some without any possessions . . . they were driven out with
> cruel beatings. . . . At midnight, I saw . . . a woman [being] dragged
> by her hair by two soldiers, a woman who was holding something in
> her arms. One of them directed a beam of light into her face, the other
> one dragged her by her hair and threw her on the pavement. Then the
> infant fell out of her arms. One of the two took the infant, raised him
> into the air, grabbed him by the leg. The woman crawled on the earth,
> took hold of his boot and pleaded for mercy. But the soldier took the
> boy and hit him with his head against the wall, once, twice, smashed
> him against the wall.[65]

Nearly four thousand Jews, including 817 children, were murdered that
night outside of Vilna.[66]

After these initial terrors, the SS generally organized the surviving
Jews into a ghetto. Both attrition and production demands were met by
the establishment of a system of forced labor which spared from death
those who could obtain the precious labor cards from the Judenrat. (This
kind of system was often instituted in the Polish ghettos as well.) Possession
of a labor card meant life, and the Judenrat faced impossible and corrupting

choices in the distribution of these cards.[67] The number of labor cards was always well below the total number of people in the community; thus the Nazis employed this system to thin out the ghettos. Periodically they swept in, checked the labor cards, and on days of terrible Jewish anguish took to their deaths a portion of those without the cards.

With each Aktion the population of the improvised Russian-zone ghettos—Vilna, Minsk, Bialystok, Lvov, Tarnopol, and others—was reduced. Meanwhile, these ghettos experienced the same kinds of losses to hunger, disease, and random killing, as occurred in the ghettos in Poland. Those surviving lived with fresh memories of their lost loved ones and constant fear. Each upcoming Aktion meant the scramble for the appropriate labor card. Those without the protection of the cards generally sought other means of survival: hiding out with non-Jews, obtaining "Aryan" identification papers or false work permits, digging a hiding place in the ghetto, fleeing to the forests, or armed resistance.[68] Most of these survival strategies involved turning to their Gentile neighbors for help; all were unlikely to succeed.

> The ability to flee, or to resist, was minimal. The Germans were armed, the Jews unarmed, while from among the local populace, especially in Lithuania and the Ukraine, hundreds could be found willing not only to round up Jews but to kill them.[69]

Finally, the ghettos were liquidated in a climactic spasm of violence, often with advancing Soviet troops only days or weeks away. One final time some Jews sought, and fewer found, a hiding place or shelter with Gentiles. Others undertook armed resistance, the most famous example being the Warsaw Ghetto revolt. Such resistance rarely hindered German plans seriously, but it did often result in the escape and survival of a handful of Jews and the deaths of a handful of Germans (as in Nesvizh). Mainly, armed resistance became a way of dying with a measure of dignity, a statement both to future generations of Jews and to an uncompassionate world.

The German historians Krausnick and Wilhelm have estimated that the *Einsatzgruppen*, other German units, and their indigenous collaborators killed 700,000 to 750,000 Jews in their initial sweep behind the German lines (June 1941 through April 1942), and 1,500,000 more in the second sweep (summer 1942 through 1943)—all told, 2,200,000 million.[70] Historians grapple for words to describe this catastrophe. Martin Gilbert: "No day now passed without Jews being murdered."[71] Lucy Dawidowicz: "Like a tornado the *Einsatzgruppen* swept through the Jewish settlements . . . in the summer of 1941, destroying age-old communities in cyclonic upheaval."[72] Michael Marrus: "This was a primitive bloodbath . . . with the widest circle of complicity anywhere in Europe."[73] By the end of 1942, excepting the tiny remnants of Jewish communities still surviving in ghettos and labor camps, those in hiding, and those who had escaped to the east, the massacre of Soviet Jewry in the German zone of occupation was complete.

The "Final Solution of the Jewish Question"

The invasion of the Soviet Union and the vast *Einsatzgruppen* killings marked a decisive and terrible radicalization of the Nazi regime and its policy toward the Jews.[74] Nazism's descent into the demonic had smashed all restraints. Hundreds of thousands of Jewish men, women, and children were now being killed without scruple. Simultaneous to (or within months of) the first slaughters in the USSR, the decision was made to extend the killings from the Russian Jews to every Jew within Germany's reach. Extermination would become the "Final Solution of the Jewish Question." All that would remain of the Jews would be their plundered possessions. Apparently the initial planning for the Final Solution occurred in July and August of 1941.[75] The next nine months were spent in the spawning of a new thing in human history—the death camps (*Vernichtungslager*): death factories which ultimately produced thousands of corpses a day.

Antecedents

Before the Holocaust, no nation had ever attempted this kind of systematic and comprehensive mass murder. Lacking precedents, Nazi bureaucrats and field operatives experimented with a variety of techniques for doing away with the Jews. Thus far in the chapter we have seen death by attrition (starvation, disease, exhaustion), by torture, by random killing, and by mass shooting. Ultimately, the Nazis came to favor the use of poison gas, administered to Jewish victims in specially constructed centers of death bearing the now infamous names of Auschwitz, Belzec, Majdanek, Sobibor, and Treblinka.

Several avenues led to this unthinkable horror. In terms of the course of the Holocaust, gassing first emerged as a technique employed by some of the *Einsatzgruppen* units in the Soviet Union. Over time, mass shootings increasingly were viewed as an unsatisfactory killing technique, due to the demoralization of the killers and the lack of efficiency and secrecy.[76] The Nazis sought a way to depersonalize the killing operations, remove them further from public view, and quicken the pace. Consequently they introduced gassing, beginning with gas vans. These killed their victims by piping carbon monoxide emissions into hermetically sealed compartments into which sixty or more Jews were jammed. Apparently thirty gas vans were used by *Einsatzgruppen* units in the course of their massacres in the Soviet Union, particularly in the southern regions of that nation.

In December 1941, after the decision had been made to exterminate all of the Jews of Europe, the vans were employed at the first death center—Chelmno, in the annexed portion of western Poland. The Nazis began to round up some of the 250,000 Jews who remained in this region and ship them to Chelmno to meet their doom. The coarse slogan of the killers at Chelmno reportedly was *"Ein Tag—ein tausend"* ("One day—one thousand")—the daily murder quota.[77] By the end of 1942, 145,000 Jews had been murdered there.[78] Some Jews survived briefly by being selected to assist in sorting the clothes (which by the end of 1942 filled 370 railroad wagons) and burying the bodies of the murdered. Though most Jews thus employed were executed, a few managed to escape to tell of these horrors.[79]

The "euthanasia" campaign in Germany itself also constituted an important path to Auschwitz. This Nazi program to eliminate the so-called *Ballastexistenz* (burdensome life) in Germany ultimately took 120,000 "lives unworthy of life." The victims of this medicalized campaign to improve the Reich's "racial stock" primarily consisted of mentally and physically disabled or "impaired" German children and adults. A committee of doctors selected the victims from inmates of mental institutions, medical facilities, and so on. They were then taken to newly constructed "euthanasia" installations, where the doctors and their assistants gassed them and then had their bodies burned in crematoria. (Some, however, were starved to death, including mentally "defective" children.)[80]

In 1940, the gassings were extended to the concentration camps. Similar procedures were followed for the classification of those considered unworthy of life. Victims included the sick, the crippled, and so on as before, but Nazi racism allowed a transition to the inclusion of Jews, Russian POWs, and others who had no health problems but were *by definition* seen as racially, and thus medically, valueless. A rare show of public resistance caused the Nazi regime to announce the discontinuation of the euthanasia program in August 1941. But the personnel, classification and killing techniques, and medicalized ideological rationale were available for transport to the east, where they provided the basis for the work of the death centers, especially Auschwitz.[81] By 1942 all of the elements were in place; several death centers equipped with gas chambers and crematoria would now systematically and rapidly destroy the Jews, who would be shipped by train from the four corners of Europe to their deaths.

The infamous meeting in Wannsee, a posh suburb of Berlin, on January 20, 1942, brought the key bureaucratic operatives together to plan the practical implementation of the Final Solution.[82] Estimates were made at this briskly efficient meeting of the numbers of Jews in Europe, and Reinhard Heydrich announced that Europe would be "combed through from west to east" for Jews, who would be "evacuated" group by group, to transit ghettos first, then onto trains to Poland. Upon arrival, a portion would be selected for hard labor and the remainder would be dealt with "appropriately." Nazi functionaries did indeed begin to comb Europe relentlessly for Jews. Henceforth the whole of Europe would become a crucial third party amidst the Nazi hunt for Jews and the Jewish fight for survival.

The European deportations

Though it is only now, at the point of inception of the deportations (1942), that our attention broadens to include Northern, Western, and Southern Europe, we must remember that by this time the war was over two years old, and Germany had dominated most of these areas for much of this time. Most of the nations of Northern and Western Europe (including Norway, Denmark, Belgium, Holland, Luxembourg, and France) had been defeated or had capitulated in the late spring and early summer of 1940. Most Southern European and Balkan nations or regions (Slovakia, Italy, Greece, Yugoslavia—divided into Serbia and Croatia—Hungary, Rumania, and Bulgaria) had quasi-independent relations with Germany, but most were within the German orbit by 1941. We have seen that the Europeans contained within the greater German Reich (Germany, Austria, the Czechs) were the first to experience Nazi rule (by 1938) and that the Jews of these lands were the first to suffer Nazi persecution; and we have seen the terrible plight of the Jews in the east—Poland, the Baltics, and the western USSR.

Though Nazi policies varied in each country, in general it can be said that from the time of occupation or domination until the deportations the Germans used what power they could muster to press for the enactment of anti-Jewish measures. They sought or imposed measures which paralleled those that had been taken against the Jews of the Reich, though this repression was normally orchestrated at a much faster pace than had been the case in Germany.[83] Thus Jews were vilified by propaganda, humiliated by petty restrictions and marking devices such as the yellow star, defined via some manner of census, stripped of political and civil rights, hit with economic hardships and finally purged from the economy, forced into ghettos and/or otherwise limited in their housing and freedom of movement, and so on. All of Europe witnessed the dismal repertoire of measures the Nazis had perfected at home, a repertoire designed to strip Jewish people of a place in society and of the basic conditions of subsistence.[84] As deportations neared, Jews were often incarcerated in transit camps, as Heydrich had announced in Wannsee. In general the Nazis operated more circumspectly in the west than in Southern or especially Eastern Europe, where they demonstrated less hesitation in killing Jews on the spot. But from 1940 to 1942/43 they had laid the groundwork for the deaths of these western Jews as well.

The scope and pace of Nazi measures in each land were strongly affected by the nature of the wartime political relationship between Germany and that nation.[85] The options included complete subjugation and occupation (such as the Reich, Poland, Russia, Ukraine, the Baltics, and, in a different way, occupied France, Belgium, Holland, Norway, and Greece), partial, quasi-, or nearly complete independence (Slovakia, Croatia, Rumania, Hungary, Vichy France, Finland, Bulgaria, Italy, and Denmark), and neutrality (Sweden, Spain, Portugal, and Switzerland). Generally speaking, the more independence a country retained, the greater ability it had to resist Nazi anti-Jewish measures *if it wanted to do so*. As well, where Germany administered a nation or region, much depended on the form of that administration—that is, on whether the army, the SS, or a civil administration ran the country. SS-dominated countries (Poland, the Baltics, Ukraine, western Russia) faced the most brutal repression and most relentless anti-Jewish measures. Complicating matters was the fact that both the level of independence and the type of German rule in each nation often shifted during the course of the war.

A crucial factor affecting Jewish survival, and most important for our purposes here, was the quality of Jewish-Gentile relations in each country. The Nazis occupied, dominated, and sought to dominate nations each with their own distinct history of Jewish-Gentile relations. Generally speaking, where the quality of those relationships was poor, and where political anti-Semitism was strongest, the Nazis found the least resistance to anti-Jewish measures and the Jews found their plight the most desperate.[86] Indeed, in many cases—such as Vichy France, Slovakia, Rumania, and Bulgaria—even nations with some degree of independence enacted their own anti-Jewish legislation with little or no prodding from Germany. Here the history of anti-Semitic politics in each nation intersects with the particular events of the Holocaust. The Nazi pressure for anti-Jewish legislation posed a severe test of the extent to which Jews were counted within the boundaries of moral obligation as fellow citizens and fellow human beings. Where Jews had been unambiguously included within those boundaries, government officials, church leaders, bureacrats, and others were most likely to resist or subvert the Germans' anti-Jewish intentions, thus dramatically increasing the chance of Jewish survival. As noted earlier, the best defense of the Jews occurred (when it occurred) at the level of effective political resistance.

To the extent that such political resistance was lacking or ineffective in completely shielding the Jews from Nazi measures, Jews were forced to rely on local help. Such help was needed from the moment Germany came to dominate a nation until the end of the war in that nation. Again, this time at the grassroots level, the historic quality of Jewish-Gentile relations was a (if not *the*) fundamental factor. Could Jews find in their Gentile neighbors the help they needed to withstand persecution? In general anti-Semitism was more raw, potent, and pervasive in Eastern Europe than in the West, and thus Jews were more likely to find hospitality in the latter nations. But, as we have seen and will see, for a variety of reasons such hospitality was often hard to find anywhere in Europe. Prior to the decision to annihilate the Jews, the closed door or the shrugged shoulder merely meant deeper pain and greater suffering. After the Final Solution began, such responses often meant capture, which meant deportation, which meant death. The Nazis were trying to reap a harvest of dead Jews, and their success depended considerably on the fertility of each local soil for the production of that terrible crop.

The large-scale deportations to the death camps began in the spring of 1942, with the transit of Jews from the Generalgouvernement (primarily Lvov and Lublin) and Slovakia to Belzec, a death center so relentless that only two out of 600,000 Jews sent there are known to have survived.[87] During this period the first five thousand Jews from France were deported to Auschwitz. In July, the 350,000 Jews crowded into the Warsaw ghetto began to be sent to Treblinka, deported at a rate of seven thousand a day for seven weeks. Over four thousand people were murdered there each day. During these deportations all Warsaw's Jews lived in terror, fearing that their street would be the next to be blockaded and that they or their loved ones would be the next to be sent to Treblinka. The roundups were terrible scenes. Adolf Berman, a Warsaw Jew responsible for many of the orphanages in the ghetto, described the scene he saw on July 22:

> On that very day, the first victims were the Jewish children, and I shall never forget the harrowing scenes and the bloodcurdling incidents when the SS men most cruelly attacked children—children roaming in the streets; took them by force to carts, and I remember, fully, those children were defending themselves. Even today the cries and shrieking of those children are clear in my mind. "Mama, Mama," this is what we heard. "Save us, mothers."[88]

The summer of 1942 witnessed a frenzy of killing—400,000 Jews were killed at Belzec, Treblinka, and Auschwitz in August alone.[89] The victims included Jews from all over Poland, from Slovakia and Croatia, as well as thousands victimized by the first major deportations from the West to Auschwitz—from France, Holland, and Belgium. Half of the 1,700 Norwegian Jews reached Auschwitz by the end of 1942 and early months of 1943 (the rest were saved by the Norwegian underground and individual rescuers—see chapter 4). The fall of 1942 also witnessed the first deportations from Theresienstadt to Auschwitz. This "model camp" had been established in the Protectorate (the former Czech lands of Bohemia and Moravia) for certain "privileged" categories of Reich Jews as well as for most of the Czech Jews. The safety proved illusory, however, as almost ninety thousand mainly Western and Central European Jews were shipped from there to their deaths in Auschwitz during the course of the war.

Even as the war's momentum shifted against Germany, the year 1943 saw annihilation efforts heightened against the Jews. In January and February, thousands of German and Austrian Jews were sent to Auschwitz (thousands more had been sent east, mainly to major ghettos in the Generalgouvernement, in 1940/41). The first Greek Jews, those in the Salonika region, were shipped to Auschwitz beginning in late March. The victims numbered approximately forty-five thousand. Some fourteen thousand Dutch Jews were sent to their deaths between January and April 1943, while smaller numbers of Jews from France, Belgium, and Luxembourg were also deported at that time. To the south, several thousand Croatian Jews were sent to Auschwitz. Numerous others had been killed in gas vans in Croatia. Eleven thousand Jews under Bulgarian control (in Serbian Macedonia and Greek Thrace) were deported to their deaths in March. Jewish efforts, as well as the resistance of public opinion and the Bulgarian churches, then stiffened the spine of the Bulgarian government. The government refused to hand over its own fifty thousand Jews for further deportations. Their lives were thus spared (see chapter 4).

In the East, Bialystok's Jews faced their doom beginning in late February. The Cracow ghetto was destroyed in March. The Jews of Lvov were sent to their deaths in June. The attempt to liquidate the Warsaw ghetto began in April, resulting in the famous uprising that lasted six terrible weeks. Thousands died in ferocious fighting there, including hundreds of Germans. This was the greatest success ever attained by armed Jewish resistance, though the Nazis finally succeeded in liquidating the ghetto. Thousands of survivors of the uprising were sent to the massive work camps Trawniki and Poniatawa, where most were executed six months later in mass shootings that took over fifteen thousand lives.[90] Another several thousand Jews were more fortunate, managing to find refuge on the Aryan side during the chaos of the Warsaw revolt.[91]

The second half of the year saw the near obliteration of the remaining Jews of Germany and those of the Salonika region of Greece. Rome's Jews were hunted in late September and October, after the German occupation of Italy. Though over a thousand were deported to Auschwitz on October 18, nine times as many Jews escaped, most with Gentile help. The Italian underground published a statement of resistance which read:

All night and throughout the day the Germans moved through Rome, seizing Italians for their furnaces in the north. The Germans would like us to believe that these people are alien to us, that they belong to a different race; but we feel that they are flesh of our flesh and blood of our blood. They have always lived, fought, and suffered with us.[92]

Similarly defiant was the nation of Denmark, which in an amazing rescue operation managed to save nearly all of its Jews from a roundup on October 1, 1943. Not a single Danish Jew was sent to Auschwitz (see chapter 4).

During the fall, ghettos in Byelorussia were liquidated, including Minsk, Vilna, Lida, and Riga. By early 1944 the killing of Jews was beginning to wind down, for most had already been destroyed and the political/military situation was turning decisively against Germany. Yet Jews from all over Europe continued to meet their deaths. Greek Jews—from Athens and the islands of Corfu, Rhodes, and Crete—met their deaths that spring and summer. The last deportations of French Jews occurred in July and August of 1944. Over 2,500 Belgian Jews were sent to Auschwitz in 1944, as well as a small number of Dutch Jews, including Anne Frank and her family.

During the spring and into the summer and fall of 1944, the complex and unique battle for the Hungarian Jews took place. Despite the strenuous efforts of Raoul Wallenberg and the less well-known rescue activities of others, over 600,000 were deported or were killed on site by the end of the year. The final three Eastern European Jewish ghettos—Shavli, Kovno, and Lodz—were liquidated in the summer of 1944. The latter cost the lives of some seventy thousand people. A final transport of Slovakian Jews made its journey to Auschwitz in late September. Finally, on the order of Himmler, the gas chambers and crematoria of the last operational death camp, Auschwitz, were shut down in October and November of 1944. Henceforth every effort would be made to destroy the evidence of two and a half years of death-camp murders.[93]

To do so proved impossible. There was no way to eliminate the traces of six million dead Jews and several million other victims. There were simply too many pairs of children's shoes to ship west. There were simply too many corpses of mothers and grandmothers, big sisters and little brothers, uncles and fathers. There were simply too many death camps and killing centers.

There were as well, from the Nazi perspective, simply too many people who lived to tell the story of what they had suffered at Nazi hands. The Nazis undertook a continent-wide search for Jews to turn into Jewish corpses. A tiny remnant of these people lived to tell us about the rides on the cattle cars, the "selections" for labor and for death at the camp entrances, the sadism and the tortures, the gas chambers and the crematoria, and the twilight existence of a death-camp inmate trying to live in a countersociety

organized on the principle of death. Auschwitz, Majdanek, Belzec, Treblinka, Sobibor. They were established to kill those deemed unworthy of
life, and they represented the final fruits of a regime organized around the
negation of every worthy human value.

The End of the Holocaust

The closing of the death camps did not mean an end to Jewish misery and
death. Many were annihilated in the final liquidations. The rest were taken
west (along with thousands of non-Jewish prisoners) with the retreating
German Army, suffering the horrendous winter 1944/45 death marches into
the collapsing German Reich. "These marches became a new form of torture, in which tens of thousands were to perish."[94] The chaos and suffering
were immense. Many Jews suffered such marches more than once, as they
were shipped from one camp to another for months. Some managed to
escape during these deportations westward and transitions from camp to
camp. Overall, "at least a third of the 700,000 inmates recorded in January
1945 lost their lives on the exhausting evacuation marches, in the transport
trains which took weeks to reach their destination, and (particularly) in
the hopelessly overcrowded reception camps in the months and weeks
immediately before the end of the war."[95] Those who survived the cold,
disease, hunger, and periodic shootings of the death marches fought for
life until (and beyond) the end of the war, May 8, 1945.

Historians estimate today that between five and seven million Jews
lost their lives during the war, with six million the generally accepted
figure.[96] Six million people—the mind reels, for it is impossible to comprehend the full scope and magnitude of the slaughter. As Judith Miller
reminds us, six million means "one by one by one" over and over again,
day after relentless day.[97] And these six million victims were accompanied
in victimization by millions more: Soviet prisoners of war, non-Jewish Poles,
Gypsies, political prisoners, homosexuals, Jehovah's Witnesses, pacifists,
and others.[98] At the same time—in a pattern all too familiar once again
today—several other nations and ethnic groups within nations were settling
old scores and attempting to reconfigure their own demographic patterns,
borders, and political situations via the massive taking of life. Meanwhile,
throughout this time a "conventional war" of unprecedented destructive-
ness was taking place. Consider the siege of Leningrad from 1941 to 1943,
in which approximately one and a half million Soviet citizens lost their
lives.[99] The world was simply drenched in blood, the worst six years of
our century of mass death. The passing of fifty years heightens rather than
diminishes the enormity of it all.

How many European Jews survived the Holocaust? Estimates vary considerably. Culling the available evidence, Michael Marrus offers the figure of one million survivors outside the Soviet Union, with no more than 100,000 of these being survivors of the camps.[100] The others had managed to defeat the Nazis' purposes for them by somehow surviving. Certainly a number of these survivors (and some who ultimately did not survive) were aided at one time or another by Gentiles.

Yet, in a final tragic and terribly illuminating footnote, many of the Jews who tried to return to their homes in Eastern Europe learned rapidly that they were not welcome. As Martin Gilbert reports, "In many towns, the killing of Jews continued long after the Germans had left, as local Ukrainians and Poles vented their own fury on Jews who sought to return to their homes and possessions."[101] Thus when the pitiful remnant of Jews trickled back from the West and emerged from hiding, many were terrorized, and some—after surviving Hitler and the full horrors of the Holocaust—were murdered. There would be no return to the status quo ante, no rebuilding of European Jewish civilization.

Conclusion: On Jewish Resistance

The Nazis meant to kill every Jew in Europe and turned a serious portion of their formidable resources to the task. From 1939 through 1944 (in the east) and 1945 (in the west), no power on earth was both able and willing to stop them. The Jews had no real chance against this onslaught.

During the war, Jewish communities—often bereft of their pre-war leadership—agonized over their response to the Nazis. Everyone wanted to save the community. Yet bitter tactical differences emerged. Some, especially until the mass deportations to the death camps began in 1942, argued that cooperation with the Nazis offered the best hope for survival. This tended to be the approach of the Judenräte. A second group, especially after those deportations, rejected this approach as an unforgivable passivity and demanded armed resistance.[102] Yet the brutality of Nazi reprisals and the essential futility of resistance under the circumstances deterred many from considering that route.[103] A third approach was that taken by those who managed to flee. While some rejected escape as an option, others saw it as an honorable way of saving a remnant of European Jewry.

A sympathetic observer must consider all of these to be defensible responses to the unprecedented Nazi assault. That none was particularly effective reveals the relentlessness of the Nazi effort, the lack of sympathy of so many locals, and the lack of intervention of outside powers. Any attempt, individual or collective, to preserve Jewish life against the Nazi onslaught was a form of resistance.[104] Understood in this way, Jewish resistance never ceased, from the beginning of the Nazi regime to the end of the "Final Solution."

As we have seen, before the war the main resistance options were emigration (where possible) and fighting for Jewish civil and political rights and economic survival. During the war, resistance actions included the following: smuggling food, building hiding places, obtaining false documents, placing one's child with a Gentile, jumping from a train or truck, fleeing to the woods, smuggling weapons, sabotaging train tracks or bridges, shooting a German, burning down one's house as the Nazis came to town, setting up family camps in the forest, organizing an underground school in the ghetto, climbing out of a mass grave, knocking on a Gentile's door to beg for help, writing a diary, enabling another Jew to survive, and running an underground newspaper. Each act was a form of resistance and an expression of the will to live. As Alexander Donat, a Holocaust survivor, has written:

> It is pure myth that the Jews were merely "passive," that they did not put up resistance to the Nazis who had decreed their destruction. The Jews fought back against their enemies. . . . They fought against hunger and starvation, against disease, against a deadly Nazi economic blockade. They fought against murderers and against traitors within their own ranks. . . . We fought back on every front where the enemy attacked . . . with every weapon we possessed.[105]

Even those occasions in which Jews simply went with dignity to their deaths marked a resistance to the Nazi stereotype of the Jew as subhuman vermin. Choosing to die with family and community rather than to escape on one's own was an act of moral courage. Many religious Jews went to their deaths without a whimper, saying the *Shema*, seeking to sanctify the name of God (*Kiddush Ha-Shem*) by dying with dignity for their faith.[106] This kind of martyr's death was a form of resistance of the spirit with roots deep in Jewish history.[107] Such behavior can be affirmed for what it was without denigrating those who chose another way. Any who dare to evaluate Jewish behavior during the Holocaust—and who dares?—must do so with the greatest of care and the tenderest of mercy.

A portion of the hunted Jews of Europe managed to slip through the Nazi net somewhere in the killing process. Their resistance almost always led to an encounter with Gentiles. Survival required that their act of resistance to the Nazis be met by a reciprocal Gentile act of resistance to the Nazis—and that their will to live be met by a Gentile act that affirmed their right to live. How Europe's Gentiles responded is the subject to which we now turn.

3

European Gentiles

❖

In the Moral Crucible

Arise and go now to the city of slaughter;
Into its courtyard wind thy way;
There with thine own hand touch,
and with the eyes of thine head,
Behold on tree, on stone, on fence, on mural clay,
The spattered blood and dried brains of the dead.
Proceed thus to the ruins, the split walls reach,
Where wider grows the hollow, and greater grows the breach;
Pass over the shattered hearth, attain the broken wall
Whose burnt and barren brick, whose charred stones reveal
The open mouths of such wounds, that no mending
Shall ever mend, nor healing ever heal.

"In the City of Slaughter"
Chaim Nahman Bialik[1]

The words excerpted from this poem of Jewish sorrow were written not in 1945 but in 1904. The "city of slaughter" is Kishinev, the Moldovan town encountered earlier as a place where twelve thousand Jews were murdered in a single day in July 1941. But Bialik's dirge concerns a day of devastation in Kishinev two generations earlier—Passover, 1903. That day, some fifty Jews were murdered in the first major pogrom of the twentieth century.

The Nazis did not introduce the world to the killing of Jews; nor was the Holocaust the first time Jews needed their neighbors' help. Recall Pharaoh's daughter, who defied her own father's death sentence on Jewish boys and rescued the infant Moses (Exod. 2:1–10). More broadly, situations in which help is desperately needed and those present must decide whether

45

to give it constitute the human condition. How people respond in such situations is a matter of great moral importance.

In this chapter we will explore the nature of Gentile behavior toward Jews in Nazi Europe during the Holocaust.[2] The basic situation facing Europe's non-Jews, vis-à-vis Jews, was outlined in chapter 1. Having defined Jews as biomedical/racial/political enemies unworthy of life, the Nazis embarked on a campaign to find and kill every single Jew they could reach. We have glimpsed the unthinkable devastation they eventually wrought. To enhance their chances of "success," the Nazis sought to involve local collaborators who shared their evaluation of Jews as beyond the boundaries of moral obligation, indeed, as unworthy of life. At the least, the Nazis hoped to create a milieu in which, for a variety of reasons, locals would not resist German actions against Jews. In chapter 2 we noted many kinds of occasions when Jews slipped through the Nazi net and encountered their local Gentile neighbors, oftentimes directly asking them for help; here we will explore what happened in those encounters. In such moments local Gentiles were placed in a most demanding moral crucible. Their response to the moral test they faced contributed either to life or to death for Jews in need.

As we shall see, there was a wide range of Gentile response, which I will analyze typologically. We will consider the behavior of perpetrators, informants, thieves, bystanders, "reward rescuers," and (very briefly, holding most discussion until chapter 4) rescuers. These categories should not be seen as frozen or rigid but instead fluid. Nor should they be seen as equivalent to the behavior of particular individuals, who could—and did—behave in varying ways during the Holocaust. Like all of us, Europe's non-Jews were not static but instead moral agents capable of both growth and deterioration—and both occurred in heightened ways during the course of the war.

Gentile Behavior Toward Jews: Wartime Factors

We begin by considering briefly some of the most important factors and wartime developments, especially Nazi policies, that affected Gentile behavior toward Jews during the war. Here one regrets the lack of space available for a review of the history of European anti-Semitism as well as of the varying, though often negative, patterns of pre-war Jewish-Gentile relations in each nation. Particularly in those regions in which anti-Semitism remained most powerful at the time of the war, this legacy must be seen as one of the central factors negatively affecting Gentile behavior during the war. Yet there were other factors peculiar to wartime that also proved quite significant in influencing behavior toward Jews—most often, for the worst.

The ravages of war

Most Europeans who experienced those years considered World War II the worst catastrophe of their lives. Not that suffering was a stranger: Europe had known a prior World War and, in the 1930s, a worldwide depression the effects of which were profound. Yet for most Europeans these ordeals appear to have been dwarfed by World War II. Any student of Gentile behavior during the Holocaust must consider the nature of the war and of the experience of all those who struggled to survive it.

Many memoirists point to the German invasion as the event that began the shattering of their world. The fearful experience of war—air-raid warnings and bombings, destroyed homes and churches, enemy soldiers marching in the streets, one's nation subjected to humiliation and defeat—deeply marked all who went through it. The experience combined both psychic shock and, often, physical suffering. Europeans lost homes and family members, security and stability, freedom and political sovereignty—indeed, most elements of the world that they had known.

Throughout the war, but especially in the beginning and again at the end, a huge refugee crisis struck Europe. People sought to avoid the Nazis by leaving their countries or moving to safer regions within their countries. They fled the sites of imminent or just-concluded military actions. They left destroyed homes and communities in search of refuge elsewhere. Millions of Europeans crisscrossed their own and foreign lands in desperate search of better and safer places (or any place at all) to abide, often moving numerous times during the war.

One cannot neglect to mention the desperate search for food and other basic necessities. The war shattered the economies of many European nations, disrupting farming cycles and food distribution patterns, taking some of the labor force from food production and turning it to war-related work, creating a black-market economy, and so on. As well, the Nazis generally sought to exploit local economic capacities for their own needs, thus perilously limiting the food and other resources available to the local population. Wartime rations often fell well short of daily needs. Some Europeans were starving to death, and most were fighting desperately against such a fate. Other basic necessities of life, such as warm clothing, electricity, water, and fuel often were lacking.

Finally, one must consider the terrifying nature of the Nazi occupation. War brought the atrocities that so often accompany a marauding army, such as torture, rape, and random murder. Further, throughout much of occupied Europe, the Nazis conscripted locals for forced labor elsewhere in Europe, from which many were never to return. For example, over 2.5 million Poles were conscripted for labor in Germany. Anyone considered at all likely to stir up political resistance was watched, incarcerated, or killed, often the latter. Organized venues of political dissent—such as the free press or political parties—were squashed. When underground movements emerged, as they inevitably did, the Nazis ruthlessly suppressed them. Acts of resistance were met with mass reprisals, on the principle of collective responsibility.

Beyond these measures, the Nazis sometimes targeted and assaulted selected portions of the local population. This was particularly the case in Poland and the Soviet Union. Earlier, we noted the murder of hundreds of thousands in the Polish elite as well as the measures against the Soviet "commissars" and the brutal murders of a staggering two million Soviet prisoners of war. Further, Nazi racial/geographical fantasies meant the uprooting of millions, such as the million Poles who were relocated to the east in the Germanization of western Poland. Many thousands of Poles lost their lives in this ruthless process.[3] Nor were the Nazis the only world power contributing to wartime devastation. In the eastern part of Poland prior to June 1941, Soviet occupation policy was remarkably similar in its murderousness—Poland was brutalized from west and east.[4]

In the midst of all of these ravages of war, many Europeans lacked the ability to discern the *particular* neediness of their Jewish neighbors, who after 1941 were targeted for systematic extermination. This problem of discernment should not be dismissed out of hand. Especially where Nazi measures against the local population were most harsh, as in Poland, a definite difficulty existed, at least for a time, in discerning any difference between the suffering of a nation's Jews and of all people in that nation.[5] Certainly among those portions of the Polish population targeted for forced labor, relocation, and execution, the plight of the Jews seemed no worse than theirs, and their own need for help as great. Many Poles too were on the run, hiding, passing under false papers, and trying to stay one step ahead of their murderers, whether Nazi or Soviet.[6]

Many other Europeans did indeed discern the particular neediness of their Jewish neighbors, but did not involve themselves on behalf of Jews. It is often the case, and first-hand accounts from the war confirm, that people's boundaries of moral obligation constrict when engaged in the struggle for personal, family, or national survival. Though it was not always a conscious decision by any means, many Europeans behaved as if they had enough to worry about in trying to keep themselves and their families alive until war's end. (Rescuers, of course, proved the exception to this pattern.) In order not to add any further risks to their own survival, they adopted a strategy toward the Jews of "purposeful uninvolvement."[7] Where the struggle between the Jews and the Nazis was concerned, these Europeans would stay out of it.[8]

Exploitation of ethnic tensions

Another wartime development of decided importance was the way in which the Nazis brilliantly exploited the ancient, multilayered majority/minority hostilities that long had afflicted Eastern, Central, and Southern Europe and continue to do so to this day.[9] In Poland, for example, the Nazis overturned the ethnic apple cart by raising the status of the local ethnic Germans (*Volksdeutsche*) and Ukrainians and enlisting their help in the occupation.[10] Members of both groups were often eager collaborators, welcoming the chance to take revenge on their former Polish masters as well as to beat on the Jews, whom many saw as partners with the Poles in their prewar oppression. Throughout these regions of Europe numerous ethnic groups, with Nazi prodding, were soon at each other's throats, their barely suppressed hatreds for one another easily inflamed by Nazi propaganda. Susceptibility to such divide-and-conquer tactics weakened overall opposition and provided the Nazis with numerous foot soldiers for their actions against the Jews and other targeted groups.

Encouragement of anti-Jewish acts

Throughout Europe, the Germans directly inflamed the already powerful anti-Semitism through propaganda and their own brutality toward Jews. Nazi propaganda endlessly played on every source of anti-Jewish sentiment—religious, economic, political, and broadly cultural. For example, during the war the Nazis published a book called *The Jewish Ritual Murders*, which was widely distributed among the ranks of the SS and in Eastern Europe.[11] This collection of ritual murder legends and other kinds of propaganda incited some to direct collaboration and for others helped to quench instincts of sympathy toward Jews.

The Nazis also directly encouraged indigenous participation in their anti-Jewish actions, thus legitimizing behavior that in some regions was already historically well established.[12] From the beginning of the occupation, especially in Poland and the Soviet Union, the Nazis essentially declared open season on the Jews. Among some people, such defenselessness stimulates brutality. Any person or group forced to live without the protection of the law is deeply vulnerable to assault.

Not only was this kind of violence against the most needy encouraged, but the reverse—sympathy and action on behalf of Jews—was brutally discouraged. Gentile accounts reveal the powerful pressures not only to avoid helping Jews but also to avoid even *appearing* sympathetic.[13] Furthermore, locals soon learned that those who helped Jews would share their fate. Execution could be expected—often particularly cruel, often public—not only for the helper but often for his or her whole family or even village.[14] Those who managed to survive the Nazi propaganda assault with sympathy for Jews intact faced this powerful deterrent to acting on such sympathy.

Economic motives

The Nazis acted as if all Jewish property rightfully belonged to the Nazi state.[15] As we saw in chapter 2, their assault on the Jews included a comprehensive program of economic exploitation. Local Gentiles were affected—indeed, tempted—by these policies in several ways. The pogroms, deportations, and ghettoization of Jews gave local Gentiles sometimes temporary and sometimes permanent access to Jewish jobs, homes, and possessions. Even Gentiles of conscience struggled to discern whether taking such things made one an accessory to Nazi crimes. Further, under conditions of wartime scarcity, Nazi bounties for tracking and killing Jews could seem enticing, as did pay received while working as a member of Nazi-recruited militias or auxiliary forces. Especially given the longstanding economic resentment against Jews, the opportunity to benefit financially at their expense was, to some, irresistible.[16]

Wartime Jewish-Gentile political tensions

An examination of the situation in the Baltic states and Ukraine is especially helpful in revealing the importance of another wartime development in some areas—Jewish-Gentile political tensions arising amidst the shifting fortunes of war. The ebb and flow of the Nazi and Soviet armies across these so-called buffer regions had devastating consequences for local Jews.

In June 1940, in accordance with the terms of the Nazi-Soviet pact of August 1939, the Red Army moved into the three Baltic states (Latvia, Lithuania, and Estonia), putting to an end some twenty years of independence. Jewish and Gentile perceptions of this turn of events differed tragically. Many of the 250,000 Baltic Jews were fairly happy to see the Red Army arrive. Well informed about German atrocities to the west, Baltic Jews saw their Soviet occupiers as the lesser of two evils. Gentiles, on the other hand, saw the Soviet occupation as an unmitigated disaster, a crushing blow to hard-won national independence. An irremediable conflict of interest existed.

Resentments stirred by this clash in perception and interests were worsened by the occupation itself. For Jews, the Soviet occupation had mixed results, but it did mean the annulment of some pre-war anti-Jewish legislation that had been imposed by anti-Semitic regimes in the Baltics. As well, positions of prominence in the occupation were available to Jewish

Communists, some of them Baltic Jews, while some Gentiles lost prestigious posts. Jews thus were viewed by some as traitorous pro-Soviet collaborators. When the Soviet armies were forced out of the Baltics under the Wehrmacht's advance, certain nationalists initiated pogroms against Jews. Once the Nazis had arrived, some nationalists were available and willing to participate in *Einsatzgruppen*-organized pogroms and later mass murder actions. According to Jewish sources, a considerable number and perhaps even a majority of the Baltic Jews ultimately murdered were killed with the active assistance of Baltic Gentiles.[17]

A similar phenomenon occurred in Ukraine, a part of which had belonged to the USSR since 1921 but all of which was rife with independence sentiment. Jewish-Ukrainian relations were chronically tense, whether in Poland, in Soviet Ukraine, or elsewhere.[18] The two worst single episodes of Jewish suffering prior to World War II had been the work of Ukrainians: the massive seventeenth-century Chmielnicki pogroms and the huge massacres of 1917–1921.[19] Meanwhile, Ukrainians nursed their own grievances received at the hands of the Stalinist USSR—dekulakization, forced collectivization, and the terror-famine, which took millions of lives.[20] Searching for someone to blame for their suffering, many Ukrainian nationalists fixed on "Judeo-Bolshevism." An increasing anti-Semitism and extremism characterized Ukrainian nationalism during the 1930s. As in the Baltics, Jews were seen as Soviet collaborators during the 1939–1941 period of Soviet control over Ukrainian eastern Poland. The brutal Soviet occupation left many Ukrainians as ready as the Baltic nationalists to attack Jews independently, and to cooperate in Nazi anti-Jewish efforts, when the Germans arrived in late June 1941.[21]

Gentile Behavior Toward Jews During the Holocaust

We now have seen some of the formidable factors and historical developments in Europe which generally made it less likely that Gentiles would help Jews during the Holocaust. I do not offer this discussion in order to excuse the multiple layers of collaboration and the fateful indifference on the part of many local Gentiles that will appear in what follows. The evidence does, however, help to identify the difficulties and place the behavior of Gentiles in much needed historical and political context.

Perpetrators

We begin our typology with the behavior of different groups of Gentiles who participated directly in the killing of Jews. Such participation included not only pulling the trigger of a machine gun but also other forms of direct involvement in the killing process.

Uniformed   Though the focus of this chapter is *local* Gentile behavior during the Holocaust, the discussion would be incomplete without some mention of the central perpetrators in this crime—members of the **German security, police, military, and camp units** whose responsibilities included occasional or regular participation in the direct killing of Jews. These constituted the paid professional staff of internationally organized mass murder. As well, it must not be forgotten that standing behind those German forces who appeared in the east was the administrative apparatus throughout the Reich that organized the destruction of European Jewry—and, behind them, the high government officials who gave them their orders. These people rarely appear on the scene, but the scene itself would be impossible without them.

In the killing fields and death centers of the east a wide array of German officials could be found. They were heavily represented by various units of the SS and police, of course, but also involved were the Army and numerous branches of the German civil service.[22] Such people were (excepting the SS) not especially trained for or inclined toward mass murder but simply "ordinary men" rotated to the east on the basis of administrative decision and expected to carry out their orders.[23] Despite occasional "lapses" into compassion or revulsion, these Germans generally remained committed to their tasks and faithful in their discharge.

Military, security, and police units of Germany's wartime allies occasionally initiated and led actions against Jews while more often serving as auxiliaries. For example, Rumanian military forces led one of the worst massacres of the war, the slaughter at Odessa, the port city on the Black Sea (see chapter 2). As a reprisal for the bombing of a Rumanian command headquarters, tens of thousands of Jews (and some others) were machine-gunned, burned alive, and bombed to death in late October of 1941. Germans functioned as the auxiliaries in this terrible massacre.[24] Normally, Nazi security forces preferred to be in charge of such killing operations, but it is a mistake to think non-German forces served solely as auxiliaries.

In regard to the killings in the Soviet zone, Raul Hilberg has noted the sparseness of German personnel in the areas of destruction.[25] Germany was fighting a two-front war by the time the extermination of European Jewry was ordered, and was also busy occupying and administering nearly the whole of Europe. Only small numbers of men could be spared for the project of killing Soviet and later European Jewry, and most of these had other responsibilities as well. Given such thin personnel levels, *Einsatzgruppen* commanders were genuinely concerned about the response of the civilian population to their mass shootings. As noted in chapter 1, the resistance of large numbers of locals would hamper their efforts; conversely, chances of success would be greatly enhanced by their cooperation. Thus the German annihilation administrators set out to win, at minimum, Gentile neutrality—and, when possible, Gentile collaboration in their program.

The most potent layer of local Gentile collaboration was direct participation in the mass killing of European Jewry. To fill out their sparse ranks the Nazis co-opted or created **indigenous Gentile security, police, and militia units** (called *Selbstschutz*) which became involved in killing Jews. Besides filling out their ranks, a key reason the Germans used local auxiliaries was to make the case later that anti-Jewish actions had the full support of the indigenous population. Another purpose was to preserve German morale by leaving some of the grimmest operations to local forces.[26] For example, German records indicate that Einsatzkommando 4a of Einsatzgruppe C used Ukrainian auxiliaries to shoot children, confining itself to the shootings of adults.[27] An example of the use of local auxiliaries can be found in the detailed personnel records of Einsatzgruppe A, operating in the north. The 990 persons who made up this unit included representatives of the Waffen-SS, the Gestapo, the SD, and other German police units. As well, eighty-seven men (9 percent of the total force) were from indigenous units of Lithuanians, Latvians, Estonians, and Ukrainians and added as "auxiliary police."[28]

Indigenous auxiliary units were especially valuable in rounding up Jews for annihilation. *Einsatzgruppen* records clearly indicate that roundups conducted with the assistance of local collaborators resulted in higher percentages of Jewish victims. As one bitter Ukrainian Jewish survivor has written, "There is not a shred of doubt that the number of Jewish survivors would have been much larger, were it not for the indifferent and collaborationist behavior of many Gentiles. After all, the Germans were strangers in the occupied territories. They didn't know and didn't easily recognize anybody who was Jewish."[29] Local Gentiles brought facility with the local language, neighborhood contacts, and personal knowledge of who was and was not Jewish in the area.

One chilling story of local collaboration from early in the Nazi occupation of Polish Ukraine is recounted in a Holocaust memoir by the Polish Jew Shlomo Kogan. Kogan recalls the time when the Germans arrived in the Volhynia region and established a Ukrainian police force in power. One night, "a military ball was arranged and the Ukrainian authorities were instructed to 'invite' fifty Jews. All but seven . . . went into hiding. These seven were subjected to an all-night orgy of torture, and then were killed."[30]

Later, Ukrainian, Latvian, and Lithuanian auxiliary forces figured prominently in the daily mass roundups and deportations from the Warsaw Ghetto in the summer of 1942. The marches to the *Umschlagplatz* (train depot) were punctuated by wanton killings, not only by German forces but also by the auxiliaries. "The people had to march at a given tempo.

He who walked too quickly was shot. He who fell on the way was shot. He who strayed out of line was shot. . . . A child who cried was shot."[31]

The roundup, deportation, and massacre of the Jewish community at Dzialoszyce in September of 1942, according to the Jewish survivor Martin Rosenblum, was carried out by the German Gestapo, the Polish police, and Ukrainians. The Poles and Ukrainians drove the carts and horses that carried the weak, young, and infirm to the site of their machine-gun massacre some distance away—and then participated in the slaughter. Two thousand Jews were killed at the massacre site, the other eight thousand shipped to Belzec and gassed.[32]

Gentiles also helped to staff labor, concentration, and death camps, often as **guards**. Some Gentiles (such as the infamous Ivan the Terrible of Treblinka) were among the cruelest participants in the worst system of organized cruelty and mass murder ever devised. One story from Treblinka can serve to represent numerous incidents. One morning a Ukrainian guard promised a Jewish woman on a deportation train that she and her four-year-old child could go free if she gave the guard a large bribe. She did so, and he let the woman and her child out of the train. As soon as she turned her back and walked down the railway embankment, he shot her. A Polish eyewitness tells what happened next:

> The mother rolled down into a field, pulling the child after her. The child clutched the mother's neck. Jews looking out of the wagons called out and yelled, and the child turned back up the embankment again and under the wagons to the other side of the train. Another Ukrainian killed the child with one blow of a rifle butt on its head.[33]

Nonuniformed   Nonuniformed perpetrators constituted a related but distinct kind of murderer. These were people who were not members of uniformed security or military units but rounded up and killed Jews in other contexts. One type of nonuniformed perpetrator might best be called the **bounty hunter**. Frequently, German forces offered a bounty to locals who would help them round up and kill Jews who had somehow slipped through the Nazi net. These bounties included products such as sugar and vodka, part of the possessions of the murdered Jews, or cash payments.[34] Many could be found who were willing to participate.

A Polish teacher has left a chilling account of the role of the local population in tracking down Jews during the roundup in the area of Lukow in 1942:

> On 5 November, I passed through the village of Siedliska. I went into the cooperative store. The peasants were buying scythes. The woman shopkeeper said, "They will be useful for you in the roundup today." I asked, "What roundup?" "Of the Jews." I asked, "How much are they

paying for every Jew caught?" An embarrassed silence fell. So I went on. "They paid thirty pieces of silver for Christ, so you should also ask for the same amount." Nobody answered. What the answer was I heard a little later. Going through the forest, I heard volleys of machine-gun fire. It was the roundup of the Jews hiding there. Perhaps it is blasphemous to say that I clearly ought to be glad that I got out of the forest alive.[35]

Another type of nonuniformed perpetrator was the **pogromist**—these were the men and women who participated in wartime pogroms against Jews. Anti-Jewish pogroms erupted early in the Nazi occupation of Poland and later of the western Soviet Union, as well as elsewhere. Discussing the Soviet territories, Raul Hilberg argues that these pogroms were not genuinely spontaneous but were all organized or inspired by German forces.[36] Other accounts contradict this assertion.[37] In any case, some of the pogroms were indisputably organized by German forces, such as the February 1940 Warsaw pogrom. The *Einsatzgruppen*, as well, managed to organize early pogroms in Kaunas (Lithuania) and Riga (Latvia). But at their worst, these pogroms included numerous Gentile participants who had had no direct contact with German forces. They turned on their Jewish neighbors with a vengeance as the pogrom spread through a town, village, or region.

It is helpful, though disheartening, to consider the behavior of nonuniformed killers who operated on their own. Such **freelance perpetrators** were individuals who killed those Jews they happened to encounter, most often as the Jews sought to flee or to hide from their Nazi pursuers. Some did so because they feared Jews, others because they hated Jews, still others, according to Mordecai Paldiel, because they sought economic gain—"they wanted to preempt the Germans and get the best loot for themselves."[38] Throughout the period of Nazi rule in Eastern Europe, it became clear to all that a Jew could be killed with impunity. The memoirs of Jews on the run reveal an intense and abiding fear of death; and Jews feared not only the Nazis but also hostile local Gentiles. The prospect of the latter was perhaps even more terrifying because it was less predictable. A Jew on the run had good reason to fear that the Gentile on the other side of the door might respond to his plea for help with a shotgun blast to the chest. That such murders occurred frequently is well documented.

Holocaust survivor Rosa Pinchewski has related the story of a terrible encounter with a local peasant. Ten-year-old Rosa, her father, mother, and brother were on the run outside of Lodz. Finally they found a peasant who hid them for quite some time, in exchange for money. At one point her father disappeared after a trip to town. Not long after, the peasant put the three in a wagon, saying he was going to take them to a safer place. On reaching a river, the peasant drowned Rosa's mother and brother. Rosa managed to escape and flee, a child now utterly alone in the world.[39]

A story with a similar ending is told by Feiga Kammer. Mother of three children, a ten-year-old girl and two sons, Kammer was seeking desperately to keep her frostbitten children alive through a snowy winter while on the run in the forests of southeastern Poland. One terrible day, while Kammer watched helplessly from a window, her daughter was caught and tortured by a Ukrainian peasant boy. Shortly thereafter, the ten-year-old was executed by Ukrainians in the forest.[40]

The effort to form small resistance groups among Jews who had fled to the forests was often hampered by local peasant killers. For example, in March 1942, in a forest southeast of Warsaw, twenty-five Jews were encamped together for some months. One day more than a hundred local Ukrainian peasants came to the camp and ordered them to leave. When the Jews refused to leave and instead put up a fight, they were rapidly captured and executed—men, women, and children—one by one. Only four of the twenty-five Jews survived.[41]

Another category of freelance perpetrators were some of the local anti-Nazi partisan bands and escaped Soviet prisoners-of-war roaming the forests of Poland, Byelorussia, and elsewhere in the east. Sometimes such groups welcomed Jewish participation in the fight against a common Nazi enemy. Often, however, they fought Jews as well as Nazis, robbing and killing Jewish partisans in the forests as well as unarmed Jews in hiding and on the run.[42] Hostile local partisan bands, when added to the dangers posed by other hostile peasants and German forces, decreased even further the slim odds that Jews who had managed to escape all prior terrors might survive in the forests.[43]

The killing did not end with Jews or liberation. In July 1944, the rescuer Jan Pauvlavicius was murdered by local Lithuanians. His crime was that he had saved the lives of Jews. Jews seeking to return home also were murdered by Poles and Ukrainians, as noted in chapter 2.[44]

Lawrence Baron has written, "Local leaders sometimes equaled the Nazis in their desire to rid their countries of Jews."[45] It was in such social milieus that the Nazis found a steady source of recruits to help them perpetrate their onslaught on the Jews.[46] The Holocaust is not only the story of assembly-line gassings by Nazi "professionals." It is also, in part, the story of local Gentile policemen, farmers, doctors, priests, and clerks taking up guns, knives, axes, and bare hands to kill Jews.

Informants

Working hand-in-glove with those who killed Jews were informants. These deadly people provided information that led to the capture and death of thousands of Jews. As with the perpetrators, a distinction can be drawn between uniformed and nonuniformed informants.

Uniformed   Nazi Germany was a totalitarian police state that took surveillance of its population to previously unheard-of lengths. During the war, the Nazis extended this surveillance apparatus across occupied Europe. Its head could be found in Berlin, with Heinrich Himmler's SS, SD, Gestapo, and other agencies. Its tentacles extended throughout Europe, through the work of uniformed officials of these and collaborating agencies and the myriad locals they recruited or encouraged. Once the hunt for Jews was on, numerous Nazi, allied, and local functionaries dug out, received, and passed along information about Jewish "fugitives." The Polish cities, for example, were full of Polish police, Gestapo agents, and other German security forces looking for Jews. Many if not most of these information-gatherers also killed Jews on occasion—the distinction between these persons and those who actually did the killing is blurry. They were all part of the Nazi annihilation staff.

Nonuniformed   Of greater interest to our study are the indigenous informants who were not part of this professional mass-murder staff but were an essential element in its success. The mass hunt for Jews opened up an economic and social niche for an entire class of what might be called **quasi-professional local informants**. There was serious money to be made in the Jew-hunting business, and informant-entrepreneurs rushed in to fill the gap. In Poland, for example, German and Polish officials were aided immensely by a group of Poles who developed the cycle of extortion and betrayal into an occupation. These were the notorious *szmalcowniki* ("fat-fleecers"—so called because they stripped Jews of everything they owned). Jews in hiding, or those trying to pass as Gentiles, lived in mortal fear of these ever-present informant/extortionists. Similar problems with informants occurred throughout most of Europe.

The szmalcowniki developed their strategy into a finely honed weapon. Their practice was to watch people constantly and look for anything out of the ordinary. Was there too much activity at the house on the corner? Unfamiliar people going in or out? Too much smoke coming from the chimney? Was a window boarded up that had not been broken? This detailed knowledge of the normal state of affairs of a home or block was most accessible to someone quite familiar with the neighborhood. Informants also became skilled at noticing unusual activity on the streets. They would walk behind someone to see if he appeared to know his way around or if he was in unfamiliar territory; they would also be vigilant for people who looked behind themselves too frequently, a telltale sign of life on the run. Did this man wear his coat collar too high up for the weather? Was this woman wearing sunglasses on a gray wintry day?

If the informant believed that he might be tracking a Jew, he usually confronted his prey. In the case of men, informants often forced them to drop their pants in broad daylight to check for circumcisions. For this reason, Jewish men were in extreme danger every time they stepped onto the streets. A number of other tests were employed to test whether the person was indeed Jewish. Informants listened for Yiddish-accented Polish and inappropriate dialects in relation to the region of the country or the job listed on one's identification card. Perhaps most hideous of all, from a Christian point of view, were the religious tests that Jews were forced to pass. Was the fugitive able to say the rosary or recite the Creed? If not, he or she could be considered a Jew. A Christian must recoil in horror at the thought of Christian faith being used as a screening device for mass murder.

Once in possession of a Jew, the informant had a number of lucrative options. He could simply turn the fugitive in to the authorities and receive the reward offered. But informants soon discovered that they could enrich themselves far more if they first blackmailed the Jew, threatening him or her with betrayal to the Gestapo unless paid protection money. After the Jew's resources were exhausted, then the blackmailer/informant still could denounce the victim to the Germans and receive the reward. Another practice was simply to rob the Jew of all of his or her possessions and then walk down to Gestapo headquarters, victim in hand. The Nazis wanted that booty, however, and did not hesitate to take it from the informant. Thus, some szmalcowniki worked in pairs; one took all of the victim's possessions, and the other turned the Jew in. Afterwards, they divided the booty.[47] The prevalence of these despicable practices is illustrated in Nechama Tec's study of Polish rescuers. She found that 71 percent of 308 Polish-Jewish Holocaust survivors reported having been blackmailed by szmalcowniki; the other 29 percent had known of it having happened to other Jews on the run.[48]

Another source of terror for Jews and rescuers was the genuinely **amateur informants**—the numerous neighbors, acquaintances, and even so-called friends ready to betray them. Especially in Eastern Europe, the streets, shops, and apartment houses contained many who were ready to denounce a Jew to the German authorities when they happened to encounter one. This "volunteer army" of informants made for a social milieu that radically limited the chance that Jews would survive. For some, financial gain was the central incentive. As we have seen, throughout occupied Europe the Nazis offered rewards for information about fugitive Jews.[49]

Those amateur informants whose motives were other than monetary are perhaps even more troubling. Greed is a familiar and well-nigh universal human problem. But the literature reveals that some betrayed Jews not for money but simply out of hatred. One Jew was told by Polish informers, after her capture, "You are Jewish and you have no right to live."[50] Such barefaced contempt for the value of another human being's life is breathtaking. Perhaps the person who made this statement had drunk far too deeply of the ideology of Poland's Nazi occupiers, who sought to create in the occupied lands precisely such contempt for Jews. Or perhaps the Nazis had little or nothing to do with it, given the anti-Semitism that long predated the Nazi arrival and deeply marked Poland and other European nations.

It is also apparent that some who informed did so not because they hated Jews but on the basis of social conformity or obedience to the authorities. Once the annihilation of European Jewry began, Jews not under Nazi control or already dead were defined as fugitives from the law. The Nazis constantly demanded that such Jews be denounced to the authorities. In much of Europe, alternative sources of social authority—such as the churches or resistance groups—did not demand that such Nazi orders be disobeyed. (When such authority figures *did* demand resistance and help for Jews, it often made a profound difference—see chapters 5 and 6.) At its worst, a social ethos emerged in which turning Jews in was seen as morally good, while sheltering Jews was seen as morally reprehensible. Such attitudes were reinforced by fear of the consequences of disobedience to Nazi dictates.

Interestingly, children and young people appear to have been particularly susceptible to the pressures of this kind of social milieu. With a regularity too steady to be coincidental, Gentile children and teenagers appear as betrayers in Jewish accounts.[51] As survivor Idel Kagan said, "The little peasant boy used to give you away."[52] The survivor Mietek Eichel recorded the story of a time when, on a Warsaw street, a Polish boy was hanging onto him and calling the Gestapo. Eichel was saved by a Pole who beat the boy off, giving Eichel a chance to escape. The rescuer was punished by having all of his possessions taken away.[53] Students of social structure and its influence on the formation of character will be struck by the way in which the nazified Eastern European milieu influenced impressionable young Gentiles.[54]

On the run, it was most difficult for fugitive Jews to distinguish friend from foe.[55] Prewar friends and acquaintances could not always be trusted. For example, on the day of the horrendous Babi Yar massacres in Kiev, one seventy-year-old Jewish man was betrayed to the Germans by the Ukrainian woman with whom he and his family had shared an apartment for many years.[56] In October 1942, a Jew who had climbed naked out of a bloody execution pit near Rakow and fled for help was betrayed to the Germans by a prewar friend of his, a local ethnic German.[57]

Memoirs about life on the "Aryan side" of the ghettos and in the forests reveal the intense and constant fear of discovery and betrayal. One story aptly reveals the depths of this fear. In November 1942, some 100,000 Jews from the Bialystok region were being kept in holding camps in preparation for shipment to Treblinka. Some Jews managed to escape from these holding camps. In one instance, a Jew who escaped decided to return voluntarily to the camp, because he was afraid of the consequences of being caught by local Gentiles. He decided he would rather face the tender mercies of the German and Ukrainian camp guards than deal with the local Gentiles in the region. On his return, he was tortured brutally and finally killed.[58]

Thieves

Some Gentiles responded to Jewish need by stealing their money and their possessions, worsening their plight dramatically.

Those Jews on the run who had managed to retain any of their prewar financial resources were easy pickings for the **blackmailers** discussed above. A variety of **con artists** also preyed on Jews. One common scheme was to offer help in return for financial reward and then take the money while reneging on the help. For example, Rosa Pinchewski, whose tale of the murder of her mother and brother was recounted above, on an earlier occasion had been offered shelter by a Polish peasant woman in return for pay. Once the money had exchanged hands, the peasant woman abandoned the ten-year-old Rosa, leaving her alone in the woods.[59] A similar betrayal happened to twelve-year-old Matti Drobless, who had escaped from the Warsaw Ghetto in March 1943 with his fourteen-year-old sister and nine-year-old brother. In "Aryan" Warsaw they found the family of a man who had worked for their father before the war. In exchange for their mother's jewelry and other valuables, the three children were promised a hiding place in this Gentile home. However, "after three days he told us we would have to leave. Otherwise, he said, he would inform on us. We cried and pleaded but to no avail."[60]

Much of the time Jews were simply robbed of their money and possessions. Historically, pogroms against Jews usually had included outright theft of Jewish possessions as well as destruction of property and loss of life. The great Jewish novelist Sholom Aleichem has left us a fictional re-creation of a 1905 pogrom scene which powerfully captures the moment and the pogromist mentality:

> A poor Jewish woman, still young, with two children—one in her arms, the other holding her hand— . . . was running, clutching a basket and being chased by two gentile women. One was grabbing for the basket and the other was tearing the shawl from the young woman's head. Tamara ran over and stopped them. "God be with you—why are you doing that?" "Today we can!" the gentile women answered her with a laugh.[61]

They robbed because, that day, it was permissible. Thirty-six years later, the Jews of Tarnopol, in Ukraine, were robbed of their possessions by Poles and Ukrainians as they made their forced move by cart and by foot into the ghetto established for them by the Nazis.[62]

Another form of thievery was the looting that occurred during and after Nazi deportations and massacres of Jews. Chapter 1 opened with the story of the action against the Jews of Nesvizh; in that account, local Gentiles descended upon the Jewish quarter to grab whatever they could get before it burned up. Similar scenes occurred all over Eastern Europe.[63] Abba Kovner described the scene the morning after the first major massacre of the Jews of Vilna:

> In the deserted streets—no Jews were in the streets—all over the streets there were scattered their belongings. Diagonally across the street there was a column of armed Lithuanians; behind them and flanking them on their sides—a multitude of men and even more women, neighbors who came from all over the area, from the suburbs. The smell of booty, of loot was in their nostrils. They saw an opportunity of gain. On the side, in polished boots and uniforms, stood the Germans.[64]

The Nazi program against the Jews included massive and total expropriation of Jewish wealth. Thus far in this section we have noted only the amateur thieves. But it was the professional annihilation staff that led the way in the expropriation of Jewish wealth, as in all else. The alert local Gentiles who managed to get a piece of that wealth somewhere in the process of expropriation and extermination were like dogs awaiting scraps from the table. The Nazi annihilation machine stole the greatest proportion of Jewish property during the Holocaust.

Bystanders

In customary usage the term *bystander* denotes "one present but not taking part in a situation or event."[65] In discussion of Gentile behavior during the Holocaust, the term generally is used to describe all Gentiles who neither directly harmed nor directly helped Jews but instead "stood by," remaining "purposefully uninvolved," as Nechama Tec says, or "escaping into neutrality," in Raul Hilberg's terms.[66] A close look at events during the Nazi assault on the Jews leads one to wonder whether it actually was possible to be a "bystander" to the Holocaust. Can it be said that those Gentiles who knew what was happening and neither helped nor harmed Jews were not taking part in that event?

That Jews asked their Gentile neighbors for help is indisputable. "Across the whole occupied territory Jews were turning to the Christian population for assistance—in vain," Hilberg says.[67] Local Gentiles may desperately have wanted to remain out of the picture, but this was impossible. To do nothing for a Jew—especially when directly asked—actually meant to turn him or her away. By providing no opportunity for the Jew to rest, to eat, to warm up, or to hide, the Gentile in effect helped the Nazis. Conversely, to offer any kind of help to a Jew enhanced his or her chance for survival. All non-Jews in occupied Europe were involved, voluntarily or not. Indeed, from a moral point of view there may be no such thing as a bystander. If one is present, one is taking part. The question is whether that inevitable "taking part" adds harm or ameliorates it.

Even so, the involvement of the bystander is distinctive. He or she is approached (directly or indirectly) by perpetrator or victim, both of whom seek the bystander's involvement on their side and identification with their cause. The bystander's response is to identify with neither but instead to try to carve out a safe space for noninvolvement and nonidentification. The Holocaust literature reveals two significant variables in the response of bystanders to Jewish need. The first has to do with the context of noninvolvement: whether the bystander rejects a direct request for help or simply fails to initiate aid. Another has to do with the level of sympathy: whether the bystander responds to Jewish need unsympathetically or with at least a glimmer of feeling.

Many Jewish accounts reveal instances in which a Jew, after making a direct request for help, was turned away coldly and unsympathetically by a local Gentile. In Nechama Tec's study of Polish-Jewish Holocaust survivors, 56 percent reported having been rejected at least once as they made a direct request for help.[68] Feiga Kammer, whose daughter's brutal murder was recounted earlier in the chapter, reported that life on the run consisted largely of a series of rejections. Much of the time she and her frostbitten children were refused entry to Gentile homes altogether; sometimes they were allowed to stay in a house for one night and then turned out. She lamented, "The children were chilled to the bone and hungry, and their cries seemed to touch no one's heart." The suffering of the children was so great that after a time they simply pleaded with their mother for an easy death and an end to their misery.[69]

In chapter 2 we noted instances in which Jews managed to survive a mass shooting and make their way, naked and wounded, out of the pit. The Jews of the Lithuanian town of Eisysky were executed by such a mass shooting in September of 1941. One survivor was sixteen-year-old Zvi Michalowski.

> At the far end of the [Jewish] cemetery . . . were a few Christian homes. Zvi knew them all. Naked, covered with blood, he knocked on the first door. The door opened. A peasant was holding a lamp which he had looted earlier in the day from a Jewish home. "Please let me in," Zvi

pleaded. The peasant lifted the lamp and examined the boy closely. "Jew, go back to the grave where you belong!" he shouted at Zvi and slammed the door in his face. . . . Near the forest lived a widow whom Zvi knew too. He decided to knock on her door. The old widow opened the door. She was holding in her hand a small, burning piece of wood. "Let me in!" begged Zvi. "Jew, go back to the grave at the old cemetery!" She chased him away with the burning piece of wood as if exorcising an evil spirit.[70]

Sometimes Gentiles encountered Jewish need not because of a direct request but by witnessing that need. To help in such circumstances required *initiating* the activity rather than responding to another's plea. Any number of stories could be cited of Jews who were in need of help and in plain sight of Gentiles who did nothing to help them. In the last chapter I cited the testimony of the Byelorussian Jew Rivka Yosselevska, who survived an *Einsatzgruppen* killing which took her whole family. She recalled Gentile shepherds passing by and throwing stones at her as she lay on the pit where her family was murdered.[71] (To Christian readers these "Christian" shepherds are strange and terrible visitants, throwing stones at a naked, wounded, and grieving Jew. For we remember other shepherds: "The shepherds returned, glorifying and praising God for all they had heard and seen.") The Gentiles of Nesvizh also present a grievous example of this failure to initiate help. With their arms full of pillaged goods, they were "wildly jumping and jeering whenever a Jew was shot," certainly demonstrating no interest in helping the Jews who were dying around them.

Jewish memoirs and some Gentile testimony reveal that many times Gentiles appeared sympathetic and wanted to help them, but in the end refused their request. M. J. Feigenbaum, a Polish Jew, spent part of the war among a group of four refugee Jews on the run in the Polish farmland and forests. Feigenbaum reported that their requests for help received mixed responses, but that some who would not help were quite sympathetic, wanted to do so, but were afraid. They answered with tears: "If it were just a fine, or prison . . . but it's our lives. We also want to get through these few weeks."[72] This way of responding has a special poignancy and comprehensibility. The risks taken in helping Jews were enormous—such behavior could and sometimes did cost the lives not only of the rescuer but also of his or her entire family. Many wanted to help but simply could not bring themselves to risk their own or their children's lives on behalf of a Jew in need. This was a painful moral dilemma for many sensitive Gentiles.[73] Sometimes one member of the family was willing to help Jews but another one did not want to take the risk. Depending on how decisions were made in such homes, the result was either a sympathetic refusal to help or, less frequently, actual helping despite one family member's objections.[74] Household divisions like this contributed to the common phenomenon of Gentiles offering help but then backing out on the brink of rescue or after a brief period of time.[75]

The famous Dutch Christian rescuer Corrie ten Boom, to whom we shall return later, related the illuminating story of a Dutch pastor's response to her request that he offer help to Jews. A Jewish woman and her infant were hiding in the ten Boom house and needed a more secure place to stay. The Dutch minister came into her father's watch repair shop one day in search of a part for his watch. Corrie took the pastor aside and asked him if he would be willing to take a Jewish mother and baby into his home. His initial response was a strong rejection: "Miss ten Boom! I do hope you're not involved with any of this illegal concealment and undercover business. It's just not safe!" But then Corrie went to the other part of the house and brought the new baby down for the pastor to see with his own eyes:

> Back in the dining room I pulled back the coverlet from the baby's face. There was a long silence. The man bent forward, his hand in spite of himself reaching for the tiny fist curled round the blanket. For a moment I saw compassion and fear struggle in his face. Then he straightened. "No. Definitely not. We could lose our lives for that Jewish child!" Unseen by either of us, Father had appeared in the doorway. "Give the child to me, Corrie," he said. Father held the baby close, his white beard brushing its cheek, looking into the little face. . . . At last he looked up at the pastor. "You say we could lose our lives for this child. I would consider that the greatest honor that could come to my family." The pastor turned sharply on his heels and walked out of the room.[76]

"Compassion and fear struggle[d] in his face." In this case, fear triumphed.

The historical evidence indicates that many Gentiles were deeply moved by the plight of the Jews. Some managed to help Jews when a request was directly presented, but did not ever initiate help. A remarkable story has been told by Sofia Nalkowska of a scene along a railroad line in Poland. One morning a badly hurt Jewish woman was discovered in the grass next to the railroad tracks. It was obvious that the woman had jumped from a deportation train. She had been shot in the knee while jumping from the train; now she was unable to move.

Throughout the morning, local Gentile peasants and workers assembled around the woman, talking to each other, sighing deeply, and then leaving. No one offered the woman any help. Finally a young Pole with compassion in his eyes approached her. She asked him for a painkiller but he refused the money she offered him and did not go to buy it for her. Later he returned to the scene, this time responding positively to a request for whiskey and cigarettes. The day wore on, crowds of onlookers came and went, but no one looked at her wounds or offered her help. "The woman lay prostrate, in full view of the onlookers, like an animal that the hunter has injured but failed to kill." At dusk, the woman still lay there where she had fallen. Finally she begged to be shot. Two Polish policemen refused; but the "gallant young Pole," back for the third time that day, killed her as an act of mercy. The narrator tells us that much sympathy for the injured woman was found in the crowds that day, but "it was a time when terror gripped every heart."[77]

Reward rescuers

Some Gentiles, of course, did indeed provide life-saving help for Jews. Those who made some kind of external reward, monetary or otherwise, a *precondition* of rescue (whom we might call "reward rescuers") are not considered by Yad Vashem to qualify as candidates for the status of Righteous Gentile.

Some rescuers helped Jews, especially children, primarily in the hope of converting them to the Christian faith. This was a matter of considerable Jewish-Christian tension during and especially just after the war. The issue is greatly complicated by the fact that those Jews who attempted to "pass" as Christians in Gentile communities needed a great deal of instruction in Christian faith to survive the inquiries of suspicious neighbors and informants. As noted above, religious tests of those suspected of being Jews were common. Rescuers thus needed to offer some such instruction; indeed, the survival of a Jew trying to pass was greatly enhanced by complete self-identification as a Christian—this was especially true for children.[78] However, a moral distinction obviously can be drawn between those who helped Jews primarily to convert them to Christianity and those who offered instruction in the faith only as a defensive measure.[79]

Another kind of reward rescuer was the paid helper. The behavior of these people raises other delicate problems. Because of the tremendous risks involved in helping Jews, some cynics have charged that all rescuers must have done it for the money. This charge is patently false, but there is no doubt that some who helped Jews did so primarily for personal financial gain. Of the paid helpers, Nechama Tec has written: "When money was the major motivating factor, the relationship between the rescuer and the rescued was less positive, less stable, and mutually less satisfactory."[80] Tec herself was sheltered by a paid helper.[81] Yad Vashem excludes such people from consideration as Righteous Gentiles. Their behavior resembles that of others who sought financial gain from Jewish suffering.

Other Gentiles accepted money because their Jewish charges insisted upon it or because they were simply too destitute to provide for Jews without receiving some financial help. A significant moral difference exists between this behavior and that of those who helped Jews as a kind of money-making operation. In the case of the former, money was simply necessary to enable rescue to happen, a means and not an end. Persons who received money on this latter basis are generally not (and should not be) disqualified from consideration as Righteous Gentiles.[82]

Rescuers (Righteous Gentiles)

Finally, we reach the Righteous Gentiles, those who risked their lives simply in order to save Jewish lives and not for monetary or other external reward. The details of their actions, of their motives, and of the implications of both, are the focus of the remainder of this work.

Conclusion: From Murder to Rescue

The historian Martin Gilbert tells a remarkable and illuminating story from Poland:

> Dana Szapira and her mother were hidden by a Polish farmer. They survived, living inside a cubby hole in his cowshed. One day the farmer heard a knock on the door: it was a Jew, holding in his arms his teenage son. "I have been hiding in the woods for months," the Jew told the farmer. "My son has gangrene. Please get a doctor." The farmer went to the Gestapo and told them about the two Jews. "He got two kilogrammes of sugar for reporting them," Dana Szapira recalled. "They were taken away and shot."[83]

How could the same Polish farmer save two Jews and betray two others? Perhaps he was morally splitting the difference, attempting to do right by his conscience by saving some Jews and to do right by the authorities by turning others in. Or it could be that the farmer could not think of a doctor he could trust to care for the gangrenous son and did not want a dying Jew to care for and later bury. Possibly he thought that four people, rather than two, were too many for him to accommodate, especially with one sick with gangrene. Maybe he feared that the Nazis (or snooping neighbors) would discover the two Jews in his cowshed and decided that the best way to avoid being raided was to demonstrate his loyalty to the Nazis by turning these new Jews in. Perhaps he felt more comfortable with Jewish women than with men and was thus willing to care for one and not the other. The story illuminates the limits of any typology, for this Polish farmer was both an informant and a rescuer. The tale also reveals the complexity of human behavior, particularly in such severe moral crisis, and indicates the importance of withholding facile moral judgments about Gentile behavior during the Holocaust.

We have studied with some care the historical context of Gentile behavior toward Jews during the Holocaust. Yet underneath all of that one is struck by the profound simplicity of the moral test facing so many European Gentiles during the Holocaust. Coming to them for help were Jews who were nearly completely powerless to save themselves from an insane regime that considered them unworthy of life. Gentiles faced the rather straightforward choice of whether or not to count these people within the boundaries of moral obligation—whether or not to be "their brothers' (and sisters') keepers." In most instances, the only thing Jews could do was to appeal for mercy and compassion and hope that such moral resources could be found in the person on the other side of the door. They usually had nothing to offer the Gentiles by way of reward, except the opportunity to affirm the value of every human life by saving another human being from death. They had much to offer the Gentiles by way of risk, including the chance that the Gentiles and their children would die.

How did the Gentiles respond in this moral crucible? The broad pattern of response is little disputed. The great majority of Gentiles did nothing to help or harm Jews directly. Whether these bystanders were predominantly sympathetic or unsympathetic is a matter of some debate, but that many were unsympathetic (especially in the east) is little disputed. A far smaller number of Gentiles were actively hostile, killing, informing on, and robbing Jews. Finally, a very small number, less than 1 percent, actively helped Jews. These are called the Righteous Gentiles of the Holocaust.

By now we have a much better understanding of the factors working against rescue and of how many other types of Gentile behavior there were during the Holocaust. In this context our admiration for those who rescued Jews grows. What can we learn from the rescuers, this less than 1 percent? To that exploration we now turn.

4

The Righteous Gentiles

❖

Partners in Resistance

While Jewish babies were being thrown alive into fiery pits, and while trucks full of naked women were making their way to the gas chambers,[1] a small number of Gentiles were working furiously throughout Europe to save babies and women and others from this unspeakable fate. In this chapter I will outline the diverse kinds of actions such Gentiles took as they joined with Jews in their fight for survival, and I will name and tell the stories of many rescuers (some stories will be presented in the text, many others in the notes). These stories will show that those who were committed to the inclusion of Jews within the boundaries of moral obligation could find myriad ways to act on that commitment. Their deeds demonstrate decisively that the claim made by some Europeans during and after the war—"nothing could be done to help the Jews"—was patently untrue. That saving Jews required moral commitment, courage, and immense hard work was indeed true, however, as we will see.

The descriptive task is daunting and historical generalizations are laden with pitfalls. Jews were hunted from the Atlantic Ocean to the Black Sea, from the Arctic to the Mediterranean. Likewise, Jews were helped by citizens in every one of the two dozen or so nations in between. The nature of their deeds varied considerably, affected by a wide variety of circumstances and factors. For example, the Nazi onslaught accelerated over time, though not at the same pace everywhere in Europe. Rescue efforts were forced to change with each twist in Nazi policy. Further, the attempt to annihilate the Jews was undertaken in different ways in each nation and was profoundly marked by each country's history, its evolving political relationship with Nazi Germany, and its own internal politics. Rescue efforts are understood best when placed in the context of each European nation's fate and behavior during the war. As well, accidents of geography such as terrain, weather, and proximity to neutral nations affected possibilities and types of rescue. Clear differences between rescue possibilities in urban and rural areas are also identifiable.[2] Though our discussion of rescue activity cannot adequately address all of these variables, it is important to keep them in view.

It should also be stressed from the outset that those now called Righteous Gentiles were not the only people engaged in relief and rescue activities[3] on behalf of Jews. Jews themselves undertook heroic and extensive efforts to save Jewish life (see chapter 2).[4] Besides the imaginative and courageous efforts of individuals to save themselves, their families, and other Jews, one must be aware of the rescue activities of European Jewish political parties and coalitions (Zionists, Socialists, etc.), self-governmental bodies, relief agencies (orphanages, hospitals, welfare groups), underground movements, partisans, individual philanthropists, and specially organized rescue groups such as DELASEM (*Delegazione Assistenza Emigranti*) in Italy. Further, Jewish individuals and groups from the *Yishuv* (Palestine) and the United States attempted to intervene (with mixed results) to help their European coreligionists.[5]

The Righteous Gentile concept by its nature focuses attention on the actions of particular individuals who saved Jews. It is important to remember, though, the larger structures both informal and formal within which most rescuers worked. Informal networks of rescue included family members, friends, work associates, neighbors, acquaintances, and even strangers who shared a commitment to saving Jews. More formal structures included those national resistance movements—like the French, Dutch, Belgian, Norwegian, and Danish—that understood helping their Jewish fellow citizens to be a fundamental part of their mission.[6] Groups organized specifically to save Jews, and usually involving both Jews and Gentiles, included the French *L' Amitié Chrétiennes*, the Belgian ONE (*Oeuvre National de l'Enfance*), the Dutch LO (National Organization for Assistance to "Divers"), the Polish Zegota, and others.[7] Certain church bodies functioning at local, regional, national, and international levels facilitated the rescue of Jews.[8] Relief agencies such as the Red Cross also became involved in rescue.[9] Finally, one must not forget the acts of states and other national and international organizations. Jews and Gentiles worked together (though not always very well) in the context of this multitude of groups to save Jews. Much could be said about the numerous failures and scattered successes of these diverse relief and rescue efforts, as well as about the actions that should have been taken but were not. While in this chapter we will focus on rescue at the local level and on the actions of individuals and small groups of rescuers, we should not forget the broader swirl of rescue activity.

Help in Maintaining a Decent Existence

Until 1938, Nazi measures against German Jewry were not normally and directly life-threatening. Instead Jews, seen as inferior aliens, were gradually stripped of the prerequisites of a decent life. Equality before the law as citizens, unhindered access to employment, participation in cultural and civic life, a sense of safety while walking the streets—these and other components of a humane and dignified existence were taken away. At each step, Jews and concerned Gentiles resisted by doing what they could to mitigate these blows and to help Jews maintain as normal an existence as possible. After the war began, this struggle was replayed at varying tempos in the lands occupied by Nazi Germany—slowly in the west, rapidly in the east. When annihilation became Nazi policy, everything changed. The first stage of Gentile help, though, was to aid Jews in maintaining a decent existence as their rights were increasingly constricted and their situation grew increasingly untenable.

Helping measures at this stage took a wide variety of forms. While by statute and propaganda the Nazis pushed for the total social isolation of Jews, many Gentile friends and acquaintances persisted in maintaining or even intensifying their relationships. Warmth, consolation, and advice were especially valuable at this time. Most Gentile spouses of Jews rejected Nazi pressures and enticements to end their marriages. Jews have recorded that in some cases they received especially kind treatment from strangers who learned that they were Jewish. One Belgian Jew, Tanya Lipski, has noted that after the introduction of the yellow star in her country in 1942 many men removed their hats in respect as she walked by on the street, and offered to give up their seats for her on trolley cars.[10] Scattered public expressions of protest were offered, such as Gentiles wearing yellow stars in solidarity with Jews, strikes, sermons, pastoral letters, and so on.[11] Such basic expressions of sympathy and support helped embattled Jews to sustain morale in the knowledge that not all Gentiles had gone mad with anti-Semitism.

As Jews were pushed out of an increasing number of professions, many non-Jews sympathetically helped them find new kinds of employment. When they were forced to sell their businesses, some friendly Gentiles bought them in name only, funneling the profits back to their rightful owner.[12] At other times, Gentiles bought the businesses at a fair price or acted as a third party to help the Jewish merchant get the best treatment possible. Similar help was rendered to Jews who were forced to sell their valuables to maintain life. Many Gentiles helped Jews to ship possessions abroad or to find hiding places for their treasured or expensive items. (Jewish defenselessness led to much fraud and exploitation by less scrupulous Gentiles in these situations.) Sometimes Gentile friends helped with child care and managing the household as Jews, pushed out of their previous employment, scrambled to find new work.[13]

Nazi restrictions on Jewish movement, limits on food purchases, and random street terror made it very difficult for Jews to sustain a decent life. Sympathetic Gentiles helped by shopping on behalf of their Jewish neighbors, going to the pharmacy for medicine, doing laundry, even making trips to the library for books.[14] Gentiles sometimes slipped extra ration tickets into the pockets of Jews on the street. Merchants helped by defying the shopping curfews and restrictions imposed on Jews.[15] Helpful Gentiles warned Jews of imminent Nazi or mob violence, sometimes providing temporary hiding places. For example, in Germany some Gentiles helped Jews to survive Kristallnacht and to avoid the mass arrests of Jews that occurred. If unsuccessful in preventing detention, some Gentiles intervened with friends and acquaintances in the German security apparatus to arrange a Jew's release; this often required a bribe.[16]

Helping Jews Leave Nazi-Occupied Europe

While the struggle to help Jews maintain a decent existence continued, many began to recognize that no such existence was possible under the Nazis. Jews who could not bear life in Nazi Germany, or who feared the worst, had been leaving since 1933, some with Gentile help. Many went to other European countries—not far enough away, it turned out. Others went abroad and were saved. In the time between Kristallnacht (November 9/10, 1938) and the onset of war (September 1, 1939), the Nazis attempted to force German Jewry out of the country while the great majority of Jews also tried to leave. The process was telescoped all the more in Austria, where Eichmann's brutal attack on the Austrian Jews after the Anschluss forced tens of thousands of Jews out of that nation before the war started. Thousands of Jews also left (and thousands more unsuccessfully sought to leave) the annexed portions of Czechoslovakia—Bohemia and Moravia.

In retrospect, it turned out that helping Jews leave Europe any time between 1933 and 1941 was a life-saving form of Gentile help. But it was only after the events of 1938 that both Jews and Gentile helpers recognized that all Jews in the German Reich were in mortal danger.[17] The years 1938 and 1939 then saw a frenzied and complex struggle rage as Jews tried desperately to emigrate from the expanded German Reich while emigration was still possible. The basic problem was a far greater demand for than supply of safe havens. Prescient and sympathetic individual Germans and Austrians, church officials, diplomats, and others[18] intervened to get as many Jews out of the Reich as possible by legal and sometimes illegal means.

For example, Samuel and Pearl Oliner interviewed a German woman with connections who got train tickets and false papers for Jews, helping them to escape to Great Britain and Sweden.[19] Gote Hedenqvist, a minister of the Church of Sweden, managed to get three thousand Jews out of Austria in 1938.[20] Captain Frank Foley, a British passport control officer in Berlin, recognized the urgency of the situation and demanded extra passports for Palestine, resisting London's policy at the time. According to the German Jew Benno Cohn, Foley "did everything in his power to enable us to bring over as many Jews as possible. One can say that he rescued thousands of Jews from the jaws of death."[21] (Foley also treated the daily queue of Jews at the passport office with compassion and dignity.) Foley's actions were representative of the handful of sympathetic diplomats who worked especially hard to facilitate Jewish emigration. But tight immigration quotas heartlessly shut out the great majority of Jews who sought to leave before Germany invaded Poland and emigration slowed to a trickle.[22]

Yet the onset of war by no means ended Jewish efforts to emigrate nor Gentile efforts to help them do so. The Nazis were known to the Jews of each nation by reputation. When they arrived—in Poland in 1939, in Norway, Denmark, Belgium, Luxembourg, and France in 1940, elsewhere later in the war—Jews fled, as did millions of Gentiles. Everywhere, the roads were lined with cars, carts, bicycles, and all manner of woebegone vehicles carrying people away from the Nazis. Whereas some Gentiles could settle down in a new location, Jews could not. Especially after ghettoization, deportations, and rumors of death in the east, Jews were constantly moving, always looking to move from less- to more-safe locations. The best place to be was out of Europe altogether. The next best was a neutral country (Spain, Portugal, Switzerland, Sweden, Turkey);[23] another possibility was a Nazi ally more friendly to Jews (Italy, Italian-occupied zones,[24] Hungary until 1944). Even within occupied Europe, a pecking order of desirability in each region spread by word of mouth. Throughout the war Jews sought to reach freedom and some Gentiles helped them, despite the illegality of this action. A review of some notable emigration efforts and the role of Gentiles in each will be helpful before moving to other forms of Gentile help.

In France, tens of thousands of Jews fled from occupied to unoccupied (Vichy) France or points farther distant during and after the Nazi conquest in May 1940. Jews crossed the demarcation line between the two zones either on false papers or by sneaking across. No Jews were legally permitted to cross, and few Gentiles had the proper transit permits, which were scarce.[25] Help was provided by a group of experts in these risky and illegal border crossings—the so-called *passeurs*. Such persons were paid extortionate rates to provide false border-crossing permits and other false documents, money, escort, and connections on the other side for food, shelter, and further transit. The majority of passeurs made a financial killing. Worse, unscrupulous persons emerged who took money and provided no services in return.[26]

Under such conditions, the rare humanitarian passeur was truly remarkable. Raoul Laporterie, a recognized Righteous Gentile, was a storekeeper who worked and lived near the demarcation line. Laporterie developed and procured the false papers necessary to slip people into Vichy France, and then escorted Jews across the line himself. He also hid Jewish valuables on one side of the line and got them to their owners on the other; hid Jews in his own home and with others; delivered mail across the zones, also strictly forbidden; and used his contacts with the French police to help Jews escape internment at Gurs. Raoul Laporterie accepted little or no money for his services, undertaking his work for reasons other than the profit motive. He emerged nearly penniless from the war.[27]

The search for emigration opportunities and a safer place of refuge is illustrated by the route traveled by some Dutch Jews. The brutality of the Nazi occupation of the Netherlands led some Jews to believe that occupied France would be a haven in comparison with their home country. Thus, some made the difficult and illegal trip across the border into occupied France. Then it was discovered that Vichy France was a safer bet than occupied France. Again, an illegal border crossing was required. Once in Vichy, neutral Spain and Portugal seemed tantalizingly close, across the Pyrenees mountains, though accessible only with the help of passeurs on both sides of the frontier. From there, North Africa, Palestine, and even America were possibilities.[28] Escape routes developed along this southerly path to move Jews from peril to less peril to freedom. Some Jews stopped and remained at various points along the way while others left Europe altogether. Lives were lost at each step.

Significant leadership in the difficult and dangerous smuggling operation from Holland was provided by young Jewish Zionists (the *Hechalutz* movement) and a select group of Gentile coworkers, in conjunction with French Zionists, the French resistance, representatives of international Jewry, and others.[29] The Jew Joachim "Shushu" Simon and the Dutch educator Joop Westerweel (Westerville) remain near-legendary figures among those familiar with this operation. Simon was caught in 1943; after being tortured, he killed himself. Westerweel was captured by the Nazis, tortured, and later murdered.[30] Haim Avni estimates that some six hundred Jews were saved through Spain in operations headed by young Dutch and French Zionists.[31]

A similarly legendary French smuggling expert was the priest Father Marie-Benoit. This resourceful and cunning Catholic cleric organized a huge operation out of his Capuchin monastery in the French port city of Marseilles. Working with the French resistance and the *Union Génerale des*

Israélites en France (UGIF—the official body representing French Jewry), his group produced thousands of forged passports and other "Aryan" documents to help Jews escape southwest into Spain and northeast into Switzerland. When those routes were closed off with the Nazi occupation of Vichy France in November 1942, Marie-Benoit helped convince Italian officials to allow Jews into the Italian zone of France (along the Riviera), despite vigorous objections from the German foreign minister himself. Thousands of Jews made the crossing into the Italian zone. After the last-minute scuttling of a grand scheme to ship fifty thousand French Jews to North Africa, Marie-Benoit was forced to flee France, ultimately moving into Rome and eventually assuming a key role, under the name of Padre Benedetti, in rescue activities there after the Germans occupied Italy and began deportations in the fall of 1943.[32]

A famous mass smuggling operation involving thousands of people and two governments was the astonishing rescue of the Danish Jews in October 1943. Warned of the imminent deportation of the Danish Jews by Georg Duckwitz, the attaché for shipping affairs in the German Legation in Copenhagen, Danish government officials helped to mobilize seemingly the whole Danish people along with the eight thousand Jews in Denmark for an escape.[33] Between September 29 and October 1, nearly every single one of these Jews was hidden and then ferried under the Germans' noses to Sweden, where the government welcomed them. Anna Christensen was a typical Danish rescuer. Getting her charges to the coast marked the climax of months of befriending, educating, hiding, and caring for forty Jewish refugee children associated with Youth Aliya, a Zionist group.[34]

In Germany itself, persecution had forced most of the remaining Jews into the major cities before the war. Mass deportations to the east began in 1941; by July 1, 1943, no Jew had the legal right to exist in Germany. Even so, some four thousand Jews lived an extremely precarious underground existence in Berlin itself, with a smattering in other cities and localities. Despite the Nazis' best efforts, operations smuggling small numbers of German Jews into Switzerland and Sweden continued throughout the war. Officials from the Church of Sweden as well as Swedish diplomats participated alongside Germans (including Dietrich Bonhoeffer) in this enterprise.[35]

Smuggling operations were most successful when the receiving countries gladly welcomed the refugees on arrival. Unfortunately, rarely was this the case. Switzerland, Spain, and Portugal, for example, officially did not accept Jewish refugees, in order to maintain their neutrality and avoid Hitler's wrath.[36] However, several diplomats who placed human need over government policy have earned praise in Righteous Gentile literature (if not in their own countries). For example, Paul Grueninger, police chief of the Swiss border town St. Gallen, disobeyed regulations early in the war by helping hundreds of Jews slip across the border. He was dismissed by the Swiss authorities and lost his pension.[37] Aristedes de Sousa Mendes, Portuguese consul in Bordeaux at the beginning of the war, worked like a man possessed in giving visas to some ten thousand Jews desperate to escape to Portugal. In doing so he publicly disobeyed direct orders. He also sheltered as many Jews as possible in his own Bordeaux home and even gave out visas while under escort back to Lisbon, while being recalled for that very act. Ultimately, Mendes lost his job and his property as punishment for his actions.[38]

Helping Jews Elude the Nazis within Occupied Europe

Getting Jews out of occupied Europe was the best kind of rescue. Tragically, emigration was possible for only a small number of Jews, primarily those in the west. While smuggling efforts continued throughout the war, the great majority of European Jews were trapped somewhere in occupied Europe and had to attempt to survive there until the end of the Nazi occupation.

By 1942, the Germans were rounding up and killing Jews in every corner of Europe. In Poland the Nazis followed the unsystematic terror of 1939[39] with the systematic deprivation characteristic of ghettos and labor camps; in 1942 and 1943 they emptied the surviving population of these incarceration centers into the gas chambers. In the Baltics and Russia, mass shootings in 1941 and 1942 took the majority of the Jews, the remaining "legal" Jews also languishing in labor camps and ghettos until their "liquidation." In the west, Jews faced a gradually worsening variety of measures, with the majority ultimately deported east in 1942 and 1943 to share the fate of their Eastern European brethren. In Central and Southeastern Europe, many Jews were killed on site (in Rumania, dismembered Yugoslavia, and Hungary, for example), but a large number were deported to death camps between 1942 and 1944 as well. All roads led to the killing centers of the east.

The struggle to survive this international maelstrom of death had a grim logic. If escaping Nazi Europe was impossible, the next best option (for those seeking escape) was to elude the Nazis *within* occupied Europe— to avoid falling into Nazi hands. The best strategy available was to convince the oppressor and his helpers that one was not among that category of people subject to Nazi persecution and annihilation—to find a way to "pass" as a Gentile (or a privileged Jew)[40] by hiding one's Jewish identity. The other option was simply to hide, physically. Scores of thousands of Jews tried one or both. Most did not survive. Most of those who did survive needed Gentile help at many points along the way.

Passing

Numerous autobiographical accounts from Jews and Gentile helpers, as well as secondary historical works, offer a rich picture of what was involved in attempting to pass the war years under false Gentile identity or to help others to do so.[41] Perhaps the fundamental prerequisite was false documentation of Gentile identity. Totalitarian Nazi Europe was extraordinarily paperwork-ridden. Every person needed an identification card (*Kennkarte*) which established their religious and racial status in the New Order, along with an employment permit, residence permit, ration cards, various transit cards, curfew exception cards, postal identification cards, and so on; even pregnancy cards were in circulation.[42] Church documents, such as baptismal and marriage records, were also important in establishing or buttressing a claim to "Aryan" identity, a prerequisite for obtaining the precious Kennkarte. (Church officials and church bodies that produced false documents of this sort were extremely helpful.)[43] Those who could not display the most important of these papers on request found themselves in mortal danger.

Jews who followed proper channels and received honest papers attesting to their Jewishness ultimately learned that their honesty had doomed them. Once this was understood, fugitive Jews and their Gentile allies scrambled to obtain or produce "false papers" on which Jews could rely when questioned by the authorities. Reports from all over Europe document the tens of thousands of people involved for profit or for mercy in the thriving black market trade in false papers. Specialists emerged who produced thousands of these papers to help thousands of Jews survive. The production of false papers became a central part of the work of organized rescue groups.[44]

Such false documents were necessary but by no means sufficient to ensure Jewish survival. Jews attempting to "pass" needed to develop the actor's ability genuinely to assume one or a succession of false identities, convincingly to *become* the various Gentile people described on their false papers. The ability to do this varied widely among those Jews attempting to pass. But over and above the acting skill of individuals, the overall level of Jewish assimilation in the surrounding society proved to be a crucial factor. Cultural, linguistic, and perceived physical differences between Jews and Gentiles generally were far less obvious in the west than in the east. Thus, native-born Jews were more likely to be able to "pass" as Gentiles/ Christians in places like France, Holland, and Germany itself than in Poland

and Ukraine, where a huge cultural and linguistic gulf between Jews and
Gentiles had long existed.[45] Those who simply could not pass as Gentiles
had to adopt the other main strategy, hiding, described in the next section.

One essential service offered by many Gentile helpers was coaching
in how to accomplish the desperately needed "Gentilization." In heavily
Catholic Poland, for example, helpful Gentiles instructed Jews in Catholic
prayers, genuflection forms, knowledge of the Mass, behavior at shrines,
and religious doctrines. Rescuers also provided properly weatherbeaten
Bibles and missals, Christian crucifixes and medallions, and other accou-
trements of Polish Catholic culture to authenticate Christian identity.[46] Similar equipping in matters religious occurred all across the continent—for
perversely, as noted in chapter 3, religious tests were common in the offices
of the Gestapo and its associates.[47]

Many other Gentilization efforts were needed. Thousands of Jews
struggled, with Gentile help, to learn how to speak Polish, Ukrainian, or
Russian without a Yiddish accent or Yiddish expressions and gestures, and
in a style appropriate to one's purported identity.[48] For most, this was
extremely difficult to accomplish. Remarkably, doctors even developed an
unprecedented operation to remove the effects of circumcision (a deadly
sign of Jewishness for men), as well as undertaking to reshape Jewish noses
in ways perceived to be more Gentile.[49] When all else failed, some Jews
and their Gentile helpers stumbled on a different passing strategy: to pretend that the passing Jew was mute, deaf, or too ill to answer questions.
Generally speaking, only those Jews with some significant level of contact
with Gentile culture before the war had much of a chance to be successful in passing as Gentiles.[50] The informants were simply too good at
their work.

Part of constructing a false Gentile identity was to develop or create
a network of Gentile friends and "relatives" willing to attest to one's non-
Jewishness to neighbors or the authorities. A nerve-wracking experience
for many Gentile rescuers was to perform such a service in the presence
of the Gestapo, who often killed those they suspected of helping Jews
survive. Without at least one friend willing to testify in this way, most
"passing" Jews could not survive interrogation.[51]

The best way genuinely to assimilate false Gentile identity was to
believe that one actually was a Gentile. Such was the strategy developed
on behalf of thousands of very young Jewish children who were placed
with Christians throughout Europe. Many Jewish parents faced the awesome task of assessing their friends and acquaintances and attempting to
determine who among them might be willing to take in their child.[52] An
approach made to someone turning out to be hostile could mean death.
Many Righteous Gentiles did indeed agree to accept Jewish children and

to raise them as their own. Jewish children and teenagers could be found passing as Christians on many a farm and in many a village and city throughout Europe. Gentile rescuers not only saved these children's lives but attempted to provide as normal an upbringing for them as possible.[53] In every case, stories had to be concocted to account to the neighbors for the sudden appearance of a child. Many single Gentile women endured vicious gossip as they pretended to be pregnant out of wedlock or the mother of a child of suspicious parentage.[54]

Many Jewish children were separated from their parents and placed in convents and monasteries, where they were raised and educated as Catholics. Some rescuers acted as go-betweens to facilitate placement.[55] Usually, officials of the institutions knew that the children were really Jewish; sometimes, however, that fact was unknown even to them, Jewish identity having been erased earlier.[56] Convents and monasteries appear to have been among the safest places for Jewish children (and some adults) to be during the war, whether Jews were passing or hiding. Numerous survivors spent at least some time in such institutions.[57]

Children raised as Christians were fortunate to have both the problem of Gentile identity and of shelter taken care of at one stroke. All Jews busy eluding the Nazis within Europe needed a place or, usually, many places to stay. Once ghettoization, deportation, and annihilation became Nazi policy, Jews *qua Jews* could not legally reside anywhere outside of Nazi control (i.e., in ghettos and camps).

But how to obtain housing? Especially in the cities, housing was extremely expensive. Those who were passing as Gentiles could sometimes fool landlords and obtain housing at these "normal" wartime rates. However, many landlords and others in control of housing were extremely careful not to rent to suspected Jews, while others would rent to them at double or triple (or more) the already high rates. Yet accounts exist of Gentile landlords or homeowners who strongly suspected (or knew of) the Jewish identity of the people seeking a room but went ahead and offered it without raising the price. Other Gentiles rented housing in their own names but used the rooms to shelter Jews.[58] Still other Gentiles simply took passing adult Jews in to share their home, developing a story to explain the presence of new members in the household. In one story from Berlin, a young Gentile couple took in a Jewish couple of similar age, declaring to neighbors that the two men were brothers.[59] This was a dangerous game, of course, as informants kept close watch on unusual housing arrangements or the appearance of never-before-seen "relatives."

Another crucial component of false Gentile existence was a job or other source of income. Jews attempting to pass as Gentiles usually could not work at their old jobs, where they were known as Jews before the war.

Thus, "passing" Jews had to find employment somehow, often in a new city and a new line of work. Finding or providing such work for a passing Jew was a crucial service that a Gentile could provide. Paid employment was needed not only to meet financial needs (which were often quite high due to black market prices for food, documents, and rent as well as the threat of blackmail) but also to fill out the false Gentile profile so carefully constructed.[60] This was particularly true for men and unattached women, on whom neighbors would be sure to look with suspicion if employment was not evident. Interestingly, when such employment did not exist, some Jews in at least one large urban area (Berlin) managed to fake it for a time by going off to "work" in the morning and coming home in the evening on a regular schedule—spending the intervening ten or twelve hours walking around the city trying to look occupied. In such cases, Gentile financial support was needed to pay not only for food and rent but also for clothing, which wore out quickly during day after day spent walking the streets.[61]

Most Jews passing as Gentiles needed at least occasional help from Gentiles in sustaining such an existence. Besides the help previously mentioned, it was the rare passing Jew who did not sometimes need help in getting food, clothing, medical care, and money for expenses. Obtaining each usually required Gentile involvement in securing the needed combination of funds, ration cards, false documents, and connections. The quest for these basic necessities was constant on the part of both Jews and their Gentile helpers. Few Jews passing as Gentiles were not hungry and weakened by illness at least some of the time.

Further, it must be remembered that Jews were being *hunted* actively by the Gestapo, and often by local officials and various informants. Like animals, people who are hunted need to stay on the move. The adult Jew who passed under a single false name and stayed in a single location throughout the Nazi period was the exception. Most faced the loss of a secure shelter from time to time as the enemy drew near, Gentile helpers grew afraid and forced a move, or the shelter was lost to bombings.[62] Many had to obtain a series of false papers and the false identities to go with them, and with the transition in identity often came the need for a new job, a new place to stay, and sometimes a new set of Gentile contacts. Berlin Jews sardonically described themselves as "U-Boats"—the image nicely conveys the pattern of hiding underground, surfacing intermittently, and going under again.[63] Gentiles could be and were of great help at these "surfacing" transition points. It is fitting that the form of help to Jews perhaps most regularly mentioned in the literature is the providing of help in moving from one place to another.[64] These transit/escort services were both a dangerous and a ubiquitous part of rescue activity, requiring both quick feet and steady nerves.

Hiding

For those unfortunate Jews temporarily or permanently lacking false papers or the other necessities of a passing existence, the only other option was to remain physically hidden. Several of the most familiar stories of wartime rescue are of this type: for example, the story of Anne Frank and her family, hidden in the annex of an office building in Amsterdam, and the rescue activities of Corrie ten Boom, who hid Jews in her family's home in another Dutch city, Haarlem.[65] Jews were hidden by Gentiles all across Europe, in myriad simple and ingenious ways. Thousands of lives were saved.

Finding hiding places was rarely easy, in some places next to impossible. This was particularly true in the east, where German terror, the threat of death for helping Jews, the problem of blackmail, and anti-Jewish sentiment combined to shut off most hiding opportunities.[66] Across Europe, both Jews and friendly Gentiles struggled to think of potential rescuers among their friends, business associates, and acquaintances. It was safer for Gentile rescuers to take the lead in approaching other prospects, though Jews often had to do so as well. Both hoped fervently that their candidates would be willing to help, fearing that instead they would be informants who would go right to the Gestapo. Jews, individual rescuers, and rescuer networks constantly worked to develop the largest possible supply of hiding places for fugitive Jews. The same relief and rescue groups which facilitated Jews passing as Gentiles also worked to find and provide these hiding places.

Once a friendly home had been found, it needed to be equipped for hiding. Some rescuers specialized in building hiding places. Those with architecture and carpentry skills were of great value in designing and constructing false walls, bunkers, and other specially designed hideouts.[67] But most rescuers had to do without a specialist's help. Some simply hid Jews in their house, having them sleep in an extra bedroom or (usually) in their own bedroom. As well, rescuers learned to find, reconfigure, or construct an ingenious array of hiding places: rooms behind false walls, spaces behind fireplaces and bookcases, in and behind couches, under kitchen sinks, in oven flues, closets, attics, cellars, barns, haylofts, chicken coops, coal cellars, storehouses, pigsties, dugouts under haystacks, manure piles, cowsheds, underground burrows, open fields, cemetery plots, even boxes big enough for small children.[68]

Life in hiding presented a different set of challenges than did passing. The need for the chameleon's ability to pretend to be a Gentile was gone; now needed was the endurance to live a completely abnormal existence burrowed into the "underground" of a nazified world. A key variable in the desirability and sustainability of a hiding situation was the freedom of movement permitted. In some remote areas, potentially suspicious Gentile neighbors were too far away to pose a constant threat. In other locales, exemplified profoundly in the case of the Protestant village of Le Chambon in France, a milieu sympathetic to the Jewish plight enabled Gentile rescuers to lower their guard to a considerable degree. Where such circumstances existed, Jews could (at least) move around their hiding places with some degree of freedom or, even better, live a life approximating normality.[69]

Such situations appear to have been exceptional. In most cases, the threat of informants was perceived to be of a severity requiring more tightly controlled movement. Some hidden Jews were required to remain in confining spaces during the daylight hours, others had to stay hidden around the clock. Sometimes Jews could move around with a bit more freedom, with the hiding places reserved for the arrival of the Gestapo, nosy neighbors, or even the rescuers' own small children.[70] Some hiding places were used only at night, for fear of Gestapo raids, which usually occurred in the middle of the night.[71] Many households practiced "raid drills" in which everyone was schooled to erase signs of Jewish presence as rapidly as possible.[72] Absolute silence was sometimes required of the hidden Jews; in other places Jews could speak, but not above a whisper. Some Jews spent every hour in the dark. Many were permanently scarred by the mental and physical strain of particularly miserable and confining hiding places.

Jews in permanent hiding often could do nothing to contribute to paying their expenses because of the impossibility of earning money. Yet extra money was needed, not only for expenses but also for bribes and blackmailers. Fortunate Jews who managed to retain some of their prewar assets could contribute to their own support. A few others, even in hiding, managed to work. For example, Fritz Croner, a German Jewish jeweler, managed to continue black marketeering in jewelry even while in hiding.[73] Many Belgian companies and governmental institutions continued to pay salaries to Jews who no longer appeared at the office because they were forced to go into hiding.[74] Sometimes, Jews and/or their Gentile rescuers would establish a household industry to raise funds via the black market. In most cases, though, extra money was still desperately needed. Gentile individuals and groups (such as Zegota, in Poland) raised and distributed money to some Jews in hiding and to their Gentile rescuers. National and international Jewish groups sometimes managed to get money in to help as well.

In many cases, however, Righteous Gentiles received no outside help. They had to make their often meager resources stretch to cover half-again as many people, or more. The most acute problem was food. Wartime food rations in occupied Europe were slim, and with the onset of the Final Solution were usually not available to Jews at all. On their own, Jews had to pay exorbitant black market rates for food. If hiding with Gentiles, Jews usually shared their rescuers' small food rations. Many hidden Jews remember with great fondness the sacrifices made by Gentiles who shared their meager food so unselfishly.

Some Gentiles involved in helping Jews contributed to ameliorating these food shortages by regularly acquiring and then distributing extra food and extra ration cards to the homes where Jews were hidden.[75] Yet extra ration cards presented their own problem—suspicious neighbors or grocers wondering why a woman shopping for a family of three was carrying extra ration cards and buying food enough for eight people. Many rescuers, mainly women in larger urban areas, spent significant portions of every day shopping at a variety of locations or at distant black market sites to avoid uncomfortable questions.[76] Some stole food when starvation for their expanded household was the alternative. Some Gentile grocers who sympathized with Jews or their Gentile rescuers asked no questions and slipped extra food into the shopping bag.

Jews in hiding often developed illnesses due to the exigencies of their situation. Gentile rescuers were called upon to tend to these needs to the best of their ability. When illness was severe, they had to take the risk of finding a reliable physician. Sympathetic doctors who would visit Jews in hiding were an indispensable part of groups helping Jews.[77] When such a physician could not be found, or when medical care could not prevent fatal illness, Gentile rescuers faced the very difficult problem of disposing of the dead. Normal procedures for doing so were out of the question. In remote areas, Gentile helpers usually buried the dead themselves; in the cities, they had to rely on other Gentiles who could help get the body to a remote location or to a sympathetic physician.[78]

Gentile helpers did what was required to keep their Jewish charges alive. Such activity ranged from the most basic daily chores to the most dramatic. Daily life involved emptying and cleaning chamberpots, shopping, preparing food, doing dishes, and washing clothes for extra members of the household. Women were usually the central participants in these daily efforts. All of these activities were undertaken amidst the tension of preparing for a Nazi raid that could come at any time. Extraordinary precautions were taken to hide the traces of extra people. For example, a family of four hiding another four Jews would, in view of a raid, usually be careful to set only four plates around the table, off of which both groups would eat. And, of course, the raids often did come. While the Jews scampered to their hiding places, the Gentile rescuers attempted to retain their composure and to lie through their teeth. Sometimes more forceful measures were required; the Dutch rescuer Marion Pritchard killed a Dutch policeman who discovered Jews in her home.[79]

As in the case of passing Jews, Jews in hiding often were forced to move from place to place rather than being able to stay in a single location.

Very frequently, Gentiles helped Jews on a temporary rather than permanent basis. When the Jew-hunters got too close, or when the Gentiles could no longer stand the strain, or just as a matter of policy, Jews were forced to find a new hiding place. Many accounts report this constant shuffling of the fugitive Jews from place to place, the Jews staying no more than a night or two in any one location.[80] A permanent, safe hiding location was the dream of every Jew. As with Jews passing as Gentiles, escort was most helpful and sometimes indispensable as Jews surfaced to make their way from one hiding place to another. False papers were important even for Jews spending most of their time in hiding—they were needed between hiding places and for when they were unable to make it into a hiding place before Jew-hunters found them in a house.[81]

Passing and hiding strategies were not mutually exclusive. As circumstances changed, so did the most desirable survival strategy. The story of a young Polish Jew named Zosia and her elderly Polish helpers Karolina and Mikolay Kmita is instructive. Zosia, an acquaintance, began her stay with her Polish rescuers by passing with false papers as a Polish relative. However, after a spate of terrifying local killings of Jews and their Gentile helpers, Mikolay Kmita decided that the risks of a passing strategy were too great. He built Zosia a hiding place in the woods of a nearby forest. Each night, Karolina Kmita very carefully walked and crawled out to this hiding place, bearing food and, occasionally, fresh clothing, blankets, vodka, and paraffin to keep pests away. Zosia survived the war in that hiding place in the woods.[82]

Helping Jews in Nazi Hands

Despite the Jewish and Gentile efforts outlined here, most Jews did not succeed in eluding the Nazis. The nightmare became reality; the hunters seized their prey and prepared for the kill. The very great majority of those in Nazi hands ended up dead. But not every one of them died, thanks partly to the efforts of Gentiles who helped Jews within Nazi control—in ghettos, holding camps, killing fields, labor camps, cattle cars, death camps, forced marches, and every other place in which Jews were incarcerated and murdered.

The ghettos in the East

Though Jews and Gentiles did not know it right away, the establishment of the ghettos in Poland and further east meant death for thousands of Jews. What *was* apparent upon ghettoization was that Jews needed various kinds of immediate relief help. As was the case elsewhere in Europe, Jews facing ghettoization were forced to dispose of business and personal affairs as rapidly as possible. Friendly Gentiles who resisted market forces (a "must-sell" situation) to give a fair price for Jewish possessions, from the family cow to the family business, performed acts of mercy.[83] The same is true of Gentiles who volunteered to hide Jewish valuables and did so honestly.[84] Most Jews never survived to retrieve their possessions. But, over the course of the war, the honest sale or barter of such valuables by a Jew or Gentile helper aided in sustaining life, at least for a time. Other Gentiles helped Jews make and execute plans to avoid ghettoization through either a passing or a hiding strategy.

Once established in the ghettos, Jews faced the nightmarish situation outlined in chapter 2. The most essential need was food. Before the ghettos were sealed off, Gentiles delivered food there openly. Some offered a fair price, others demanded exorbitant rates. After the ghettos were sealed, and severe penalties inflicted upon those caught providing food to ghettos, some Gentiles persisted in smuggling food in anyway. Certain Gentile merchants made extra quantities of food and established contact with ghetto smugglers to get the food in. Other Gentiles with access to the ghetto hid food on their persons or with their cargo and distributed it once inside. Some Gentiles bartered Jewish goods that were smuggled out of the ghetto for food and other items.[85] Polish and Jewish children, small and quick, worked their respective sides of the ghetto walls.[86] The quantity of food smuggled in was by no means enough to ensure Jewish survival, but it did slow down the rate of attrition in the ghettos.

Other items and services were provided by smugglers and those with legal access to the ghettos. Desperately needed medicines saved lives, as did forged labor cards, which permitted their holders the (temporary) right to survive through work. False identification cards enabled some Jews to be smuggled out to the Aryan side. Such escapes were usually carefully planned in advance by persons on both sides of the wall.[87] Information was a prime commodity as well; couriers informed ghetto leaders of developments in other ghettos and of imminent plans for roundups, liquidations, or partisan actions. Small quantities of arms also were funneled to armed resistance groups in various ghettos, especially from 1943 on.[88] Some extraordinarily committed Gentiles chose to live in the ghettos voluntarily, to be better able to help. In each case, the help offered could not nearly counteract the murderous Nazi chokehold on the ghettos, but these measures did help to sustain life and fortify resistance to some degree.

Perhaps the quintessential helper of ghettoized Jews in all of Europe was Ona (Anna) Šimaite of Vilna (Lithuania). Šimaite, mentioned with reverence in numerous memoirs and histories, was a librarian at the University of Vilna and a longtime friend of the Vilna Jews. To gain uninhibited access to the ghetto, she convinced the Germans of the need to collect library books from Jewish students there. Free to enter, Simaite visited the ghetto daily, bringing all of her bread, jam, margarine, and cheese to children at the ghetto orphanage. She ran important errands for hundreds of Jews, such as tracking down Jewish clothing and valuables in Gentile possession and reclaiming them for their Jewish owners. (This provoked the wrath of many of the Gentiles holding the valuables.)[89] Simaite also smuggled in false papers, military information, and weapons and their instruction books, acting as a courier between ghetto Jews and forest partisans. She became a regular attendee at ghetto cultural events as a sign of her solidarity with Jews and commitment to Jewish cultural survival. She smuggled religious and cultural treasures out of the ghetto and hid them. She saved dozens of children by smuggling them out of the ghetto and finding homes for them, including her own. One time, she saved a young Jewish girl from a mob of Latvian and Lithuanian auxiliaries intent on murder. Her flagrant help noticed, Simaite was caught and tortured, sent to Dachau and other camps, and finally survived the war. In 1953, she said of the war years, "Those were the happiest days of my life."[90]

The transit camps in the West

In 1942, as the Nazis began rounding up and deporting western Jews to the east, they established several transit camps in which to hold Jews until ready to ship them to their deaths. Among the most prominent of these camps were Westerbork and Vught in Holland, Malines in Belgium, and Gurs and Drancy in France.

Both Jews and Gentiles worked desperately to offer relief and even to rescue Jews from these and other holding camps. Relief work included providing food and medicine when possible, communicating with a Jewish prisoner's relatives, and undertaking other activities to maintain contact and support. At the same time, desperate efforts were made to try to get Jews released from these camps or to facilitate an escape. Loyal Gentile friends petitioned for the release of particular Jews; remarkably, they were sometimes successful. Inevitably, bribery soon proved to be an even more likely route to success. Jews and Gentiles worked together to identify candidates for bribery among the camp guards and officials and to approach them with an offer. These various approaches bought freedom for some Jews, though not many, before the trains rolled to death in the east.[91]

Labor camps

The Germans established hundreds of labor camps during the war, in which they worked Jews to death and often killed them for pleasure (see chapter 2). Yet labor camps varied greatly in the severity of the work and the brutality of the overseers. Gentiles employed in the camps at various levels often had the opportunity to help preserve the lives of their Jewish laborers, and some did so. Other concerned Gentile contractors and business owners attempted to gain access to Jews for labor and thus to save them.[92]

Wladislaw Misiuna was the nineteen-year-old Polish foreman of a rabbit farm established near Radom to provide rabbit skins for German soldiers on the Eastern front. As labor camps went, the work was fairly light. However, as in all German camps, sanitation was primitive and food was scarce, especially for Jews. Misiuna used all means at his disposal to help his (primarily young female) Jewish prisoners. He violated orders by giving them food that was supposed to go only to the rabbits, and bought other food for them out of his own pocket. "You are human beings and must therefore eat," he said. He worked hard to keep his charges healthy, for disease was rampant and no medical care was permitted for Jewish prisoners. In one extraordinary case, he purposely infected himself with the illness of a sick young Jewish woman so that the camp doctor would bring him medicine. He then proceeded to share the medicine with the woman and they both recovered. Through these and other efforts, including purposeful attention to keeping their spirits up, Misiuna managed to keep most of the Jewish girls alive until the end of the war. He saved more than ten people.[93]

The more power a Gentile had in the camp hierarchy, the greater were his or her opportunities to help Jews. (The principle is true more broadly—the more power an individual had or seized in areas of Nazi annihilation efforts, the greater were the opportunities to help Jews. Certainly, tens of thousands more Jewish lives would have been saved if more of those in positions of power to help great numbers of Jews had done so.)[94] German and Austrian industrialists in charge of labor installations in the east sometimes worked feverishly to provide decent food and working conditions, to employ as many Jews as possible, and to attempt to prevent the liquidations of their installations and the deportation of their prisoners to the death camps.

Julius Madritsch, for example, was an Austrian contractor in charge of two textile plants in Cracow. He was a secret anti-Nazi who treated his Jewish workers well, employed as many as he possibly could, and allowed them to meet with Poles to barter their possessions for food. When the Cracow ghetto was liquidated and his workers sent to work in the dreadful Plaszow camp in March 1943, Madritsch managed to save these workers by convincing the SS to let him keep his Cracow factories open and to allow his Jews to commute to Plaszow. Meanwhile, Madritsch became involved with a group of people smuggling survivors of the liquidated Cracow ghetto into his workshops and then on to other ghettos or to (temporary) safety in Hungary.[95]

Sometimes soldiers, military officials, and politicians found themselves in a position to help labor-camp Jews. The Hungarian colonel Imre
Reviczky (Revicky) was a commandant in charge of Jewish labor battalions
from 1940 to 1944. (The Jews of Germany's lukewarm ally Hungary were
subject to forced labor but not annihilation before Germany's takeover of
the Hungarian government in 1944.) Reviczky helped the Jews under his
command in numerous ways. Unlike other camp commanders, he allowed
the wives of Jewish prisoners to appeal to him on their husbands' behalf.
He let Jews take leave for religious holidays and certain other occasions.
He helped those Jews accused of leaving camps without permission. Reviczky and his wife opened their own home to Jews and employed as many
there as they could. He delayed transport of Jewish labor battalions to the
Russian front, as he assumed the Jews would be murdered there. Once
deportations to the death camps were ordered, he opened his work camps
to Jews who would otherwise have gone to their deaths. Once, in mid-
1944, he disobeyed orders by sending wood and timber instead of 2,500
Jews on a train to the east. These and other ingenious efforts to save Jews
led to his imprisonment when pro-German Hungarian fascists took power
late in 1944.[96]

Death camps

Gentile help was even offered in the very belly of the beast, the death
camps. Those most able to offer help were Gentile political prisoners who
almost always had an easier lot than their Jewish campmates. Anna Binder,
once a Czech diplomat, had been arrested for helping to hide Jewish property and ship it abroad. In March 1942 she was sent to Auschwitz, where
she was put to work in the administration of the women's camp, assigned
to find prisoners to work in the Plant Cultivation Commando, a much more
desirable location than the regular slave-labor brigades. She picked women
for her unit to save them from a far worse fate. In several other ways she
helped Jews, siding with them in disputes with SS personnel, finding decent
living quarters for them, teaching them various languages, and providing
moral support. As a consequence of these actions on behalf of Jews, the
SS finally took away her privileged status and sent her to do hard labor at
Birkenau, paving roads in the mud and snow in early 1944. Binder fell ill
and, like many other Holocaust survivors, barely survived the ensuing year
of labor, transfer from camp to camp, illness, and massacres. She did indeed
survive the war.[97]

Charles Coward was a British POW held in Monowitz, an industrial
installation associated with Auschwitz. Coward, camp liaison officer with
the Germans and the Red Cross, devised an ingenious plan to help Jews
escape from Auschwitz. By bribing a German officer and working clandestinely with Jewish prisoners, Coward managed to help several Jews

escape from Auschwitz labor brigades. Coward was also involved in smuggling arms to the Jewish resistance at Birkenau for a sabotage operation.[98] These kinds of efforts complemented Jewish efforts to escape and to sabotage the operations of the death camps.

Mother Maria of Paris (Elizabeth Skobtsova), a Russian nun, was arrested for her strenuous activities on behalf of Jews in France (see note 57). She was sent to Ravensbruck camp for women in April of 1943. For nearly two years, she lived in a vermin-infested cell block with 2,500 other women, most of them Jewish. Because she was a Gentile and thus of privileged status, she survived for quite a long time, daily witnessing the last moments of her Jewish cellmates who were dragged to their deaths before her eyes. She helped as she could, sharing food and moral support, though powerless to do more—until the last day of her life, probably March 31, 1945. On that day, she too was dragged off to the gas chamber. Her last act was to slip her Gentile identification card to a Jewish woman, in the hope of saving her life. She had attempted to help a Jew even at the hour of her death.

Conclusion

In the next chapter we will begin considering the character and motivations of those who rescued Jews during the Holocaust. Before proceeding, though, perhaps we should pause to reflect very briefly on the moral shape of the deeds just outlined.

Rescuers were people who included Jews within the boundaries of moral obligation (whether or not they would have described their actions in such language). They refused to stand by and do nothing to help people threatened with imminent death. As will be shown, the reasons why they arrived at this position varied dramatically. But whatever the reasons, their commitment to saving Jews came to require of them what might be called an "earthly ethic of survival."

The Nazis forced Jews to redirect their lives to the quest for survival. Higher pursuits were largely postponed as Jews attempted to endure and survive while having the necessities of life progressively stripped from them. With each tightening of the Nazi noose and each step in the Nazi plan, survival became more difficult. The effort to resist their murderers and fight for survival lay at the heart of the Jewish moral situation until the end of the Holocaust. The inability to do so very successfully continues to gnaw painfully at Jewish consciousness. Rescuers were those who chose to abandon relative safety and throw in their lot with Jews. Their decision to work for Jewish survival meant that their own survival was threatened.

In the eyes of the Nazis, the rescuers' decision to help Jews reduced them to the status of Jews. They had forfeited their privileges as "Aryans," which included their right to live; if caught, they could be murdered without scruple, just like the Jews. Once embarked on rescue, then, the Righteous were also forced to redirect their lives toward the quest for survival—both for themselves and for their Jewish charges. How and why anyone would voluntarily take on such a perilous situation is a question that has preoccupied many who have considered the phenomenon of the rescuers.

The fight for survival required that rescuers practice a most earthly ethic. They needed to learn how to be cunning and clever, how to lie and deceive, how to operate by stealth and by night, sometimes even to kill. They needed to learn the skills of underground life, common to those who do not play by society's rules, but unfamiliar to those who are accustomed to a normal existence in a decent social order. Many rescuers found the moral ambiguity of this shadowy ethic troubling. Most could not easily adjust to life in the underground as outlaws in a social order gone horribly awry. Yet most did adjust, uneasily, until such a moral practice was no longer necessary.[99]

Theirs was also an earthly ethic in terms of the sheer physical effort, stamina, and endurance that rescue required. One reason why rescue stories were slow to emerge after the war is that in most cases they were the stories not of dramatic street rescues but of immense daily effort within the boundaries of a household. Even when dramatic initial rescues occurred, survival then required months and sometimes even years of doing dishes, washing clothes, buying food, fixing meals, caring for the sick, emptying chamberpots, and so on. Only in retrospect did six months or a year or four years of such extra efforts seem heroic. The silence was also undoubtedly related to the fact that most often it was women who carried these household burdens, adding them to shoulders already hunched over with too much work.

Rescuers began with the commitment to save a life or several lives. This was fundamental. The earthly ethic of survival that would be required to save these lives was not necessarily clear at first. It emerged over time, as rescuers daily defied those who sought to kill the innocent.

5

Many Paths to Righteousness

❖

Why Rescuers Helped Jews

The path of the righteous is like the first gleam of dawn, shining
ever brighter till the full light of day. (Prov. 4:18)

The Righteous Gentiles were those Europeans who counted Jews
within the boundaries of moral obligation while the most powerful nation
in Europe was putting to death every Jew it could find. In welcoming
hunted and hated strangers they risked the destruction of themselves and
their loved ones. Such actions marked a reversal of all-too-customary human moral practice. Most often, loved ones are helped and protected at
all costs, while equally needy strangers—especially those defined as "enemies"—are ignored or shunned. Rescuers were those who considered it
morally obligatory to offer safe haven to the needy stranger, even though
the action might mean death for those whose well-being mattered the most
to them. Though the propriety of risking a loved one's life to save a stranger
was hotly debated in many homes during the war, those who study the
rescuers today agree that such actions approach the pinnacle of moral
conduct and aspiration. The rescuers are aptly named Righteous Gentiles,
for this was righteousness of a very high order.

Why did the rescuers risk their lives to help Jews, when the great
majority of their neighbors did not? The question runs like a scarlet thread
through every discussion of the Righteous Gentiles. Other questions follow,
such as: What, besides the fact that they rescued Jews, set these people
apart from those around them? Were they raised differently? Were they
members of particular social classes or partisans of particular political ideologies? Were they people of a certain personality type? Were they less (or
more) inclined to religious conviction, or religious conviction of a certain

91

type? What motivated their behavior? Or was motivation irrelevant, and coincidental situational factors more significant instead? Are all such "why" questions simply impossible to answer?

For many years, and still today, these questions have been pondered privately by those Jews fortunate enough to have been saved by rescuers during the Holocaust. The contrast between the goodness of their rescuers and the brutality and indifference of their rescuers' neighbors has made such queries inevitable. Likewise, as we have seen, over the years a substantial body of published reflection and research on the rescuers has appeared. Whatever form this material has taken—memoir, interview, film, biography, tribute, oral history, or formal research project—the question of *why* rarely has been absent. Those writing about the rescuers have believed that the answer to that question matters a very great deal.

In this chapter, we will examine and assess a portion of the rescuer literature that directly explores the question of why the rescuers helped Jews. We will focus on the work of just over a dozen scholars who have undertaken formal research projects on rescuers.[1] Most of this research has been done by university-based social scientists, though a variety of other kinds of researchers also have initiated similar projects, some of which will be considered here. The social scientific studies generally obtain their data through structured interviews or other forms of direct contact with persons verified as rescuers by Yad Vashem. Some studies have included interviews with Holocaust survivors who were helped by rescuers, and a handful of researchers have managed to interview Gentile nonrescuers as a kind of control group. We will examine what these researchers have discovered or hypothesized concerning rescuer socialization, sociological characteristics, personality traits, and motivations, as well as the impact of situational factors. We will find that this research provides some important insights into the factors that contributed to the behavior of the Righteous Gentiles of the Holocaust—as well as tantalizing hints about the development of people who today might act with courage and compassion on behalf of others in need. Rescuer research of the social scientific genre does not offer the only legitimate avenue to insight about the rescuers, nor are its methodologies or findings beyond critique, as we shall see. And yet this largely unknown body of research is worthy of careful consideration, by Christians and others who are morally concerned.

Socialization

Most rescuer projects have attempted to identify dimensions of socialization that may have set the rescuers on a different life path from those of nonrescuers. The findings tend to be fairly consistent with one another and with current social scientific research on socialization and the development of altruism.[2] Here we can sketch them only very briefly.

Parent-child relationships

Altruism researchers consistently find that "parental warmth and nurturance are prerequisites for the development of empathy."[3] Parents who treat their children with love, care, and solicitude provide the foundational sense of security upon which normal emotional development is built. Likewise, studies show that children who are abused or otherwise maltreated tend to be less capable of altruism in childhood or later in life.[4] Samuel and Pearl Oliner find that rescuers characterize their early family relationships as close more often than nonrescuers do (78 percent vs. 55 percent).[5] Psychotherapist France Grossman's small sample of rescuers also reports an upbringing permissive of affection and communication between parent and child.[6] Stanley Coopersmith argued on the basis of his early research that the parents of rescuers were not necessarily warm with their children; however, they did communicate their acceptance and love.[7]

Discipline

One of the findings the Oliners consider most significant is that parents of rescuers relied less on physical punishment as a form of discipline than did parents of nonrescuers (32 percent vs. 40 percent).[8] (The small difference between these two figures does raise questions about how seriously they should be taken.) Other researchers report similar findings, however. For example, Grossman and Eva Fogelman both report low levels of physical punishment and, more generally, parental authoritarianism.[9] As well, very few rescuers in the Oliner study (under 1 percent) report that their parents treated them with *gratuitous* violence; that is, violence unrelated to their own behavior (vs. 9 percent of bystanders). Further, rescuers' parents relied more on reasoning with their children as a form of discipline than did parents of nonrescuers (21 percent vs. 6 percent). The Oliners theorize that reasoning or "inductive" discipline fosters altruism. By focusing children's attention on the consequences of their behavior for others, this method encourages the "role-taking" that is essential for the development of empathy. Further, when parents, who have nearly total power over children, "voluntarily abdicate the use of [physical] power in favor of explanation and reasoning, they are modeling appropriate behavior toward the weak on the part of the powerful."[10]

Role modeling

Parents do, in fact, serve as the first and usually most important role models for their children. They set an example both with regard to the moral norms they articulate and their daily actions in the home and beyond it. Parents who consistently respond to others' needs in a caring and giving fashion tend to show their children the way to altruism. Many studies confirm this pattern.[11]

The significance of parents as role models for the Righteous Gentiles is generally confirmed in the rescuer studies. In his pioneering work, Perry London concluded that rescuers identified themselves intensely with a parent who "tended to be a very strong moralist—not necessarily religious, but holding very firm opinions on moral issues and serving as a model of moral conduct."[12] His associate Coopersmith reaffirmed this finding, emphasizing that these parents both preached and practiced "ethical, altruistic, and moral values," and that rescuers later consciously imitated a specific role model.[13] The same is true in Douglas Huneke's sample; he emphasizes the role of moral instruction in the home, whether rooted in Christian resources like the Bible, or in folk wisdom, or in other sources.[14] In Eva Fogelman's sample of one hundred rescuers, a parent who behaved altruistically appears almost universally.[15] There is also some evidence of the "learning-by-doing" phenomenon: rescuers, as children, became involved in their parents' actions on behalf of others and thus apprenticed in altruism.[16]

Content of moral instruction

Another critical dimension of childhood socialization is the content of the moral norms stressed in the home, which tend to be internalized and carried into adulthood.

For example, *tolerance* appears steadily in rescuer reports concerning the moral norms learned in childhood. Both Fogelman and the Oliners report that rescuers were far less likely to have heard anti-Jewish slurs in their homes than were bystanders (3 percent vs. 16 percent, Oliner), and more likely to have been taught the value of tolerance.[17] The Oliners also emphasize that rescuers were, by and large, instructed to assess Jews as individuals rather than as group members. It is important to note that there was no statistical difference in their study between rescuers and nonrescuers in the communication of *positive* views of Jews as a people, but only in the absence of negative ones and the emphasis on the common humanity of people of all groups.[18] In short, most rescuers were not taught to love Jews in particular, but they were taught not to have contempt for any human being.

A closely related emphasis at home was what the Oliners call *inclusiveness*—"a predisposition to regard all people as equals and to apply similar standards of right and wrong to them without regard to their social status or ethnicity."[19] This was related to a commitment to the concept of justice as equity, in which rescuers were taught that they had the moral obligation to treat all human beings in ways consistent with basic standards of fairness. Such themes were emphasized in 70 percent of rescuers' homes in the Oliner study, but only 56 percent of nonrescuers' homes.[20] Framed another way, while 39 percent of rescuers' parents taught their children that moral values were to be applied universally—to all human beings—this was the case for only 13 percent of bystanders' parents.[21] Training in extending the boundaries of moral obligation began early for many rescuers, as others likewise received training in constricting those boundaries.

Another element that reappears in several studies is parental teaching (and modeling, as noted above) concerning the obligation to care for people in need. The Oliners find that while the importance of being generous, loving, hospitable, concerned, and helpful was stressed in 44 percent of rescuers' homes, the same was true for only 21 percent of bystanders' homes.[22] Again, the boundaries of caregiving were broad ones—28 percent of the rescuers said that their parents taught them that the obligation to give such care extended to every human being in need, whereas only 5 percent of bystanders' parents did so.[23] A parental emphasis on, and practice of, caring for other people is also noted in the research of Coopersmith, Huneke, Fogelman, and Grossman.[24]

Independence, self-reliance, personal competence, and high self-esteem appear frequently among the personal traits and moral virtues stressed by rescuers' parents and thus often embodied by rescuers. Coopersmith, Grossman, Fogelman, and Nechama Tec all find that parents of rescuers encouraged this cluster of traits in their children.[25] The Oliners appear to contradict the other studies in finding no statistically significant parental emphasis on independence. However, they do find that the value of obedience was *less* stressed by rescuers' parents than by parents of bystanders (1 percent vs. 12 percent).[26] Most researchers reason that an independent orientation was significant in enabling rescuers to do what they considered obligatory despite the risks and, frequently, a lack of social support.

A parental emphasis on high self-confidence and a related sense of competence and self-reliance in their children are inextricably linked to an actual parenting style that fosters these traits, which we have already identified as more common among rescuers' parents than nonrescuers' parents. This cluster of self-esteem characteristics has been found to be correlated with altruism in the broader altruism literature as well.

Childhood loss

Both Huneke and Fogelman find that a large number of their rescuers experienced a major encounter with suffering or death and/or a significant personal loss in childhood.[27] Fogelman notes that such an experience was well-nigh universal in the days of less advanced medicine as well as during the first World War. Thus, she especially emphasizes the importance of the transforming of this grief into an enriched capacity for empathy and a commitment to ease the pain of others, through the influence of a trusted adult who models altruistic behavior at this time. The lack of such a model appears to diminish sharply or eliminate the constructive capacity of such an experience.[28]

The ingredients of successful childhood socialization that tentatively emerge from these rescuer studies do not seem heroic, saintly, or contrary to common sense. Essentially, one can conclude that children should be treated with love, warmth, and respect. They should be reasoned with rather than beaten, *especially* when such physical violence is unrelated to their own behavior. They will learn by watching the trusted adults in their lives, so adults should attend to the example they are setting. Children will listen to the content of the moral instruction in their homes. If this instruction emphasizes justice, care, and tolerance for all human beings, children will probably internalize those moral norms. Further, children who are taught and parented toward self-esteem and personal efficacy will likely arrive there as adults. These findings are fully consistent with the best Christian approaches to childrearing and moral development and ought to reinforce the church's convictions about the fundamental importance of the family. The research also inspires confidence because its results largely conform with the results of broader work in child development.

Yet the findings do not leave one without questions. Even the most generous reading of the data requires the conclusion that healthy childhood socialization does not prove to be a *necessary* cause of rescuers' behavior. These socialization characteristics rarely appear in 100 percent of any of the samples of rescuers, and usually far fewer than that. For example, in the Oliners' study, only 21 percent of rescuers report that their parents reasoned with them as a mode of discipline. While this is significantly higher than the nonrescuers' 6 percent, it still leaves 79 percent of rescuers who did not report this kind of parenting.[29] The findings do not justify the claim that "rescuers were reasoned with as children" or any claim of similar strength.

Moreover, one has to believe that more than some 100,000 European Gentiles alive during World War II experienced the kind of socialization that the research studies have discovered. Surely, at least 10 percent of all Europeans were treated with love and warmth by their parents, shown a pattern of caring deeds by a role model, taught to be just and caring, and so forth. If this is so, then such socialization is not a *sufficient* cause for rescue behavior either, or "we should be counting [rescuers] in [the] hundreds of thousands, if not millions, not as is the case, in [the] thousands."[30]

Any finding on "rescuer characteristics" (socialization or any other) is susceptible to this kind of death-by-specific-counterexample and the empirical reality that no factor identified in rescuer research thus far proves formally necessary or sufficient for rescue.[31] While this does not destroy the value of rescuer research or theories, it should create considerable modesty about their comprehensive explanatory power. Perhaps the most that ought to be claimed here is that this pattern of socialization has a greater tendency to nurture the human capacity for altruism than its alternatives; but by itself it cannot promise such behavior. The same modesty is appropriate for other claims emerging from this research, as we shall see.

Sociological Variables

Did rescuers differ significantly from nonrescuers in such classic sociological variables as age, gender, occupation/social class, political affiliation, or religion? The relative insignificance of these variables emerges from the research.

Age

Manfred Wolfson's study of seventy German rescuers finds that 84 percent of them had been born before 1910 and thus had achieved adulthood prior to the Hitler era.[32] Frances Henry reports that those in her pseudonymous Bavarian town of "Sonderburg" who helped Jews tended to be over forty at the time.[33] Sarah Gordon's study of Gestapo files also finds that the so-called *Judenfreunde* (friends of Jews) tended to be older, between the ages of forty and fifty-nine, especially fifty to fifty-nine. Gordon suggests that the disproportionate representation of older Germans was rooted partially in the lack of financial and other rescue resources among the younger generation, and perhaps in higher levels of anti-Semitism among the impressionable young.[34] Yet moving to the broader European situation, Fogelman discovers a significant group of child rescuers (12 percent under the age of twenty) in her sample,[35] and there is abundant historical evidence for rescuers of all ages. Age appears unlikely to have been a significant factor for rescue, though perhaps there is some evidence that rescuers were disproportionately older, at least in Germany.

Gender

Both Wolfson and Gordon find that more men than women appear in their sample of rescuers.[36] Henry reports that the opposite is true for her group. She surmises that the gender differences occur because "most of the aid given [in Sonderburg] involved the provision of food—women's work, as opposed to administrative help with papers, passports, and the like, which is associated with men."[37] Such a specialization of rescue labor along gender lines, if it existed in Sonderburg, does not appear to be generalizable to all rescuers. In his early study, Philip Friedman highlighted the role of women in rescue, particularly the rescue of children, and claimed that "women are more easily moved by their emotions than men" and that this contributed to rescue.[38] Eva Fogelman set out to test Friedman's hypothesis in her 1987 study; she reports that emotionally oriented responses were not in fact more common among women than men.[39] As we did in the last chapter, Pierre Sauvage calls attention to the fundamental role of women in rescue, arguing that "it was often women who were faced with the first all-important decisions as to whether or not to take a stranger into their . . . homes," and that in Le Chambon women were the "backbone" of rescue efforts.[40] On balance, it does not appear that gender is a helpful predictor of involvement in rescue, nor does it illuminate much about the nature of that involvement.

Occupation/social class

Whether rescuers differed from nonrescuers in social class and occupational patterns is an ideologically weighty question that has attracted considerable attention. Considerable anecdotal evidence has long suggested that rescuers ranged from the very rich to the very poor. The studies now seem to bear this out. Though Henry's study of "Sonderburg" helpers of Jews finds that they tended to be middle-class (like the Jews they helped), and Gordon finds a disproportionate number of "independents" and white-collar workers, Wolfson, Fogelman, and the Oliners all discover no evidence that rescue was proportionally more prevalent in any one social class or occupation.[41] Fogelman does note that intellectuals appear prominently in one of her several rescuer categories (the "ideological-network" rescuers), but are not disproportionate overall.[42] Nechama Tec, in her study of Polish rescuers, also points to a high number of intellectuals but fears that a disproportionate number of them may have come to her attention.[43] The Oliners conclude that "at best . . . occupations and economic status favored a few rescuers," but that these "were not a critical factor influencing the decision to rescue."[44] This seems a judicious verdict.

Politics

Anecdotal evidence has led some to claim that Gentiles associated with the political and economic left were disproportionately involved in rescue activities. But the bulk of the research seems to suggest that most Europeans, rescuer and nonrescuer, were relatively apolitical. The Oliners report that only 21 percent of the rescuers and 10 percent of the bystanders said they had a political affiliation before the war.[45] Tec's evidence reveals a similar lack of political affiliation and involvement.[46] Tec concludes that "by no means were the politically active more inclined toward helping Jews than the rest," a conclusion that the Oliners' evidence also demands.[47]

But might there still be a pattern of political ideology among that segment of rescuers who *do* claim political affiliation? That at least a handful of rescuers emerged from all political parties, even the anti-Semitic ones, is well documented. Tec gives special attention to what she calls "the rare case of the anti-Semitic helper," showing that (in Poland) a very small number of political anti-Semites ended up engaging in rescue despite their feelings about Jews.[48] Wolfson reports that his sample of rescuers was distributed evenly across the political spectrum, and Fogelman also remarks on the wide range of political affiliations among her rescuer sample, though she highlights the disproportionate presence (16 percent) of members of religious political parties.[49]

Tec and the Oliners come to different conclusions about the political tendencies of the affiliated. Tec finds that most of the politically affiliated rescuers in her Polish sample were Communists and Socialists.[50] The Oliners, on the other hand, find that membership in political parties committed to democratic pluralism rather than a leftist ideology was characteristic of the affiliated rescuers (80 percent).[51] However, their sample of politically affiliated rescuers (forty) and nonrescuers (thirteen) is so small as to make this evidence of limited significance. Further, they seem to assume that partisans of the political left are by definition other than proponents of democratic pluralism. On the whole, one must conclude that political affiliation per se tells us little about rescuers—though the evidence would support the modest claim that among the politically affiliated, those in democratic and leftist parties were more likely to rescue than those on the right.

Religion

The role of religion in rescue is an especially important one for the Christian researcher. Here, it is necessary only to sketch the basic sociological data that has emerged.

All who study the rescuers have noted that some cite their religious faith as a factor in their behavior. But a close look at the statistical picture painted by several studies shows that no measure of religious affiliation or commitment differentiates rescuers from nonrescuers. According to the Oliners, 93.7 percent of rescuers and 95.2 percent of nonrescuers were affiliated with the Christian religion while growing up.[52] The parents of 45 percent of both rescuers and nonrescuers sent their children to religious or parochial elementary schools. Similar percentages of rescuers (85.4 percent) and nonrescuers (86.4 percent) described their mothers as "very" or "somewhat" religious; the pattern also holds for the fathers of rescuers (64.3 percent) and nonrescuers (62.3 percent). Around 15 percent of both rescuers and nonrescuers described religion as a "primary value" learned from their parents.[53]

Most importantly, perhaps, rescuers again differ little from nonrescuers in terms of their own sense of religious commitment over time. In the Oliner study, approximately 70 percent of both groups describe themselves as "very" or "somewhat" religious growing up, just before the war, and today. Interestingly, within this 70 percent, more rescuers than nonrescuers describe themselves as "very" religious (rather than "somewhat" religious) at each stage. Similar percentages (around 10 percent) of rescuers and nonrescuers tend to describe themselves as "not at all" religious. Again, of some interest here is that the highest percentage in the "not-at-all" religious category are *rescuers* describing their level of religiosity today (15.5 percent).[54] Thus, it appears that rescuers may have stronger convictions about religion, positive or negative, than do nonrescuers.

The import of the Oliners' figures and other similar data is that, just like age, gender, class, and politics, religion does not prove to be a significant predictor of rescue behavior. This is true across the board, from religious background and education to personal levels of religious commitment. A Jew in need could not expect that, simply because a Gentile was "religious," the Gentile would help the Jew. Because the religiosity under discussion here is Christian faith, this is a very humbling finding for the church. However, the evidence converges that *certain kinds of religiosity*—a certain understanding and practice of Christian faith—sometimes did prove extremely helpful for rescue. Sauvage, Tec, Eva Fleischner, and the Oliners notice this qualitatively distinctive dimension to some rescuers' religiosity and search for words to describe it.[55] We will take up this crucial issue in chapter 6.

Situational Factors

Having seen that age, gender, class, politics, and religion do not offer much help in predicting who would rescue Jews, we turn briefly to situational factors. The hypothesis can be offered that rescue behavior emerged accidentally—that nothing distinguishes rescuers from nonrescuers except luck, fate, or circumstance. Several rescuer researchers have pointed to the importance of factors such as knowledge of what was happening to the Jews, risk, various skills and resources for rescue, and the accident of simply being asked when others were not.[56] Historians are also quick to emphasize the pressures of broader social, political, and historical forces on people's behavior. Further, an influential school of thought ("situationalism") in social psychology has argued that people behave as they do solely because of the situation they are in, rather than out of personal convictions or internal psychological forces.[57] The Oliners have taken situational factors particularly seriously and tested their sample for several of them.

Knowledge

The Oliners' data show that rescuers had more friends, coworkers, and neighbors who were Jewish than did nonrescuers. Thus they may have had greater opportunity to find out what was happening to Jews. However, more rescuers than nonrescuers were generally *aware* of the presence of Jews around them, so this difference in contact with Jews may be illusory. In any case, there appears to have been little difference between rescuers (99 percent) and nonrescuers (93 percent) in their comprehension of what was happening to the Jews during the course of the war. There were other sources of information about what was going on, and both rescuers and nonrescuers were exposed to them. The Oliners conclude that the difference was in the "credibility and significance" of the knowledge. Rescuers began to perceive facts about the plight of the Jews in a personal way and began to focus concentrated attention on specific people in need.[58] This says more about the rescuers themselves than about their access to the necessary information.

Risks

Another finding is that rescuers were no less free than nonrescuers from risks that would be incurred in undertaking rescue. The objective risk of being caught pivoted on such factors as geographical location, distance from neighbors, hostility of neighbors to the rescue of Jews, size of household, and presence of children in the household who might have trouble keeping the rescuing secret. Testing these factors, the Oliners find that little difference existed between rescuers and nonrescuers.[59] Further, both rescuers and nonrescuers knew that the consequences of being caught were extreme; rescuers were not somehow deluded about the risks of their actions, nor were they unafraid. They were different, however, in being able to persevere despite the fear that such risks produced.[60] A word for perseverance in the midst of fear and risk is courage.

Resources

Besides financial resources, which were implicit in the earlier discussion of occupation and social class, other relevant resources for rescue included adequate shelters and a supportive network of people with which to work. No significant differences were found between bystanders and rescuers in such shelter factors as the presence of houses of adequate size, or of cellars and attics in which to hide. There was a difference, though, in the presence of a supportive network. *It was not that rescuers knew more people than non-rescuers, but that the people they knew were more likely to be supportive of their rescue activities.* In a striking finding, 60 percent of rescuers in the Oliner study reported that at least one other family member was involved in rescue, while this was true for only 20 percent of bystanders' families.[61] Later we will consider the importance of corporate acts of rescue emerging from voluntary associations and even small communities, such as Le Chambon. For now it should be noted that the presence of a network or community collectively committed to rescue was a crucial resource available to some rescuers,[62] even though many rescuers went ahead with rescue despite the lack of such a supportive group of people.

Opportunity

While 67 percent of rescuers report having been asked by either a Jew or an intermediary for help, only 25 percent of nonrescuers say they were ever asked for help.[63] If these figures are believed, then the accident of whether one was asked to help would seem to be a crucial factor in determining who became a rescuer and who did not. But the Oliners, as well as historical evidence, suggest that who was asked for help was no accident. Jews and rescuers chose their potential helpers very carefully, as we saw earlier, because they feared the consequences of misjudgment.[64] Further, because rescuers were parts of formal and informal networks either involved in or friendly to rescue, opportunities for rescue would have emerged more naturally from within those groups. It seems likely that many potential rescuers had given some indication that they might be open to helping Jews, or they would not have been asked to help.[65] Further, it may very well be that the number of nonrescuers who were asked to help and declined may be far higher than those who will admit it or who recall it many years later.

Still, there can be little doubt that these and other situational factors proved relevant to whether a person became a rescuer, especially at the beginning of rescue efforts.[66] In their attempt to establish the primacy of personal/psychological considerations, the Oliners probably understate the significance of situational factors. Yet the evidence is also clear that many Gentiles who acted to help Jews had most situational factors stacked against them. More generally, it seems to be a mistake to reduce rescue to an accident of circumstance. There was something about them as people that required rescuers to help.

Personality Traits

We turn to personality traits. There is no single way that the terms "personality" or "personality traits" are used in rescuer research, which makes it a bit hard to compare the work these studies have attempted in this area. In general, most rescuer researchers appear to intend by the term "personality" those distinctive personal attributes and predispositions developed during childhood and relatively stable through adulthood that are fundamental in shaping a person's consciousness and behavior.[67] This definition overlaps to a considerable degree with key aspects of the term "character" as it is employed in Christian ethics.[68] Indeed, "character" is occasionally used in rescuer literature as if interchangeable with "personality." It seems to this ethicist that what are often identified in rescuer studies as personality traits are better described as character traits. In any case, rescuer studies consistently have sought to identify what personality traits, if any, appear to have been distinctive among rescuers.

Adventurousness

London's early study of rescuers offered two personality trait hypotheses which his successors have been chasing ever since. The first proposal is that rescuers were distinctively adventurous—besides the desire to help, they tended to seek and enjoy "inherently exciting activities."[69] Douglas Huneke also finds that rescuers had a "proclivity for adventure," though they were not "reckless or impulsive."[70] Most other researchers have rejected London's claim or at least sharply modified it. In Fogelman's sample, 57 percent identified themselves as adventurous, but this proves statistically less significant than several other factors. She grants that adventurousness may have affected the *style* of rescue activities.[71] The Oliners weave adventurousness into their profile of one type of rescuer but do not claim its presence more broadly.[72] The overall picture appears to be that some rescuers, though by no means all, can be described as particularly adventurous, and that the willingness and ability to take risks and endure them, though better described by the term "courage," was indeed an important skill or trait for rescue.

Social marginality

London also suggested that rescuers were, or felt themselves to be, socially marginal.[73] Huneke at first confirmed the social marginality hypothesis but later modified his view, citing definitional deficiencies.[74] Tec prefers to label this characteristic "individuality" or "separateness," and affirms that she finds it in her sample of rescuers.[75] Fogelman rejects this view, finding that a low 29 percent of her sample describe themselves as feeling marginal.[76]

The Oliners test this thesis by asking their sample about their sense of belonging in the community, the number of friends they had while growing up, and their perception of the friendliness of their neighbors during child-hood. They find no statistical difference between rescuers and nonrescuers on any of these measures. Fully 80 percent of their sample of rescuers felt a sense of belonging in their community.[77] Mordecai Paldiel also finds no evidence for a disproportionate presence of the socially marginal in rescue activities.[78]

Thus the evidence on this issue of social marginality is mixed. A significant part of the problem is, indeed, a definitional deficiency. As employed in rescuer theory, the term "social marginality" mixes testable sociological variables, such as level of social integration, membership in a minority group, or language differences, with an internal psychological state—the *feeling* of being marginal, of being an outsider. This latter feeling can occur regardless of whether one is or is not marginal by any sociological measure. The position is confused even more by Tec's combining of such characteristics as adventurousness, independent-mindedness, and indi-viduality with social marginality.[79] In the end, nearly anything can be cited as "evidence" for marginality (including, circularly, rescue itself), and thus the definition empties of meaning. On balance, the evidence can support only the modest claim that some rescuers were socially marginal and/or perceived themselves as such, and that their behavior was fueled by re-sources drawn from this social location and/or perception.[80]

Social responsibility and empathy

Personality tests conducted by the Oliners offer other evidence concerning rescuer personality traits. Rescuers score higher than nonrescuers on the Social Responsibility Scale, a measure assessing the individual's sense of responsibility toward other people and sense of duty to contribute to the well-being of others and the community.[81] A version of the Empathy Scale is employed to test whether rescuers are generally more responsive to others' emotions. Interestingly, the only dimension of the Empathy Scale on which rescuers score higher than nonrescuers is in their responsiveness to others' *pain*.[82] The Oliners theorize that the combination of a sense of personal responsibility for others and high empathy for pain is reflected in the rescuers' greater tendency to get and stay involved in activities on behalf of others in need.[83]

This consistency in helping the needy has been indicated by several studies as well as other evidence.[84] The Oliners test the level among their sample of rescuers of seven kinds of helping activities during the year preceding the interview. Despite being in poorer health on average than nonrescuers, rescuers had been involved in every kind of help with greater frequency than nonrescuers.[85] This finding appears to offer powerful evidence for the consistency of character over time. Many rescuers are simply the kinds of people who help others. Perhaps this finding helps to explain why so many rescuers describe their wartime actions on behalf of Jews as unremarkable and completely natural, "what anyone would have done."[86]

Self-esteem and independence

Most of the rescuer studies have found a cluster of related traits: self-esteem, sense of competence, self-confidence, self-reliance, willingness to stand up for beliefs, and independence.[87] We have already seen how such characteristics were encouraged by many rescuers' parents. The self-esteem-oriented traits appear to have borne fruit in the rescuers' ability to believe that they could successfully defy the mighty Nazis. Nonrescuers were more likely to throw up their hands in despair, believing that "nothing could be done," that they were at the mercy of external forces.[88] Independence-related traits proved important in enabling rescuers to act despite lack of support from neighbors, church, and government, when that was the case. Rescuers do not appear to have been people easily swayed by the misgivings of others.

Motives (Reasons for Rescue)

The last category to be considered is the first and only one that is sometimes mentioned—motives, to be defined narrowly here as *the reasons given to researchers by the rescuers themselves in response to the question of why they rescued Jews.* The study of motives is quite problematic. The approach I have taken thus far has been rooted in the view that a range of factors contributed to rescue, besides the reasons a rescuer can articulate. Further, the difficulty of identifying the existence, strength, and relative importance of motives from a rescuer's self-report is a very serious one.[89] Yet, surely, the rescuers' declared reasons for rescue are worth considering, even *ex post facto.* Rescuers were those Gentiles who refused to allow the Nazis to define Jews as outside the boundaries of moral obligation. The reasons rescuers give for including Jews within the gates of refuge vary in fascinating and important ways.

Personal ties with Jews

Memoirs long have shown that some rescuers knew the Jews they rescued prior to the Holocaust. Likewise, every rescuer researcher has noticed that personal ties between particular Jews and Righteous Gentiles were in many cases important for rescue.[90] Some have assumed on this basis that *most* rescuers behaved as they did in order to help a friend. Though a claim of this strength cannot be sustained, it appears that the positive presence of Jews in a rescuers' world (or worldview)[91] was indeed important for rescue.

The kinds of personal ties that existed between Jews and Gentile rescuers varied in intensity. The closest and most obvious were family ties, such as those that existed between Jewish-Gentile couples and between a Gentile parent and "half-Jewish" children. A full range of other family ties were also put to the test. Romantic relationships between unmarried Jews and Gentiles were significant for rescue. Close personal friendships between Jews and Gentiles led to rescue, as did less intense acquaintanceships. Professional relationships also were helpful, such as those between office colleagues, trading partners, household servants with their families, and landlords with tenants. Childhood friends, schoolmates, neighbors, local grocers, and a variety of others sometimes helped Jews. Of course, for far too many Jews help was not forthcoming from any of these friends and relations.

The Oliners find that before the war 59 percent of rescuers had Jewish friends, whereas only 34 percent of nonrescuers had any such friends.[92] Rescuers also report that they lived near Jews, worked with Jews, and that their spouse had Jewish friends, in higher percentages than do nonrescuers.[93] These findings may be taken to mean that rescue was simply situational, a matter of certain Gentiles having more Jewish friends and acquaintances than did other Gentiles. Yet, given the anti-Jewish prejudice and Jewish/Gentile distance in much of Europe prior to the war, it seems likely that it was no accident that these Gentiles had more Jewish friends than did other Gentiles.[94] This judgment is supported by data showing that the rescuers did not differ from nonrescuers in the *opportunity* to make Jewish friends while growing up, but they did differ in the percentage who *actually had* close Jewish friends (46 percent vs. 35 percent).[95] It appears that the tolerance for differences and inclusivity that rescuers were taught at home was embodied in the breadth of their friendships. Interestingly, rescuers were also more likely to have crossed social class lines in their childhood friendships (62 percent vs. 45 percent).[96]

Still, only 16 percent of the rescuers in the Oliners' study report that they acted on the basis of care for a personal Jewish friend as even one of their reasons for rescue.[97] Tec reports that 36 percent of her sample of Polish rescuers assert that friendship motivated their actions.[98] For Fogelman the figure is 28 percent, but this number includes those who acted on the basis of a philo-Semitic ideology, not just friendships.[99]

Many friendships between Jews and Gentiles were put to the test during the Holocaust. The great majority of those relationships had not, before the war, reached a level of intensity and commitment in which either party would consider risking their lives for the other an obvious moral obligation. Paldiel is wise to label rescues of this type "evolutionary altruism."[100] The preexisting friendship provided the initial open hand or open door for a limited kind of help. Over time—in those relationships that proved durable and survived the test—relief evolved into rescue, and relationships of varying intensity evolved into bonds of partnership and resistance for mutual survival.[101]

Once engaged in life-saving work involving such transcendent commitment, the significance of exactly *who* the Jew was began to diminish for most rescuers. It became impossible to draw a defensible moral distinction between the Jewish friend worth saving and the Jewish stranger one could allow to die. Thus, only a minority of rescuers who began with a friend stopped there. Over 90 percent of the rescuers in the Oliners' sample report that they helped at least one stranger.[102] Several researchers have noted this "foot in the door" phenomenon—those Gentiles who were willing to help even a single Jew, friend or stranger, were soon inundated with requests from others. Most rescuers acceded to these requests whenever possible, and experienced considerable agony when further rescue efforts were not possible.[103]

Lawrence Baron has reminded the Jewish community of the extreme value of Jewish social integration in Europe during the Holocaust. Where Jews were embedded in a network of Gentile friends, colleagues, and neighbors, they were more likely to be able to find help.[104] There is a message in these findings for Christians as well. Interreligious, interethnic, and interclass ties between Christians and with non-Christians should be nurtured consciously, beginning in the home and in the congregation. Christians should be the kinds of people who can be found around both the dinner table and the communion table with the stranger. The Jesuit biblical scholar John Dominic Crossan argues that this was at the heart of the ministry of Jesus of Nazareth.[105] An "open table" of this sort is fundamental to expanding the boundaries of moral obligation.

Intra-group ties

Sometimes Gentiles rescued Jews because they were fellow members of a group. This category deserves more attention than it has received in rescuer research.

The most prominent form of intra-group rescue was that undertaken by Christian leaders, laypeople, and institutions on behalf of Jewish converts to Christianity and partners in mixed marriages. The historical literature is full of references to these rescue efforts.[106] When the Nazis defined "Jewishness" along racial rather than religious lines, their definition posed a direct challenge to the theology and institutional interests of the churches.

The churches faced the deportation and annihilation of members of their own flocks; to the churches, these persons were "Christians" rather than "Jews" and thus should not have been subject to Nazi anti-Jewish measures. Strenuous efforts were undertaken to force a redefinition and to exempt converts from persecution. Though any effort to save any Jew from the Nazis should be applauded, this one suffers from an obvious deficiency. When the churches' rescue efforts were restricted to people whom they considered Christians, they tacitly (and sometimes explicitly) legitimized Nazi efforts against "real" Jews. The boundaries of moral obligation were construed too narrowly, as has all too often been the case in the history of the church.[107]

Another prominent form of intra-group rescue occurred among the elites. Much evidence reveals that special pains were taken to try to save the "cream" of Jewish life. Among intellectuals, these efforts tended to be spearheaded by university or other professional Gentile colleagues and sometimes by students. Leading Jewish cultural figures were also of special importance to their Gentile colleagues and other admirers. Besides personal ties, these actions appear to have been motivated by the hope of preserving a remnant of Jewish leadership to help rebuild Jewish and/or national life after the war.[108]

A variety of other intra-group rescue activities have been noted. Yehuda Bauer refers to rescue activities by Gentile Scouts on behalf of their Jewish colleagues.[109] Some Gentiles rescued members of the same social class, others acted on behalf of a native of the same town or region.[110] Active members of political parties made special efforts to help their own—Gentile Communists rescuing Jewish Communists, and so on.[111] Uniting all rescue activities of this type are intra-group ties between Jews and Gentiles that predated the Nazi onslaught and managed to be of life-saving significance. As fellow group members, certain Jews were seen as within the boundaries of moral obligation. Perhaps less morally exalted than the rescue of complete strangers, intra-group rescue seems, correspondingly, more accessible to the average person. It points, again, to the importance of involving people of disparate religious, ethnic, gender, class, and racial identities with one another in meaningful relationships. The church can and ought to be a major place where this takes place. Other opportunities should be cultivated as well.

Reference group influence

Some Gentiles rescued Jews at least in part because some person or group of importance to them influenced them to do so or even demanded it, and they acted in conformity with these pressures.[112] The Oliners categorize over half of their sample as "normocentric" rescuers—people whose first rescue act took place due to a feeling of obligation to a valued social-reference group.[113] These groups included family, church, friends, resistance networks, neighbors, and community leaders. Though the label "normocentric" is unfortunate here, and the category suffers from definitional problems,[114] the high percentage of people grouped into this category remains remarkable.

Douglas Huneke has written most perceptively of the importance of what he calls "communal rescues," which he considers one of the three major types of rescue. Huneke defines communal rescues as those carried out by groups of people living in close proximity to one another, sharing common, long-established values, functioning as a cohesive group prior to the war, associating with one another voluntarily, and establishing an intentional rescue plan and network. He emphasizes the immense capacity of such groups for rescue on a scale not possible to one person or a small number of individuals.[115] One reason for this, as Helen Fein notes, is that the risk of being caught was always lower when a community was united in its commitment to rescue—just as it is impossible to destroy a guerrilla movement when it receives universal support from the populace.[116] The activities of the Chambonnais villagers leap immediately to mind, as well as those less well-known villages and neighborhoods that engaged in collective rescue. Similarly, one thinks of the natural rescue networks provided by monastic orders and other church groups, which proved so valuable when employed for rescue.[117]

Sometimes rescue occurred in submission to church authority. Fleischner describes the activities of those French Catholics who were ordered to participate in rescue by a higher-up in the church.[118] She also notes that some Catholics understood the papal encyclical *Mit brennender Sorge* (1937) to demand anti-Nazi activity of them. Sometimes an influential mentor or teacher asked a Gentile to help in rescue activities and it seemed impossible to refuse.[119] One is reminded that even hierarchical authority structures, when directed to moral ends, can be morally fruitful. Commentators long have noted the potential for Christian action in Europe if more church authorities had demanded action on behalf of Jews. The same holds true for political authorities asking for relief and rescue behavior from citizens. Conformity is a powerful factor in human behavior. When respected religious, moral, and civic authorities failed to exemplify and demand help for Jews, social pressures toward conformity with Nazi ideology and practice went disastrously unimpeded (see chapter 3).

The Oliners report that nearly every rescuer was involved in some kind of supportive network. Slightly under half of their sample was involved with formal resistance or rescue groups (44 percent); almost all of them relied to some extent on informal networks of friends, family, neighbors, and other rescue coworkers.[120] Here it is difficult to distinguish between a reference group's instrumental (problem-solving) and authoritative (behavior-reinforcing) role. When individuals already committed to rescue formed groups simply to facilitate their work, their behavior cannot be said to have been *compelled* by the influence of that group.[121] On the other hand, even committed rescuers benefited from the help, shared moral norms, and mutual accountability available in a rescuer network of whatever type.

The importance of rescue as the activity of communities, then, must be highlighted.[122] Oriented as it is to individual "personality" and behavior, rescuer theory often overlooks the extent to which rescue was frequently a group act. One hopes that future researchers in the field will broaden the scope of their inquiry, asking about the activities of groups as well as asking how such groups—neighborhoods, villages, churches, families, even a nation in the case of Denmark—developed the character that led to their conduct. The next question, of course, is how that kind of corporate character and conduct might be consciously nurtured in such groups today. Huneke's definition of communal rescues poses a challenge, in particular to the churches. How many churches consist of people—to follow Huneke's categories—who live in proximity to one another, share a common commitment to love, justice, and mercy, can be described as cohesive, associate with one another voluntarily, and have the skills to undertake a liberating action on behalf of people who are oppressed or persecuted?[123]

Patriotism and political ideologies

It is now apparent that a considerable number of rescuers acted on the basis of patriotism and various other political ideologies. Nearly all of the rescuer studies have identified this explicitly political kind of motivation for rescue.[124]

Some Gentiles rescued Jews because they hated the Nazis and simply wanted to thwart them at every opportunity. Helping Jews was one way of fighting the nation's enemy, a struggle to which these people were committed above all else. Those acting on this basis were more likely to have been involved in general underground resistance activities—such as sabotage, gun-running, armed actions, and so forth—and rescued Jews as one part of their underground work. The Oliners claim that 17 percent of their sample had hatred of the Nazis as at least one of their motives.[125]

Other Gentiles saw the rescue of Jews particularly as a defense of fellow citizens and national values. The Nazi attempt to tear the fabric of national life by identifying, isolating, deporting, and destroying a nation's Jews was seen by some as a murderous assault on the entire society, with resistance a matter of national self-defense.[126] This response was more likely to occur where Jews had won full and unequivocal citizenship rights before the war and where there existed little or no political sentiment in favor of disenfranchisement—in other words, where Jews were already counted within the crucial boundaries of national moral obligation.[127] But it occurred elsewhere as well, among a small number of perceptive Gentiles in places like Poland and Lithuania (and Germany itself) who viewed the murder of the Jews as an assault on their fellow citizens, and local killers as a national embarrassment.[128]

The Oliners argue that 8 percent of their sample acted on the grounds of patriotism.[129] Tec finds that 55 percent of her Polish rescuers cited patriotism or resistance to the Nazis as one reason for rescue, while Fogelman groups 22 percent of her rescuers in a roughly similar category ("ideological-network rescuers").[130] There is no evidence that rescuers were quantitatively more patriotic than nonrescuers, or that patriotism was emphasized more strongly in rescuers' homes as they grew up. The difference, according to the Oliners, appears to be in the *kind* of patriotism espoused by the rescuers. Rescuers were more likely to believe in democratic pluralism—the full acceptance of diverse groups in national life in relationships of equality—as a central national value. The institutionalization of an inferior status for Jews was an assault on this core value and had to be resisted.[131] For these Gentiles, the ties that bound them to Jews were ties of national identity and co-citizenship. They were unwilling to abandon fellow citizens to the enemy.

Other political ideologies also proved to be motives for rescue. Socialists and Communists, for example, cited their universalist and anti-Fascist ideologies as a motive for rescue. They also sometimes proved adept at analyzing the dynamics of Nazi oppression and sensing the need for early, vigorous, militant opposition. An underground network and history of resistance activities prior to the war prepared some of these groups well for wartime efforts on behalf of Jews.[132] Sometimes persons who espoused a democratic ideology acted on this basis even when many of their fellow citizens did not. For example, the French revolutionary ideals—liberty, equality, fraternity—were cited by some French rescuers, though it can by no means be said that the Vichy political leadership acted on this basis.

These findings imply that those who are tempted to consider patriotism and any kind of political ideology outside the boundaries of the Christian moral life must rethink their stance. An inclusive, democratic, life- and justice-affirming patriotism and political orientation should instead be viewed as a potentially powerful force for sound personal behavior—even for Christians—as well as crucial for national character and conduct. Rather than withdraw from debate over the shape of national values and the responsibilities of citizens, the churches should weigh in for a particular kind of values and citizenship, beginning with their own membership.

Moreover, the practice of habits of political discernment, resistance, and solidarity should be highlighted. For the churches, so many of them wedded to a passive and unquestioning patriotism founded on cultural captivity and a misreading of Romans 13 and other biblical texts, this is a much needed word. Churches need to be communities in which discernment of the political signs of the times is a well-refined art. Such discernment sometimes will lead to resistance, in whatever form is both consistent with biblical norms and most appropriate to the situation and the faith-community's skills. Most compellingly demonstrated in the case of the rescuers is solidarity, the kind of resistance in which those with relatively more power and freedom stand with those who are most vulnerable, working in partnership with them for survival and ultimately liberation.[133] This should be understood as activity characteristic of genuine patriotism.

Religion

A surprisingly low percentage of rescuers cite religion as even one of their motivations. According to Tec, only 27 percent of her sample attributes their behavior to religious motivations—this, in heavily Roman Catholic Poland![134] Fogelman classifies only 12 percent of her sample as "religious-moral rescuers," people who acted out of an explicit sense of religious duty.[135] The Oliners report that 15 percent of their rescuers list religion as a motivation.[136] Block and Drucker find religious motivations among 25 percent of the people they interviewed.[137] The validity and importance of these numbers need to be considered carefully and critically; moreover, the wide variety of religious resources upon which some rescuers did draw is worthy of careful examination. These will be our focus in chapter 6.

"Humanitarian motives"

It has been important to consider those motives rooted in particular ties between rescuers and those they rescued. Such motives are often neglected in the rush to discuss what are often considered more profound—the purely "humanitarian" motives that tended to be at work when Righteous Gentiles rescued strangers. In these cases, the Jewish stranger was rescued, not because of any particular connection, but simply because the stranger was a victim and the rescuer considered himself or herself morally obliged to offer help. Such motives for rescue require the careful attention they have received, even though they are not the only kinds of motives that matter.

While some rescuer theorists do not push beyond the fairly weak term "humanitarian" to describe this kind of motive, others attempt to break down humanitarian motives into a variety of types. The lack of a well-developed and widely shared moral vocabulary in the social sciences hampers these efforts considerably and makes any statistical comparison of the findings very difficult. However, the importance of this matter demands an effort to work through the various findings and theoretical proposals.

At least three different but overlapping styles of moral response within the broad category of "humanitarian motives" can be identified. Interestingly, they correspond with important dimensions of moral theory.

Some humanitarian rescuers employ the language of an *inclusive, principled moral commitment to justice and human rights* to describe the motives for their action. In this case, rescuers responded with outrage as they witnessed the mistreatment of Jews, which they considered a violation of the victims' fundamental rights as human beings. Most rescuers, of course, were not moral philosophers who had developed a theory of human rights. It was the witnessed *violation* of those rights that demonstrated or reaffirmed for the rescuer their very existence as well as the requirement to defend them.[138]

Varying formulations of these convictions appear in the research. Some rescuers objected most profoundly to governmental prosecution of those who had done nothing wrong, on the principle that innocent people should not be punished and should be left alone to live in dignity and peace. The indignation was especially powerful with regard to Jewish children.[139] Other rescuers pointed to the repugnance of Nazi racial doctrine positing Aryan racial superiority and Jewish inferiority, and its embodiment in laws denying basic human rights to Jews. Rescuers rejected the purported qualitative racial inferiority of the Jews and believed that all human beings are equal and have the right to fair and equal treatment. Whatever the particular formulation, some rescuers acted to help Jews because Nazi actions were seen as a fundamental violation of justice, understood as the basic right of every human being to a decent and free existence as an equal member of the human community.[140] (Recall the communication of such moral principles in some rescuers' childhood homes.) This style of moral reasoning—a reasoned ethic of rights—corresponds with the dominant strand of the western liberal tradition. What sets these rescuers apart is that a commitment to moral principles clustered around justice-as-fairness and human rights was enough to demand action of them. These moral convictions were sufficient to bring Jews within the boundaries of moral obligation.

Other rescuers employ the language of "care" to describe the motives for their actions. Here the emphasis is not on rights but on "the need to be responsive to others, to provide care to them, to prevent harm and maintain relationships."[141] Following Carol Gilligan, the Oliners call this the "ethics of care" and ascribe such motives to a full 76 percent of their sample, far more than those who acted on the basis of an ethic of rights.[142] They consider this a major discovery. The Oliners group under this category those motives rooted in a self-conscious commitment to act with kindness, benevolence, mercy, and generosity to those in need, even the stranger.

They carefully distinguish between such motives and the less personal and relational motives rooted in notions of justice and human rights. Earlier, we saw how instruction in the ethics of care took place in a disproportionate number of rescuers' childhood homes; here we perhaps see its fruits.

A third form of "humanitarian" motive can be labeled *emotional/empathetic*. Both the ethics of rights and the ethics of care are articulated by rescuers as reasoned moral convictions. But many rescuers did not act on the basis of articulated moral convictions; instead, they were moved to the depths of their emotions by the plight of suffering Jewish human beings and acted—often spontaneously—to alleviate that suffering. Once again, the moral importance of the emotions is demonstrated, as well as the enormous error in Western ethics of making reasoned moral convictions the single normative way of either doing ethics or being moral.[143]

The broken, emotional English of the Polish rescuer Alex Roslan may be the best illustration:

> When I am going to the [Warsaw] ghetto. I get stiff, I not believe, what was there, so many children was laid down, already dead. You walk blocks and blocks, dead children, dead and they covered by paper, just. They so skinny, the children, and the men stay and the woman sit down, like ready to die, the fly eat from the nose, from the mouth. I was there, I, I, I, I never believed it can be like that. . . . And the Jewish children tag at your jacket. "Hey mister give me something, give me something," then my friend say, "Hey, don't give nothing, because they no got a chance." But I say, "How can you not give?" How much money I had, I not remember, but I [give] everything. After I come home and I explain for my wife. My wife say, "You know, maybe me take a child from somebody."[144]

It is far more difficult to disentangle and name the elements of such an emotional response than to recognize its immense power. One thinks of the terms sympathy and pity, which convey the experience of understanding and being moved by another's suffering, or of empathy, which is the human capacity to put oneself in the place of the suffering other and viscerally experience his or her pain and sorrow. Mercy, benevolence, and care connote action rooted in empathy or sympathy on behalf of a person in need. Then there is compassion, a word that appears again and again in rescuer literature. Understood in its richest sense, compassion can be an emotion, an attitude, a character trait, a moral commitment, and a quality of action on behalf of a hurting other. The Good Samaritan, seeing the beaten man, "took pity on him. He went to him and bandaged his wounds, pouring on oil and wine" (Luke 10:33-34). Finally, in considering these gracious ways of being and doing one is pointed toward love. Here we have reached the heart of the Jewish and Christian moral and theological traditions.[145]

Rescuer Research: Methodological Concerns

It is not at all difficult to raise significant questions about the presuppositions undergirding Righteous Gentile research or about the scientific validity of the findings.

(a) Any attempt to identify the causes of a human being's behavior is problematic. A single act likely has multiple "causes"; in some cases, no discernible cause whatsoever can be identified. We have already pointed to the difficulty in interpreting a person's self-reported motivations. There is an irreducible dimension of mystery to human behavior that practitioners of the social sciences do not always appear to acknowledge.

(b) These research projects operate on the assumption that "the rescuers" are a discrete group of people, a part of whose wartime behavior—rescuing Jews—identifies them as somehow different from their neighbors. Rescuer studies are efforts to isolate and identify the content of that differentness. It can be questioned whether this single dimension of the wartime behavior of these Europeans should be artificially divided from the rest.

(c) Rescuing behavior, as shown in chapter 4, took a variety of forms, in an array of contexts, at different levels of risk to the rescuers. It may be that this diversity is too great to allow meaningful grouping of the people involved.[146] No rescuer study has been able to avoid lumping together people whose contexts and deeds were vastly different.

(d) The problem of *ex post facto* research is a serious one. Most rescuer studies were undertaken fully forty years after the events in question. Obviously, one doubts that memory is completely reliable at such a distance. Moreover, it may be that the experience of having rescued Jews changes the people who performed such acts, coloring their answers to the questions posed to them. This points to the general question of the consistency of personality and character over time.

(e) Another fundamental problem is sample size and generalizability. London interviewed 27 rescuers, Grossman 9, Tec 31, Fogelman 100, Fleischner 46, Monroe 13, Block and Drucker 105. Even the Oliners interviewed only 406 rescuers. Accepting Mordecai Paldiel's estimate of 100,000 European rescuers as safely conservative, the Oliner sample represents less than one-half of 1 percent of all rescuers. Even this small percentage does not constitute a statistical random sample, as such a sample for rescuers is impossible to obtain.

(f) Further, each discipline that has concerned itself with the Righteous Gentile phenomenon brings not one but several theoretical models, exploratory techniques, and languages to the effort. This diversity makes any straightforward comparison and interpretation of the research findings difficult. Each study slices the behavior, as it were, with a different knife. This reminds us that inherent in the diverse "findings" are sometimes incompatible foundational assumptions, over which these sociologists, psychologists, anthropologists, and so on, long have argued.

Even with these problems, this research and theory concerning the Righteous Gentiles is a body of literature of considerable significance. Though the evidence should be seen as "soft data" rather than "hard science," that soft data is nonetheless interesting and suggestive—both for those who study the past and especially for those seeking to shape character and conduct today. It needs to be brought into dialogue with those laboring in many different academic disciplines. This is the first such dialogue attempted by a Christian ethicist. Perhaps this survey of the terrain will lead to follow-up efforts. Obviously, there is much ground to cover.

Conclusion

Why did Righteous Gentiles invite Jews to safe haven within the boundaries of moral obligation? What resources gave them the strength to risk their lives? The evidence rules out any explanation that completely reduces rescue to an accident of circumstance or of sociological characteristic like age, gender, or class. Important clues can be found concerning the shape of rescuer socialization as well as personality, but the evidence is modest, suggestive rather than conclusive. Articulated motives for rescue range all over the map—relational, political, ideological, emotional, principled, religious, and idiosyncratic, with a wide variety of permutations within and among these categories. The breadth of these motives surprises us, though if we reflect on the diverse human beings we have known we will not be all that surprised.

Perhaps the best summary that can be made is simply that although the destination was the same—rescue—those who traveled there took many different paths. This should come as no surprise to the church or to Christian ethics, neither of which has settled on a single way of describing the path to, or the content of, moral goodness. What we do know is that the rescuers demonstrate such moral goodness as well as a number of the many paths to righteousness. They challenge each of us to consider whether we are journeying along even one of those paths.

6

Compelled by Faith

❖

Religious Motivations for Rescue

One does not have to look very hard to find sweeping denunciations of Christianity emerging from the Holocaust. Jewish theologian Eliezer Berkovits, for example, has charged "the moral bankruptcy of Christian civilization and the spiritual bankruptcy of Christian religion." He asserts:

> After nineteen centuries of Christianity, the extermination of six million Jews, among them one and a half million children, carried out in cold blood in the very heart of Christian Europe, encouraged by the criminal silence of virtually all Christendom including that of an infallible Holy Father in Rome, was the natural culmination of this bankruptcy. . . . This has been a moral and spiritual collapse the like of which the world has never witnessed . . . for contemptibility and inhumanity.[1]

Proclamation of "the spiritual bankruptcy of Christian religion" is neither a welcome nor a familiar message for the church. Most Christians are utterly unaware that such charges are in circulation, or that a considerable number of morally concerned people consider our whole enterprise a disaster. The churches have closed their ears to these angry cries of indignation and shut their eyes to the evidence—Holocaust-related and otherwise—upon which this indignation is based. It is a remarkable example of moral complacency.

With regard to the Holocaust, perhaps the substance of the indictment and the fury behind it can be illuminated a bit by the following memorable examples of Christian theology and morality during those awful days. These few stories represent many others that could also be cited.

The following is reported to have been the warm, pastoral response of the Archbishop of Slovakia when approached by a rabbi in 1942 for help in preventing the imminent expulsion of the Slovakian Jews.

This is no mere expulsion. You will not die there of hunger and disease. They will slaughter all of you there, old and young alike, women and children, at once—it is the punishment that you deserve for the death of our Lord and Redeemer, Jesus Christ.[2]

Such sentiments were not restricted to the clergy. One day a Jew escaped from the death camp Majdanek and asked for help from a local Pole. The Pole's response: "If God takes no pity on your people, how can you expect pity from a human being?" With that, he turned the Jew away from his door.[3]

A Jewish survivor had this to say about the religious habits of the Polish policemen who participated in the September 1942 massacre of the two thousand Jews of Dzialoszyce: "On the following Sunday, they went to church with their families, as if nothing had happened. They suffered no guilt feelings. After all, they were only murdering Jews, with the blessing of their priests, who inflamed them from their pulpits on Sundays."[4]

After the war, another Jewish survivor asked his neighbor why she had brought Gestapo agents to his mother's hiding place. Her answer: "It was not Hitler who killed the Jews. It was God's will and Hitler was his tool. How could I stand by and be against the will of God?"[5]

The untimely death of Leopold Socha, a Lvov Gentile who had been a professional thief before he became involved in the rescue of Jews, occasioned local Christian comment. Shortly after the war, he was accidentally run over by a truck. Halina Wind, one of those who had been rescued by Socha, reports: "As he lay on the pavement, with the blood dripping into the sewers, the Poles crossed themselves and said that it was God's punishment for hiding Jews."[6]

In the last chapter, we saw that researchers consistently find that a minority of rescuers cite religion as at least one of the reasons they aided Jews during the war. With rare exceptions, it is the *Christian* faith to which these religious rescuers refer, citing it as both a source of motivation and an empowering resource for rescue. Yet it is undeniable, as the few examples cited above attest, that down the street and around the corner other Christians were finding in their faith the motivation either to do nothing for Jews or to help the Nazis destroy them. Our task in this chapter is to discover, if we can, what was different about the faith of religiously motivated Christian rescuers. Stated more formally, our task here is to probe in detail the religious resources that were drawn upon by rescuers who demonstrate or assert that their Christian faith motivated them to rescue Jews during the Holocaust. We do so in order to see what we can salvage from the wreckage, not to engage in any kind of misguided and historically unwarranted celebration of Christian moral goodness during World War II.

Jewish researcher Pierre Sauvage asks a haunting question. Considering the case of devout Christian rescuers in Le Chambon and elsewhere, he wonders: Were they "rare but legitimately representative embodiments of exemplary Christian faith or merely . . . marginal, possibly accidental successes of a disastrously ineffective [faith]?"[7] If the latter is the case, there is little hope for the church. But if the former is true, a Christian may still dare to hope and must immediately embark on an intense search to discern the characteristics of such "exemplary Christian faith." Why? So that such a version of the faith might be purposefully encouraged among Christian people today. Nechama Tec has said that devout rescuers were "religious in a special way," that they exhibited "a certain kind of Christianity."[8] What exactly is the content of this "certain kind of Christianity"? We will try to find out by carefully exploring relevant evidence in Righteous Gentile research as well as memoirs, biographies, and other kinds of rescuer materials. It is my hope that a Christian researcher, one who lives and works within this community of faith, might be able to understand and describe these resources with a certain degree of insight.

Sense of Special Religious Kinship with Jews

Perhaps the religious resource most remarked upon in rescuer literature is *a strong sense of religious kinship with Jews as a people.*[9] Given the appalling history of Christian anti-Judaism, the existence of such a sense of religious kinship and its moral efficacy during the Holocaust is both surprising and welcome news. Evidence for such Christian philo-Semitism crops up frequently in both rescuer research and other rescuer literature, though in broader perspective it was surely a very rare phenomenon in World War II Europe.

Sometimes this sense of religious kinship with Jews was exceptional within a Christian's particular context. For example, Germaine Bocquet was a French Catholic woman who in tandem with her husband hid the Jewish historian Jules Isaac for more than a year. Interestingly, Isaac is best known for identifying and expositing the Christian "teaching of contempt" for Jews. In the course of his time with the Bocquets, Isaac discussed this project with Germaine and showed her some of the virulently anti-Jewish Christian texts with which he was working. She was surprised and deeply distressed, never having been exposed to theological anti-Judaism. As she told the researcher Eva Fleischner:

> The religious education I had received had instilled in me respect for
> the Jewish people, and gratitude that they had given us the prophets,
> the Virgin Mary, Christ, and the apostles. Jews were for me people of

the Covenant, of God's promises. Jesus, the Messiah, was a faithful son of the Law, which he had come to bring to perfection, not to abolish. I had never heard the Jews spoken of as Christ-killers; I had been taught that *our* sins crucified Jesus.[10]

Fleischner was struck by the absence of anti-Judaism in Germaine Bocquet's marvelous rendering of the Jewish role in the Christian story of origins. Probing further, she discovered that Bocquet had been raised in a home in which Catholic (and other) religious influences were absent, and that when she later received religious instruction her mentors consciously had abandoned the anti-Judaism so prevalent in many French Catholic circles. Bocquet came into adulthood imbued with a version of Christian faith in which Jews play a special and positive role.[11]

The statements of a handful of Christian bodies and individual Christians during the war reveal that Bocquet's support for the Jews on the basis of a special sense of religious kinship was not wholly exceptional. For example, in the midst of the dramatic Danish rescue of the Jews, the Bishop of the Lutheran Church of Denmark proclaimed:

> Wherever persecutions are undertaken for racial or religious reasons against the Jews, it is the duty of the Christian Church to raise a protest against it . . . because we shall never be able to forget that the Lord of the Church, Jesus Christ, was born in Bethlehem, of the Virgin Mary into Israel, the people of His possession, according to the promise of God. The history of the Jewish people up to the birth of Christ includes the preparation for the salvation which God has prepared in Christ for all men [and women]. This is also expressed in the fact that the Old Testament is a part of our Bible.[12]

In October 1940, representatives of the six major Protestant denominations in the Netherlands cited the fact that Christ was born of the Jewish people as one reason for their protest against the dismissal of Jewish civil servants.[13] Donald Dietrich has noted occasional references in German Catholic documents along similar lines. In one pastoral letter, Jesus is referred to as "king of the Jews." Another flyer, written by a priest, quotes the New Testament text that "salvation comes from the Jews" to resist the anti-Semitism of the *Deutschen Christen*.[14] These and all similar efforts strove to affirm a special religious kinship between Christians and Jews in order to encourage Christians to support their persecuted Jewish neighbors.

Of a different order of magnitude is the discovery that the theological perspective of a handful of Protestant Christian groups in several nations was characterized by a profound sense of religious kinship with Jews. In such Christian communities, philo-Semitism was more likely to be the rule and anti-Semitism the exception, though both were often present. The most prominent of these groups in the research is the Dutch Reformed, who will receive most of the attention here. But French Protestants (predominantly Reformed but also sectarian fundamentalist), Ukrainian Baptists, Hungarian Methodists, and German Plymouth Brethren all have been identified in this regard.[15] It is no overstatement to say that rescuer researchers have been stunned to discover European Christian subcultures in which an almost awestruck respect for Jews quietly has been passed on for generations as a dimension of traditional faith.

Samuel and Pearl Oliner quote four different Dutch Reformed rescuers whose words reveal aspects of this special sense of religious kinship:

> When it came to the Jewish people, we were brought up in a tradition in which we had learned that the Jewish people were the people of the Lord.
>
> The main reason [for rescue] is because we know that they are the chosen people of God. We had to save them.
>
> Like I told you, we always liked the Jewish people because the Jewish people are God's people.
>
> My background is Christian Reformed; Israel has a special meaning for me. We have warm feelings for Israel.[16]

The autobiography of the Dutch rescuer Corrie ten Boom helps to illustrate some ways in which this deeply felt sense of kinship with Jews was nurtured.[17] These are worth discussing here at some length, because the ten Booms' form of piety was not unique within the Dutch Reformed community, and because undergirding it seem to have been elements of orthodox Calvinist theology and practice that contributed to rescue outside of the Netherlands as well.

One important factor was clearly the extensive Bible reading that occurred in the ten Boom home. The significance of this family tradition is at least twofold. First, *The Hiding Place* makes clear that daily meditation on the Bible profoundly marked the moral character and conduct of Corrie ten Boom and other members of her family. Particular biblical narratives and moral injunctions both helped to shape the family's moral consciousness prior to the war and became empowering resources as the ten Booms struggled to meet the challenge of rescue work. This aspect of the Bible's capacity to form the believer's moral character and empower his or her conduct will be discussed in a later section.

More central for our purposes here, the ten Boom family read and knew well the entire Bible and thus was immersed in the earliest formative texts of the Jewish religious tradition as embedded in what Christians call the Old Testament. Corrie ten Boom emphasizes that the Old Testament was deeply cherished in their home, and that immersion in it contributed to the family's profound sense of religious kinship with Jews. The dramatic tales of the Hebrew patriarchs and matriarchs, the poetry of the psalms, the prophets' cry for justice, the moral injunctions of the Decalogue—all of the nooks and crannies of the Old Testament apparently were as dear and familiar to her father Caspar as they were to the rabbi of Haarlem. For this family, at least, a love for the Hebrew Scriptures directly nurtured a love for the Jewish people.

It is also important to note Caspar ten Boom's oft-repeated belief that the Jews are God's chosen people, "the apple of God's eye," as he told Corrie.[18] A lively belief in the chosenness of the Jewish people is a consistent theme in *The Hiding Place* and other memoirs and interviews with Dutch Reformed rescuers, as well as in accounts concerning some other theologically conservative Christian rescuers. This belief, drawn from the well-springs of biblical Judaism, is an important feature in most forms of traditional Christian faith as well, even today. However, by no means do all conservative Christians speak of the chosenness of the Jewish people as a *present* as well as a past reality, as so many of the Dutch Reformed rescuers seem to do. Corrie ten Boom, anticipating the need to help Jews, prays: "Lord Jesus, I offer myself for *Your* people. In any way. Any place. Any time."[19] A Jewish woman comes to the door one night looking for help; Corrie's father says, "In this household, God's people are always welcome."[20] References to "My people" (from God's perspective), "Your people" (when addressing God in prayer), and "God's people" appear again and again among Calvinist rescuers in referring to Jews. Such a designation for Jews appears self-evident and obvious to those who used it, but it was bewildering to many Jews and by no means a common practice in most Christian circles.[21]

An examination of the piety of the ten Boom family and the comments of other Reformed rescuers perforce leads one to ask some questions about the Calvinist tradition. Is there (or was there) something about that particular strand of Christian faith that contributed disproportionately to rescue? It is widely recognized that Calvin found more continuity between the Old and the New Testament than have many other Christian theologians. Calvin wrote, "God exhibits to us nothing in his only begotten Son but what he had formerly promised in the law."[22] Thus, Christians are enjoined to search the Hebrew Scriptures with all diligence for revelation concerning Christ, who is the very foundation of those Scriptures. Perhaps this contributed to a greater respect in this tradition for Jewish faith and Jewish people than is the case for many other Christians.

Moreover, Calvin argued for the importance of Old Testament moral law and its continuing validity for Christians.[23] For example, he described the Ten Commandments as "a perfect pattern of righteousness" and the "one everlasting and unchangeable rule to live by."[24] This emphasis became embedded in the Reformed tradition, while many other strands of Christian faith juxtaposed Old Testament "law" with New Testament "grace," denigrating and deemphasizing the former. Interestingly, even today the Ten Commandments are read weekly from the pulpit in many Dutch Reformed churches, a practice unknown in most other Christian denominations.[25] It may well be that this distinctive Calvinist stance has helped those following in his line to appreciate rather than to deride continuing Jewish fidelity to biblical laws.

Also needed is a fresh look at Calvin's view of the status of the covenant between God and the Jewish people after the coming of Christ. A central element of Christian theological anti-Judaism has been the fateful belief that, because of Israel's unwillingness to embrace Jesus as the Messiah, the church has superseded or displaced the Jewish people as God's elect and covenant partner, and thus the Jews have been utterly abandoned by God.[26] Such convictions are common among many Christians even today; they see a past but not a present nor a future relationship between God and the Jewish people. Did Calvin manage to avoid this Christian supersessionism? He did argue that an unchangeable God could not and did not abandon the covenant with the Jewish people. He was sure that "God's purpose of election" remains with the Jewish people even as the Gentiles are adopted into the covenant. Further, he did find evidence from as early as the call of Abraham (Gen. 12:1-3) that all that has occurred vis-à-vis the Jews and Jesus has unfolded according to God's eternal decree. Yes, for Calvin God's purpose remains that redemption in Jesus Christ should come to Israel.[27] But many rescuers seriously nurtured in the Calvinist tradition held this view while retaining a profound and morally constructive sense of God's continuing and unique relationship with the Jewish people.

The evidence available about Calvinist rescuers by no means demonstrates that all Calvinist Christians were philo-Semites, or that it was impossible for Calvinists to construe their tradition in an anti-Semitic manner. It does seem to be the case, though, that resources for a positive view of Jews were both available and relatively prominent in that particular strand of the Christian tradition. Moreover, the historical record now amply demonstrates that Jews in desperate need found among many Calvinist Christians a profound respect and solidarity precisely *because* they were Jews. These Calvinists, as well as adherents of certain other forms of very conservative Christian theology, viewed Jews as religious kin in a way that most Christians simply do not. For them, saving Jews constituted a kind of intra-group rescue. It was the rescue of people whom they saw as a special kind of religious kin, fellow believers in the God of Abraham and

Sarah, Isaac and Rebekah, Jacob, Leah, and Rachel—brothers and sisters in faith. Because they were Jews (though, often, not *only* because they were Jews) these hunted people were definitely within the boundaries of moral obligation.

A terrible irony here is that the Nazis seemed to understand the fundamental religious kinship between Jews and Christians better than most Christians did. They at least feared its potential for blocking their plans and used every means possible to discourage Jewish-Christian rapprochement. But they had less to worry about than they thought. Historic Christian theological anti-Judaism had left the majority of European Christians with little or no sense of particular and positive religious ties between Christians and Jews—quite the contrary, in fact. Where protests were made and rescue undertaken by most Christians, even the devout, this rationale was usually absent.

The Calvinist rescuers (and others with a similar sense of Jewish-Christian religious kinship) remind us that historic Christian attitudes toward Jews actually run the spectrum from virulently negative to profoundly positive. The Jewish origins of the Christian faith make it less likely that serious traditional Christians will adopt a casual stance toward Jews than that they will hold an emotionally charged conviction at one pole or the other. These philo-Semitic rescuers were indeed "legitimately representative embodiments" of *one strand* of historic Christian faith. Tragically, so were those anti-Semites who hated Jews on the basis, in part, of a different strand of that same Christian faith.

One concern some have raised about this form of Christian solidarity with Jews is its rooting in a belief in the chosenness and special historic destiny of the Jewish people. While many secular Jews find this belief antiquated or even incomprehensible, some Jewish and Christian theologians also have perceived dangers. For example, Richard Rubenstein in his groundbreaking book *After Auschwitz* demanded abandonment of the belief in the chosenness of Israel and traced murderous Christian and Nazi anti-Semitism to the effects of this "Christian mythology of history" that is rooted also in traditional Jewish faith.[28] He pleaded with Christians to see Jews simply as normal human beings, not as either "Jesus or Judas," as has so often been the case.[29] One wonders whether the evidence presented here concerning Christian philo-Semitic rescuers might move Rubenstein to reconsider his view. It may be that anti-Semitism, so often related to or rooted in religion, is best confronted by an equally religious philo-Semitism. In any case, it seems completely unrealistic to hope that serious adherents of the three Abrahamic faiths (Judaism, Christianity, Islam) will ever be able to view one another through other-than-religious lenses. This means that those of us working with and in such communities of faith must try to grind the hatred out of these religious lenses rather than attempt to discard them altogether.

One does not have to be enthusiastic about every aspect of orthodox Calvinism to acknowledge that those who teach, preach, and write Christian theology must promote the positive sense of Christian kinship with Jews embodied by such rescuers. There are ways of understanding and discussing Judaism and the Jewish people that can both be true to historic Christian faith and create that sense of kinship. This is the lesson that the religious philo-Semitic rescuers teach us so profoundly, for they risked their very lives on the strength of that sense of kinship. We cannot afford to ignore their witness.

While exploring the importance of this sense of special religious kinship with Jews, the church must also consider those theological and moral resources which may be of more general applicability. We want to see Christians act with compassion toward *anyone* who is vulnerable, threatened, and in need, and thus we seek resources in the faith that might lead to such compassion. The testimony of the Christian rescuers reveals the presence of a wide range of faith-based resources that compelled them to become rescuers.

The Remembered Experience of Religious Persecution

Researchers on the rescue activities in and around the French village of Le Chambon, as well as in the nearby Cévennes region, have drawn attention to the historic Huguenot experience of religious persecution in France and the way in which the memory of that experience became a crucial resource for these Protestant rescuers.[30] In a little-noticed parallel observation, Yehuda Bauer has claimed that the small Baptist minority in Lithuania and western Ukraine stood out with regard to the extent of its rescue activities, and that their historic experience of persecution was a central factor: "Themselves persecuted as a religious minority, they saw the Jews as the Agnus Dei, to be helped and succoured whatever the risk and whatever the cost."[31] No research exists to demonstrate that members of religious minorities were disproportionately involved in rescue across Europe. But there are tantalizing hints—and it is clear from the activities of the French Protestant rescuers that the experience of religious persecution and minority status could and sometimes did provide powerful impetus for rescue. This phenomenon deserves exploration.

Several powerful resources related to the Huguenot experience of religious persecution should be noted. The first is identification with all

suffering people. The history of Protestantism in France had been a history
of suffering. For some three hundred years, with brief exceptions, the tiny
Protestant minority had faced brutal persecution at the hands of Catholic
France. This long period of repression is known in Protestant circles by the
graphic name *Le Désert* (the Wasteland). Protestants had been murdered
en masse in such tragedies as the St. Bartholomew's Day Massacre of 1572
(which took over three thousand lives), and throughout these years had
been enslaved and imprisoned for their beliefs. Protestant temples had
been destroyed and their pastors sometimes executed for their leadership
of these illegal sects. In 1598, King Henry IV promulgated the Edict of
Nantes, which finally offered religious toleration to French Protestants. But
eighty-seven years later, this freedom was cruelly revoked by King Louis
XIV, which led to a fresh outbreak of religious persecution. Many Huguenots left France after the revocation in 1685 (including my ancestors on my
father's side, who settled in New England). For those who remained, religious freedom was finally restored over one hundred years later, after
the French Revolution. Yet the memory of their suffering had been seared
into the Huguenot consciousness and was then passed down through the
generations.[32]

This heritage appears to have been one of the reasons why the residents of Le Chambon, in particular, had long involved themselves in
actions on behalf of people in need. Philip Hallie reports that this predominantly Protestant village had not only experienced the persecution of its
pastors and people for hundreds of years, but also had been a haven for
almost a thousand Protestant newcomers seeking refuge after the revocation in 1685.[33] These people settled in Le Chambon and most of their
descendants stayed in the town in succeeding generations. In the early
1900s, the Chambonnais welcomed sick working-class children from nearby
cities to their community. In the 1930s, Le Chambon sheltered refugees
from the Spanish civil war and received more refugees of all types as World
War II loomed and then began.[34] Thus ample precedent existed for the
decisions of scores of Chambonnais families to welcome Jews and other
refugees into their homes during the war. The collective memory of persecution was foundational for the community's consistent practice of hospitality to the needy, a practice that simply continued during the Holocaust
even as the risks increased.

A related resource for French Protestant rescuers was their sense of
identification *with Jews in particular* as a suffering religious minority. French
Protestants knew the bitter taste of religious persecution, and many considered what was happening to the Jews a parallel to the suffering of their
own Huguenot ancestors.[35] They were peculiarly well equipped to reject
the legitimacy of religious (or quasi-religious) persecution and to reach out

to its victims. Further, these rescuers remembered that in their history the persecution had been an attempt to force them to renounce their faith. Perhaps this is one reason why André Trocmé (pastor of Le Chambon's Reformed congregation) and other French Protestant rescuers consistently chose not to take advantage of the Jewish plight by proselytizing their charges.[36] Pierre Sauvage has noted that *Judaism* was sheltered in Le Chambon, as well as Jews.[37] For many of the French Protestant rescuers (some Reformed, some in evangelical or fundamentalist groups), their stance toward the Jewish refugees also was affected by their deeply respectful view of the Jews as God's chosen people, as discussed in the previous section.[38]

State-sponsored religious persecution had helped to create within the French Protestant community an appropriately critical eye toward government. Through vividly remembered experience, they knew that governments do indeed sometimes pass and enforce unjust laws. Having suffered such injustice, they had developed a carefully constrained theological understanding of the role and limits of governmental authority. One of the most dramatic wartime events in Le Chambon was the visit of the Vichy official Georges Lamirand in the summer of 1942. The Chambonnais leadership made clear to Lamirand its view of the appropriate obedience due to the state. Two different speakers, one reflecting on Romans 13, argued that Christians owe obedience to the state, but that such obedience is sharply constrained by the commandment to love one's neighbor. When the governing authorities attempt to force people to harm their neighbors or otherwise to violate the laws of God or their own consciences, they are no longer owed obedience.[39] This view of the state and the limits of Christian obedience to it played a crucial role in leading to rescue in Le Chambon, in the Cévennes, and elsewhere in Europe—while a theology inculcating passive and uncritical obedience proved to be a particularly devastating impediment to rescue all across the Continent.[40]

French Protestants also knew that governmental injustice must be not just rejected but resisted, and had inherited a legacy of such resistance. During *Le Désert*, Huguenot resistance to religious persecution had taken a variety of different forms. The most militant resistance had occurred in the early eighteenth century in the Cévennes, where an armed group known as the Camisards fought the French government for several years before their rebellion sputtered in 1710. This resistance is an important part of the historical consciousness of the Protestant Cévenols.[41] In Le Chambon, historically, resistance had taken a quieter form—Hallie calls it the resistance of "silence, cunning, and secrecy," peculiarly well suited to mountain people and their circumstances (also well suited, one might add, to those who lack any hope of matching firepower with the oppressor).[42] Especially this latter form of resistance reappeared during French Protestant rescue work, as rescuers creatively and often nonviolently defied Nazi and Vichy racial laws.

Finally, the effect of religious persecution on the shape of pastoral leadership was crucial. French Protestant pastors traditionally led the resistance to religious persecution and often paid for it with their lives. For example, in 1529 a Chambonnais Protestant pastor was burned alive for his preaching—and this was not an isolated case.[43] Their courage in continuing to hold their despised flocks together in the midst of the storm earned them the profound respect of their people. When the Nazi terror arose, it was natural for the Protestants of Le Chambon and the Cévennes to unite quietly around their pastors as these communities once again defied government decrees.[44] Fortunately for the several thousand Jews rescued, pastors like André Trocmé in Le Chambon, Marc Donadille in the Cévennes, and others proved worthy heirs to the Huguenot pulpits of southern France.

Religious persecution is sought neither by Christians nor by any other group. But such suffering, when it occurs, often serves as a refiner's fire for the church. Those faint in faith and courage drop off, leaving a more highly committed remnant who cleave passionately to one another and to God for courage and strength. The experience of having been oppressed and wounded can lead to a commitment to liberate, to heal, and to do justice. This theme, in fact a divine command for the people of faith, resounds throughout the Old Testament (see Exod. 22:21-24). Persecution at the hands of the state quickly leads to or deepens an appropriately critical stance toward government and nation (see Rev. 13), one that enables a purer devotion to Jesus Christ and an immunity to national idolatry. The churches learn skills of resistance that prove powerful in surviving oppression and helping others to survive it. The pulpit rings with a moral passion incarnated in the minister's moral practice.

Many Christian thinkers have concluded that the church took a fateful wrong turn when it ascended to power with the emperor Constantine. They recall with wistful pride the martyred minority church of the first three Christian centuries. Though there are advantages and disadvantages to every power position for the church, the resources available to the minority church with a memory of persecution are powerful. A history of having been oppressed obviously cannot be created out of whole cloth, nor should contemporary persecution be sought for its own sake. But the churches can choose to identify with the persecuted and all suffering people and to work with them for justice, and can choose a stance of theologically constrained distance from the nation. When this path is taken, the church is more faithful—and more likely to taste persecution, as its Lord did.

The Incompatibility of Nazism and Christian Faith

Some Christians became convinced that Nazi ideology and policy were fundamentally incompatible with Christian faith. Some of those who perceived this incompatibility responded by involving themselves in anti-Nazi activities. And some of those who became involved in such religiously motivated anti-Nazi efforts engaged in the rescue of Jews. This theme—the incompatibility of Nazism and Christian faith, which demanded Christian resistance—appears frequently in statements of the German religious resistance, both Protestant and Catholic, as well as in documents and accounts offered by theologians and ministers in other countries.[45] But it also appears in the testimonies of Christian rescuers with little or no theological training or even formal education. What all of these have in common is a religious revulsion against Nazism and a sense of compulsion to resist it wherever possible. For some such religious rescuers, it was the racist war against innocent Jewish people that epitomized the depths of Nazism's evil and demanded the most vigorous resistance. Tragically, though, other Christians who succeeded in seeing Nazism as a mortal enemy failed to embrace fully its foremost victims, the Jews.[46]

This simultaneous success and failure was apparent in the now-famous Barmen Declaration of May 1934, which first enunciated theological resistance in Germany to Nazism and its penetration into Protestant church life. The focus of the declaration was precisely the incompatibility of Nazism and its policies with the church's self-understanding. In their statement, those gathered in the first Confessing Church Synod implicitly but clearly rejected any belief that God's revelation was occurring through Adolf Hitler and the Nazi regime, as some pro-Hitler Christians (the *Deutschen Christen*) asserted. They dismissed the claim of "other lords" than Jesus Christ in any area of the Christian's life, thus rejecting the idolization of Hitler (the *Führerprinzip*), the Aryan race, the German *Volk*, or any other false god. They expressed their resistance to any synchronization (*Gleichschaltung*) of church order or doctrine with Nazism and its program. They decried the Nazi state's attempt to become the "single and totalitarian order of human life" and to co-opt the church as an organ of the state (*Reichskirche*).[47] Accordingly, they implicitly (but obviously, in the context) rejected the "Aryanization" or racial "purification" of the church through the imposition of anti-"non-Aryan" decrees and associated theological/moral norms. The fateful omission of any response to the state's mistreatment of German Jews *qua* Jews demonstrated even the Confessing Church's limited recognition of the fundamental theological and moral importance of Nazi anti-Semitism.[48] But the Declaration did at least lay a solid theological foundation for resistance to Nazism as an alien and anti-Christian ideology. Some who thus understood the nature of the enemy became involved in rescuing those it victimized.

It was Dietrich Bonhoeffer who offered the most penetrating theological reflection in Germany both on the radical and dangerous perversity of Nazism and on the necessity for Christians to aid the Jews (and not only the church's Jewish converts). His writings on Nazism ranged widely from 1933 to 1945, addressing with great insight the kinds of theological issues raised at Barmen.[49] But it was his discussion of the church's responsibility in the Jewish crisis that was particularly unique in his context. As early as 1933 he argued that the church's responsibility in any state is to call government to task when it violates its divinely given vocation. Bonhoeffer described Hitler's early political measures as what they were—illegal nullifications of the constitutional rights of the German people, especially Germany's Jews—and called for the church to confront the state at this point.[50] In the same 1933 essay, Bonhoeffer declared that the church has a responsibility to offer unconditional aid to the victims of state action, in this case the Jews of Germany.[51] Bonhoeffer's theological reflections on Judaism and Jewish-Christian relations *per se* are complex, evidencing both elements of historic Christian anti-Judaism and also, especially in his *Ethics*, traces of a new and more constructive approach.[52] Whatever his limits here, however, his theology proved morally worthy both in its clearsighted anti-Nazism and in its demand that the Jews be helped. Bonhoeffer is remembered with such great respect today not only for his insight on these crucial issues, of course, but also for his moral practice. He both participated in a plot to kill Adolf Hitler (thus attacking the evil directly) and also involved himself in efforts to smuggle Jews into Switzerland. Arrested and imprisoned for his anti-Nazi activities, he met his death at Nazi hands on April 9, 1945.

Theological reflection on the incompatibility of Nazism with Christian faith occurred elsewhere in Europe as refugees and later the war reached different lands. Sometimes an awareness of the incompatibility of fascism with Christian faith preceded the Nazi arrival. In the Netherlands, the orthodox Christian Reformed Church decided in their synod in Amsterdam in 1936 that members of the Dutch fascist party (the NSB) should be prohibited from receiving communion and eventually excommunicated if necessary.[53] This decision was courageously reaffirmed after the Nazis occupied Holland in 1941 and brought the NSB into a considerably more powerful position. Not coincidentally, Christian Reformed congregants tended toward a strong belief in the special religious kinship between Christians and Jews, as discussed above. According to Lawrence Baron, members of this religious community accounted for only 8 percent of Holland's population but a full 25 percent of the rescues of Jews in that country.[54]

Just as in the Germany of 1933, one of the first tests of Dutch Christian solidarity with Dutch Jewry came when the Aryan paragraph was imposed. In the Netherlands, this crisis occurred in the fall of 1940. All Dutch civil servants were required to declare their "Aryan" or "non-Aryan" identity. All non-Aryans were dismissed in short order. The weak resistance to this measure in Holland was important in paving the way for the Final Solution in the Netherlands. But some did oppose this first major step. One who sensed the moral and religious issues at stake was N. H. de Graaf, supervisor of Social Youth Services in the government bureaucracy. De Graaf told his coworkers that he would refuse to enforce the Aryan Declaration in his department. According to Pieter De Jong, de Graaf asserted that "every form of preference of one person to another because of race or nation [is] in conflict with the deepest roots of faith in Jesus Christ."[55]

During the course of the occupation, official Christian statements in the Netherlands consistently noted the "discrepancy between the Gospel and the totalitarian religion of National Socialism."[56] One leader of this Dutch religious resistance was clergyman/theologian K. H. Miskotte, who drafted several thoughtful statements for the Dutch Reformed Church as it engaged in its own "church struggle" against the Nazi occupiers. Miskotte's particular strength was his analysis of the neopagan religious roots of the Holocaust. In a May 1945 sermon, for example, Miskotte argued that the Nazi attempt to destroy the Jewish people was at its deepest level an idolatrous assault on the God who had chosen Israel. By destroying the people of God the Nazis sought to annihilate God. Their desire to annihilate the God of Jewish and Christian faith stemmed from their embrace of the gods of Germanic pagan tribalism. For Miskotte, Nazism was a pagan faith and the struggle against it an awesome "faith against faith" encounter. Thus the Nazi effort at divine and human holocaust had demanded the church's resistance, and one key reason was that the God under attack was God of the Christian church as well as of the Jews.[57] Here again we see a theological analysis of Nazism leading both to recognition of its fundamental irreconcilability with Christian faith and to solidarity with Jews.

In retrospect it seems hard to believe that this irreconcilability was not immediately obvious to most German (and then other European) Christians. However, in the case of Germany, Hitler was at first careful to reassure the churches of his support for religion and his benign intentions toward them. He emphasized the points (i.e., anti-liberalism and anti-Communism) where their interests appeared to overlap. He called on their patriotism, which most Germans were ready to understand as demanding unquestioning support for him and his program of national reconstruction. The visibility of his stormtroopers served as a deterrent to opposition, as did the very human inclination of most Germans to try to be both "good

Christians" and "good Germans."[58] On our side of World War II and the Holocaust, however, the overall failure of Christian theological discernment in Nazi Germany can be viewed as nothing less than an unmitigated disaster.

As we inspect these ruins, we are reminded of how difficult it is for Christians to discern the political signs of the times, especially when those signs demand a resistance that might prove personally or institutionally costly. Christians appear to be just as susceptible to the charms of the charlatan-demagogue and just as lacking in courage as everyone else.. Yet the church has produced persons of discernment and moral courage, as we have seen. In Barmen and in Bonhoeffer, in the Christian Reformed Church and in K. H. Miskotte, we see evidence that such discernment and courage can happen as Christians keep their eyes fixed on the one God and commit themselves without reservation to serve that God alone. "I am the Lord your God. . . . You shall have no other gods before me" (Exod. 20:2-3). In their obedience to this, the First Commandment, some Christians found a way to preserve both their souls and the lives of Jews in Nazi Europe.

The Equality and Preciousness of Every Human Life

The Nazis preached and practiced an ideology that radically elevated the value of some human beings over others. In the Nazi scheme, a primordial ontological gulf existed between groups of people, one that fundamentally affected their relative worth. To those classified as racially superior ("Aryans" and their close kin) rightly belonged all power, security, land, wealth, and civic and political rights. To those classified as inferior (non-"Aryans") rightly belonged no power, no security, no land, no wealth, and no rights. In stark contrast, some Christians rescued Jews from death because of their theological commitment to the equal worth of every person and to the preciousness of every human life. Of great interest are the various ways in which this commitment emerged from the Christian faith.

Some Christians offered a theological rationale for rescue grounded in a version of the doctrine of creation. A formal rendering of this view was given in a famous pastoral letter by Pierre-Marie Théas, bishop of Montauban, France:

> I must make heard the indignant protest of the Christian conscience, and I proclaim that all men [and women], aryan or non-aryan, are brothers [and sisters], *because they are created by the same God*; that all, whatever their race or religion, are entitled to respect from individuals and the State.[59]

The Confessional Synod of the Old Prussian Union offered a similar opinion, though from a different angle of vision, when it proclaimed: "The right to exterminate human beings because they belong to . . . another race, nation, or religion was not given by God to the government. The life of men [and women] belongs to God and is sacred to him."[60]

Less formal statements to this effect appear in the accounts of several Christian rescuers. One Dutch rescuer asserts, "Once I knew of a Jew in risk of losing his life, nothing else made any difference. Our Lord had created the Jew just as he had created me. That was enough for me."[61] According to one of the rescuers quoted by the Oliners, "I could not comprehend that innocent persons should be persecuted just because of race. We all come from the same God."[62] Fela Steinberg reports that her Polish rescuer was torn by conflicting religious teachings concerning whether to rescue Jews. One resource leading him to think he should help was the teaching that "all were God's children . . . all are made in God's image."[63]

Two central biblical texts from the book of Genesis appear (sometimes directly, sometimes by allusion) in many of these accounts: "So God created humankind in his image, in the image of God he created them, male and female he created them" (Gen. 1:27 NRSV); "Then the Lord God formed the man from the dust of the ground, and breathed into his nostrils the breath of life, and the man became a living being" (Gen 2:7 NRSV). The latter is best interpreted as affirming that it is God who breathes life not only into that first human being but into every human being, thus placing extraordinary value on each life. The former offers the audacious assertion that human beings—all of them—share something of the worth of God by sharing in the *imago dei*. Both, as these Christian rescuers rightly understood, demand rejection of a view that places higher value and worth on some people's lives than on others. There are no "children of a lesser God," no theologically defensible ontological gulf between groups of human beings.

Some Christian rescuers offered a Christ-centered or church-centered rationale for their belief in the equality and worth of every person. The Dutch civil servant N. H. De Graaf, mentioned above, offered this theological rationale for his refusal to circulate the Aryan paragraph: "In Jesus Christ, God Almighty, Creator of heaven and earth, was willing to reveal himself to all [humankind]; before [Jesus Christ] everyone has equal status."[64] The Nazis put Germany's churches to the test precisely on this point when they sought to impose the Aryan/non-Aryan distinction throughout ecclesiastical life. One splendid early proclamation of resistance to this effort was offered by the Confessing Church of the Old Prussian Union in 1933:

> If the church would refuse the baptism of a Jew because of race-political reasons, then it would claim a power over the sacrament which is not

given to it. It is bound to the mission of Christ. The realm of Christ in
which we are adopted by baptism does not know the differences of
race and sex which have their limited meaning in the natural sphere
of this world. There is, in Christ, no Jew or Greek or German![65]

The Holy Synod of Bishops of the Bulgarian Orthodox Church also offered
a ringing declaration along these lines:

> The Holy Synod [has] informed the government that the principle of
> racialism cannot be justified from the point of view of the Christian
> doctrine, being contrary to the fundamental message of the Christian
> Church, in which all who believe in Jesus Christ are men and women
> of equal worth. "There is neither Jew nor Greek, there is neither bond
> nor free, there is neither male nor female; for you are all one in Christ
> Jesus" (Gal. 3:28).[66]

This particular text, Galatians 3:28, proved to be extraordinarily pro-
ductive in motivating Christians to resist Nazi racism and support Jews.
Numerous references to it are found in the literature of Christian resistance
and in the accounts of rescuers.[67] Interestingly, Helen Fein has argued that
many of these Christian statements stretch the original meaning of the
Galatians text.[68] Yet the church has rightly come to understand that Paul's
assertion—that ethnic, gender, class, and national distinctions among
Christian believers are transcended in Christ—has broader social and political implications as well. If all human beings are equal in Christ, then all
human beings are equal, period. Thus, one could argue that the Old Prussian Union statement appropriately understood and employed the original
meaning of the text, while the Bulgarian Synod also appropriately discerned
its broader theological implications. The text proved morally empowering
for Christian rescuers beyond what might reasonably have been expected.
This is something for the church to ponder.

Another avenue toward Christian affirmation of the equal worth of
every human being was found in the language of human rights. The use
of this language, whether on the part of the average Christian on the street
or in the public statements of churches, seems to have emerged most
frequently in immediate response to a particularly traumatic violation of
the rights of Jews. As noted in the last chapter, it was the brutal violation
of human rights that called forth strenuous assertions of the existence of
those rights.

An important example of this phenomenon is provided by an eloquent
pastoral letter dated August 23, 1942, and written by the French Archbishop
Jules-Gérard Saliège. Writing immediately after the brutal roundups of
foreign Jews in Paris, Saliège wrote:

> There is a Christian morality and a human ethic which impose duties
> and recognize rights. Both rights and duties are parts of human nature.

They were sent by God. They can be violated. But no mortal sin can suppress them. The treatment of children, women, fathers, and mothers like a base herd of cattle, the separation of members of a family from one another and their deportation to unknown destinations, are sad spectacles which have been reserved for us to witness in our times. . . . Jews are men and women. Foreigners are men and women. It is just as criminal to use violence against [them] as it is against anyone else. They too are members of the human race.[69]

Such protests were heard in Germany as well. Strong and effective opposition was first offered to the Nazi "euthanasia" program on these grounds. Cardinal Faulhaber of Munich wrote that "even during wartime, one may not discard the everlasting foundations of the moral order, nor the fundamental rights of the individual."[70] The Pope himself weighed in with a decree indirectly but unmistakably calling the euthanasia program "contrary to both the natural law and the divine positive law."[71] Tragically, the persecution of the Jews did not evoke opposition of comparable strength. However, statements were issued such as the following by Cardinal Preysing of Berlin in 1942:

Every human has rights that cannot be taken from him by an earthly power. . . . Primitive rights, such as the right to live, to be free, to have possessions, to marry whom one chooses, etc., cannot be denied him simply because he is not of our blood. . . . We must realize that depriving him of those rights is a grave injustice.[72]

The principles behind the behavior of Christian pacifist rescuers should also be mentioned. There appear to have been very few pacifists of any kind in World War II Europe. Broadly speaking, people in aggressor states tended to be inflamed with militarism and people in occupied states inflamed with hatred of the oppressor. Further, the dominant Christian traditions sanctioned participation in "just wars," and most people in both aggressor and victimized nations were convinced of the justice of their cause. Thus one does not find many Christian rescuers who acted on the basis of pacifist principles, though one does find some.[73] One of these was André Trocmé.[74] Fortunately, his thinking is as well documented as that of any Christian rescuer of Jews.

Trocmé, like all Christian pacifists, believed that "human life [is] too precious . . . to be taken for any reason, however glorious and vast though that reason might be."[75] The dignity, worth, and supreme value of every human life are unexceptionable. For Trocmé this conviction was theologically grounded both in the Sixth Commandment—"Thou shalt not kill" (Exod. 20:13)—and in an understanding of the meaning of the life, death, and resurrection of Jesus Christ.[76] Trocmé and his associates in Le Chambon perceived pacifism as an aggressive and creative strategy for resisting evil and doing good. He believed in the immense power of the "weapons of the Spirit" (2 Cor. 10:4; Eph. 6:10-17) if unstintingly employed. As Hallie asserts, Trocmé's was an ethic of nonviolent combat, not of passivity.[77] Ultimately, it was grounded in the belief that God's love is more powerful than any human force, even the most evil. Several thousand Jews were saved in Le Chambon by several thousand Christians armed only with those weapons of the Spirit.

It seems appropriate to close this section with the wondrous story of Jan Sagan, a Polish farmer who rescued eighteen-year-old Morris Krantz. Krantz had witnessed the massacre of his whole family and was alone in the forest—hungry, homeless, grieving, and cold. Searching his memory for a potentially trustworthy Gentile, he settled on Jan Sagan, a business associate of his father. Early one morning he approached Sagan and begged for his help. The farmer hesitated, fearing retribution on his wife, children, and parents. But then he decided to help him. After the war, Sagan told Krantz of his struggle:

> That morning will not leave me as long as I live. I was startled by the sight of you—overgrown hair, face swollen from the cold, all in rags—a ghost, a wild man, a barely human creature. When I asked you to leave, I was reacting to my first impulse, to shock. I was in turmoil over it for two days. I considered it the biggest crisis of my life, to jeopardize my family by allowing you to stay, or to turn you out to certain death. . . . *You made me aware of what a precious gift life is and of the God-given power in it.* When I considered your presence on the farm and its effect on me, I suddenly realized that whatever I had done for you had resulted in as much good for me—more. I had never felt so good, so alive. I was convinced that it was the work of a higher power.[78]

Biblical Teachings on Compassion and Love

Another crucial set of resources for rescue were biblical texts enjoining love of neighbor and compassion for the wounded and oppressed. Reference to these biblical injunctions appears constantly in official church statements, interviews with rescuers, autobiographies, and so on. They clearly had a profound impact on the behavior of many Christian rescuers. Below we will review several of the biblical texts that appear most frequently in rescuer literature.[79]

The parable of the Good Samaritan (Luke 10:25-37)

". . . But a Samaritan while traveling came near him; and when he saw him, he was moved with pity. He went to him and bandaged his wounds, having poured oil and wine on them. Then he put him on his own animal, brought him to an inn, and took care of him. The next day he took out two denarii, gave them to the innkeeper, and said, 'Take care of him; and when I come back, I will repay you whatever more you spend.' Which of these three, do you think, was a neighbor to the man who fell into the hands of the robbers?" He said, "The one who showed him mercy." Jesus said to him, "Go and do likewise." NRSV

"Go and do likewise." This was a command that cut like a knife through the hearts of a number of Christian rescuers, stilling their doubts and impelling them to help Jews. Eva Fogelman tells the story of a woman she identifies as Christina R., a devout Dutch Christian from Friesland. One day, a friend came to her with a four-year-old Jewish girl. The little girl's father had been shot, her mother and brother had fled; she had been shoved into a closet and told to wait for help from Christians. Christina, the mother of five children under the age of eight, took the child in without being able to consult her husband about it. That night, when he came home from work, he expressed his deep discomfort with her decision.

> My husband . . . was afraid. "Chrissie, Chrissie, what are you doing?" he asked. "Remember this," I answered. "We call ourselves Christians. We cannot put this little girl out on the street. She will be gassed." My husband was not convinced. "I have to take care of my own," he said. Later . . . we talked it over. "Remember the story of the Good Samaritan?" I asked. "Martin, do you want to be like the first two who looked away and turned their backs? Or do you want to be like the third, who, no matter what the cost, said, 'Okay, I will help'?"[80]

They agreed to take the little girl in, the first rescue of many they successfully undertook in the next few years.

The impact of the Good Samaritan story was felt keenly in Le Chambon. According to assistant pastor Édouard Theis, this story and the Sermon on the Mount were André Trocmé's favorite biblical passages. According to Philip Hallie, both texts were preached quite frequently during the rescue, to remind the villagers of the central driving force behind their clandestine efforts and to fortify them for the struggle.[81] Gabrielle Barraud ran one of the several boardinghouses in Le Chambon. She sheltered several Jewish boys in her home without pay. When Hallie asked her why she took the risks she did, she replied that the Good Samaritan story was one of the major influences on her thinking.[82]

Love of God and neighbor (Matt. 22:34-40)

"Teacher, which commandment in the law is the greatest?" He said to him, " 'You shall love the Lord your God with all your heart, and with

all your soul, and with all your mind.' This is the greatest and first
commandment. And a second is like it: 'You shall love your neighbor
as yourself.' On these two commandments hang the law and the prophets." NRSV

Mordecai Paldiel tells the story of Tadeusz Soroka, a Polish employee
of the Lithuanian railroads. Soroka initiated the daring rescue of Aaron
Derman, a Jew incarcerated in the Grodno ghetto, and rescued other Jews
later. In 1982, Soroka was brought to the United States and honored by
the Jewish community. When asked why he helped Jews, Soroka responded, "We were all taught the second great commandment, 'You shall love
your neighbor as yourself.' So I knew what I must do. . . . It was no big
thing."[83]

References to this command appear in several declarations of Christian
resistance. A May 1936 memorandum to Hitler from the Confessing Church
rejects the hatred of Jews because of the command to love one's neighbor.[84]
The dean of St. Hedwig's Cathedral in Berlin, Bernard Lichtenberg, asserted
in 1941: "If it is said that Germans, by supporting Jews, commit treason,
I enjoin you not to be misled by such unchristian sentiments, but to act in
obedience to Christ's commandment, and to love your neighbor as yourself."[85] That the command to love demanded the rescue of Jews was apparent to numerous Christians. Accounts to this effect can be found in the
work of most rescuer researchers.[86]

The Great Judgment (Matt. 25:31-46)

". . . Then the king will say to those at his right hand, 'Come, you that
are blessed by my Father, inherit the kingdom. . . . For I was hungry
and you gave me food, I was thirsty and you gave me something to
drink, I was a stranger and you welcomed me, I was naked and you
gave me clothing, I was sick and you took care of me, I was in prison
and you visited me.' Then the righteous will answer him, 'Lord, when
was it that we [did these things for you]?' . . . And the king will answer
them, 'Truly I tell you, just as you did it to one of the least of these
who are members of my family, you did it to me.' " NRSV

Several rescuers have cited or alluded to the influence of this powerful
text upon their actions during the war. Fritz Graebe, the well-known German rescuer, told his biographer that this passage was one of the central
biblical texts emphasized by his devout mother in the religious instruction
she gave him as a child.[87] The Polish rescuer Zofia Kossak-Szczucka, a well-
known writer of historical novels and an avowed anti-Semite, provides

another intriguing use of this text. In one of her wartime writings, Kossak-Szczucka creates a conversation between two strongly anti-Semitic Poles; one is involved in rescuing Jews, the other not. The rescuer offers this biblical allusion in explaining his actions:

> Christ stands behind every human being and watches how we react to him. He stretches his hand to us through a runaway Jew from the ghetto the same way as he does through our brothers. He is close to everyone.[88]

Kossak-Szczucka's actions give every indication that this speaker represents her own views.

Pieter Miedema was a Dutch Reformed minister from Friesland who struggled to enlist his congregation and others in his rescue efforts, and did so on explicitly Christian grounds. Andre Stein reports the following conversation between Miedema and his father-in-law. It reveals both the positive impact of the passage from Matthew 25 and the ability of Christians to resist it. The excerpt begins with the father-in-law (FL) expressing his rejection of Pieter's (P) rescue activities and any such activities on his own part.

> *FL:* You have a child now; you owe all your responsibility to her and to her mother. You can't get involved with the lives of every little Jew. What are those people to us anyway? Why should I risk my peace and tranquility for someone who means nothing to me?

> *P:* What if Christ himself came knocking on your door, father? Would you send him away, too?

> *FL:* Of course not. How can you compare the two? One is our Savior, the other is just a nobody. I don't see the connection at all. You as a minister, you should be the first one to know that, Pieter.

> *P:* And you, father, as a Christian and an elder in our Church, you should be more familiar with the words of Jesus Christ: "The things you do to the least of my friends, you do to me." Do you recall that Jesus was nothing more than a little Jew?

> *FL:* It's still different. I will risk nothing for a stranger.[89]

The Golden Rule (Matt. 7:12)

Do to others what you would have them do to you.

This simple injunction from the Sermon on the Mount may be the most familiar Christian moral teaching (and in slightly different form is well known in the Jewish tradition, as is the command to love God and neighbor). It stands as a perennial challenge to Christian people and is often cited in the churches. The Golden Rule proved to be a resource for some Christian rescuers during the Holocaust. As they opened their door to a cold, shivering, hunted Jew asking for refuge, these Christians heard "Do unto others . . .", and knew that if they were in a similar position, they certainly would want the person on the other side of the door to let them in. Two examples will serve to represent many others. Zofia Kossak-Sczuzcka's Polish anti-Semitic rescuer cites the Golden Rule in the same passage discussed above:

> Today the Jews face extermination. They are victims of unjust murderous persecutions. I must save them. "Do unto others what you would have them do unto you." This commandment demands that I use all the means I have to save others, the very same ways that I would use for my own salvation.[90]

Jan Sagan, the farmer who rescued Morris Krantz, also alluded to the Golden Rule when he explained his motivations in the following way: "People should not inflict on others what is not good for themselves."[91]

My Brother's Keeper (Gen. 4:8-10)

The LORD said to Cain, "Where is your brother Abel?" "I don't know, he replied. "Am I my brother's keeper?" The LORD said, "What have you done? Listen! Your brother's blood cries out to me from the ground."

Just after the end of the war, Pieter Miedema was transferred to the community of Dwingelo. In his first sermon, he reflected on his well-known wartime rescue activities and made clear that he would continue working for justice.

> "Am I my brother's keeper?" generations of Cains have asked with irate indifference toward the plight of others. There are countless ways to answer this simple question. But there is only one that makes sense to me: "Not only am I my brother's keeper, my brother is *my* keeper." Without this tacit contract, I am as vulnerable as he is without me.[92]

The elders in Dwingelo preferred not to hear such sermons, and Miedema eventually left that church. But fortunately there were some Christians who found this text important in shaping their behavior. One such person is quoted in the Oliner study:

> When you see a need, you have to help. Our religion was part of us. We are our brother's keeper. It was very satisfying for us.[93]

Christian Commitment and Spirituality

Theological and biblical resources for compassion and moral goodness do not stand alone. Obviously, they are not somehow automatically compelling for all who say they are Christians. Even when a person is committed to an appropriately compassionate version of Christian faith (other versions do exist), that faith must be infused by the kind of religious commitment and spiritual vitality that makes it come alive in practice. Most of those Christian rescuers who explicitly cite biblical passages or other resources of faith simultaneously reveal a personal religious experience that proved empowering to them. An exploration of some empowering elements of Christian commitment and spirituality seems necessary to give a fully accurate impression of the religious resources at work in the lives of Christian rescuers.

Some Christian rescuers saw their fundamental daily responsibility as the discerning and doing of the will of God. They assumed that God was active in the world and in their lives. Some believed that little if anything happened to them by chance. They were vigilant as they watched and waited for God's next intervention in their lives and for guidance on how to respond. Thus, in that fateful moment when a Jew came to them asking for help, their inclination was to ask whether offering such help was what God wanted them to do. It was difficult for those with a compassionate version of Christian faith to believe that the answer was No.

Rooted in this worldview, some Christian rescuers interpreted the opportunity to help as a message or signal from God. One Belgian rescuer was Father Hubert Celis, a Catholic priest. One day, very early in the war, he attended a meeting in which his bishop urged all the priests present to help their Jewish neighbors in any way they could. On the way home, a woman from his parish told him of a Jewish family nearby whose children were in urgent need of shelter. Celis's interviewer writes:

> Father Celis is convinced that this urgent request for help, coming as it did just after he had received his bishop's instructions, was a sign from God that he must aid the Jews. "Send the family to me," he said without hesitation. "I will help them, even if it costs me my life."[94]

The Polish rescuer Leokadia Jaromirska was convinced that the infant she discovered crying in the woods one morning was saved by God and divinely delivered into her safekeeping. She named her new "daughter" Bogumila.

> Bogumila—it means the one whom God loved—because God stood at her side and did not allow her to share the fate of thousands of other

children who were murdered in the most cruel way. I lived with her and for her.[95]

Convinced that God somehow had intervened to involve them in rescue, these Christians could not fail to believe that rescue was God's will for them. This conviction had a powerful effect. For many devout Christians, if God wills something, the Christian has no choice but to obey. One Dutch rescuer asserts:

> It's not because I have an altruistic personality. It's because I am an obedient Christian. I know that is the reason why I did it. I know it. The Lord wants you to do good work. What good is it to say you love your neighbor if you don't help them. There was never any question about it. The Lord wanted us to rescue those people and we did it.[96]

Numerous rescuers report this sense of Christian duty as the reason they rescued Jews. They did not view their actions as the free choice of a person of altruistic inclinations but instead as an act of obedience to God. In that obedience they accepted a role as a special instrument of God's will. The Oliners quote a rescuer who asserts, "My husband said right after the war started that we had to do something to help our people against the Nazis. It was our Christian duty—we should help as many as we could."[97] The language of obedience, obligation, and duty can be found in many Christian rescuer accounts.[98]

Related to this, one finds among some Christian rescuers a vivid sense that God watches human actions, ultimately rewarding those who do right and punishing those who fail to do so. A related but distinct conviction is that Christians can trust that after death they will have eternal life with God. It is hard to know which of the two was at play when Christina R., the Dutch rescuer discussed above, said to a German officer who had raided her house along with twenty soldiers, "You may shoot me—but I am not afraid. You will shoot only the body, while my spirit goes straight to heaven."[99] This confidence in her eternal destiny clearly had an effect on her response to the Germans, and in the context of the story it seems that it may well have saved her life.

Embedded in traditional Christian faith is a vivid scene drawn from the Bible and richly embroidered in the religious imagination: the moment in which the person faces God and is asked to give an account of his or her life. A few rescuers, like Christina R., hoped for or were confident of eternal life, and this enabled them to face the risks of rescue with some serenity. More who allude to this judgment by God indicate their fear of divine disapproval if they failed to help Jews. One who thought along these lines was Hela Horska, an avowed Polish anti-Semite who became involved in the rescue of Jews. Horska told Nechama Tec:

> I am a deeply religious person and I believe that the world became so horrible, so cruel, that when we would have to account before God one would at least have to point to a few good deeds in this hell on earth. Someone had to help these persecuted Jews. And so they stayed with us.[100]

One Dutch rescuer became tormented during the early days of his rescue activities when he had difficulty answering his Jewish charge's question: "What [is] in it for you to risk sharing the fate of the Jews? Why, Bill, why?" Finally, among the reasons he listed was the following:

> Can you imagine Judgment Day? The Lord would ask me: "What did you do, Bill Bouwma, when the Nazis were tormenting my people?" And I would have to answer sheepishly: "Nothing, my Lord. I had other things to do."[101]

Several rescuers believed that God here and now rewarded their efforts to do God's will by placing them under special protection. This belief empowered them to overcome their fears of discovery and punishment. Sometimes it led to breathtaking courage, even recklessness. "I gave it up to the Lord. It was in God's hands. . . . I know the Lord protected us," said one Dutch rescuer.[102] A different Dutch rescuer engaged in the following exchange with a Jewish woman whose nephew he was about to rescue. The woman says:

> "Thank you, thank you in advance. I guess the rest is in the hands of fortune."
> "No, Sylvia, fortune has nothing to do with it. The matter is in my hands, and I'm in the hands of the Lord."[103]

As the bombs rained down on Berlin in the latter days of the war and several Christian leaders called the terrible devastation God's punishment for what Germany had done,[104] others were convinced that homes had been spared in which Jews were being saved. One of these rescuers was Frau Jauch. A devout fundamentalist Christian, Jauch sheltered Hans Rosenthal for months in her home. During one bombing raid, three homes around her were destroyed, while her own survived. She and several neighbors were convinced that this was God's reward for sheltering Jews.[105]

A crucial religious resource for rescue was the sustenance that can be found in prayer, Bible reading, worship, and other acts of Christian spirituality and piety.

Corrie ten Boom writes of a crisis one night in her family's rescue work. A young member of the network had been caught and arrested. The

family feared that he had divulged crucial information about the ten Booms'
activities.

> Once again we considered stopping the work. Once again we discovered
> we could not. That night Father, Betsie, and I prayed long after the
> others had gone to bed. We knew that in spite of daily mounting risks
> we had no choice but to move forward. This was evil's hour: we could
> not run away from it. Perhaps only when human power had done its
> best and failed, would God's power alone be free to work.[106]

Nechama Tec tells a story that reveals the potential of a different kind
of piety—devotion to the Virgin Mary. Ada Celka and her sister were
unmarried Polish women in their forties, both devout Catholics. Unemployed due to the war, living with their paralyzed father in a one-room
apartment, they struggled to subsist. One day a Jewish friend asked them
to save her eight-year-old daughter. In the words of Ada Celka:

> My first reaction was to refuse. After all, we had no room, father was
> paralyzed. People around us knew that we lived alone without children.
> What would we do if someone came? What could we say about a child
> here? But then my sister and I knelt in front of Mother Mary's picture,
> asking her to enlighten us. When we got up from our prayers we both
> said: "We must take the child."[107]

One little-noticed dimension of the story of Le Chambon is the role
of the *responsables*—an inner circle of thirteen parish leaders who met every
two weeks with André Trocmé and then weekly with small groups throughout the parish. According to Hallie, these thirteen leaders became the
backbone of organized rescue efforts in Le Chambon. Their activities were
inspired and sustained by their corporate meetings. They spent these ses-
sions in lively and practical Bible studies and powerful communal prayer.
Wrote Trocmé of the meetings:

> It was there . . . that we received from God solutions to complex
> problems, problems we had to solve in order to shelter and hide the
> Jews. . . . Nonviolence was not a theory superimposed upon reality; it
> was an itinerary that we explored day after day in communal prayer
> and in obedience to the demands of the Spirit.[108]

Christina R. and her reluctant rescuer husband spent crucial time in
prayer together after deciding to shelter the little Jewish girl. Eva Fogelman
reports that "to transcend their fears, Christina and her husband prayed
and read the Bible together, especially Psalm 91." This psalm reads, in part:

> You who live in the shelter of the Most High,
>   who abide in the shadow of the Almighty,

> will say to the Lord, "My refuge and my fortress;
>   my God, in whom I trust . . ."
> Because you have made the Lord your refuge . . .
> no evil shall befall you.[109]

Here we see another hint of the hope, perhaps even the assurance, that God would provide protection for them as they tried to save this little girl's life.

This leads to a final resource of Christian spirituality—the Bible. Along the way we have reviewed a number of key biblical texts that proved important for rescue. Most of these would be seen by the hypothetical objective observer as texts that logically should be of importance in this situation. But devout rescuers, the kind who knew their Bible well and turned to it often for comfort and strength, found a remarkable range of texts upon which to draw. Only a few can be cited here. They will suffice to show that the Bible comes alive in unpredictable ways in the hands of those who turn to it searching for guidance.

For example, notice the biblical reference to Judas' betrayal of Jesus (Matt. 26:14-16 and parallels) in the Polish teacher's story quoted in chapter 3, concerning a roundup of Jews:

> The peasants were buying scythes. The woman shopkeeper said, "They'll be useful for you in the roundup today." I asked, "What round-up?" "Of the Jews." I asked, "How much are they paying for every Jew caught?" An embarrassed silence fell. So I went on. "They paid thirty pieces of silver for Christ, so you should also ask for the same amount."[110]

Several rescuers found the sixth commandment of immense importance: "Thou shalt not kill" (Exod. 20:13). In September 1943, the German Catholic bishops wrote: "Killing is wrong in itself, even when allegedly exercised in the interest of the common good against the innocent and defenseless weak and infirm . . . or on men [and women] of another race and origin."[111] This commandment was also important in shaping the behavior of André Trocmé. Not only was it central in forming his own pacifism, but it seemed to him to demand rescue in order to prevent *others* from sinning by violating God's commandment.[112] Pieter Miedema, the Dutch minister, discussed the importance of this text in a sermon: "By staying idle at a time when we are the last resort for innocent people condemned to die, we blaspheme against God's commandment against killing."[113]

Another important set of texts were Old Testament passages concerning the granting of sanctuary to fugitives (Num. 35:9-29; Josh. 20:1-9; Deut. 19:1-13). These were crucial for Trocmé and Le Chambon but appear elsewhere as well.[114] The passage from Deuteronomy mandates the establishment of "cities of refuge" in which anyone who has accidentally killed another person can find safety from the wrath of an avenger. By extension, the passage demands that "innocent blood" not be shed in the land of Israel; indeed, the death penalty is decreed for anyone who kills a person being sheltered in a city of refuge. Trocmé considered Le Chambon a contemporary city of refuge and took very seriously the command to prevent the shedding of innocent blood in that city.[115]

Among the many other passages that could be cited, emphasis should be placed on a cluster of texts concerning Jesus. Some Christians saw in the hunting of Jews a parallel to what had happened to Jesus, Mary, and Joseph when Herod sought to find and kill Jesus (Matt. 2:16ff.). One night, confronted by a young Jewish girl half mad from the strain of life on the run, a Dutch Christian woman said, "There was once another innocent child born to a Jewish mother, tormented and tortured by cruel people. He turned out to be our Savior."[116] The image of humanity as the body of Christ was important for some rescuers. It helped to create a sense of the oneness of all human beings, the wrongness of allowing any member of that sacred body to suffer, and the demand to go to that member's aid.[117] The suffering inflicted on the Jews struck some Christians as "another nail in Christ's body."[118] Pieter Miedema saw the murder of the Jews as the grievous "crucifixion" of a number of "Christs," an image that has come to the minds of other Christian interpreters of the Holocaust.[119] A statement issued by Polish rescuers warned the Poles against becoming "Pilates" who "deny all guilt" for the murder of their Jewish neighbors. The authors cry out, "We do not want to be Pilates."[120]

Conclusion

In a 1955 essay, Jewish historian Philip Friedman made a perceptive comment that is acutely relevant to our topic:

> For the first time in the history of humanity, mass murder, with millions of victims, was carried out, by the Nazis, in a methodical, efficient, cold-blooded manner. . . . Anyone who opposed the murderers and sought to rescue the victims was treated as a dangerous criminal. . . . All previous ideas of law, justice, and morality were abolished. It is understandable that this policy had to be opposed by all organizations, especially the Church, whose basic *Weltanschauung* was threatened by that legal and moral revolution. The Church had to oppose the Nazi ideology, not so much for their "love of Mordecai" as for their "hatred of Haman."[121]

"The Church had to oppose the Nazi ideology." Friedman was right, and in this chapter we have reviewed very strong evidence for the truth

of his assertion. Within the Christian faith there existed a powerful manifesto for compassion and rescue, a manifesto drawn not from the margins
but from the living center of the faith. Christians should have been able
to see that the Jewish people are our kin in faith, not our enemies; that
people who are being persecuted must be sheltered by the church, not
turned away; that the policies of unjust and evil governments must be
resisted, not acquiesced to; that Nazism and its racist ideology were fundamentally incompatible with Christian faith, not complementary; that
every human life is equally precious, not racially graded in value; that the
center of the ministry and teaching of Jesus was compassionate love for
all, even the "least of these," not just love for me and my kind.

What can we learn from the religious rescuers about the nurture of
Christians who will understand and practice this kind of faith, a rescuing
kind of faith? Such a faith seems to begin with people deeply committed
to the God they have met through Jesus. Their commitment is nourished
and strengthened by encounter with that God. Such encounter is available
in prayer, biblical reflection, worship, the experience of Christian community, and other practices of the Christian life. Such people earnestly
want to discern and to do God's will in their lives. They want God to be
pleased with them, here and in the hereafter. They believe that they will
face God someday to give account of their lives. They are trying to be ready
for that day.

In many cases, the religious rescuers were people who read the Bible
and knew it well. They were confident that important direction for their
lives could be found in the Bible's pages. Some of them learned a special
love for Jews through that reading as mediated in their particular strand
of the Christian tradition. More were taught to cherish and focus on the
heart of the teaching of the Bible and especially of Jesus: God created every
human being and loves each one dearly. God detests violence and the
taking of innocent human life. God desires our unabashed love for God
and for our neighbor—who is any human being, especially any human
being in need. When we treat our neighbor with loving compassion we
treat Jesus that way; when we fail to do so, we likewise fail Jesus himself.
These were people who studied the life story of Jesus in search of clues
for how they themselves should live. They wanted to be "servants worthy
of their hire" (Luke 10:7).

Most of these devout Christian rescuers were people deeply rooted
in a particular historic faith community. They were Dutch Reformed who
were indeed taught to "love Mordecai" and cherish the Old Testament.
They were French fundamentalists whose zeal for the faith led to a fiery
commitment to doing God's will. They were Italian Catholics who drew
strength from the Mass, from a statue of the Virgin Mary, from the authority

of the bishop draped in black, from time spent on their knees in penitent prayer. They were Ukrainian Baptists and French Huguenots whose experience of suffering had been a refiner's fire. They were German Lutherans who knew when the state had stopped performing its appointed function and begun to demand what only God may rightly demand.

The church has been charged with moral and spiritual bankruptcy in the Holocaust. There is much truth in this charge, much for the church to repent, much in its theology and practice for the church to change. But perhaps we have seen in this chapter that the church has assets as well as liabilities. We grieve that so few Christians made use of those assets when they were most needed. Perhaps those Christians who did use those assets can help the rest of us to improve the Christian moral balance sheet today.

7

The Quest for Righteousness

❖

Implications of the Righteous Gentiles for the Church

Can Gentiles Be Righteous? Jewish Reflections

Rabbi Harold Schulweis has asserted that "the memory of the Holocaust has left the surviving Jewish community a battered people still working out its shock, sense of abandonment, resentment and disillusion. . . . Jews are still grieving."[1] Jews mourn incalculable losses—of parents and children, brothers and sisters, aunts, uncles, and friends. They mourn the homes and villages they once lived in, the civilization they once inhabited—gone forever. Some mourn their loss of faith in God and humankind. Fifty years after the catastrophe, the Holocaust remains an inescapable dimension of Jewish life. But its place is not settled. As the generation of the survivors passes from the earth, a struggle is occurring among Jews over the nature of the Holocaust's legacy—over what might be called the hermeneutics and politics of Holocaust remembrance. Almost all agree that Jews must *remember*. But how to remember, and what to remember, and what to do with that memory today?

A central element of the struggle concerns how Jews should think about and relate to non-Jews. The long history of anti-Semitism, which erupted with unsurpassed deadliness in the Holocaust, provides powerful support for the view that the *goyim* (non-Jews) are eternally and implacably committed to the destruction of the Jewish people. The constant state of war in which the fledgling nation of Israel has existed since its birth, and which only now shows any signs of changing, has reinforced this thinking. The profound sense of isolation and abandonment Jews experienced during the Holocaust (and often before, and sometimes after) has led some to

149

make Jewish solitariness and Gentile hostility an eternal, quasi-metaphysical principle. In this view, Jews always have been and always will be alone in a hostile Gentile world. Gentiles always have sought and always will seek a world "free of Jews"—*Judenrein*. No partnership or help can be expected from Gentiles, nor should any be sought. Jews will have to guarantee their own survival by their own devices.[2] The Israeli governments of both Menachem Begin and Yitzhak Shamir were vocal in expressing such views, rooting them deeply in the Holocaust experience and using them to undergird their national security policies.

Yet some Jews vigorously reject this line of thinking. Some do so because they believe such a perspective is inimical to Jewish moral well-being; others because they think it harms Israel's true political interests; still others because they see it as untrue to historical reality; and some for all three reasons. Among the latter is Harold Schulweis, dean of rescuer studies. Schulweis has decried those who have found in the Holocaust

> confirmation of a primitive fissure in the human species, a primordial split between them, the perennial persecutors, and us, the eternal victims. . . . Such thinking does not properly memorialize Jewish history. On the contrary, it endows anti-Semitism with immortality.[3]

Pointing to rescuers of Jews during the Holocaust, Schulweis pleads with Jews to avoid demonizing all Gentiles. Instead, he urges a "double memory of the worst and the best,"[4] in which the names of Gentile murderers like Hitler and Eichmann are accompanied by those of Gentile rescuers like Ona Simaite and Raoul Wallenberg. Both sets of names and both kinds of deeds must reside permanently in Jewish remembrance of the Holocaust. Such assertions frequently appear in the writings of Jews who study and celebrate the rescuers.[5] A broader political polemic often is apparent.

Those who conceived Yad Vashem, the Holocaust memorial in Jerusalem, seem to have shared Schulweis's vision of the way the catastrophe should be remembered. Though the central task of Yad Vashem always has been to provide a "place and name" for the six million dead, the law establishing the museum also called for remembrance of those "high-minded righteous who risked their lives to save Jews."[6] As noted in chapter 1, this 1953 law designated rescuers *hasidei ummot ha-olam*—commonly translated "Righteous Among the Nations," or "Righteous Gentiles."[7] This term was well chosen, for it linked these particular righteous Gentiles with the righteous Gentiles visualized in a significant (though not undisputed or univocal) strand of Jewish religious thought. The term reminds Jews of aspects of their tradition that could easily be abandoned as a result of the Holocaust. These aspects are worthy of discussion due to their importance for the Christian reflections that are to follow, as well as for their inherent interest.

Woven into the Jewish religious tradition across the centuries is the affirmation that morally worthy persons can be found among the non-Jews of the world. The Jewish community has no monopoly on righteousness, nor on the God who is its ultimate source and who rewards righteous conduct. Given the centrality of righteousness in Jewish thought, this is a crucial claim. Such a view encourages the recognition of the fellow-humanity and moral potential of all other human beings. In so doing, it expands the circle of those who can be counted within the boundaries of "us," the people of faith. In light of the extent to which Jews have been victimized by non-Jews, the generosity of this theological conviction is striking.

The earliest roots of the concept of the *hasidei ummot ha-olam* can be traced to the biblical concept of the *ger-toshav* (the "resident-alien" or "semi-proselyte"). The *ger-toshav* laws prescribed the behavioral requirements for non-Jews who lived under Jewish political sovereignty, and regulated how such persons could be converted to Jewish faith and identity. Much later, the changed circumstances that prevailed with the loss of Jewish self-rule required the rabbis to adapt the *ger-toshav* rules and to develop others for relating to Gentiles. Such an undertaking occurred in a major way during the formative years of rabbinic Judaism—the late first and early second centuries of the Christian era. Central in what emerged was the concept of the "seven laws of the children of Noah." These "Noachide laws" have since provided the basic legal, moral, and theological framework in Judaism for relating to non-Jews and for understanding Gentile moral obligations.[8]

From a Jewish point of view the Noachide laws are not particularly demanding, especially in comparison with the rigorous requirements of the Torah. They describe the minimum moral obligations incumbent upon all human beings. Exegetically, the rabbis rooted the laws in the moral requirements imposed upon Adam (Gen. 2:16ff.) and Noah (Gen. 9:4ff.) and, through them, upon all humanity. In some respects, the concept functions as a species of natural-law thinking.[9] As enumerated by the rabbis, the seven Noachide laws prohibit blasphemy, idolatry, homicide, illicit sexual relations, theft, and eating the limb of a living animal, and require the establishment of a just court system.[10] As codified by Moses Maimonides in the twelfth century, the *hasidei ummot ha-olam* qualify for this status by observing these seven basic commandments of Noachide law.[11]

However, despite the centrality of the Noachide law framework and the work of Maimonides, Jewish tradition does not speak in a single voice concerning the conduct that qualifies a Gentile as one of the *hasidei ummot ha-olam*. Some authorities speak in general terms, not delineating a particular legal requirement. For example, the Zohar, a medieval kabbalistic text, states that all Gentiles who do not hate Israel and who deal justly with the Jews qualify as righteous.[12] Other texts refer to Gentiles who "remember God," who are "pious," who "desire to know God," who "walk uprightly," and so on. The term *hasid* itself (as well as another important term related to righteousness, *zedakah*) most commonly connotes the living out of a higher ethic, an ethic not only of obedience to Torah but of conduct well beyond the letter of the law—especially with regard to the practice of benevolent deeds on behalf of human beings in need.[13] This meaning is especially significant for our study. Such a standard far exceeds that of obedience to Noachide Law. Whatever the posited criteria, the central point is that a strand of the authoritative Jewish religious tradition steadily carves out theological space for "righteous among the nations." To use the concise definition of righteousness employed in the *Encyclopedia Judaica*, Gentiles, like Jews, are viewed as having the ability to "fulfill . . . all legal and moral obligations" incumbent upon them.[14]

How is it possible that Gentiles, who by definition have not taken Torah upon themselves, are nonetheless capable of righteousness? Theologically, an answer begins with Jewish belief in God as Creator of each human being. The Talmud states that despite the depth of human sinfulness and rejection of God, God's "hand is always stretched forward to receive all those who come into the world."[15] God is "God of all flesh" (Jer. 32:27) and "King of the nations" (Jer. 10:7). As such, God has never ceased to be concerned with the well-being of "strangers" and other nations, even while offering special care to Israel. One day, all nations will call upon the name of the Lord as does Israel now. On that day, the kingdom of God will be fully realized. "Turn to me and be saved, all the ends of the earth! For I am God, and there is no other. . . . To me every knee shall bow and every tongue shall swear" (Isa. 45:22-23; cf. Phil. 2:10-11). God's purposes are not limited to the people Israel, though Israel plays a crucial role in bringing to fruition God's intentions for all humankind.

One sign of God's provision for all, according to several rabbis, is that the Torah was given in "open places, in the free desert, so that every [person] feeling the desire might receive it."[16] The view that God offered the Torah to all nations, but only Israel accepted it, serves as an important part of the concept of Israel's election. The Torah is not the exclusive possession of the Jewish people and never was intended to be. Only the Jews took up the awesome challenge and committed themselves to bear witness to Torah. The nations did not, primarily (according to the rabbis) because they found its moral demands too rigorous.[17] Yet the Torah was originally meant for all people, remains available to all, and one day shall be obeyed by all.[18]

But the hope for Gentile righteousness is a present and not solely an eschatological hope. Even now, God's overtures to the Gentiles sometimes receive positive response. Israel is called to "open the gates, so that the righteous *goi* who keep the truth may enter in" (Isa. 26:2). Even now, the rabbis say, one can find righteous Gentiles. In fact, Israel occasionally faces the challenging assertion that some Gentiles are more faithful to God than are some Jews. "Not because you are greater than other nations did I choose you, nor because you obey my injunctions more than the nations; for they follow my commandments, even though they were not bidden to do it, and also magnify my name more than you"[19] (compare Deut. 7:7; Mal. 1:11).

When Gentiles meet their obligations, their deeds are to be celebrated. Such righteous ones should be seen not as strangers but as a kind of religious kin, equal with Jews in the eyes of God. One text reads, "Behold . . . one of other nations who fulfills the Torah is as [good as] the very high priest."[20] A medieval text declares, "Every true pious gentile is equal to a 'son of Israel.' "[21] In another place it is written, "The just among the peoples of the world are priests of God."[22] Moses Maimonides equated "all human beings who ardently seek God . . . desire to worship him, to know him, and to walk uprightly in his ways" with priests and levites.[23]

As thinking about the hereafter developed, the rabbis included a place for righteous Gentiles. As early as the Tosefta we read, "The righteous of the nations of the world have a share in the world to come."[24] Leo Trepp argues that the traditional rabbinic emphasis on *mitzvot* (acts of moral goodness in obedience to God's command), rather than the content of doctrine, laid the foundation for an openness to other ethical faiths as a way to God. Those of whatever faith who practice *mitzvot* are friends of God, here and hereafter. One rabbinic text reads: "I call heaven and earth to witness that on every person, be he Jew or non-Jew, man or woman, or servant, the divine spirit rests on him according to his deeds."[25] Maimonides opened heaven's gates to all Gentiles who observe the Noachide laws.[26] The recognition that Gentiles can be righteous led to the affirmation that Jews will share the hereafter with those Gentiles who, in fact, are righteous.

Rabbinic tradition also develops the theme that a remnant of righteous people plays a decisive role in preserving the world. A formative text is the story of Abraham's bold bargaining with God over the fate of Sodom (Gen. 18:22-33). In this story, Abraham challenges God to spare wicked Sodom from utter destruction if even a small number of righteous people can be found there. Ultimately, he ventures the question, "Suppose ten are found there . . . ?" God answers, "For the sake of ten I will not destroy it" (v. 32). Alas, the ten cannot be found, and Sodom and Gomorrah receive "sulfur and fire from heaven" (Gen. 19:24).

Yet the principle has been established. God will forbear from destroying this world, so full of evil, for the sake of a handful of righteous people.[27]

To their sorrow, the rabbis recognized that the righteous are scarce. But enough exist to prevent utter destruction. One text asserts that God "plants" or distributes these few righteous persons across each generation. In a creative interpretation of 1 Samuel 2:8, the righteous of every generation are described as "the pillars of the earth" who form the moral foundation of the world.[28]

The legend of the *lamed vav zaddikim*, found first in the Babylonian Talmud and popular especially in the Kabbalah and Hasidic sources, is closely related. The *lamed vav* are the thirty-six (or perhaps more) unknown righteous people, scattered within Israel and among the nations. The survival of humanity depends upon their presence on the earth, for God allows the rest of us to live on the basis of their merit.[29] Those reckoning with the Righteous Gentiles of the Holocaust often have turned to this tradition, seeing the rescuers as the *lamedvovniks* (a Yiddish term) of our own age—the proverbial "thirty-six" who prevented God from finally "sweep[ing] us clean from the earth."[30]

It seems to this Gentile observer that the term *hasidei ummot ha-olam*, so rich in its traditional meanings, aptly describes rescuers of Jews during the Holocaust. They were indeed "righteous" in the sense of the term *hasid*, not merely doing no harm but instead risking their lives actively to do good, to save human beings from murderers.[31] In fact, some were also "pious" in the sense also implicit in *hasid*, conducting themselves on the basis of a transcendent commitment to love God by loving the neighbor in need. They embodied and fulfilled the spirit of both Noachide Law and Torah, behaving in a way recognizably virtuous in any moral tradition. They "dealt justly with Jews" when an entire political order was organized around injustice toward Jews. And they were "Gentiles," persons on the other side of the fateful dividing line between Jews and non-Jews, a dividing line exploited so masterfully by the Nazis. Refusing to recognize the ultimacy of this division, rescuers instead viewed any needy human being as a "neighbor" within the boundaries of moral obligation.

The depth of Jewish victimization and the extent of Jewish abandonment by non-Jews probably made a categorical anti-Gentile backlash inevitable. But the rescuers' actions cannot be erased from the historical record. They will be enshrined permanently at Yad Vashem and elsewhere. Perhaps, over time, their witness can begin to bridge the chasm between Jews and Gentiles after the Holocaust.[32] Perhaps even now the *hasidei ummot ha-olam* can be a resource for those Jews struggling to articulate a way of relating to Gentiles other than the familiar role of perennial victim and the more recent possibility of tough victimizer.[33] Perhaps the role of the Righteous Gentiles in the Holocaust story can become part of a more politically and morally constructive Jewish hermeneutic of the Holocaust.

Can Christians Be Righteous?

But what are Christians to make of the Righteous Gentiles of the Holocaust? What place will they play in our own hermeneutic of the Holocaust? This ground is far less well traveled. Few Christians know the term, fewer still have thought about what the Righteous Gentiles might mean for Christian theology or ethics. What follows are some guideposts for further Christian reflection and action, drawn from the evidence discovered in the course of this study.

Not so long ago, the Christian ethicist James Gustafson wrote a book entitled *Can Ethics Be Christian?* His purpose was to discuss the distinctive characteristics (if any) of Christian ethics. After undertaking my own study, I am inclined to turn his question around and ask it another way: Can Christians be ethical? Or, to use the terminology with which we have been working here: Can Christians be righteous? After the Holocaust, this question is worth asking.

As we have just seen, the rabbis have debated the question for centuries. Prior to the birth of Christianity, the *goyim* under discussion were people of a wide variety of nations and religious traditions. After the fateful split between the church and the synagogue, and especially in the European setting, the discussion increasingly focused on Christians. As a result, rabbinic writings sometimes employ the terms "Gentile" and "Christian" interchangeably; contemporary rescuer literature often does so.[34] This usage is inaccurate, because not all Gentiles are Christians. Nor were all rescuers Christians. Some were Muslims, some were atheists and agnostics, and some distantly related to the Christian church would not qualify as Christians by any standard that most churches would use.

As a Christian ethicist, my concern focuses on the moral behavior of those who are indeed Christian people, defined rather broadly here as those who profess belief in Jesus Christ, identify themselves as Christians, and (usually) participate in communities of Christian faith. The rabbis were well acquainted with such people, who were the source of much Jewish suffering. Can they be righteous? An affirmative answer was not always easy for the rabbis to give. Discrimination, pogroms, and expulsions at Christian hands did not provide much positive evidence. On the whole, however, the rabbis generously continued to affirm that even though the church and cultures dominated by it were responsible for a great deal of Jewish anguish, Christians can be righteous. The rabbis even expected to share the hereafter with exceptional members of their persecutors' tribe.

Can Christians be righteous? How shall the church answer? Perhaps, in good rabbinic fashion, with more questions: Were Christians righteous during the Holocaust? How did Christians fare in the moral crucible of

Nazi Europe? Did they "fulfill all moral obligations" incumbent upon them? We are now prepared to address these questions directly. Along the way, we will have the opportunity to reflect upon and knit together some issues raised in earlier chapters.

The unrighteous Christians

Reflecting on Gentile/Christian behavior toward Jews in Lithuania during the Holocaust, Sarah Neshamit has written:

> We cannot demand from others that they risk their lives on our behalf. Each person must decide that question for himself. Yet we cannot forgive the Lithuanian people for the large number of Lithuanians who collaborated in the murder of the Jews, for their beastly cruelty in torturing their victims before they killed them, and for their serving as hangmen for the Germans even outside their native lands.[35]

Neshamit draws an important moral distinction here. She does not claim that to rescue Jews was morally incumbent on Gentiles, but instead argues that one cannot require others to risk their lives. (We will revisit this important question below.) Her word of judgment is reserved for those who actively helped the Nazis destroy the Jews or sought to benefit from Jewish vulnerability. Her judgment on this matter cannot be disputed. Indeed, a Christian observer cannot fail to be distraught over the behavior of those decidedly "unrighteous Christians" who took up axes and pitchforks to kill Jews, raced to loot Jewish homes, turned in Jews to the Nazis for fun and profit, or cheered on others who did such deeds. Those Christians who did such things demonstrate, as if proof were needed, that Christians can be utterly unrighteous. In the last chapter, we saw the numerous resources in the Christian faith that some Christians drew upon in rescuing Jews. Taken together, they seem to offer a powerful manifesto for rescue. But those professing, churchgoing Christians who harmed rather than helped Jews bear awful witness to the impact of other powers as well as to the existence of morally disastrous versions of Christian faith.

The unrighteous Christians illustrate with great clarity that the forces set loose in particularly troubled historical situations often overwhelm moral resources for compassion and decency. To the despair of the ethicist, dismal and seemingly immutable patterns of human behavior emerge in times of historical crisis. For example, when war, oppression, or natural disaster disrupts the supply of food and other necessities to an area, price gouging follows like night follows day. The law of supply and demand performs its inexorable work, and compassion disappears. Earlier we indicated that some Gentiles took advantage of Nazi discrimination against Jews to hike prices for food, apartments, false identification cards, and so on, and discussed how these inflated prices proved to be a major detriment to Jewish survival. But Nazi Europe held no monopoly on such behavior. Not so long ago in this country a major hurricane that struck southern Florida led to the very same phenomenon. Despite strongly worded government threats against price gougers, apartment and food prices skyrocketed. Many of those who practiced price gouging in Nazi Europe were churchgoing Christians. Undoubtedly, the same was true in southern Florida.

Further, when law and order break down under such circumstances, looting and other property crimes inevitably follow. During the Holocaust, looting became a part of the landscape as soon as the Nazis made Jews powerless to protect their property or to receive just treatment before the law. Many ordinary Gentiles joined in. The same kind of conduct occurred in Los Angeles during the May 1992 riots there, and in Florida after the hurricane. The prospect of getting something for nothing and the perceived lack of risk in doing so turns many a law-abiding citizen into a common thief.

Moreover, when Jews became "fair game" and those who harmed or killed Jews received no punishment, many people with no history of assault and murder turned to that ugly work. The vulnerability of another person or group tends to inflame the basest instincts of the human being. People begin to thirst for the blood of those whom society has left unprotected. In such cases, no teaching of mercy, no moral resources seem able to prevail against the temporary lunacy provoked by lawlessness and another's prostration. Abuse of the most vulnerable is as common as the local playground; children often mistreat the most vulnerable among them.

In the case of the Holocaust, one must add to these general consequences of war and disaster the legacy of historic anti-Semitism which, as we have noted, was deliberately inflamed by the Nazis. The net effect of these factors, as many wartime observers recorded, was a marked and rapid deterioration of Gentile behavior toward Jews in much of Europe. In chapter 3 we pointed to such a deterioration with respect to the Gentile children who eagerly collaborated with the Nazis. But it happened to some of their parents as well. Martin Gilbert notes that as early as 1938, "the Germans who carried out the atrocities and cruelties had already become corrupted by their tasks; laughing when inflicting pain, and drawing in passers-by to laugh with them."[36] The Polish diarist Zygmunt Klukowski wrote in 1942:

> Generally, a strange brutalization has taken place regarding the Jews. People have fallen into a kind of psychosis: following the German example, they often do not see in the Jew a human being but instead consider him a kind of obnoxious animal that must be annihilated with every possible means.[37]

Metropolitan Andrei Sheptyts'kyi, leader of the Ukrainian Uniate Church in Galicia, also saw the dehumanizing impact of Nazism on the local Ukrainian population, especially the youth. In a November 1942 pastoral letter, Sheptyts'kyi lamented the "murder addiction" that had taken hold in his region.[38] A Lithuanian Righteous Gentile, Helena Kutorgiene, remarked in her diary:

> The coarse Lithuanian mob . . . acted with such beastly cruelty that by comparison, the Russian pogroms seemed like humanitarian deeds. . . . I cannot believe my eyes and ears. I am totally shaken by the force of blind hatred which they cultivate to satisfy the most base instincts.[39]

Certainly a tiny number of any group of people are sociopaths, murderers, and criminals. The highest Nazi leaders were such people and offered like-minded Gentiles punishment-free opportunities to act on their instincts. But more terrifying is the moral deterioration effected among many other Gentiles who by no means had been sociopaths or murderers before the war. By legitimizing murder and cruelty and inviting the locals to participate, the Nazis contributed to widespread Gentile moral deterioration. Teachers, priests, doctors, and farmers became, for a time, thieves and murderers. That so many of these Gentiles/Christians lacked the moral resources to withstand the Nazi moral assault on European civilization—for that is what it was—is a matter of the gravest concern. Their failure illustrates the profound effect of social structure on character and behavior. Moral resources for compassion and decency, however considerable, do not easily flourish in the midst of social structures that suppress such resources.[40]

But is it too much to expect that people who profess belief in Jesus Christ might be able to rise above these dismal patterns of mass behavior and social structure and act in a manner that at least faintly resembles the way Christians are supposed to act? The Christian ethicist dare not cede this ground, even while recognizing the profound importance of social and moral order (and disorder) for human behavior. Christian leaders must work both for communities of faith that will act with justice and mercy when social and moral order breaks down or is perverted, and for healthy politics and social morality. No person or group must be placed in the position of having to rely for his or her survival on the moral decency of people who are not also compelled to respect the other's rights by force of law.[41] By the time rescuers are needed, it is too late. Paradoxically, we can celebrate and try to nurture the rescuer's kind of decency while working to ensure that on a mass scale it is never required again.

We let the church off too easily, though, if we do not remind ourselves that *one place many Christians learned to hate Jews was in church.* Clearly, many people find it difficult to resist their worst instincts when circumstances present the opportunity to benefit from the plight of others. In such circumstances, moral and religious teachings commanding and cajoling us toward compassion, mercy, and justice constitute a crucial resource for fortifying people to resist those instincts. Such teachings (obviously) should be offered in Christian churches, for they constitute the heart of the teaching of Jesus. When such teaching does not occur—or, more frequently, when the church sends a mixed message by teaching contempt for other groups along with the love of Jesus—the church fails not only itself and its Lord but also society. It does the latter by weakening one of the few bulwarks that society has available to keep the flood of human evil from engulfing us all. The rest of society needs the church to do better than this.[42]

The "average" Christians

What are we to make of those Christians who possessed some measure of pity and compassion for Jews but for one reason or another did not help them? Surely such people numbered in the millions. The data lead me to conclude that more Europeans responded in this way to the Jewish plight than in any other single way. Their behavior may be the most easily comprehensible to the observer. Was this the kind of response that most "normal" or "average" people could be expected to make? From a moral point of view, was it enough simply to feel sympathy and to do no harm? Did that "fulfill all legal and moral obligations" incumbent upon Europe's Gentiles during the Holocaust? Or was an attempt to help Jews during the Holocaust morally obligatory, especially for those claiming Jesus Christ as their Lord?

One trembles before such questions. They were the subject of anguished soul-searching and debate in many Christian homes during the assault on the Jews. Often, Christians in good conscience decided that they should not (or could not) try to help Jews. Some wanted to help but believed they lacked sufficient opportunity and resources to do so. They lived across the street from Gestapo headquarters, or next door to Nazi sympathizers; they were old and feeble, or poor. Others felt profound sympathy for Jews but simply could not muster the courage to risk their own lives on Jews' behalf. Every one of us wants to live. Few human beings easily risk their lives for another, especially for a stranger. The historical record indicates that many a Gentile offered help but then backed down when the risks became clearer, and others stood on the brink of rescue but finally turned away in fear of the consequences. Finally, many thoroughly decent people chose not to rescue, not because of a lack of courage but due to the moral conviction that their obligations to their own families and neighbors were primary. They believed that to risk their loved ones' and their neighbors' lives on behalf of strangers would be morally irresponsible.

Interestingly, some Holocaust survivors are not at all sure that Christians had a moral obligation to help them. Joseph Lichten was a Warsaw Jew who lost his entire family to the Nazis. His comment about the behavior of Polish bystanders is illuminating:

> It is hard not to remember the millions who remained indifferent to what was going on. . . . We know that they could have been executed for giving help; we know that it is difficult to transform ordinary men [and women] into heroes. We are willing to be rational about the situation, but our hearts object.[43]

Lichten's *cri de coeur* assumes that because they risked their lives, those who offered help to Jews performed acts of heroism that went beyond the realm of the "ordinary." Yet Lichten retains a nagging sense, from the "heart," that most of his Gentile neighbors failed him and his people at the hour of their greatest need. Though ambivalent, he does not appear willing to abandon the conviction that they had some kind of moral obligation to help.

Felix Zanman and his daughter Sabina were Polish Jews hidden by the Catholic Anna Pulholsky, a mother of five children. According to Sabina Zanman, Pulholsky was well aware of the risks to herself and her family but proceeded with rescue because she considered it "the Catholic thing to do." Though Felix Zanman deeply appreciates his rescuer, he asserts that her actions were "logically irresponsible." To risk the lives not only of herself but of her five children was something she should not have done, though he calls her "a saint." Zanman claims that he would not have done the same thing in her situation.[44] Felix Zanman is clearly convinced that those who risked their lives (and especially their families) to rescue Jews had no moral obligation to do so. His comments suggest that her actions were at the same time both extraordinarily commendable and in a sense morally irresponsible.

The ancient concept of supererogation offers important insight into the moral shape of the deeds of both nonrescuers and rescuers. Traditionally, a "work of supererogation" is an act that is not obligatory in terms of the basic moral duties incumbent upon every human being, but is nonetheless laudable. Failure to perform such an act would not normally bring criticism upon one's head, but at the same time the performance of this act would bring the highest praise.[45] An act in which one risks one's life for another, especially for a stranger, might best be described as a work of supererogation. Those observing such acts do not fail to praise them; and yet, most would hesitate before arguing that such actions are part of the "rock-bottom duties that are duties for all and from every point of view."[46] This kind of response to the deeds of the rescuers is quite common—their actions were laudable, worthy of study and imitation, but at the same time exceptional actions that soared well beyond what normally can be expected of human beings.

The righteous Christians

Most rescuers, however, believe that their actions were in fact both morally obligatory and not especially commendable. Their obligation to help Jews seemed perfectly clear, and from their perspective a person deserves no praise for fulfilling an obvious obligation. Again, the concept of supererogation is helpful. Those who perform works of supererogation do not necessarily consider their actions worthy of praise. Gene Outka calls this phenomenon "agent-stringency."[47] An action that appears to an observer to be above and beyond what can be expected of people often appears to the agent to be fully and legitimately obligatory—at least for the agent *himself or herself*. The agent's standards are more stringent than the observer's. He or she not only accepts basic "rock-bottom" standards of moral obligation but supplements these with what appears to the observer to be an extraordinary commitment to the neighbor's well-being, while this commitment appears to the agent to be self-evidently morally obligatory.

Many rescuers express profound discomfort when asked why they helped Jews. Some researchers have attributed this discomfort to personal modesty. The concept of agent-stringency helps to illuminate its real source. For many rescuers the question is almost unintelligible; one might just as well ask why the rescuer breathes. People were in need; it is obligatory to help people in need, regardless of the risk; so they helped the people who needed help. What is there to understand? Moreover, many rescuers fear that even to ask the question somehow participates in the nazification of moral values they so strenuously opposed during the war. The statement of the Danish rescuer Poul Borchsenius nicely illustrates this view:

> Danish action was spontaneous, unanimous and had the support of practically the entire nation. Its motives were purely humanitarian. We saw in our midst a defenseless and outlawed minority about to be murdered, and we could rescue them. *As a matter of course we helped. When a neighbor's house is on fire everybody helps to fight the flames.* The Nazis' failure to understand that ordinary Danes were ready to risk their lives on behalf of Jews, merely illustrates the gulf between free [persons] and doctrinaire totalitarians.[48]

When an act's obligatory character is obvious, one commonly asks about the *nonperformance rather than the performance* of that act. Thus, those who believe that rescue was morally obligatory often turn the familiar "why" question on its head. One hears that striking inversion in this question from the late German leader Willy Brandt: "What . . . *hindered* those who had gone to school with Jewish neighbors, who had worked with them in offices, schools, factories and hospitals, who had spent leisure time with them in coffeehouses . . . what kept them from standing up for their friends and neighbors of Jewish faith?"[49]

Daniel Carpi, a Jewish historian, concludes a technical article on the Italian rescue of Jews in Croatia with an unexpected statement most germane to this discussion. Considering the question, Why did the Italians do what they did? Carpi responds:

> The query always pains me because . . . it is an indication of the profound distortion in our thinking regarding the period of the Holocaust. The logical and natural question is not, "Why did so and so refuse to participate in cold-blooded murder or even try somehow to stop it?", but rather, "How was it that so many people, and even entire nations, directly or indirectly sanctioned such deeds?" . . . The criteria by which one measures human behavior cannot be arbitrarily changed to suit the character of this or that period. . . . Basic and universal moral norms are always binding, even in times of crisis, even when the majority of [hu]mankind ignores them, and the devotion to these norms requires no explanation.[50]

The oft-quoted statement found in *The Plague*, the great novel written by Albert Camus during his wartime sojourn in Le Chambon, reveals a similar spirit: "The essential thing was to save the greatest number of persons from dying and being doomed to unending separation, and to do this there was only one resource: to fight the plague. There was nothing admirable about this attitude; it was merely logical."

"When a neighbor's house is on fire, everybody helps to fight the flames," argued Poul Borchsenius. In the light of the flames of Auschwitz, the image is terrifyingly appropriate. The great majority of European Gentiles did not, in fact, help their Jewish neighbors as their house burned down around them. Why not? Some didn't consider Jews their neighbors. Some refused to believe that the house was on fire. Others knew the house was on fire, and were concerned, but were afraid of being burned. Others were glad to see both the house burned up and the Jews within it. Only a small minority risked their lives to join their neighbors in fighting the fire. Only these saw their moral obligation with full clarity. This acute moral perception was fundamentally important in leading them to "fulfill all of the legal and moral obligations" incumbent upon them. Only those who helped to fight the flames were worthy of the term "righteous." Some of these righteous ones were Christians.

Can Christians be righteous? The rabbis had it just about right. Christians can be righteous—but not many of us were during the Holocaust, and not many of us are today. Righteous Christians are the exception. Some

Christians harm a person in need. Some feel no stir of compassion. A great many others feel compassion but do not do anything about it. A small minority are both compassionate and active to help persons in need.

This rather depressing distribution of behavior is not unique to Christians. The rabbis knew this as well. In one place, the Talmud divides human beings into three classes of people: the thoroughly wicked (*resha'im gemurim*) the average (*beinonim*) and the thoroughly righteous (*zaddikim gemurim*), acknowledging that the majority of men and women will be found among the *beinonim*.[51] Jewish thinking about the human propensity for good or evil leans heavily on the concept of the *yetzer ha-ra* (broadly, the inclination to do evil) and the *yetzer ha-tov* (the inclination to do good). These are seen as engaged in a struggle for dominance over one's heart and thus over one's character and conduct.[52] One passage in the Talmud states that the thoroughly wicked are governed by the *yetzer ha-ra*, the thoroughly righteous (*zaddikim*) are governed by the *yetzer ha-tov*, and the average person by both inclinations.[53] Jewish religious thought has held up the *zaddikim gemurim* as the model toward which Jews should strive, while recognizing the great difficulty in moving the mass of men and women from the ranks of the average into the *zaddikim*. To use this language, it can be said that Christian ethics is about increasing the number of Christian *zaddikim* the churches produce. This must be our quest, despite those stubborn forces within and around the human person (and the Christian church) that so often block the attainment of authentic righteousness.

Can Christian Faith Produce Righteousness?

Is the Christian faith, as embodied and taught in Christian churches, up to the task of nurturing righteousness? In other words, can Christian faith produce righteousness? Or should those who yearn for righteousness look elsewhere? Research on the Righteous Gentiles provides important evidence for addressing these crucial and perennial questions.

Religiosity not correlated with rescue

Earlier, findings from the Oliners, Nechama Tec, and Eva Fogelman were cited, all to the same effect—that rescuers are not distinguishable from nonrescuers in any quantifiable measure of religious faith, affiliation, and commitment. The fault line dividing rescuer from nonrescuer does not run between the religious and the less religious (or the nonreligious) but cuts across categories of religiosity. Researchers must turn to a qualitative understanding of religious commitment to identify resources for rescue. But the quantitative finding itself is profoundly important.

Most Christian ministers and teachers nurture the hope that instruction in the Christian faith, participation in the life of a community of faith, and especially personal commitment to Jesus Christ will lead Christians to a high quality of moral character and conduct. Surely, in the context of the Holocaust many might imagine churches in which numerous members would have construed rescue as their moral obligation and acted upon that conviction. As we have seen, the Scriptures and Christian tradition offer multiple resources for compassion and courage. Moreover, the Bible offers the promise of divine help in the moral journey. For example, in the thought of the apostle Paul, God is seen as empowering the believer to live as he or she ought to live, through the power of the Holy Spirit (Gal. 5:5, 5:22ff., et al.).[54] Many Christians have believed that through this power of God at work in their lives, Christian people not only should but do experience moral transformation. By extension, some have claimed that this "community of the transformed" attains a level of moral quality in its character and conduct not matched outside the church.

Christian behavior and misbehavior during the Holocaust leads to the conclusion that while we must hope earnestly and work incessantly for faith communities of high moral quality, claims to Christian moral superiority are exceedingly inappropriate. In genuine and repentant humility, the church must turn to God and beg for the development of genuine Christian righteousness in our faith communities. Meanwhile, our task is to return to our Scriptures and tradition and relearn authentic Christian faith, a faith that does justice, loves the stranger, and goes to the aid of the most vulnerable. Eva Fleischner has written, "What is asked of Christians is not to love better than others, but simply not to pervert the teaching of Jesus and what is best in their own tradition."[55] Christian behavior during the Holocaust should give the church ample reason to be humble about its virtue, and ample reason to ask for help in obeying the teaching of the One we call Lord.

Insignificance of Christian resources for Christian rescuers

Research on rescuers offers another finding that is worthy of careful consideration: the rather low percentage of rescuers who cite religion as even one of their reasons for rescue. The figures were reported in chapter 5: Tec, 27 percent; Oliner, 15 percent; Fogelman, 12 percent; Block and Drucker, 25 percent.[56] If we believe these figures, the vast majority of European rescuers—94 percent of whom affirm an affiliation with the Christian church as children, 70 percent of whom describe themselves as "very" or "somewhat" religious in the Oliner study—drew not on their Christian faith but exclusively on other resources for rescue.

The validity of these findings legitimately can be questioned. The percentages have been determined on the basis of the reasons that rescuers articulate for their behavior and the classification choices made by the researcher. Both have their limits. It is impossible to know the extent to which rescuers who did not explicitly cite religion were shaped by religious influences. As Eva Fleischner points out, humanitarian motives such as care and compassion may well have been undergirded, or even rooted, in exposure to church teachings that enjoin such behavior.[57] Further, coding rescuers' responses is to some degree subjective, and researchers may have neglected religion in coding motives, as Richard Neuhaus argues.[58] Religious resources may well have played a more profound role than the theorists depict.

On the other hand, the data retain at least partial validity. Loyalty to the church must not obscure the important truths to be learned from this disappointing record. *The irrelevance of Christian faith for many self-identified Christian rescuers in so-called Christian Europe is an extraordinary finding.* Despite broad cultural and other kinds of exposure to Christian teaching, as well as serious religious commitment in many cases, most Christian rescuers apparently drew solely on resources other than their Christian faith. What does this have to teach the church?

Most painfully, these findings speak a word of judgment. The historical record reveals that some rescuers saved Jews *despite* some of the teaching they received at church. Whatever ought to remain of the gap between the number of rescuers affiliated with Christianity and the far lower number citing their faith as a reason for rescue, one source of that chasm is Christian anti-Jewish teaching. Consider the story of the devout Polish Catholic Lech Sarna, who hid David Rodman and his family. Rodman says of his rescuer:

> Essentially a highly moral and good person, he changed after each visit to Church. At such times, he would grumble, swear, and scream at us and his wife. "I am sure to lose in both worlds. They will kill me for keeping Jews and then I will lose heaven for helping Jews." He would go on and on arguing with himself, with his wife, feeling totally miserable. We tried to comfort him. He usually calmed down after a while until the next sermon.[59]

It is extremely difficult for most of us to imagine a Christian pastor teaching that those risking their lives to help Jews also risk eternal damnation. But apparently the local priest offered this kind of religious instruction to Lech Sarna and his fellow congregants while the Nazis murdered their Jewish neighbors. It is very likely that Lech Sarna had also received religious instruction on the necessity of acting in compassion and love. Perhaps his anguish flowed from these internally contradictory messages—

from one side of its mouth the church encouraged compassion and love, and from the other it discouraged the practice of compassion and love toward Jews. With some Christian churches at best sending such mixed signals, it makes sense that some European Christians would not have cited religion as a motivation for rescue. And it makes sense that the charge of Christian moral bankruptcy resounds to this day.

These findings also remind us that the church does not exercise exclusive jurisdiction over the moral formation of even its most committed members. Especially in our time—but not only now—Christian people simultaneously function as members of a number of other communities. These other communities serve as sites in which moral formation and action, for good or ill, also take place. The findings outlined here, especially in chapter 5, reveal the importance of such formative communities as families, friendship networks, neighborhoods, workplaces, professional associations, political parties, and nation-states. Only those Christians who withdraw completely into separatist Christian communities avoid any involvement in these other groups. On the contrary, most Christian people find their affiliations with communities other than the church a meaningful and important dimension of their lives.

Any approach to Christian ethics that presumes that the church must form airtight communities is an unconstructive utopianism.[60] The church should nurture the slightly less utopian hope that Christians will construe allegiance to Jesus Christ as their single most significant commitment, and the Christian community as their single most significant community. Some Christians indeed will do so. Many of the devout Christian rescuers discussed in chapter 6 seem to be people of this type. Overall, however, the findings of our study help to demonstrate that for many Christians (perhaps even the majority), their Christian allegiance will not occupy such an exalted role.

Realism thus demands that Christian ethicists, ministers, and teachers recognize the involvement of not only the "average Christian" but also themselves in other commitments and communities. Christians are also part of their families, workplaces, political parties, neighborhoods, and nations. An appropriately rich understanding of Christian discipleship grants Christian involvement in these other communities, while seeking to ensure that such involvement relates with integrity to the Christian's primary allegiance to the Christian community.[61]

An even stronger claim can be made here. The church must acknowledge the fact that communities and resources other than itself sometimes bear decisive moral significance, both for Christians and for society at large. Indeed, the evidence here suggests that for most Christian rescuers, other moral resources proved more compelling than those available through the

Christian faith. Some rescued Jews as an act of patriotism; others as an act of solidarity with a fellow socialist; others in allegiance to the moral climate of their friendship group; others because they believed it was what their parents would have wanted them to do; others because their heart burned with pain at the plight of another.

The church must learn to welcome moral resources and moral allies wherever it can find them, without ever losing its vigilance to the corrosive and idolatrous possibilities inherent in patriotism, political ideologies, friendship networks, family loyalties, and any other human community or worldview. As Christians we should be thankful that moral potential and moral goodness are not confined within our communities. Instead, they burst forth from unexpected places (including our own hard hearts) at unexpected times, like oases in the desert. Christians should be prepared to see the faith occasionally play a supporting rather than a lead role when other communities fulfill their moral potential and direct people toward right moral action. This by no means diminishes the church's obligation to be the kind of moral community that its Lord calls it to be.

A Christian Faith That Nurtures Righteousness

While acknowledging the importance of extra-ecclesial moral resources and influences, this study has demonstrated that the church can and sometimes does nurture both righteous people and righteous deeds. Not that it always does so, obviously. But this much is certain—week after week and year after year, hundreds of millions of human beings gather together in hundreds of thousands of congregations to worship God in the name of Jesus Christ. The fundamental vocation of Christian ethics is to encourage the members and leaders of these churches in their attempt to be faithful to the God they worship every week. Christian ethics seeks to serve the churches' quest for righteous character and righteous conduct, believing that progress indeed can be made despite daunting obstacles. Thus, our study closes by offering a few constructive suggestions, rooted in the findings of this study, for churches seeking to "conform to the image" of Jesus Christ (Rom. 8:29), and for the discipline of Christian ethics as it pursues its vocation of service to this quest.

Rediscover character, redefine the virtues

The evidence cited in this study demands affirmation of the growing emphasis in Christian ethics today on character and its formation.[62] We have noted a remarkable consistency among rescuers in finding it difficult to give the motives for their actions; in describing their "decision" to get involved in rescue as "no decision at all," but rather as a spontaneous or natural (re)action; and in viewing their rescue activities as transparently morally obligatory and not particularly commendable. All of these comments tend to point to the centrality of character rather than decision making in the genesis of both extraordinary acts of rescue and, in all likelihood, most actions of moral significance. It seems to require a "certain kind of person" to internalize such "agent-stringent" values and then to act on them, risking life and limb to rescue another. Churches, ministers, and Christian educators ought to find in the Righteous Gentiles important evidence for the centrality of character formation in the development of Christian disciples.

The researcher Pierre Sauvage was so impressed by (what we are calling) the primacy of character over decision that he said in a 1989 interview with Bill Moyers, "Those who agonize don't act; and those who act don't agonize."[63] Like any overall statement about the characteristics of the Righteous Gentiles, this one requires qualification. Many rescuers did, in fact, agonize over what to do. But a great many did not do so—their actions came naturally to them, as an expression of their character. Given the magnitude of the risk, this is remarkable. If any potential action should require agonizing decision making, an action risking death at Nazi hands was surely one of them.

Recognizing the centrality of character, however, is necessary but not sufficient. Character by itself is an empty vessel. Reasonable people can agree on the importance of character but disagree violently on its normative content. The churches must not only recognize the importance of character but also work more carefully to define the *kind* of character they want to produce. Findings outlined earlier about the Righteous Gentiles, especially in chapters 5 and 6, can contribute to a rethinking of the normative content of the virtues churches should seek to cultivate.

Sound Christian character must include the fixed perception that every other human being is my equal—in fact, my kin—and thus equally precious and worthy of a decent life. The Christian must be schooled to see that despite important differences among human beings, ultimately our common humanity bears more significance than that which divides us. Christian theology provides several rich ways in which this perception can be grounded, as we saw in chapter 6. However theologically grounded, this perception must be of such rigor and resiliency that attempts by others to classify human beings as superior and inferior (on whatever basis) will not penetrate it. Such a view also assumes a person's own worth before God and neighbor, which helps to develop the self-esteem necessary for morally healthy relating with other human beings and with God.

Rooted in this impermeable perceptual commitment, the Christian should develop a disposition toward others characterized by what might best be called "openheartedness." Such openheartedness signals a basic life-stance of accessibility to all other people, an openness to receiving and interacting with the other's joy, pain, sorrow, or whatever else the individual brings to the encounter. Such a stance requires a willingness to be vulnerable before and with the other. This will sometimes mean receiving hurt at the hands of those who exploit openheartedness; often, it will mean rich possibilities of encounter, connectedness, and relationship.

An essential dimension of openheartedness for Christians must be a consistent alertness to the needs of the other. This faculty requires careful nurture, for the evidence discussed in this study reveals how easily we can blind ourselves to others' needs as we seek to protect our own loved ones and to look after our interests. Moreover, this alert disposition must be extended into a permanent life-commitment to try to meet the needs we discover. One of the most striking findings of the Oliner study is that rescuers were more likely than nonrescuers to have been involved in helping activities before the war and after the war, as well as during the war. Wartime rescue, despite its qualitatively different level of risk and other unique aspects, was for many rescuers mainly one more opportunity to help people who needed help. As such, it was taken up as a matter of course.

These meditations could be extended. But perhaps they suffice to show that the church must not only recover a self-conscious commitment to the formation of sound Christian character, but must also sharpen and even reconceive its understanding of what kind of character it wants to see formed. The Righteous Gentiles can help us here. One major reason the ethics of character fell into disrepute in many Christian circles was that the most heavily emphasized Christian moral virtues often were peripheral to the most basic concerns of the life and teaching of Jesus. Prudence and diligence, for example, are simply less significant virtues for the church than are openheartedness and compassion. A recovery of the ethics of character requires a simultaneous recovery of the core of the ethics of Jesus.[64]

Nurture a spirituality that does justice

One of the most significant findings I have outlined in this book concerns the resources that some rescuers found in Christian spirituality and piety as they struggled to save Jews from the Nazis. The ancient repertoire of Christian devotion proved vital in helping Christians both to understand their moral obligation and then to "go and do" what they understood they must do. This repertoire included staying alert to communication from God, initiating communication with God through prayer, reading the Bible for guidance and strength to endure, searching for God's will and being utterly devoted to its performance, desiring to please God and avoid God's displeasure, experiencing a sense of God's living and providential presence in one's life, and involving oneself in a group of Christians doing rescue and together seeking sustenance in the faith.

Today, the American church scene witnesses a resurgence of interest in Christian spirituality and spiritual formation.[65] One senses a growing hunger for encounter with God and for a peaceful heart, in response to a world that often feels both bereft of God's presence and dominated by clamor. This renewed interest in spirituality and mysticism reflects the particular needs of our troubled age. Yet it is also rooted in the nature of the human being, who perennially seeks to make contact with the God who inhabits our "inmost parts" and is ultimately responsible for our existence. As Augustine said, "Our hearts are restless, until they find rest in Thee."

An ethicist finds this surging interest in spirituality both an alarming and a promising trend. Concern arises because some of those seeking to encounter God and find peace do so by withdrawing from that alert concern for the neighbor and his or her needs which constitutes normative Christian character and conduct. Indeed, exhaustion from social, moral, and/or political effort sometimes inspires Christians toward interest in spiritual renewal. However, a peaceful heart cannot be won with integrity by shutting the door and stopping one's ears to the violence and injustice that take place just outside and around the corner. As Kenneth Leech argues, an appropriate Christian spirituality must take place in "the eye of the storm" of injustice and the costly struggle against it.[66]

The devout Christian rescuers provide an inspiring example of the kind of spirituality that serves the quest for justice rather than detracts from it. For those concerned with the moral possibilities of the "average" congregation, the simplicity of many Christian rescuers comes as good news. These were not sophisticated theoreticians of justice, liberation, or spirituality, but practitioners of basic Christian discipleship, of love of God and neighbor. When history presented them with the momentous moral challenge of whether or not to try to help Jews, and the extremely draining and dangerous months and years that followed if they answered Yes, their faith proved to be a source of living power. These were real resources that contributed concretely to the saving of innocent human life.

A Christian ethicist must be concerned not only with helping the church to discern what following Jesus requires, but also with cultivating the resources that enable Christians actually to do what they know they must. Because the basics of the Christian spiritual life can help Christians to be righteous, their cultivation must be on the agenda of Christian ethics. The same is true of the church. Education on matters of peace, justice, and liberation must be coupled with cultivation of those spiritual resources that empower Christians actually to act on behalf of others.

Rediscover the constructive moral power of the Bible

The Christian rescuers also bear witness to the constructive moral power available in the Bible for the people of faith. This power revealed itself not only in the sophisticated reflection of the cleric and church body but also in the creative reading of the unschooled Christian layperson. The former tended to find biblical texts and themes that directly and profoundly addressed the moral situation in which Christians found themselves vis-à-vis Jews. The latter discovered both these texts and other resources in the Scriptures whose relevance no one could have predicted. For both, the Bible helped them to discover the content of Christian fidelity in this terrible moral crucible, and empowered them to do what faithfulness required.

Among other lessons to be derived from this evidence, it serves as a reminder to Christian ministers and educators to return central biblical teachings on compassion and love to the forefront of Christian proclamation and education. Again and again, Christians need to hear the parable of the Good Samaritan, the commandment to love God and neighbor, the Golden Rule, the parable of the Sheep and the Goats, and related texts. Sometimes church leaders assume that these familiar passages are so well known as to require little attention. But our findings suggest that these texts form something of a biblical constitution for the Christian moral life. They should be the subject of regular reflection, proclamation, and application, with less central themes and texts falling into place around them.

On another level, the devout rescuers reveal the importance of reinvigorating the reading of the whole Bible. The witness of Corrie ten Boom and others like her seems to demonstrate that a Christian immersed in the Scriptures is far more likely to find moral resources in its pages than one who does not read the Bible regularly or know it as well. Only people immersed in the Bible likely will run across or recall an unexpected text that serendipitously proves to be of moral value and power. Christians are more likely to be able to act like disciples if they immerse themselves in the narratives of the people of faith—people whose words reveal their struggle to be worthy disciples themselves—and seek encounter with the God who can be met through Scripture's testimony.

A recovery of the constructive moral power of the Bible requires committed and skillful local church leadership. A very great deal of harm has been done in the name of the Bible. All one has to do is consider the misuse of the Bible in the development of Christian theological anti-Judaism, as well as in the hateful teachings heard from some Christian pulpits and Christian lips during the Holocaust itself—let alone other glaring instances of the destructive misuse of the Bible, such as in the legitimation of slavery. But a great deal of good has been done in the name of the Bible and in its power, and this too occurred during the Holocaust. The local church must be a place in which this kind of morally constructive reading of the Bible can take place. This requires the existence of a community of such a character that the reading of the Bible will nurture love and compassion rather than hatred and exclusion. This kind of community character itself is formed, in part, through an appropriate reading of the Bible. Where the Bible can come alive in Christian congregations in morally healthy ways, the church adds a crucial "weapon of the Spirit" to the arsenal of resources it can deploy in the quest for Christian righteousness.[67]

Articulate a diverse vocabulary of neighbor-love

The Bible and Christian faith overflow with terms and images that together constitute a diverse Christian vocabulary of neighbor-love. The rich portfolio of terms mentioned in this study includes the following: love, justice, care, mercy, pity, relationship, hospitality, humanitarianism, openheartedness, sympathy, inclusiveness, tolerance, friendship, benevolence, compassion, fellow-humanity, liberation, partnership, solidarity, resistance, empathy, rights, lovingkindness, and righteousness. Each term highlights a different dimension of the love of neighbor that Jesus described as the second greatest commandment (Matt. 22:34-40).

Rescuer research demonstrates that no single moral paradigm accurately captures the conduct or motivations of all Righteous Gentiles. We saw in chapter 5 that at least three different moral styles or paradigms can be delineated within the broad motivational category of "humanitarian rescue"—an ethic of rights, an ethic of care, and an empathic response. Further, a great number of rescuers acted on the basis of other than strictly humanitarian motivations. One implication of these findings is the need for tolerance in Christian ethics and the church of the different languages and paradigms used to describe the motives or characteristics of Christian action on behalf of others. A kaleidoscope of terms and paradigms is available to describe loving and just treatment of the neighbor. Different paths toward such a just love, and different terminology to describe each path, are appropriate for different historical and corporate contexts. Given the desperate importance of neighbor-love in a world full of suffering and needy neighbors, all paths that *genuinely lead Christians in love's direction* should be accorded legitimacy and warmly welcomed. Likewise, all paths that lead Christians to hatred, indifference, injustice, and exclusion should be rejected. The shadow of death that this century casts over our planet's future makes arguments over the superiority or profundity of any particular moral paradigm, term, or model seem like a waste of ink and time.[68]

The church should consider a related lesson. The local church must be a place in which clergy and laity learn to articulate together the rich and diverse Christian vocabulary of neighbor-love. From the pulpit and in the classroom, the second great commandment must be heard and the whole of the moral kaleidoscope that flows out of it. This should happen not simply because the church must hear the command to love the neighbor, and not simply because the words enrich our spirits and nurture the character of our communities. These words should be spoken and discussed, in all of their diversity, so that they can help Christian people name that nudging in the direction of neighbor-love which God inspires within their souls, and name it in a way appropriate to themselves, their gifts, and their particular contexts. From there, the Christian vocabulary of neighbor-love can serve as the congregation's lingua franca as it attempts to incarnate love within its community and in its mission to the world.

Identify competent moral leadership

Numerous commentators, both Jewish and Christian, have pointed to the collapse of Christian leadership during the Holocaust. For example, most standard treatments of the subject condemn the Vatican's failures.[69] Those historians who take the grassroots view note that local church leaders tended to reflect rather than shape the sentiment and conduct of their rank-and-file. Anti-Semitic populations tended to find their prejudices reinforced by anti-Semitic clergy, and so on. Horrific evidence from a variety of sources illustrates the casual anti-Semitism and callous disregard for Jewish life that poisoned the teaching and behavior of high church officials and local clergy in various lands. A handful of priests and ordained ministers even participated directly in murdering Jews! Far more common and widespread was the lack of courage demonstrated by church officials who, at critical moments, failed to seize the opportunity to guide their flocks in the direction of rescue. From every quarter come reports on the failure of Christian leadership. Christian ministers are called to lead their flocks in the way of following Jesus and to be distinctively committed and distinctively faithful. Instead, as Yehuda Bauer writes, "the priests ranged from martyrs to murderers, just as all the rest of the people did."[70]

Our overview has presented several stories of church leaders who resisted all manner of pressures by providing courageous and competent moral leadership in this *kairos* moment for the Christian churches. A study of the behavior of these Christian leaders (and the behavior of those who failed to lead) should become part of the curriculum for anyone seeking to become a high official, cleric, bureaucrat, or other kind of leader of a Christian body. The resplendent regalia, lofty titles, and glorious ordination services enjoyed by Christian leaders perhaps have obscured the fact that when Christ calls a person to Christian leadership "he bids him come and die," as Dietrich Bonhoeffer said. Those who take upon themselves the mantle of Christian leadership must be prepared to suffer and die in the service of Christian moral fidelity. Those who seek out and appoint Christian leaders must take care to find people who appear capable of providing the moral leadership the church requires in order to be an authentic people of God.

Conclusion

Those who write about the Holocaust find themselves affected by a penetrating sadness. Grief and horror mingle in the soul. Even though the rescuers provide perhaps the only spark of light in the Holocaust tragedy, I too have been penetrated by this sadness. Without question, the shadows overwhelm the light.

As a lifetime churchgoer, ordained minister, and Christian ethicist, I find the dismal overall performance of the Christian churches during the Holocaust to be a significant source of the pervasive sadness that this subject enkindles in me. The New Testament offers the church a breathtaking portrait of its special character and mission in the world. We are "a chosen people, a royal priesthood, a holy nation, a people belonging to God" (1 Pet. 2:9); we are the bride of Christ (Eph. 5:22ff.), the community of saints, the redeemed, sanctified, and transformed people of God, evangelists to a lost world (Matt. 28:19-20). We are the firstfruits of God's new creation (James 1:18), a sign to the world of the cosmic redemption that God has inaugurated in Jesus Christ. We will even stand at the right hand of God and join in the judgment of the nations (Rev. 20:4).

The church revealed during the Holocaust bears so little resemblance to the church described in the Bible. At its worst, we see a church in which believers are taught to hate people of different creed, "race," or ethnicity. We see priests and ministers discouraging their congregants from saving human lives. We see Christians (including some sophisticated theologians) lost in complete ideological confusion as they give their souls over to the Third Reich and its cauldron of hatreds.[71] We see self-proclaimed followers of the compassionate One react with utter coldness of heart when another human being needs their compassion. We see morally powerful sacred texts create faint stirrings of compassion, only to watch them be damped by raw fear. We see Christian leaders fall far short of their calling to lead the people of God in the way of Jesus Christ, which is the way of unmitigated love of neighbor, which is the way of the cross.

Royal priesthood? Holy nation? Community of saints? Transformed people of God? Firstfruits of God's new creation? How broad and deep is the gulf between who we are in Christ and who we were during the

Holocaust. How base and unholy, how unsaintly and untransformed we showed ourselves to be! Our house stands in ruin. A deep silence must descend on us, the silence of self-examination and repentance. Then we must go back to school, back to the classroom of Jesus Christ, and try to learn all over again what it might mean to bear that name in this world; try to learn the shape of authentic Christian righteousness and how to live it. The Righteous Gentiles of the Holocaust—those few Europeans who acted like Christians are supposed to act—have a fundamental role to play in our reeducation.

Notes

Preface

1. Eva Fleischner, "Catholics in France Who Saved Jews during the Holocaust," *Journal of Philosophy and Theology* 3 (Fall 1988), 46.

2. Irving Greenberg, "Cloud of Smoke, Pillar of Fire," in Eva Fleischner, ed., *Auschwitz: Beginning of a New Era?* (New York: KTAV, 1977), 23.

Chapter 1: Christian Ethics and the Righteous Gentiles

1. From 1921 to 1939, Nesvizh was part of eastern Poland, very near the western border of the Soviet Union. During the war, it was taken first by the Soviet Union, then by Nazi Germany, then again by the Soviets. After the war, it remained part of the USSR, in the republic of Byelorussia. With the demise of the Soviet Union, Nesvizh now is part of the fledgling nation Belarus. The case of Nesvizh helps to illustrate the maxim that in Eastern Europe it is normally borders that move rather than people, with all of the ethnic and nationalist tensions that this causes. All geographical references in this study will use the political/geographical term appropriate to the period under discussion.

2. Shalom Cholawski, *Soldiers from the Ghetto* (San Diego: A. S. Barnes, 1980), 69–70. See also Martin Gilbert, *Atlas of the Holocaust*, rev. and exp. ed. (New York: Morrow, 1993), 77, 108.

3. Ibid.

4. Michael Marrus, *The Holocaust in History* (New York: New American Library, 1987), 23.

5. Ruth Leger Sivard, *World Military and Social Expenditures 1986* (Washington, D.C.; World Priorities, 1986), 26, estimates 19.6 million deaths; Mortimer Chambers

et al., *The Western Experience*, 3d ed. (New York: Knopf, 1983), 937, offers a lower estimate of between ten and thirteen million fatalities.

6. Leo P. Kuper, "The Turkish Genocide of Armenians," in Richard P. Hovannisian, ed., *The Armenian Genocide in Perspective* (New Brunswick, N.J.: Transaction Books, 1988); cf. Mark D. Bedrossyan, *The First Genocide of the 20th Century* (Manasquan Park, N.J.: Voskedar Publishing, 1983). Following Kuper, I define genocide here as "a coordinated plan of different actions aiming at the destruction of the essential foundations of the life of national groups, with the aim of annihilating the groups themselves." Leo P. Kuper, *Genocide* (New Haven: Yale Univ. Press, 1981), 22, quoted in Marrus, *The Holocaust in History*, 21.

7. Sivard, *World Military and Social Expenditures 1986*, 26; cf. Bruce Lincoln, *Red Victory* (New York: Touchstone, 1989).

8. Robert Conquest, *The Harvest of Sorrow* (New York: Oxford Univ. Press, 1986), 299–308.

9. Robert Conquest, *The Great Terror: A Reassessment* (New York: Oxford Univ. Press, 1990), 484–89. The total number of casualties in the Stalin era is now placed between twenty and forty million.

10. Estimates of World War II fatalities vary. This figure is drawn from Marrus, *The Holocaust in History*, 24.

11. Ibid.

12. Ibid., 23–24; cf. Sivard, *World Military and Social Expenditures 1986*, 26.

13. This important theme was introduced and developed by Jonathan Schell, *The Fate of the Earth* (New York: Avon Books, 1982), especially 181ff.

14. This date is a matter of dispute. For discussion, see chapter 2. Marrus claims that the commitment to destroy *every single Jew* is one of the features that sets the genocide against the Jews apart from the murder campaigns against other groups during the war as well as during other historical periods. *The Holocaust in History*, 24. Cf. Yehuda Bauer, *The Holocaust in Historical Perspective* (Seattle: Univ. of Washington, 1978), 35–36.

15. Some prefer other terms for naming this catastrophe. Alternatives from the Jewish religious tradition include *Shoah* and *Churban*. Terms without religious connotation include the Nazis' own term "Final Solution." Some prefer to avoid abstract terms, speaking instead of "the destruction of the Jews," "the war against the Jews," and so on. We will settle on the term "the Holocaust," because it appears to be the term most commonly employed by Jews themselves to discuss the catastrophe. Further, we will restrict the meaning of that term to the attempted annihilation of the *Jews*, rather than include all other civilian victims of Nazi measures, such as Gypsies, Russian prisoners-of-war, non-Jewish Poles, and homosexuals. Most Holocaust scholars use the term in this more restricted way. See Martin Gilbert, *The Holocaust* (New York: Henry Holt, 1985), 18; Bauer, *The Holocaust in Historical Perspective*, 3, 30–35; Lucy S. Dawidowicz, *The War Against the Jews, 1933–1945* (New York: Bantam Books, 1975), xxxvii. This does not indicate a lack of interest in or concern for the suffering of other Nazi victims, merely a recognition that this term emerges from the Jewish tradition and best denotes the Jewish experience at Nazi hands. Yet one fears that the suffering of all the "others" will be forgotten or downplayed if not included in the term "Holocaust." This is a matter of considerable

sensitivity. There exists a disheartening debate today concerning the interpretation and contextualization of the catastrophe of European Jewry vis-à-vis the suffering of other groups during World War II. The argument is important both historically and morally. It has to do with the formulation of a historically accurate perspective on events, as well as with the transmission of a just and inclusive historical memory to future generations. Yet the debate is disheartening because of its pettiness in the context of the suffering it seeks to remember. Millions died at Nazi hands for ideological and other nonmilitary reasons; millions more died as a result of "regular" wartime suffering. World War II was a time of exceptional human savagery. How unseemly that people should spend time today arguing over degrees of victimization. However, anyone who today isolates the Holocaust, the particular suffering of the Jews, must be prepared to give reasons for this decision in the context of the massive suffering of others. Later in this introductory chapter this is done by highlighting the particular importance of the Holocaust as an experience in Christian-Jewish relations. Meanwhile, the victimization of many people, especially other Europeans, will be considered both significant and relevant throughout this study.

16. The continued dominance of these categories is illustrated by the recent publication of a book by one of the preeminent scholars of the Holocaust, Raul Hilberg, under the title *Perpetrators Victims Bystanders* (New York: HarperCollins, 1992).

17. For a discussion of some of these other bystanders, see Hilberg, *Perpetrators Victims Bystanders*, chs. 21–23, and Leni Yahil, *The Holocaust* (New York: Oxford Univ. Press, 1990), ch. 20.

18. Bauer, *Holocaust in Historical Perspective*, 52.

19. Raul Hilberg, *The Destruction of the European Jews*, 3 vols., rev. ed. (New York: Holmes and Meier, 1985), 1003.

20. For this concept see Otto Dov Kulka, "Major Trends and Tendencies in German Historiography on National Socialism and the 'Jewish Question' (1924–1984)," *Leo Baeck Institute Year Book* 30 (1985), 234; cited in Marrus, *The Holocaust in History*, 15.

21. This concept, fundamental to this study, is adapted from the work of Helen Fein, *Accounting for Genocide* (New York: Free Press, 1979). Her actual formulation of the phrase is "sanctified universe of obligation" (4). Remarkably similar concepts, using different language, appear throughout the literature on altruism and rescue. The sociobiologist Edward O. Wilson uses the language of "ingroup and outgroup"—"Human beings are consistent in their codes of honor and endlessly fickle with reference to whom the codes apply." The distinction is "between the ingroup and the outgroup, but the precise location of the dividing line is shifted back and forth with ease." Wilson, "Altruism," *Harvard Magazine* (Nov.–Dec. 1978), 27, quoted in Marie Augusta Neal, "The Future of Altruism," *Cross Currents* 36 (Winter 1986/87), 427. Morton Hunt speaks of the destructive human tendency toward "we/they" thinking and action. Morton Hunt, *The Compassionate Beast* (New York: William Morrow and Co., 1990), 87–93. Social psychologist Ervin Staub prefers to speak of the "range of applicability" of values such as caring and the responsibility to ease others' suffering, and the human propensity to limit that range so that some people are excluded from compassion. See Staub, "The Roots of Altruism and Heroic

Rescue," *The World & I* (July 1988), 398. Inclusive boundaries of moral obligation are seen in the concept of the "species self," borrowed by rescuer researcher Eva Fogelman from Robert Jay Lifton: A species self "is capable of integrating a human identity which goes far beyond concepts of nationalism and race." Fogelman, "The Rescuers: A Socio-psychological Study of Altruistic Behavior During the Nazi Era," Ph.D. diss, City University of New York, 1987, 216–17. Similarly, Samuel and Pearl Oliner employ the language of "extensivity" and "inclusiveness" to connote the rescuers' tendency to regard Jews and all other human beings as equally worthy of rights and care. Oliner and Oliner, *The Altruistic Personality* (New York: Free Press, 1988), 165 and elsewhere. Kristen Monroe prefers to speak of the rescuers' "identity perception as part of a common humanity," which demands of them action on behalf of any human being in need. See Monroe et al., "Altruism and the Theory of Rational Action: Rescuers of Jews in Nazi Europe," *Ethics* 101 (October 1990), 117–18. Under the rubric of "universalistic perceptions," Nechama Tec describes the rescuers' moral conviction that the dependence and helplessness of a victim are the only salient factors, and that these demand action on any human victim's behalf. Tec, *When Light Pierced the Darkness* (New York: Oxford Univ. Press, 1986), 176ff. Both the Jewish and Christian moral traditions—in their best voice—seek to nurture such broadly inclusive understandings of moral obligation and patterns of moral practice. See Neal, "The Future of Altruism," 431; Mordecai Paldiel, "Hesed and the Holocaust," *Journal of Ecumenical Studies* 23, no. 1 (Winter 1986), 90–106, and chs. 6 and 7 of this study.

22. Bauer, *Holocaust in Historical Perspective*, 52.

23. See Kulka, "Major Trends and Tendencies in German Historiography on National Socialism and the 'Jewish Question,' " 234; Neal, "The Future of Altruism," 431; Mordecai Paldiel, "Hesed and the Holocaust," 90–106. A thorough discussion of Christian theological resources for such an inclusive understanding of the boundaries of moral obligation is offered in chapter 6.

24. In a study of European rescuers and nonrescuers of Jews during the Holocaust, Samuel and Pearl Oliner found that approximately 95 percent of both groups were affiliated with a Christian church while growing up, and approximately 72 percent of both groups said they were either "very" or "somewhat" religious while growing up. Sixty-nine percent of rescuers and 64 percent of nonrescuers said they were either "very" or "somewhat" religious just before the war. Oliner, *Altruistic Personality*, 289 (Table 6.4) and 291 (Table 6.6). This data helps to place in perspective the relative decline of Christian influence in Europe by 1939. The churches may have reached the "nadir of their influence" during World War II, as Hilberg notes (*Perpetrators Victims Bystanders*, 260), but that influence remained considerable nonetheless, at least at the grassroots level. Reflection on the importance of the Oliner findings will be offered in chs. 5–7.

25. Hilberg, *Destruction of the European Jews*, 309.

26. For example, Hilberg speaks of "a relatively large number of indigenous collaborators [who] were employed in shooting operations in Eastern Europe," in *Perpetrators Victims Bystanders*, 21.

27. "Righteous of the Nations," *Encyclopedia Judaica* (henceforth *EJ*), vol. 14 (Jerusalem: Keter Publishing House, 1972), 184; "Righteous among the Nations,"

Encyclopedia of the Holocaust (henceforth *EH*), vol. 3 (New York: Macmillan, 1990), 1279. Extensive reflection on the ancient theological and moral roots of the term is offered in ch. 7.

28. Mordecai Paldiel, director of the Department for the Righteous Among the Nations, Yad Vashem, in interview with author, December 1991; "Righteous Among the Nations," *EJ* 3, 1279–80. Another statement of the official criteria for qualifying for Righteous Gentile status includes the following: "extending help in saving a life; endangering one's own life; absence of reward, monetary and otherwise; and similar considerations which made the rescuer's deeds stand out above and beyond what can be termed ordinary help." Tec, *When Light Pierced the Darkness*, 4. The criteria are seen as flexible, and case-by-case judgment is required. In a March 1993 conference at Princeton University sponsored by the Jewish Foundation for Christian Rescuers/ADL, Paldiel discussed some of the difficult, "gray area" cases that his office faces, indicating that as a general principle Yad Vashem "bends over backwards" to accept rather than reject nominees for Righteous Gentile status.

29. Diana Stein, Associate Director of the Jewish Foundation for Christian Rescuers/ADL, telephone conversation with author, October 1992.

30. "Righteous among the Nations," *EH* 3, 1280.

31. Mordecai Paldiel, interview; Diana Stein, telephone conversation.

32. Mordecai Paldiel, interview.

33. A book emerging from that meeting is *The Courage to Care: Rescuers of Jews during the Holocaust*, Carol Rittner and Sondra Myers, eds. (New York: New York University, 1986). For contemporary reporting on the event, see Eugene J. Fisher, "Faith in Humankind: Rescuers of Jews during the Holocaust," *Journal of Ecumenical Studies* 21 (Summer 1984), 636–37; "Holocaust Heroes Honored," *Christian Century* 101 (October 17, 1984), 952.

34. See Harold M. Schulweis, "The Bias Against Man," *Jewish Education* 34, no. 1 (Fall 1963), 6–14; "Remember the Righteous Redeemers," *Jewish Digest* 9, no. 1 (October 1963), 65–69; "In Praise of Good People," *Jewish Spectator* 48, no. 1 (Spring 1983), 16–18; "They Were Our Brothers' Keepers," *Moment* 11, no. 5 (May 1986), 50; "Remembering the Rescuers: The Post-Holocaust Agenda," *Christian Century* 105 (December 7, 1988), 1126–28. Schulweis is widely recognized as the dean of rescuer studies, and the impact of his vision has been considerable on almost all rescuer research.

35. Stanlee Stahl, Director of the JFCR/ADL, telephone conversation, July 1994.

36. The phrase is from Eva Fleischner, "Can the Few Become the Many? Some Catholics in France Who Saved Jews during the Holocaust," in *Remembering for the Future*, vol. 1 (New York: Pergamon Press, 1989), 233–47.

37. Mordecai Paldiel, interview.

38. It is relevant to note here that the new United States Holocaust Memorial Museum, which opened its doors to the public in Washington on April 26, 1993, includes a section on rescuers.

39. For the important though disturbing concept of a "usable" Holocaust, see Michael Berenbaum, "The Nativization of the Holocaust," *Judaism* 35, no. 4 (Fall 1986), 447–57.

40. Schulweis, Foreword, in Oliner and Oliner, *Altruistic Personality*, ix.

41. David Novak, "A Jewish Theological Understanding of Christianity in Our Time," *First Things* 9 (January 1991), 30.

42. Bruce C. Birch and Larry L. Rasmussen, *Bible and Ethics in the Christian Life*, rev. and exp. ed. (Minneapolis: Augsburg, 1989), 36.

43. This is the burden of the argument of Stanley Hauerwas in *A Community of Character* (Notre Dame: Univ. of Notre Dame Press, 1981), see esp. 92.

44. See Franklin Littell, *The Crucifixion of the Jews* (Macon, Ga.: Mercer Univ. Press, 1975); Harry James Cargas, *When God and Man Failed* (New York: Macmillan, 1981); Alice and A. Roy Eckardt, *Long Night's Journey into Day* (Detroit: Wayne State Univ. Press, 1982); Richard Rubenstein and John K. Roth, *Approaches to Auschwitz* (Atlanta: John Knox Press, 1987), ch. 7; A. Roy and Alice Eckardt, eds., *Remembering for the Future: Jews and Christians during and after the Holocaust* (Oxford: Pergamon Press, 1989). The annual "Scholars' Conference on the Holocaust and the Churches," for many years under the leadership of Franklin Littell and Hubert G. Locke, has provided regular opportunity for reflection on Christian moral failure during the Holocaust. See Littell and Locke, eds., *The German Church Struggle and the Holocaust* (San Francisco: Mellen Research University Press, [1974] 1990). The history and consequences of Christian theological anti-Judaism are seen as a fundamental part of Christian responsibility for the Holocaust and thus moral failure. For a listing of sources on anti-Judaism and anti-Semitism, see below. Many Jewish scholars of the Holocaust also speak sharply of Christian moral failure during those events. See Richard Rubenstein, *After Auschwitz* (Indianapolis: Bobbs-Merrill, 1966), esp. ch. 3; Eliezer Berkovits, *Faith after the Holocaust* (New York: KTAV, 1973), esp. ch. 1; Greenberg, "Cloud of Smoke, Pillar of Fire," 12.

45. The term "anti-Judaism" is used here to convey Christian theological rejection of Judaism. "Anti-Semitism" refers generally to hatred of the Jewish people. They are profoundly related but at least conceptually distinct phenomena. The literature on both anti-Judaism and anti-Semitism is vast. On the former, major works include James Parkes, *The Conflict of the Church and the Synagogue* (New York: Atheneum, 1969); Malcolm Hay, *Europe and the Jews* (Boston: Beacon Press, 1960); Jules Isaac, *The Teaching of Contempt: Christian Roots of Anti-Semitism*, ed. Claire Huchet-Bishop, trans. Helen Weaver (New York: Holt, Rinehart, and Winston, 1964); Edward Flannery, *The Anguish of the Jews* (New York: Macmillan, 1964); Gregory Baum, *Is the New Testament Anti-Semitic?* (New York: Paulist Press, 1965); A. Roy Eckardt, *Elder and Younger Brothers* (New York: Scribner, 1967); Alan Davies, *Antisemitism and the Christian Mind* (New York: Seabury, 1969); Rosemary Radford Ruether, *Faith and Fratricide* (Minneapolis: Seabury Press, 1974); A. Roy Eckardt, *Your People, My People* (New York: Quadrangle, 1974); Alan T. Davies, ed., *Antisemitism and the Foundations of Christianity* (New York: Paulist Press, 1979); Paul M. Van Buren, *A Theology of the Jewish-Christian Reality*, 3 vols. (New York: Harper and Row, 1980–88); John Gager, *The Origins of Antisemitism: Attitudes Towards Judaism in Pagan and Christian Antiquity* (New York: Oxford Univ. Press, 1985); John Pawlikowski, *Jesus and the Theology of Israel* (Wilmington, Del.: Michael Glazier, 1989); Darrell J. Fasching, *Narrative Theology after Auschwitz* (Minneapolis: Augsburg Fortress, 1992). On anti-Semitism generally, see Leon Poliakov, *History of Anti-Semitism*,

4 vols. (New York: Viking Press, Vanguard Press, 1965–86); Arthur Hertzberg, *The French Enlightenment and the Jews: The Origins of Modern Anti-Semitism* (New York: Columbia Univ. Press, 1968); Hannah Arendt, *Antisemitism* (New York: Harcourt, Brace, and World, 1968); Jacob Katz, *From Prejudice to Destruction: Anti-Semitism, 1700–1933* (Cambridge, Mass.: Harvard Univ. Press, 1980); George Mosse, *Toward the Final Solution: A History of European Racism* (Madison: Univ. of Wisconsin Press, 1978); Gordon Allport, *The Nature of Prejudice* (Reading, Mass.: Addison-Wesley, 1979); Theodor W. Adorno et al., *The Authoritarian Personality* (New York: Norton, 1950); Jean-Paul Sartre, *Anti-Semite and Jew* (New York: Schocken, 1948); Uriel Tal, *Christians and Jews in Germany: Religion, Politics, and Ideology in the Second Reich, 1870–1914* (Ithaca: Cornell Univ. Press, 1975); Robert S. Wistrich, *Antisemitism: The Longest Hatred* (New York: Pantheon Books, 1991).

46. Most histories of the Holocaust focus attention on this question. See Raul Hilberg, *The Destruction of the European Jews*, ch. 10; Dawidowicz, *The War Against the Jews*, Part 1. Specialized studies include Gitta Sereny, *Into That Darkness* (New York: Vintage Books, 1974); Robert Jay Lifton, *The Nazi Doctors* (New York: Basic Books, 1986); Heinz Höhne, *The Order of the Death's Head* (New York: Ballantine Books, 1969); Peter J. Haas, *Morality after Auschwitz* (Philadelphia: Fortress Press, 1988); Ernst Klee et al., *"The Good Old Days"* (New York: Free Press, 1991); Christopher R. Browning, *Ordinary Men* (New York: HarperCollins, 1992); John Sabini and Maury Silver, *Moralities of Everyday Life* (New York: Oxford Univ. Press, 1982), ch. 4; Hilberg, *Perpetrators Victims Bystanders*, Part 1; Hannah Arendt, *Eichmann in Jerusalem* (New York: Penguin, 1977); Rudolf Höss, *Commandant of Auschwitz*, trans. Constantine Fitzgibbon (London: Pan Books, 1974); Birch and Rasmussen, *Bible and Ethics in the Christian Life*, ch. 5. The head perpetrator, of course, was Adolf Hitler. Among the numerous biographies, see Joachim C. Fest, *Hitler* (New York: Vintage Books, 1975).

47. Guenther Lewy, *The Roman Catholic Church and the Third Reich* (New York: McGraw-Hill, 1964); John F. Morley, *Vatican Diplomacy and the Jews during the Holocaust, 1939–1943* (New York: KTAV, 1980); Saul Friedlander, *Pius XII and the Third Reich* (New York: Alfred A. Knopf, 1966); Gordon Zahn, "Catholic Resistance? A Yes and a No," in Littell and Locke, eds., *German Church Struggle*, 203–37.

Chapter 2: The Holocaust

1. Nazi party platform in J. Noakes and G. Pridham, eds., *Nazism: A History in Documents and Eyewitness Accounts, 1919–1945* (New York: Schocken Books, 1990), 14–16.

2. Fein, *Accounting for Genocide*, 33.

3. Hilberg, *Destruction of the European Jews*, 32.

4. Ibid.

5. Noakes and Pridham, *Nazism*, 12–14. See Dawidowicz, *The War Against the Jews*, 17; Yahil, *The Holocaust*, 44.

6. Dawidowicz, *The War Against the Jews*, 18. A fuller statement of Hitler's anti-Semitism is found in his autobiography, *Mein Kampf* (Boston: Houghton Mifflin,

[1925] 1971). For analysis, see *The War Against the Jews*, ch. 1; Marrus, *The Holocaust in History*, pp. 13–18; Yahil, *The Holocaust*, ch. 2.

7. Yahil, *The Holocaust*, 44; Hilberg, *Destruction of the European Jews*, 20.

8. Dawidowicz, *The War Against the Jews*, ch. 2; Marrus, *The Holocaust in History*, 9–13; Mosse, *Toward the Final Solution*, Part 1.

9. Marrus, *The Holocaust in History*, 9. France, Russia, Poland, Rumania, and Hungary are among the European nations in which modern political anti-Semitism was also quite potent. See Yahil, *The Holocaust*, 38–39; Mosse, *A History of European Racism*.

10. Marrus, *The Holocaust in History*, 12. The extent of Hitler's popular support before he took power should not be overestimated. He and his party never gained more than 37 percent of the popular vote in an election before January 1933. Dawidowicz, *The War Against the Jews*, 48.

11. Yahil, *The Holocaust*, 62.

12. Hilberg, *Destruction of the European Jews*, 49.

13. Yahil, *The Holocaust*, 62.

14. Dawidowicz, *The War Against the Jews*, 52.

15. Ibid., 54–55.

16. Gilbert, *The Holocaust*, 41.

17. This eyewitness report was included in British diplomatic correspondence of the time. Quoted in Gilbert, *The Holocaust*, 37.

18. Dawidowicz, *The War Against the Jews*, 174–79; Yahil, *The Holocaust*, 73–86.

19. *The Manchester Guardian*, April 3, 1934, quoted in Gilbert, *The Holocaust*, 42.

20. Yahil, *The Holocaust*, 71. In November, after months of internal debate in government circles, a Jew was defined as a person with at least three Jewish grandparents or, under certain circumstances, two Jewish grandparents. Provisions were also worked out for classifying two different kinds of "part-Jews" (*Mischlinge*). The arcane distinctions between these "racial" categories meant the difference between life and death when annihilation began. See Yahil, 72–73; cf. Hilberg, *Destruction of the European Jews*, ch. 4.

21. British diplomatic report, quoted in Gilbert, *The Holocaust*, 49.

22. Dawidowicz, *The War Against the Jews*, 97–98.

23. Gilbert, *The Holocaust*, 58–63; Yahil, *The Holocaust*, 109.

24. Dawidowicz, *The War Against the Jews*, 196.

25. Dawidowicz, *The War Against the Jews*, 100–102, is the source of these estimates. Gilbert, *The Holocaust*, 69–73, counts 191 synagogues burned and ninety-one Jewish deaths. The exact numbers will never be known.

26. Francis H. Schott, "Kristallnacht in Solingen," *The New York Times*, November 9, 1988.

27. Dawidowicz, *The War Against the Jews*, 104.

28. Ibid., 189.

29. The secret pact worked out between Hitler and Stalin, which carved up Poland between Germany and the USSR, resulted in the Nazis gaining territory that contained two million Jews. The Soviets took lands holding the remaining 1.3 million.

30. Dawidowicz, *The War Against the Jews*, 200.

31. Ibid.

32. Leon Poliakov, *Harvest of Hate* (New York: Holocaust Library, [1951] 1979), 40.

33. Gilbert, *The Holocaust*, 87.

34. Abraham Isaiah Altus, "The Nazi Invasion of Raciaz," in Gilbert, *The Holocaust*, 90.

35. Dawidowicz, *The War Against the Jews*, 201.

36. Historians now make sure to place the Holocaust in the context of this overall Nazi population policy. See Marrus, *The Holocaust in History*, 51–54.

37. Dawidowicz, *The War Against the Jews*, 114; For a more comprehensive discussion, see Hilberg, *Destruction of the European Jews*, ch. 6.

38. After decapitating Polish society by murdering the elite, the Nazis planned to use the remaining Polish population as uneducated laborers. See a memo from SS chief Heinrich Himmler dated May 15, 1940, entitled "Some Thoughts on the Treatment of the Alien Population in the East," in Noakes and Pridham, *Nazism*, 932–34. Both Marrus, *The Holocaust in History* (24) and Poliakov, *Harvest of Hate* (264f.) estimate that three million non-Jewish Poles were killed. Some place the figure closer to two million. The suffering inflicted on the non-Jewish Poles is fundamentally important in understanding Polish behavior during the Holocaust.

39. Gilbert, *The Holocaust*, 95.

40. Hilberg, *Destruction of the European Jews*, 215.

41. Christopher Browning, "Nazi Ghettoization Policy: 'Attritionists' vs. 'Productionists,' " paper presented at the German Studies Association Conference, Albuquerque, N.M., September 1986; quoted in Marrus, *The Holocaust in History*, 60.

42. Yahil, *The Holocaust*, 159–71.

43. See Dawidowicz, *The War Against the Jews*, 206–13; Alexander Donat, *The Holocaust Kingdom: A Memoir* (New York: Holt, Rinehart, 1965), for an excellent memoir of life in the Warsaw Ghetto; Lucjan Dobroszycki, ed., *The Chronicle of the Lodz Ghetto, 1941–1944* (New Haven: Yale Univ. Press, 1984), and numerous other memoirs and accounts.

44. For an interview with Karski, see Gay Block and Malka Drucker, *Rescuers: Portraits of Moral Courage in the Holocaust* (New York: Holmes and Meier, 1992), 170–75.

45. Jan Karski, *Story of a Secret State* (Boston, 1944), quoted in Marrus, *The Holocaust in History*, 120.

46. Chaim Kaplan, *Scroll of Agony* (New York: Macmillan, 1965), 244–45.

47. Quoted in Dawidowicz, *The War Against the Jews*, 222. A similar story is found in Gilbert, *The Holocaust*, 155.

48. Philip Friedman, *Roads to Extinction*, ed. Ada June Friedman (New York: Jewish Publication Society, [1955] 1980), 44, describes life in Nazi forced labor as being "slowly tortured to death." The multitudes of forced labor camps, as well as forced labor in the ghettos, death camps, execution sites, and elsewhere, were a central and daily part of Jewish existence under Nazi rule. Numerous valuable firsthand accounts exist of the agonies of such labor. Cf. Sala Paulowicz with Kevin Klose, "The Wache," the story of a women's slave labor group, in Jacob Glatstein et al., eds., *Anthology of Holocaust Literature* (New York: Jewish Publication Society,

1969), 206–15; also Primo Levi, *Survival in Auschwitz* (New York: Collier Books, 1961), 58–64.

49. Hilberg, *Destruction of the European Jews*, 269.

50. For a fine survey of Nazi foreign policy documents to this effect, see Noakes and Pridham, *Nazism*, ch. 25.

51. The *Kommissarbefehl* (Commissar Order) of June 6, 1941, distributed to top army officers, illustrates the nature of the instructions given to the German military. "The troops must be advised: 1. In this struggle consideration and respect for international law with regard to these elements [political commissars] are wrong. They are a danger for our own security and for the rapid pacification of the conquered territory. 2. The originators of barbaric Asiatic methods of warfare are the political commissars . . . accordingly, whether captured in battle or offering resistance, they are in principle to be disposed of by arms." Quoted in Dawidowicz, *The War Against the Jews*, 123; see also the collection of Nazi documents in Noakes and Pridham, *Nazism*, 1086–92.

52. On this point, see Bauer, *Holocaust in Historical Perspective*, 14; Dawidowicz, *The War Against the Jews*, 90–91.

53. This question is still disputed, but that the decision to murder the Jews was part of the Operation Barbarossa planning process is the conclusion of the foremost scholars of the *Einsatzgruppen* activities in Russia, Helmut Krausnick and Hans-Heinrich Wilhelm, *Die Truppe des Weltanschauungskrieges: Die Einsatzgruppen der Sicherheitspolizei und des SD, 1938–1942* (Stuttgart: Deutsche Verlags-Anstalt, 1981), quoted in Marrus, *The Holocaust in History*, 39–40. Raul Hilberg argues that the instructions were at first understood to mean that only Jewish men should be murdered; thus no women or children were killed by the *Einsatzgruppen* from June to August 1941. Beginning in September, however, all Jews were subject to death by shooting: *Perpetrators Victims Bystanders*, 17.

54. Poliakov, *Harvest of Hate*, 121. See *Einsatzgruppen* reports and editors' commentary in Noakes and Pridham, *Nazism*, 1092–94.

55. The army leadership had strongly resisted cooperation with the SS *Einsatzgruppen's* killings during the Polish campaign, but their official stance and behavior on the ground changed during the Russian campaign, much to their shame. See Noakes and Pridham, *Nazism*, 1090; Yahil, *The Holocaust*, 256.

56. Martin Gilbert, *Atlas of the Holocaust*, 67. Historians differ on these exact figures.

57. Shlomo Kogan, "The Long Road," in Leo W. Schwarz, ed., *The Root and the Bough* (New York: Rinehart and Co., 1949), 100–101.

58. Gilbert, *Atlas of the Holocaust*, 68.

59. Gilbert, *The Holocaust*, 175, emphasis in the original.

60. Gilbert, *Atlas of the Holocaust*, 76. Numerous Rumanian Jews were also killed by *Einsatzgruppe D*, in conjunction with the Rumanian army. The course of the Holocaust in Rumania was unique. Of the 600,000 Jews in Rumanian territory in 1941, some 300,000 were killed. Some were killed by the Germans, others by the Rumanian army, still others in pogrom-style killings. Many died of illness, hunger, exposure, and suffocation due to ill-prepared Rumanian-organized deportations. Yet 300,000 survived, in part, because Rumanian authorities refused to

countenance German requests that these be deported to Poland. See Dawidowicz, *The War Against the Jews*, 384–86; Yahil, *The Holocaust*, 344–48.

61. It appears that Jewish communities were often taken by surprise during the first wave of *Einsatzgruppen* killings but generally knew what was coming during the second sweep.

62. Friedman, *Roads to Extinction*, 200, n. 34.

63. Testimony of Rivka Yosselevska, Eichmann Trial, May 8, 1961, quoted in Gilbert, *The Holocaust*, 421–25.

64. For an example from the Ponary killing grounds, outside Vilna, see Gilbert, *The Holocaust*, 194. Jews survived these mass shootings and climbed out of mass graves frequently enough to attract the attention and dissatisfaction of officials in Berlin.

65. Testimony of Abba Kovner, Eichmann Trial, May 4, 1961, quoted in Gilbert, *The Holocaust*, 192.

66. Ibid., 193.

67. Dawidowicz, *The War Against the Jews*, 281.

68. Ibid., 287.

69. Gilbert, *The Holocaust*, 172.

70. Estimates vary widely concerning the total number of Jewish victims of the *Einsatzgruppen*. The Krausnick and Wilhelm estimates, quoted in Noakes and Pridham, *Nazism*, 1102, are the highest figures I have seen. Other estimates include the following: Bauer, *Holocaust in Historical Perspective*, 15—between one and two million; Dawidowicz, *The War Against the Jews*, 125—two million; Hilberg, *Destruction of the European Jews*, 390—1.3 million.

71. Gilbert, *The Holocaust*, 161.

72. Dawidowicz, *The War Against the Jews*, 279.

73. Marrus, *The Holocaust in History*, 65.

74. For this interpretation, see Marrus, *The Holocaust in History*, 46.

75. Here I adopt the view taken by Christopher Browning, "The Decision Concerning the Final Solution," in Francois Furet, ed., *Unanswered Questions: Nazi Germany and the Genocide of the Jews* (New York: Schocken Books, 1989), 105.

76. Ibid., 110.

77. Gilbert, *The Holocaust*, 287.

78. Yahil, *The Holocaust*, 323.

79. See the testimony of Michael Bodhalevnik (Podkebnik), Eichmann Trial, June 5, 1961, quoted in Gilbert, *The Holocaust*, 247–48; cf. Yahil, *The Holocaust*, 321.

80. Yahil, *The Holocaust*, 309.

81. See Lifton, *The Nazi Doctors*.

82. Estimates of the importance of this meeting vary with the historian's view of when the decision to kill all the Jews of Europe was actually made. Most scholars now see Wannsee merely as an administrative working session to iron out details of a policy decided several months earlier. See Bauer, *Holocaust in Historical Perspective*, 15. For minutes of the meeting, see Noakes and Pridham, *Nazism*, 1127–34.

83. Yahil, *The Holocaust*, 172.

84. Ibid., 288.

85. Ibid., 172; Dawidowicz, *The War Against the Jews*, 357ff; cf. Fein, *Accounting for Genocide*, 35 and throughout.
86. Fein, *Accounting for Genocide*, esp. ch. 6; Yahil, *The Holocaust*, 172; Dawidowicz, *The War Against the Jews*, 357; Hilberg, *Perpetrators Victims Bystanders*, ch. 18; Friedman, *Roads to Extinction*, ch. 17; Bauer, *Holocaust in Historical Perspective*, ch. 3.
87. Gilbert, *The Holocaust*, 302.
88. Testimony of Adolf Berman, Eichmann Trial, May 3, 1961, quoted in Gilbert, *The Holocaust*, 388.
89. Gilbert, *The Holocaust*, 417.
90. For a survivor's extended account of these executions, see Gilbert, *The Holocaust*, 627–32.
91. Yahil, *The Holocaust*, 446–47.
92. Quoted in Yahil, *The Holocaust*, 427.
93. For a stunning account of a Jew put to work cleaning up the gas chambers and crematoria of Birkenau (Auschwitz II) in the last days before the Russians arrived, see Irene Schwarz, "The Small Still Voice," in Leo W. Schwarz, ed., *The Root and the Bough* (New York: Rinehart and Co.), 189–200.
94. Gilbert, *The Holocaust*, 757.
95. Quoted in Marrus, *The Holocaust in History*, 196.
96. Raul Hilberg, *Destruction of the European Jews*, 1219–21, retains the most conservative estimate, 5.1 million. Yehuda Bauer, *Holocaust in Historical Perspective*, 30, offers the figure of 5.8 million; Dawidowicz, *The War Against the Jews*, 403, estimates 5.93 million.
97. Judith Miller, *One by One by One* (New York: Simon and Schuster, 1990).
98. See Michael Berenbaum, ed., *A Mosaic of Victims* (New York: New York Univ. Press, 1990).
99. Harrison E. Salisbury, *The 900 Days: The Siege of Leningrad* (New York: Da Capo Press, 1990).
100. Marrus, *The Holocaust in History*, 198.
101. Gilbert, *The Holocaust*, 711.
102. For a first-hand account of this argument in Warsaw, see Bernard Goldstein, "Girding Our Strength," in Schwarz, ed., *The Root and the Bough*, ch. 2.
103. See Philip Friedman, "Jewish Resistance to Nazism," in Glatstein, ed., *Anthology of Holocaust Literature*, 275–90. See also Marrus, *The Holocaust in History*, 133–40.
104. See Marrus, *The Holocaust in History*, 136–40, for a good overview of the discussion of Jewish resistance among historians. Here I differ from those who limit the term "resistance" to armed uprisings against the Nazis.
105. Donat, *The Holocaust Kingdom*, 8.
106. Ibid., 184–85.
107. Cf. Friedman, "Jewish Resistance to Nazism," 279–80.

Chapter 3: European Gentiles

1. Chaim Nahman Bialik, "In the City of Slaughter (1904)," trans. A. M. Klein, in David G. Roskies, *The Literature of Destruction* (New York: Jewish Publication Society, 1989), 160–68.

2. The focus of the chapter, as of this entire study, is local Gentile behavior. (Here we focus especially on the Eastern European killing zones.) There were other kinds of Gentile onlookers, though, particularly at the political and international level. These included the governments and political and military officials of Allied and neutral nations, the international press, international church bodies such as the hierarchy of the Roman Catholic Church, international relief organizations such as the Red Cross, and Jewish organizations in Palestine, America, and elsewhere. The behavior of these and other relevant parties to the tragedy is controversial and has been much discussed. Our study assumes the overall failure of such bodies and organizations to prevent the annihilation of the Jews, fully recognizing the fatefulness of that failure. Given that failure, however, our study focuses its attention on the local non-Jews who were forced to deal with the assault on the Jews as a matter of conscience.

3. Tec, *When Light Pierced the Darkness*, 52.

4. Several hundred thousand Poles died in Soviet labor camps, in exile, or in massacres at Soviet hands. The most famous of these mass killings today is the Katyn massacre of April and May 1940, in which fifteen thousand Polish prisoners of war, a cross section of the nation's elite, were murdered. Stalin appears to have had the same strategy as Hitler with regard to the Polish elite—to destroy it. See Robert Conquest, "First the Slaughter, Then the Lie," review of *Katyn*, by Allen Paul, *New York Times Book Review* (September 1, 1991), 11–13.

5. Gilbert, *The Holocaust*, 277, tells the fascinating story of Poles living near Chelmno telling a fugitive Jew, "They are gassing Jews and Gypsies at Chelmno, and when they have finished with them it will be our turn." Numerous Poles thought their plight was as bad as that of the Jews, or worse; the same was true in Soviet territories. For Poland, see Margaret O'Brien Steinfels, "On the Outskirts of Auschwitz," review of *The Convent at Auschwitz*, by Wladyslaw T. Bartoszewski, *New York Times Book Review* (September 8, 1991), 15. For the USSR, see Zvi Gitelman, "History, Memory, and Politics: The Holocaust in the Soviet Union," *Holocaust and Genocide Studies* 5, no. 1 (1990), 23–38.

6. For a personal account of the suffering of a Polish aristocratic family, see Christine Zamoyska-Panek, *Have You Forgotten?* (New York: Doubleday, 1989), especially pp. 66, 81.

7. Tec, *When Light Pierced the Darkness*, 40.

8. For several examples of the articulation of this reason for not rescuing, see Oliner, *The Altruistic Personality*, 140.

9. Friedman, *Roads to Extinction*, ch. 17, offers a fine discussion of the importance of Nazi efforts to instigate ethnic conflict in the areas under occupation.

10. See Gilbert, *The Holocaust*, 141–42, on the ethnic Germans and their significant level of collaboration in Poland; and 151 for the involvement of Ukrainians. See also Raul Hilberg, *Destruction of the European Jews*, 313–14.

11. Hilberg, *Destruction of the European Jews*, 1021–22.

12. Marrus, *The Holocaust in History*, 94. See also Poliakov, *Harvest of Hate*, 121.

13. Gilbert, *The Holocaust*, 360, 409.

14. For example, the death penalty for helping Jews was instituted in occupied Warsaw on October 15, 1941. It was no idle threat. Documents record numerous

executions of those who helped Jews along with the Jews who were helped. See Gilbert, *The Holocaust*, 132, 188, 504, 532, 583 for examples.

15. Hilberg, *Destruction of the European Jews*, 1008.

16. Lawrence Baron, "The Historical Context of Rescue," in Oliner, *The Altruistic Personality*, 27–29. On economic motives see also Bauer, *Holocaust in Historical Perspective*, 54; Poliakov, *Harvest of Hate*, 62ff.

17. Dov Levin, "On the Relations Between the Baltic Peoples and Their Jewish Neighbors before, during, and after World War II," *Holocaust and Genocide Studies* 5, no. 1 (1990), 53. See also Gilbert, *The Holocaust*, 155–56, on the killings in the interregnum between the exit of the Soviets and the entry of the Germans; and 172 on Lithuanian and Latvian involvement in the Holocaust generally. See also Hilberg, *Destruction of the European Jews*, 310–14.

18. Here I follow Shimon Redlich, "Metropolitan Andrei Sheptyts'kyi, Ukrainians and Jews during and after the Holocaust," *Holocaust and Genocide Studies* 5, no. 1 (1990), 39–51.

19. For a detailed discussion of the massacres in Ukraine during the Russian Civil War, see Lincoln, *Red Victory*, ch. 9.

20. See Conquest, *Harvest of Sorrow*.

21. A collection of Jewish accounts of Ukrainian collaboration in the Holocaust can be found in B. F. Sabrin, ed., *Alliance for Murder* (New York: Sarpedon Pubs., 1991). See particularly 23 and 44.

22. The best discussion of these German units has been offered by Hilberg, *Destruction of the European Jews*, see esp. ch. 10.

23. For a stunning account of the ordinary men of Reserve Police Battalion 101, who were directly responsible for the deaths of eighty-three thousand Jews in Poland, see Christopher R. Browning, *Ordinary Men*.

24. Gilbert, *The Holocaust*, 217–18; Hilberg, *Destruction of the European Jews*, 306–7.

25. Hilberg, *Destruction of the European Jews*, 1003.

26. Ibid., 313–14.

27. Ibid., 314.

28. Ibid., 289.

29. Abraham Ochs, "The Dark Clouds," in Sabrin, *Alliance for Murder*, 29.

30. Kogan, "The Long Road," 101.

31. David Wdowinski, *And We Are Not Saved*, 65–66, quoted in Gilbert, *The Holocaust*, 390–91.

32. Testimony of Martin Rosenblum, quoted in Gilbert, *The Holocaust*, 444–46.

33. Testimony of Franciszek Zabecki, quoted in Gilbert, *The Holocaust*, 399.

34. On prizes for turning Jews in, see also ch. 2. Information also provided by Paldiel, interview with author.

35. S. Zeminski, diary entry, quoted in Gilbert, *The Holocaust*, 493.

36. Hilberg, *Destruction of the European Jews*, 312.

37. Compare Sabrin, ed., *Alliance for Murder*, 23; Levin, "On the Relations": 53–66.

38. Paldiel, interview with author.

39. Rosa Pinchewski, "Rosa's Journey," in Schwarz, ed., *The Root and the Bough*, 299.

40. Feiga Kammer, "Winter in the Forest," in Glatstein, ed., *Anthology of Holocaust Literature*, 155–57.

41. Testimony of Hersh Werner, quoted in Gilbert, *The Holocaust*, 301.

42. Baron, "The Historical Context of Rescue," 28; See Shmuel Krakowski, *The War of the Doomed: Jewish Armed Resistance in Poland, 1942–1944* (New York: Holmes and Meier, 1984), 28. Compare Gilbert, *The Holocaust*, 590.

43. On the difficulties of surviving in the forest, see Yitzhak Arad, "Jewish Family Camps in the Forest: An Original Means of Rescue," in Yisrael Gutman and Ephraim Zuroff, eds., *Rescue Attempts during the Holocaust* (Jerusalem: Yad Vashem, 1974), 333ff. See also Kazimierz Iranek-Osmecki, *He Who Saves One Life* (New York: Crown Books, 1971), 60ff.

44. For the murder of Pauvlavicius, see the testimony of Miriam Krakinowski, quoted in Gilbert, *The Holocaust*, 702–3. See p. 711 on the killing of Jews after liberation.

45. Baron, "The Historical Context of Rescue," 18.

46. Ibid.

47. Much of this information was provided by Mordecai Paldiel, interview with author. Cf. Iranek-Osmecki, *He Who Saves One Life*, 250ff.; Peter Hellman, *Avenue of the Righteous* (New York: Atheneum, 1980), 28–29, 137ff.; Joseph Kermish, "The Activities of the Council for Aid to Jews (Zegota) in Occupied Poland," in Gutman and Zuroff, eds., *Rescue Attempts*, 379–82. The blackmailing/informing situation was also appalling in Berlin. See Leonard Gross, *The Last Jews in Berlin* (New York: Touchstone, 1982). In general, Jews throughout Europe were vulnerable to informants.

48. Tec, *When Light Pierced the Darkness*, 47.

49. For examples, see Gilbert, *The Holocaust*, 200, 479. Rewards appear to have been publicized widely on the brink of Nazi actions against Jews.

50. Tec, *When Light Pierced the Darkness*, 42.

51. For examples, see Gilbert, *The Holocaust*, 360, 408, 492.

52. Quoted in Gilbert, *The Holocaust*, 407.

53. Mietek Eichel, "Warsaw and After," quoted in Schwarz, ed., *The Root and the Bough*, 287.

54. See Birch and Rasmussen, *Bible and Ethics in the Christian Life*, ch. 5.

55. An illuminating discussion of this terrifying reality can be found in Tec, *When Light Pierced the Darkness*, ch. 2.

56. Testimony of Victoria Shyapeltoh, in Gilbert, *The Holocaust*, 203.

57. Gilbert, *The Holocaust*, 509.

58. Meir Peker, "In the Bielsk Ghetto and the Camps," quoted in Gilbert, *The Holocaust*, 490–91.

59. Pinchewski, "Rosa's Journey," 298.

60. Quoted in Gilbert, *The Holocaust*, 545. For such behavior in Lithuania, see Sarah Neshamit, "Rescue in Lithuania during the Nazi Occupation (June 1941–August 1944)," in Gutman and Zuroff, eds., *Rescue Attempts*, 316. For an example from France, see Hellman, *Avenue of the Righteous*, 137. For another example from Poland, see Iranek-Osmecki, *He Who Saves One Life*, 253.

61. Sholom Aleichem, *In the Storm*, trans. Aliza Shevrin (New York: New American Library, [1917] 1984), 205.

62. Ochs, "The Dark Clouds," 25. Cf. Iranek-Osmecki, *He Who Saves One Life*, 259–60.

63. See Gilbert, *The Holocaust*, 360 (Hrubieszow); 383 (Nesvizh); 429 (Rembertow). Sometimes Jews were robbed when they jumped from deportation trains. See Iranek-Osmecki, *He Who Saves One Life*, 261.

64. Testimony, Eichmann Trial, May 4, 1961, quoted in Gilbert, *The Holocaust*, 193.

65. *Webster's New Collegiate Dictionary* (Springfield, Mass.: Merriam-Webster, 1979).

66. Tec, *When Light Pierced the Darkness*, 40; Hilberg, *Destruction of the European Jews*, 308.

67. Hilberg, *Destruction of the European Jews*, 308.

68. Tec, *When Light Pierced the Darkness*, 34. For other examples from the Polish setting, see Iranek-Osmecki, *He Who Saves One Life*, 130. For direct quotations of Gentiles from a research study, see Oliner, *Altruistic Personality*, 140.

69. Kammer, "Winter in the Forest," 155–56.

70. Yaffa Eliach, *Hasidic Tales of the Holocaust* (New York: Vintage Books, 1982), 53–55.

71. Testimony of Rivka Yosselevska, Eichmann Trial, May 8, 1961, quoted in Gilbert, *The Holocaust*, 421–25.

72. M. J. Feigenbaum, "Life in a Bunker," in Schwarz, ed., *The Root and the Bough*, 144.

73. For an interesting quotation to this effect from a Gentile, see Oliner, *Altruistic Personality*, 187.

74. Gilbert, *The Holocaust*, 403.

75. Mordecai Paldiel, interview with author. See also Joseph Lichten, Foreword, in Iranek-Osmecki, *He Who Saves One Life*, ix; Iranek-Osmecki, 130–31; Hellman, *Avenue of the Righteous*, 24.

76. Corrie ten Boom, *The Hiding Place* (New York: Bantam Books, 1971), 99.

77. Sofia Nalkowska, "At the Railroad Tracks," in Glatstein, ed., *Anthology of Holocaust Literature*, 361–63.

78. Many Jews who passed as Christians during the Holocaust have experienced severe identity problems since. This was illustrated by a workshop entitled "Who Am I, Christian or Jew?" offered at the first "Hidden Child Conference," New York, May 1991.

79. For a discussion of this situation in Lithuania, see Neshamit, "Rescue in Lithuania during the Nazi Occupation," 314–15.

80. Tec, *When Light Pierced the Darkness*, 97.

81. Nechama Tec, *Dry Tears: The Story of a Lost Childhood* (New York: Oxford Univ. Press, 1984).

82. This is the position taken by Tec, *When Light Pierced the Darkness*, 89, and according to Mordecai Paldiel (personal interview with author) is the stance of Yad Vashem as well.

83. Quoted in Gilbert, *The Holocaust*, 492.

Chapter 4: The Righteous Gentiles

1. One account of the babies is in Elie Wiesel, *Night* (New York: Bantam, [1958] 1982), 30. Concerning the women, see Renee Fersen-Osten, *Don't They Know the World Stopped Breathing?* (New York: Shapolsky Publishers, 1991), 176.

2. This partial list of general factors affecting the possibility of rescue is influenced by Fein, *Accounting for Genocide*, 31–49, and Baron, "The Historical Context of Rescue," 13–21.

3. The terms "relief" and "rescue" will be used here, as in the literature, to delineate two distinct but clearly overlapping aspects of helping activities during the Holocaust. In common parlance, "rescue" is the stronger term, referring to acts freeing a person or persons from imminent danger. Yet no Jew in Nazi Europe was genuinely free from danger; only acts enabling Jews to leave occupied lands altogether would constitute rescue in the customary sense. "Relief" generally denotes temporary measures to aid persons in need, such as the provision of food and medical supplies to a drought-stricken area. Most historians consider the plight of the European Jews to have been so extreme that any act taken to aid Jews was a form of rescue, even if it could not *free* Jews from danger. The rescue of Jews was built brick-by-brick upon daily acts of relief, rescue in the full sense not becoming a reality until Jews had lived to see the end of the Nazi occupation. In keeping with this judgment, my usage of the terms will recognize their overlap. For discussions of this question, see Dalia Ofer, "The Activities of the Jewish Agency Delegation in Istanbul in 1943," in Gutman and Zuroff, eds., *Rescue Attempts*, 444–45; cf. Lucien Steinberg, "Jewish Rescue Activities in Belgium and France," in *Rescue Attempts*, 603.

4. A question that seems not to have been resolved is whether Jews who rescued Jews should be counted among the "rescuers" and the "righteous." At the May 1991 "Hidden Child" conference the problem was evident. Whereas Gentile rescuers were feted uniformly and on several occasions, "Jewish rescuers" were honored only once, and the appropriateness of this was questioned privately by several conference participants. It appears that the problem lies in the assumption that Gentiles who risked their lives for Jews performed an extraordinary deed for a different people, whereas Jews who saved fellow Jews did what was only natural. Yet numerous Gentile rescuers refused to draw a "peoplehood" boundary between themselves and Jews and described their deeds as "the natural thing to do." See Tom Tugend, "Coping with Goodness," *Hadassah* (November 1990), 18.

5. The effectiveness of Jewish self-help efforts during the Holocaust is an enormously touchy subject, one which cannot be discussed further here. One fine treatment of the inner workings particularly of Eastern European Jewish communities during the Holocaust is found in Dawidowicz, *The War Against the Jews*, Part 2. As well, the effectiveness of the rescue attempts made by various international Jewish organizations is also a painful subject in the intra-Jewish Holocaust literature. Among the organizations involved in rescue efforts were the World Jewish Congress (WJC), the American-Jewish Joint Distribution Committee (the "Joint" or JDC), the *Halutzim* (Zionist pioneers), the "Rescue Committee" of the Jewish Agency (representing Jews in Palestine), and the Hebrew Sheltering and Immigrant Aid Society

(HIAS-HICEM). Self-appointed individuals from abroad also were a factor. These organizations and individuals worked in conjunction with one another and with local Jewish and non-Jewish bodies involved in relief and rescue work. The lack of unity in these rescue attempts and the rivalries among the groups is blamed by many observers for their relative lack of success. See several articles in Gutman and Zuroff, eds., *Rescue Attempts*. See also Yahil, *The Holocaust*, chs. 20 and 21.

6. On the French and Belgian resistance and rescue organizations, see Steinberg, "Jewish Rescue Activities in Belgium and France," 603ff. One unique aspect of Belgian resistance was the successful armed attack on an April 1943 convoy, the twentieth carrying Jews to their deaths in the east. Several hundred Jews were saved. Cf. Philip Friedman, *Their Brothers' Keepers* (New York: Holocaust Library, [1957] 1978), 69–70.

7. On the French groups see Michael R. Marrus and Robert O. Paxton, *Vichy France and the Jews* (New York: Schocken Books, 1983); Anny Latour, *The Jewish Resistance in France (1940–1944)*, trans. Irene R. Ilton (New York: Holocaust Library, 1981); Emil C. Fabre, ed., *God's Underground* (St. Louis: Bethany Press, 1970); Ernst Papanek and Edward Linn, *Out of the Fire* (New York: Morrow, 1975); Joseph Ariel, "French-Jewish Resistance to the Nazis," *Judaism* 18, no. 3 (Summer 1969), 299–312. On the Belgian groups, see Friedman, *Their Brothers' Keepers*, 68–71; Anna Sommerhausen, *Written in Darkness* (New York, 1946). For information on the Dutch groups, see Werner Warmbrunn, *The Dutch under German Occupation, 1940–1945* (Stanford: Stanford Univ. Press, 1963). On Zegota, see Kermish, "The Activities of the Council for Aid to Jews (Zegota) in Occupied Poland," 367–98, in Gutman and Zuroff, eds., *Rescue Attempts*, and Yisrael Gutman, "The Attitude of the Poles to the Mass Deportations of Jews from the Warsaw Ghetto in the Summer of 1942," in *Rescue Attempts*, 399ff., especially 413–14. (See also the minutes of the discussion that followed those presentations, 451–59.) Both Kermish and Gutman criticize the overly enthusiastic discussion of Zegota and of Polish help generally by the Polish writer Iranek-Osmecki, *He Who Saves One Life*; see especially ch. 6. Another well-known Polish account is provided by Wladyslaw Bartoszewski and Zofia Lewinowna, *The Samaritans: Heroes of the Holocaust* (New York: Twyne Pubs, 1970). Zegota makes an interesting case study. Its work was organized into seven departments—the categories are illuminating: material aid (money to Jews in hiding), legalization (false papers), children (placement in homes and institutions), medical (care for hidden Jews), housing (hiding places), propaganda (nurturing Polish sympathy and help for Jews), and action against blackmail (shaming, threats of death to blackmailers). Though Zegota was by no means a grand success and was always hampered by lack of serious funding from the Polish government-in-exile, one can see in its history and even in the organization and structure of its work the superior potential inherent in organized rescue groups over the scattered efforts of individuals or small networks. Adolf Berman, Secretary-General of Zegota, claimed that the organization aided six thousand Jews in Warsaw and through its branches in other Polish cities. Gutman and Zuroff, eds., *Rescue Attempts*, 454.

8. Among the church groups participating in rescue were the Protestant CIMADE in France, Caritas Catholica in Germany, headed by the honored rescuer Dr. Gertrud Luckner, and various Catholic monastic orders. Many other religious

individuals, congregations, communities, and groups participated on their own or in broader resistance or rescue movements. Several examples of such activity will be discussed herein. Religion as a motivating factor for rescue will be discussed in chs. 5 and 6. See Marrus and Paxton, *Vichy France and the Jews*; Philip Hallie, *Lest Innocent Blood Be Shed* (New York: Harper and Row, 1979); Sam Waagenar, *The Pope's Jews* (LaSalle, Ill.: Alcove, 1974); Alexander Ramati, *The Assisi Underground* (New York: Stein and Day, 1978); H. D. Leuner, *When Compassion Was a Crime* (London: Oswald Wolf, 1966); Sybil Milton, "The Righteous Who Helped Jews," in A. Grobman and D. Landes, eds., *Genocide: Critical Issues of the Holocaust* (Los Angeles: Simon Wiesenthal Center, 1983), 284.

9. The activities of the Red Cross are discussed in Meir Dworzecki, "The International Red Cross and Its Policy vis-à-vis the Jews in the Ghettos and Concentration Camps in Nazi-Occupied Europe," in Gutman and Zuroff, eds., *Rescue Attempts*, 71–110.

10. Hellman, *Avenue of the Righteous*, 16. The Dutch rescuer Marion Pritchard records that the Dutch also reacted to the imposition of the yellow star on Jews by giving up their seats on trolley cars as a sign of respect and sympathy. "A *Moment* Interview with Marion Pritchard," *Moment* 9, no. 1 (December 1983), 26.

11. B. A. Sijes, "Several Observations concerning the Position of the Jews in Occupied Holland during World War II," in Gutman and Zuroff, eds., *Rescue Attempts*, 548. Marion Pritchard records that her twelve-year-old brother and his friends were among those Dutch people who wore yellow stars in protest. Pritchard, "It came to pass in those days . . . ," *Sh'ma* 14 (April 27, 1984), 98. Such acts occurred in other countries, but both in Holland and elsewhere the Nazis swiftly crushed any public signs of resistance.

12. Oliner, *Altruistic Personality*, 51–52.

13. This is the case in the memoir by Jacqueline Wolf, *"Take Care of Josette":
A Memoir of Occupied France* (New York: Franklin Watts, 1981), 27–28. When Mr. Wolf, Jacqueline's father, was called into the French armed forces, and Mrs. Wolf was forced by the Nazis to give the family business to a Gentile, a Gentile friend (Marie Collins) stepped in to help take care of the children while Mrs. Wolf began a new job requiring extended absences from the home.

14. Oliner, *Altruistic Personality*, 50.

15. One such grocer was the German Robert Jerneitzig. This Berliner defied Nazi regulations by allowing the Jew Hella Riede to shop outside of the allowed hours; then when this became impossible he took food to her apartment and often did not charge for it; he also arranged with her to get some food after the store closed. When the mass deportations threatened Hella and her husband in 1943, it was Jerneitzig who arranged for their hiding place. Gross, *The Last Jews in Berlin*, 57. On the other hand, Wolf, *"Take Care of Josette,"* 38, tells the story of a shopowner of long acquaintance who did the reverse, humiliating her mother when she tried to buy one item a few minutes after the Jewish shopping curfew expired. Given such restrictions and humiliations, those Gentiles who shopped on behalf of Jews performed a real service.

16. Bribes to ransom Jews were sometimes successful even at the height of the Holocaust. According to Gross, ministers from the Church of Sweden regularly

managed to bribe SS officials into releasing Jews—in the heart of the Reich, Berlin. *The Last Jews in Berlin*, 193.

17. Abraham Margaliot, "The Problem of the Rescue of German Jewry During the Years 1933–1939," in Gutman and Zuroff, eds., *Rescue Attempts*, 264–65.

18. The rescue-via-emigration possibilities available to a single determined and creative individual are exemplified by the activities of the Dutchwoman Gertrud Wijsmuller-Meyer, who is credited with the rescue of ten thousand Jewish children. In 1938, when the escape of several thousand Jewish children to Great Britain hinged on German cooperation, she traveled to Vienna and spoke with Adolf Eichmann himself—garnering a collective exit visa for six hundred of these children. In August 1939, mere weeks before the German invasion of Poland, she traveled to Danzig and organized fifty transports of Jews to Holland and Belgium. During the war, she engaged in many of the relief and rescue activities described in this chapter— providing escort, finding hiding places, providing false papers, even bringing food to the transit camp Gurs in France. Edward Lynne, "Brave Lady from Holland," *Jewish Observer and Middle East Review* 16, no. 16 (April 21, 1967), 9.

19. Oliner, *Altruistic Personality*, 62–63.

20. Gross, *The Last Jews in Berlin*, 200.

21. Quoted in Gilbert, *The Holocaust*, 74–75. Tragically, the British tightened restrictions on legal Jewish emigration to Palestine at precisely the moment of greatest need.

22. Margaliot, "The Problem of the Rescue of German Jewry," 265. Henry Huttenbach has documented the frustrated attempt of the Jews of Worms to emigrate from Germany in 1938 and 1939. Of the 191 Jews who had not left the country by the winter of 1941, only five Jews can be classified as having remained in Germany voluntarily. Huttenbach, "The Emigration of Jews from Worms (November 1938– October 1941): Hopes and Plans," in Gutman and Zuroff, eds., *Rescue Attempts*, 266–88.

The story of the German Jews Fritz and Marlitt Croner makes for an instructive case study. After witnessing Kristallnacht in Berlin, Fritz Croner reversed his plans and decided that he and his wife must emigrate immediately. After much standing in line he managed to obtain visas to Palestine through the Aliya office and booked passage. They shipped most of their possessions to Palestine and deposited much of their money in an Amsterdam bank (to avoid confiscatory Nazi emigration charges). On March 20, 1939, the Croners were told to take a train to Marseilles where they would board an illegal transport to Palestine. Two hours later another caller told them that there was no room on that transport. All other efforts were fruitless; they were trapped in Berlin, ultimately among the few who survived the war there. See Gross, *The Last Jews in Berlin*, 27–28.

One unexpected haven for Jews at this time and later was Shanghai, under Japanese control, in which some seventeen thousand German Jews were welcomed. Some two thousand Polish Jews made it to Kobe, Japan, through Siberia, between 1940 and 1941. Of these, one thousand could not find another country willing to take them in, so the Japanese allowed them to go to Shanghai as well. All told, eighteen thousand Jews survived with Japan's acquiescence and help. The strange circumstances behind these developments are described by David Kranzler, "How

18,000 Jews Survived the Holocaust While Europe Burned," *Jewish Life*, vol. 1 (new series), (1975), 29–39.

23. Neutral Turkey is rarely mentioned in popular discussions of the rescue of Jews, but as the only neutral country near the eastern and southeastern parts of Europe, it was inevitable that Jews would make considerable efforts to escape to Turkey. Those who managed to do so often went ahead and settled in nearby Palestine. For example, it is estimated that some three thousand Greek Jews were smuggled to Palestine via Turkey by Greek partisans. Steven Bowman, "Jews in Wartime Greece," *Jewish Social Studies* 48, no. 1 (Winter 1986), 56. The Rescue Committee of the Jewish Agency of Palestine responded to the opportunity by establishing an office in Istanbul. See Dalia Ofer, "The Activities of the Jewish Agency Delegation," 435–50.

24. One of the few pleasant turns of events in the terrible story of the Holocaust was the behavior toward Jews of the Italian political and military authorities and the population. Italian authorities resisted vigorous German entreaties to deport their Jews, and this attitude extended to zones of Italian military occupation in southern France, Yugoslavia, Greece, and Albania. Consequently, Jews flooded Italian-occupied zones. Local army commanders generally allowed Jews to cross into Italian territory. In one remarkable story, Italian occupation authorities acted to protect Jews in occupied Croatia, against the wishes of many in the local population, the fascist Croatian government, and Germany itself. Their actions saved between 2,500 and 3,000 Jews. The story of one of those Jews is told by Ivo Herzer, "How Italians Rescued Jews," *Midstream* 29, no. 6 (June/July 1983), 35–38. For an extended historical overview, see Daniel Carpi, "The Rescue of Jews in the Italian Zone of Occupied Croatia," in Gutman and Zuroff, eds., *Rescue Attempts*, 465–507. The realization that Italian behavior toward Jews during the Holocaust ranks with the best was slow in developing. Eugene Fisher, "Faith in Humankind: Rescuers of Jews during the Holocaust," 636–37. Systematic studies of this matter include Leon Poliakov and Jacques Sabille, *Jews under the Italian Occupation* (New York: Howard Fertig, 1983), and Susan Zuccotti, *The Italians and the Holocaust* (New York: Basic Books, 1988).

25. For two first-hand accounts of what was involved in making the harrowing illegal exodus to the south, see Fersen-Osten, *Don't They Know the World Stopped Breathing?*, 25–31, and Wolf, *"Take Care of Josette,"* 23–25.

26. An illuminating first-hand account of negotiations with passeurs is offered in Fersen-Osten, *Don't They Know the World Stopped Breathing?*, 38–43. In this account, the negotiations break down because of Fersen-Osten's father's unwillingness to leave his elderly mother behind, and the unwillingness of the passeurs to take her through the treacherous Pyrenees mountains. Cf. Friedman, *Their Brothers' Keepers*, 55. Wolf, in *"Take Care of Josette,"* 37, refers with contempt to those who, having promised to get Jews into Spain, took them up into the Pyrenees, robbed them, and left them stranded there. Fraudulent passeurs are also described in Hellman, *Avenue of the Righteous*, 137.

27. See the extended profile of Laporterie in Hellman, *Avenue of the Righteous*, 118ff. A border-crossing network operating out of a family-owned cafe, involving several people on both sides of the border, is remembered fondly in Wolf, *"Take*

Care of Josette," 57–63. One Gentile who lost her life because of such activities was twenty-three-year-old Marianne Cohn. Arrested by the Nazis while smuggling a group of Jewish children from France into Spain, Cohn was given the opportunity to go free in exchange for abandoning her charges to the Nazis. She refused to do so, and was executed by firing squad on July 8, 1944. Friedman, *Their Brothers' Keepers,* 188.

28. Jacqueline Wolf's family was a single day away from flight to Vichy France and then a planned trip to North Africa when her parents were taken by the Gestapo. *"Take Care of Josette,"* 37. Haim Avni documents this evaluation of the desirability of each situation in his "The Zionist Underground in Holland and France and the Escape to Spain," in Gutman and Zuroff, eds., *Rescue Attempts,* 562. For the Zionists, of course, Palestine was the ultimate goal.

29. Avni, "The Zionist Underground in Holland and France," 555–90. Avni says that the international Jewish groups involved included the Joint Distribution Committee, the Jewish National Fund (JNF), the World Jewish Congress, and the Rescue Committee of the Jewish Agency. Again, coordination and cooperation among these groups was a problem. See also Marie Syrkin, *Blessed Is the Match: The Story of Jewish Resistance* (New York: Jewish Publication Society, 1976); Steinberg, "Jewish Rescue Activities in Belgium and France," 603ff.

30. Arieh Bauminger, *The Righteous,* 3d ed. (Jerusalem: Yad Vashem, 1983), 50–52. Wilhemina Westerweel, Joop's wife, was also caught, tortured, and sent to Ravensbruck. She survived the war. See also Friedman, *Their Brothers' Keepers,* 65–66.

31. Avni, "The Zionist Underground in Holland and France," 584.

32. Bauminger, *The Righteous,* 39–41. Cf. Friedman, *Their Brothers' Keepers,* 55–59; Fernande Le Boucher, *The Incredible Mission of Father Benoit* (New York: Doubleday, 1969).

33. On the role of Georg Duckwitz, see Moshe Bejski, "The Righteous among the Nations and Their Part in the Rescue of Jews," in Gutman and Zuroff, eds., *Rescue Attempts,* 640–42. Cf. "German Who Saved Danish Jewry," *Israel Digest* 14, no. 8 (April 18, 1971), 5.

34. On Anna Christensen, see Bauminger, *The Righteous,* 30–33; on the rescue generally, see Harold Flender, *Rescue in Denmark* (New York: Simon and Schuster, 1963); Leni Yahil, *The Rescue of Danish Jewry, Test of a Democracy,* trans. Morris Gradel (New York: Jewish Publication Society, 1969); Aage Bertelsen, *October '43* (New York: Putnam, 1954); Peter Freuchen, *Vagrant Viking* (New York: 1953); Friedman, *Their Brothers' Keepers,* 149–58; Poul Borchsenius, "The Rescue of the Danish Jews," *Jewish Spectator* 34, no. 6 (June 1969), 7–10. About nine hundred Jews were also smuggled into Sweden from Norway, where resistance to anti-Jewish measures was also strong, despite Quisling. See Bauminger, *The Righteous,* 64–66, for the story of Inge Sletten, a Norwegian who managed to get fourteen Jewish children into Sweden. Sweden received Jewish refugees from several different directions. For an account of Sweden's activities, see Steven Kolbik, *The Stones Cry Out: Sweden's Response to the Persecution of the Jews* (New York: Holocaust Library, 1988). Trenchant commentary on the significance of the actions of these Scandinavian nations is offered by Trude Weiss-Rosmarin, "Heroism and Martyrdom," *Jewish Spectator* 38, no. 3 (March 1973), 2–4.

35. The smuggling activity of the Church of Sweden in Berlin is reconstructed in Gross, *The Last Jews in Berlin*, ch. 23 and elsewhere. Indeed, the book is an important source of information about the relief and rescue activities on behalf of the Berlin Jews, some examples of which are used throughout this chapter. Another testimony to rescue activity in Berlin is noted in Moshe Bejski, "The Righteous Among the Nations," 640.

36. However, at least by the second half of the war Spain was in practice permitting Jews to cross the border. Political considerations were paramount here, as Spain and Portugal both were surrounded by Allied forces on three sides by the end of 1942 and had to take their wishes seriously. Not that the Allies were demanding border privileges for Jews—what was demanded was access to Spain and then on to North Africa for the thousands of young Frenchmen streaming there to join the Free French forces. In agreeing not to block this flow of people, Spain effectively had to permit entrance to all who sought it, including Jews. See Haim Avni, "The Zionist Underground in Holland and France," 556.

37. Bejski, "The Righteous Among the Nations," 645–46. On Switzerland's policies toward Jews during the war, see Alfred Haesler, *The Lifeboat Is Full: Switzerland and the Refugees, 1933–1945* (New York: Funk and Wagnalls, 1969).

38. Bejski, "The Righteous Among the Nations," 646–47. Cf. Harry Ezratty, "The Consul Who Disobeyed," *Jewish Digest* 13, no. 12 (September 1968), 54–56.

39. The German invasion of Poland marked the beginning of disaster for Polish Jewry. Gentiles who helped Polish Jews in the first stage of anti-Jewish measures (prior to ghettoization) often began by providing or locating temporary shelter during the Nazi arrival in various Polish towns and villages, or during Nazi and collaborator killing sprees. The hidden Jews needed to be fed and cared for. At other times, Gentiles warned Jews of imminent disaster, providing them time to flee or to find or build a temporary hiding place. Some Gentiles discouraged their neighbors from collaborating with the German killers; others demonstrated sympathy for Jews or protested directly to the Germans, very risky acts. As random and then systematic expropriation developed, some Gentiles helped Jews sustain life. Occasionally, a Pole directly saved Jews from death; in one story from Bialystok, a Polish porter saved several Jews from a synagogue in which they were being burned alive. Gilbert, *The Holocaust*, 160. Gentiles also helped Jews to flee to the east, providing food and other necessities for some of the 300,000 Jews making this desperate move. Non-Jews as well as Jews in eastern Poland and further east provided food and shelter for these fleeing Jews.

40. The Nazis and their anti-Jewish predecessors struggled long and hard to define who was a Jew (see ch. 2). Ultimately, Nazi Germany defined a Jew as any person with even a single Jewish grandparent. Yet complexities abounded, and exceptions to anti-Jewish clauses were made in certain cases. For example, Jews married to German women were exempt from deportation; when the Nazis rounded up some of these men in Berlin, their wives successfully protested, and the men were released—a rare coup in totalitarian Germany. (A small number of women and children were also released as a result of this so-called "Rosenstrasse 2–4 Protest.") See "Women's Resistance to Gestapo to Be Commemorated in Stone," *The Week in Germany* (March 13, 1992), 7. The specifics of anti-Jewish legislation,

including the technical definition of who was a Jew, varied from country to country during the war. In any case, certain categories of Jews were "privileged," treated as if they were not Jewish. Jews attempting to "pass" sometimes could do so by successfully assuming the identity of one in the privileged category. On the definition of Jews, see Dawidowicz, *The War Against the Jews*, 59–60, as well as nearly every work on the Holocaust. The Dutch rescuer Marion Pritchard describes efforts to have Jews declared "privileged" in "It came to pass in those days," 99.

41. Some of the sources that form the basis for the following account include Wolf, *"Take Care of Josette"*; Fersen-Osten, *Don't They Know the World Stopped Breathing?*; Friedman, *Their Brothers' Keepers*; Hallie, *Lest Innocent Blood Be Shed*; Gross, *The Last Jews in Berlin*; Hellman, *Avenue of the Righteous*; Bauminger, *The Righteous*; ten Boom, *The Hiding Place*; Tec, *When Light Pierced the Darkness*; Zamoyska-Panek, *Have You Forgotten?*; Oliner, *Altruistic Personality*, as well as numerous articles, conference lectures, and personal conversations, all listed in the bibliography.

42. These were the documents required of Berlin Jews. See Gross, *The Last Jews in Berlin*, 32. Some configuration of "papers" akin to this list was established throughout Nazi Europe.

43. On the involvement of officials of the Church of Sweden in producing false church documents, see Gross, *The Last Jews in Berlin*, 203–4. The production and authentication of false religious documents was a ubiquitous part of the relief and rescue work of ministers and church groups, a central contribution such groups could make to Jewish survival. Examples can be cited from all over Europe. So too, unfortunately, can examples be cited of church officials cooperating with the Nazis in providing confirmation of Aryan/Christian identity or especially the lack thereof, which meant death.

44. Besides those mentioned elsewhere, government officials willing to produce and distribute false papers were particularly helpful. Numerous figures in the Belgian bureaucracy, for example, did such work. See Friedman, *Their Brothers' Keepers*, 68, and Hellman, *Avenue of the Righteous*, 25. Zegota, the Polish rescue group, established a separate "legalization" department which produced thousands of false papers of a very high level of workmanship. Ingenious techniques for producing false papers are also described in Gross, *Last Jews in Berlin*, 194–95.

45. See Hellman, *Avenue of the Righteous*, 24. In Belgium, according to Hellman's sources, foreign-born Jews usually had to adopt a hiding strategy, whereas their native-born children could attempt to pass. For the situation in Poland, see Tec, *When Light Pierced the Darkness*, 40–52.

46. Kermish, "The Activities of the Council for Aid to Jews in Poland," 375. Tec, *When Light Pierced the Darkness*, 34. Mordecai Paldiel, interview with author.

47. Both Wolf, *"Take Care of Josette,"* and Fersen-Osten, *Don't They Know the World Stopped Breathing?*, describe the instruction in Roman Catholicism given to them in France. In Wolf, see esp. 84–85; Fersen-Osten, who spent most of the war years in a convent, refers to religious instruction throughout. For a tragic story of a Gestapo religious test of a six-year-old child, see Tec, *When Light Pierced the Darkness*, 35.

48. Tec, *When Light Pierced the Darkness*, 36–37; Paldiel, interview with author.

49. For a first-hand account from a physician who performed such operations, see Felix Kanabus, "Address at the J.N.F.," in Glatstein, ed., *Anthology of Holocaust Literature*, 392–95.

50. Tec, *When Light Pierced the Darkness*, 38–39.

51. Ibid., 34.

52. This agonizing process is well exemplified in the story of the Belgian Jew Abram Lipski's decision to ask a single woman named Henriette Chaumat to raise his three-year-old son, Raffi, as her own. Chaumat agreed without hesitation and saved the child's life. See Hellman, *Avenue of the Righteous*, 27ff. Sometimes Jewish children were not handed directly to Gentile rescuers but were found abandoned. Hellman (170–267) gives a bittersweet account of the Polish rescuer Leokadia Jaromirska, a thirty-four-year-old woman who found a Jewish baby abandoned near her village by parents fleeing the liquidation of the Jewish ghetto in Legionowo. Accepting an enormous risk, she took the child in, had her baptized, and raised her as her own, despite strong suspicions on the part of her neighbors that the child was Jewish. Jaromirska sacrificed enormously to keep herself and the beloved child Bogusia alive throughout the remainder of the war, which they both barely survived. The story is bittersweet because Bogusia's father, who survived the Holocaust, tracked his daughter down and ultimately took her away to Palestine.

53. Jacqueline Wolf offers a delightful account of life with her rural French rescuers, the Lassalas family. See *"Take Care of Josette,"* 78ff. The stories of the raising of Raffi Lipski by Henriette Chaumat (Belgium) and of the little girl Bogusia by Leokadia Jaromirska (Poland) are also illuminating. See Hellman, *Avenue of the Righteous*. In the latter case, it becomes apparent how basic parenting problems such as the need for child care were exacerbated considerably when the child in question was a brand new arrival of suspicious origin. For a story of a Belgian priest (Hubert Celis) and his efforts to rescue several Jewish children through a "passing" strategy, see Alfred K. Allan, "The Priest Who Came to the Bar Mitzvah," *Reconstructionist* 34, no. 19 (Jan. 31, 1969), 20–24. A Dutch couple who raised two small Jewish children along with their own three young children is lauded by the father of one of the Jewish children in Werner Weinberg, "A Dutch Couple," *Christian Century* 100 (June 22–29, 1983), 611–15.

54. Henriette Chaumat, rescuer of Raffi Lipski, faced such gossip. See Hellman, *Avenue of the Righteous*, 31–34. She reports enduring it gladly, for if the neighbors believed that she had a new "love child," the real identity of the boy became even more safe from discovery. Marion Pritchard became the purported mother of three Jewish children during the war, accidentally registering two of these "births" within five months of each other. Pritchard, "It came to pass in those days," 100.

55. One rescuer whose name appears fairly often is Jeanne Daman-Scaglione, a Belgian schoolteacher. Early in the war, she had served as the principal of an underground school for Jewish children in Brussels. Later, she worked with the Jewish Defense Committee in Belgium to help place children in convents and with Christian families. See Friedman, *Their Brothers' Keepers*, 68–69, and Hellman, *Avenue of the Righteous*, xiii–xiv.

56. Wolf, *"Take Care of Josette,"* 34, indicates that at more than one stage in the war she was enrolled in private Catholic boarding schools under a false name—

and no one in the institution knew her true identity. In the case of Fersen-Osten, only the head of the Toulouse convent and the mother superior knew that she was Jewish. Fersen-Osten, *Don't They Know the World Stopped Breathing?*, 49.

57. Among the many stories documenting these rescue efforts, see Ramati, *The Assisi Underground*. In this dramatic instance, Franciscan monks in Assisi placed many Jews in local convents and monasteries, where they were taught how to pass as Catholics. Orthodox monasteries and convents also helped Jews. Bauminger, *The Righteous*, 84ff., tells the story of Olga and Dragica Bartulovic, Yugoslav partisans who provided false papers and helped a Jewish woman to pass as an Orthodox Christian in the Marian convent in the city of Split. Though it will not be discussed specifically below, it should be noted that convents, monasteries, seminaries, and churches also served regularly as temporary or even permanent *hiding* places as well as *passing* locations. See the story of the rescue of one hundred Jews in the Italian village of Nonantola in Bauminger, 56–59. The head of the theological seminary there hid a number of children in the seminary itself, after a year of caring for them in other ways, and before helping them escape to Switzerland on false papers. This case illustrates the fluid, changeable nature of the relief and rescue activities needed at different points in the war.

The story of Mother Maria of Paris (Elizabeth Skobtsova), a twice-divorced Russian woman who had become a nun, is also instructive. Mother Maria used a small convent in Paris to hide Jews who were on their way to more secure hiding places. This was only a small portion of her multifaceted rescue operation. Taking leadership of a rescue organization established by Greek Orthodox priests, Mother Maria collected food and clothing for Jews in the Drancy camp outside Paris, presided over the production of false documents, and established contact with other groups to facilitate rescue. Both she and her son Yuri were murdered by the Nazis. Friedman, *Their Brothers' Keepers*, 30–32. Schulweis, "Remember the Righteous Redeemers," 66–67. Her helping activities continued even in Ravensbruck, until her death. See p. 89.

58. The Dutch rescuers Joop and Wilhelmina Westerweel at one point had rented three apartments in their name for Jews to live in. Bauminger, *The Righteous*, 50.

59. The Jews were Kurt and Hella Riede, their rescuers Joseph and Kadi Wirkus. Gross, *The Last Jews in Berlin*, 59. Hellman, *Avenue of the Righteous*, 72ff., tells the lovely story of the rescue of twenty-three-year-old Nurit Hegt by Frisian villagers in the town of Ferwerd. Friesland appears to have been a particularly hospitable location in which to pass or to hide, due to its remoteness and other logistical blessings, but also because of the strong local sympathy for Jewish refugees among the devout Christian Frisians (see ch. 6).

60. See the story of Ida Altman, a Belgian Jew helped by Leopold Ros, who appointed her supervisor of a summer school and provided false documentation to enable her to pass as a Gentile. The arrangement was not permanent, but was one stage in the help Ros offered to Altman during the war. Bauminger, *The Righteous*, 18–20.

61. Gross, *The Last Jews in Berlin*, 113.

62. Dozens of instances of Gentiles taking Jews in for a night and then forcing them to leave appear in the literature. The daily and nightly bombings of Berlin

after the middle of 1943 cost many hiding places. Jews who after much trouble had managed to find good passing (or hiding) arrangements often lost them to these raids. As well, Jews were not wise to go to public bomb shelters during air raids, because the ubiquitous Gestapo checked documents even there. See Gross, *The Last Jews in Berlin*, 152ff.

63. Ibid., 113.

64. Tec, *When Light Pierced the Darkness*, 74, confirms this observation with regard to her research in Poland.

65. *Anne Frank: The Diary of a Young Girl* (New York: Washington Square Press, [1947] 1967). A memoir by one of the people who helped to hide the Frank family, Miep Gies, is *Anne Frank Remembered* (New York: Simon and Schuster, 1987). Corrie ten Boom tells her story in the famous *The Hiding Place*.

66. For example, Kermish indicates that the "housing" department of Zegota was not very successful in comparison with its other departments. See "The Activities of the Council for Aid to Jews in Poland," 377.

67. Ten Boom, *The Hiding Place*, 85–88, tells of the work of a "Mr. Smit," a brilliant architect and member of the underground, who designed the famous "hiding place" in the ten Boom home with the assistance of a small army of carpenters, plasterers, painters, and other workers.

68. Each of the hiding places mentioned in this list appears in the memoirs of Jewish survivors. Cf. Oliner, *Altruistic Personality*, 75–76. Jacqueline Wolf and her four-year-old sister Josette were saved from a Gestapo raid by hiding in a trench dug under a manure pile for just such an occasion. See Wolf, *"Take Care of Josette,"* 53–54. A detailed account of the transformation of an attic into a permanent hiding place is found in Hellman, *Avenue of the Righteous*, 35–36. The Polish Jew Felix Zanman and four others were hidden for some five hundred days in a five-by-three-by-four-foot hole. Testimony given on "Sixty Minutes," 1991. The Polish rescuer Alex Roslan built a hiding place for his eight-year-old Jewish charge Jacob Gilot under his kitchen sink. This saved the boy's life during a Nazi raid. Michael Halperin, "He Who Saves One Life," *Moment* 6, no. 7 (July/August 1981), 39. On Roslan, see also notes 85 and 87. One Polish Jew, Fania Paszht, was hidden, successively, in the flue of a country oven, a cellar, a chicken coop, and an attic, where she was forced to lie down for four months. Each of these hiding places was in different homes; fearful rescuers, Gestapo raids, and informants forced the moves. "The Rescue of Fania Paszht," translated from the Yiddish by Abraham Ingber (her son), *Moment* 11, no. 5 (May 1986), 48–49.

69. Stories from Holland, France, and even a few from Poland indicate that some villages and neighborhoods banded together informally to save Jews. The most famous instance of this phenomenom is the now well-known story of Le Chambon, the small French Huguenot community which cooperated to save several thousand Jews. See Hallie, *Lest Innocent Blood Be Shed*. The newly documented rescue activities of the people in the Cévennes region were a similar phenomenon. See Philippe Joutard, editor, *Cévennes: Terre de Réfuge, 1940–1944* (Presses de Languedoc, 1990). A summary of the activities of the villagers of these two regions is offered in Pamela Oline, "Rescuing the Hidden Story," *Books and Religion* 18, no. 2 (Summer 1991), 4ff. For more on these rescue activities, see chapter 6. Another

story from France concerns the village of Haut-Biol. The entire little village knew that the Argoud family had taken in two young Jews, yet no one ever disclosed their presence to the Germans who scoured the area looking for Jews. David Bedein, "The Righteous of Haut-Biol," *Israel Scene* 6, no. 15 (December 1985), 20–21. In one village in Holland (Nieuwlande), every single family concealed at least one Jew, despite the lack of any formal organization. See Bejski, "The Righteous among the Nations," 633. Iranek-Osmecki reports that in the Polish village of Osiny, the peasants agreed collectively to shelter a Jewish girl, taking turns so that all would share the responsibility and thus none would tell the Germans. For this and other stories, see *He Who Saves One Life*, 59–60. In such marvelous milieus, those hiding Jews could be a little less careful in the degree to which Jews were kept out of sight.

70. Gross, *The Last Jews in Berlin*, 224–27, tells the harrowing story of a raid on the apartment of the rescuer, Maria Countess von Maltzan ("Marushka") and her Jewish lover, Hans Hirschel. In preparation for just such a day, Maltzan had rigged up a daybed into which Hans could climb rapidly on the arrival of the Gestapo. Every morning, she put a fresh glass of water and a cough suppressant inside the daybed. On the day of the Gestapo raid, the hiding place worked. Gestapo agents looking directly at the daybed and attempting to open it did not discover Hans. Both Hans Hirschel and Maltzan survived the war in Berlin. Compare Block and Drucker, *Rescuers*, 153–57. Several accounts indicate that rescuers feared that their small children, not knowing any better, would disclose the presence of Jews to their neighborhood friends. Thus some rescuers hid their Jews from their own children, only allowing them freedom of movement around the house when the children were out or asleep. See Hellman, *Avenue of the Righteous*, 35. A Roman Catholic family dealt with this fear by every night making their children stand before a crucifix and promise not to tell anyone about the people living with them. B. A. Sijes, "Several Observations concerning the Position of the Jews in Occupied Holland," 551.

71. Renee Fersen-Osten and her older sister were saved from sure death because a Gentile woman routinely kept them at night when they were home from the convent on breaks; one night, their apartment was raided and her parents were taken, but the Gestapo did not find the children. See *Don't They Know the World Stopped Breathing?*, 79–81.

72. Ten Boom, *The Hiding Place*, 104–6.

73. Gross, *The Last Jews in Berlin*. Croner's survival strategy varied, like that of many other Jews. Sometimes he passed, other times he hid. Another hiding Jew who managed to stay employed was the Belgian engineer Abram Lipski. Though Lipski's Gentile employer was forced to dismiss him from his job at a rubber factory, he continued to employ Lipski clandestinely throughout the war. The income earned was crucial in keeping the Lipski family alive. Hellman, *Avenue of the Righteous*, 35–36.

74. Steinberg, "Jewish Rescue Activities in Belgium and France," 607. Steinberg also documents the swirl of high-level activity on behalf of Jews in Belgium. Leading banks, social and cultural institutions, hospitals, asylums, monasteries, and schools provided money, hiding places, and other help. Around twenty-five thousand Jews survived the war in Belgium.

75. One beloved rescuer who did this kind of work was an illiterate, poor Lithuanian named Bronius Gotautas, a devout Catholic who lived on the grounds of the local monastery. Gotautus transformed his job of delivering religious literature into an opportunity to deliver food to the needy and to Jews in hiding. He also got involved in the work of smuggling false papers and finding hiding places for Jews. Neshamit, "Rescue in Lithuania during the Nazi Occupation," 315.

76. For example, Leokadia Jaromirska, the Polish rescuer of a year-old infant, traveled five hundred miles round-trip to Cracow *every weekend* to barter stolen goods for food. She also clandestinely purchased extra coal for heat, walking long distances with sixty-five pounds of it on her back. Hellman, *Avenue of the Righteous*, 180–81. For another such story, see Iranek-Osmecki, *He Who Saves One Life*, 55.

77. Kermish, "The Activities of the Council for Aid to Jews," 377. Zegota established a special medical section for this purpose. Cf. Tec, *When Light Pierced the Darkness*, 36.

78. For a stunning story illustrating this problem, see Tec, *When Light Pierced the Darkness*, 76–77.

79. Pritchard, "It came to pass in those days," 101. Also on Pritchard, see "A *Moment* Interview with Marion Pritchard," 25–31.

80. See Gross, *The Last Jews in Berlin*, 221; Hellman, *Avenue of the Righteous*, 23–24. In the latter case, the Belgian Jews Abram and Tanya Lipski spent their first twelve days underground moving desperately from place to place, staying no more than a night or two at any single location.

81. Iranek-Osmecki, *He Who Saves One Life*, 49.

82. This story is told in Bauminger, *The Righteous*, 67ff. Shmulek (Samuel) Oliner, a twelve-year-old Polish Jew, was hidden by a friendly Gentile peasant named Balwina after escaping the Bobowa ghetto. Assessing his looks and command of the Polish language, she decided that his best hope for survival was to pass as a Gentile. After several days of instruction in the Catholic catechism and written Polish, he went off to work for a family several miles away. He survived the war and is the coauthor of the major text on the Righteous Gentiles, *The Altruistic Personality*. See pp. xvi–xvii. Numerous other stories of rescue by hiding are available in the literature, far more than can be incorporated into this chapter. See Bauminger, 45–48 for a story from Greece, as well as the longer article by Bowman, "Jews in Wartime Greece"; Iranek-Osmecki, *He Who Saves One Life*, 52–57, for the hiding experiences of the Jews Ludwig Hirszfeld, Bernard Goldstein, and Oskar Pinkus. See Neshamit, "Rescue of Jews in Lithuania during the Nazi Occupation," 289–332, for several stories of Lithuanians who hid Jews.

83. Oliner, *Altruistic Personality*, xvi. Cf. Iranek-Osmecki, *He Who Saves One Life*, 124.

84. One Lithuanian couple who performed this service was Antanas and Marija Macineviciene. They also brought food to the nearby Kovno ghetto to their friend Chana Brava, whose possessions they were guarding. See Neshamit, "Rescue in Lithuania during the Nazi Occupation," 301–2.

85. Alex Roslan, the Warsaw Pole, was one who did this kind of work. See Halperin, "He Who Saves One Life," 38. See also note 87.

86. See Friedman, *Their Brothers' Keepers*, 113; Iranek-Osmecki, *He Who Saves One Life*, 125.

87. Engineering escapes from the ghettos was an important and extremely dangerous form of rescue work. Before the ghettos were sealed, some Gentiles managed to slip false papers, money, and a change of clothes to Jews, who then had a chance of simply walking out of the ghetto passing as Poles. After the ghettos were sealed, escapes were even more difficult. The best chance was to escape with the labor brigades that exited and entered the camps every day. The help of a sympathetic labor boss or employer who allowed Jews to escape saved many lives. Escapes were facilitated on a humanitarian basis by concerned individuals. A few escapes were the work of relief and rescue groups. Paid smugglers and those guards and soldiers open to bribes facilitated escape on a for-profit basis. See Kermish, "The Activities of the Council for Aid to Jews," 375–76, 399.

Alex and Mela Roslan are much-honored rescuers. Alex Roslan, spirited through an underground tunnel into the Warsaw ghetto in 1943 by a friend, became determined to rescue some Jewish children after seeing their wretched condition. He managed to smuggle eight-year-old Jacob Gilat out of the ghetto; later, younger brothers Shalom and David followed. Jacob and David Gilat survived to the end of the war in the Roslans' care; Shalom Gilat died of scarlet fever. Alex Roslan was the subject of a 1991 segment of "60 Minutes." Their story is also told by Halperin, "He Who Saves One Life," 37–41; in the 1979 Anti-Defamation League film *Avenue of the Just*; by Harold M. Schulweis, "In Praise of Good People," 16; and by Block and Drucker, *Rescuers*, 186–91.

88. One extraordinary arms smuggler was Anna Borkowska, mother superior of a convent near Vilna. She and several other nuns scoured the countryside searching for knives, guns, bayonets, hand grenades, and so on, delivering what they found to the ghetto. The convent became a place of refuge for Jewish underground and partisan leaders like Abba Kovner and Abraham Sutzkever. Many children were saved as well. The activity and the passionate support of these nuns on behalf of the Vilna Jews is remembered fondly in several memoirs and accounts. See Sutzkever, "Never Say This is the Last Road," in Schwarz, ed., *The Root and the Bough*, 66–94. Friedman, *Their Brothers' Keepers*, 26–27; Tec, *When Light Pierced the Darkness*, 140; Schulweis, "Remember the Righteous Redeemers," 66.

89. Gentiles who would not return the valuables entrusted to them appear to have been legion. Cf. Wolf, *"Take Care of Josette,"* 51–52. Gentiles who attempted to pry these possessions loose on behalf of their rightful owners took a real risk and performed a valuable service.

90. Bauminger, *The Righteous*, 60–63. See also Friedman, *Their Brothers' Keepers*, 21–25; Neshamit, "Rescue in Lithuania during the Nazi Occupation," 303–4; Levin, "On the Relations Between the Baltic Peoples and Their Jewish Neighbors," 58. A moving personal tribute offered by a Vilna survivor is Dina Abramowicz, "Anna Simaite, Lifeline to the Ghetto," *Keeping Posted* 24, no. 2 (October 1978), 15–18.

91. One tragic story illuminating both the possibility and the difficulty of escape from Drancy is found in Wolf, *"Take Care of Josette,"* 51–52, 74–76. The author, a fourteen-year-old at the time, received a letter from her father while he and her mother were interned at Drancy in 1942. The letter instructed her to retrieve the family valuables, hidden with various Gentile friends, and to send the proceeds to him at the camp via a Gentile intermediary. With this money he hoped to "buy

their freedom" by bribing a German, which others had done. Most of the Gentile friends named in the letter denied having been given valuables; further, the money that was sent to the intermediary never reached the author's father. In a note thrown out of a cattle-car on the way to Poland and death—the final communication between Jacqueline and her father—he reproached her for not following his instructions. Wolf writes: "It was impossible for anyone to console me after I read that letter. My parents thought that I had deserted them. I was suffocating in guilt . . . they left believing that I had failed them."

92. The German civilian contractor Heinrich (Fritz) Graebe became involved in rescuing Jews after hearing of and then actually seeing a mass killing in the Dubno area of Ukraine. His eyewitness account of that killing is one of the most moving statements to come out of the war. (See Noakes and Pridham, *Nazism*, 1100–1101.) Graebe requisitioned Jews for work and established an underground escape route through Ukraine. See Schulweis, "In Praise of Good People," 16; Rittner and Myers, *The Courage to Care*, 38–43. A full-length account is provided by Douglas Huneke, *The Moses of Rovno* (New York: Dodd, Mead, 1985).

93. Bauminger, *The Righteous*, 71–74. Some Gentiles purposely worked their way into the labor camps so that they could help Jews there. One such story is told in Tec, *When Light Pierced the Darkness*, 73–74. This latter story also illuminates the importance of helping persecuted Jews sustain the will to live.

94. An example of what the energetic diplomat could do was the work of the famed Raoul Wallenberg, whose remarkable efforts saved over thirty thousand Jews. See Bauminger, *The Righteous*, 78–81; John Bierman, *Righteous Gentile* (New York: Viking Press, 1981), among other sources. An illuminating memoir of the Jewish situation in Hungary from the Jewish side is Bela Ungar, "Surviving in Nazi Hungary," *Jewish Spectator* 34, no. 6 (June 1969), 18ff. This account is especially helpful in demonstrating the strenuousness of Jewish efforts at self-help. A less well known but amazing story from Hungary at this time is the tale of Giorgio Perlasca, an Italian who ended up representing Spain in the chaotic Hungary of late 1944 and managed to save perhaps ten thousand lives. Michael Ryan, "A Simple Deed with Awesome Power," *Parade* (August 19, 1990), 4–7.

95. Arieh Bauminger, *The Righteous*, 13–17. Later, when the Plaszow camp was sealed and his workers prevented from leaving, an action that presaged their annihilation, Madritsch bribed SS leaders to get permission to reopen his workshops in the Plaszow camp itself. When Plaszow was destroyed in August 1944 and its inmates sent to concentration camps, Madritsch and a helper enabled a few to escape to safer camps. He was arrested in November 1944 but survived the war. A more famous rescuer-industrialist was Oskar Schindler, who, besides treating his Cracow Jewish workers well, successfully undertook similar efforts to save them when the ghetto was liquidated. Later, he followed this rescue with extraordinary measures to save both his workers and their wives and children (from Auschwitz) as the collapsing Reich pulled the men toward Germany. His cunning and courageous efforts saved some 1,200 Jews. Bejski, "The Righteous Among the Nations," 642–45. A historical novel telling Schindler's story is Thomas Keneally, *Schindler's List* (New York: Penguin Books, 1983). Steven Spielberg's 1993 film by the same name also tells Schindler's story. The film dominated that year's Academy Awards

and did much to raise public awareness of the Righteous Gentiles. Another German factory owner who helped Jews (in Bialystok) in wide-ranging ways was Otto Busse. See Yehuda Bauer, *A History of the Holocaust* (New York: Franklin Watts, 1982), 287.

96. On Reviczky, see Bauminger, *The Righteous*, 53–55. Cf. Katherine M. Ruttenberg, "A Righteous Gentile," *Jewish Spectator* 48, no. 2 (Summer 1983), 60–61. A political official who helped Jews was the Rumanian Traian Popovici, whose story is told in Bauminger, 75–78. Mayor of the city of Cernauti, Popovici vigorously opposed the ghettoization, murder, and deportation of Rumanian Jews, in public and in letters to his superiors. In October 1941, Popovici managed to protect twenty thousand Jews from expulsion by persuading higher Rumanian authorities to spare certain groups from deportation, mainly professionals. He also added thousands of names to official lists of exempted Jews.

The rescue of fifty thousand Bulgarian Jews is an important and dramatic story, one of whose leading personae is Dimitur Peshev. Vice-president of the Bulgarian parliament (the Sobranie), Peshev countermanded the order to deport the Jews of Bulgaria. But the Jews were not out of danger yet, as the Germans continued to press for their deportation. Peshev's continued protest and opposition were joined by leading figures in the Bulgarian Orthodox Church and among the intelligentsia. Public opinion as a whole opposed the deportations. Though dismissed from his post, Peshev played a crucial role in successfully preventing the deaths of these Bulgarian Jews. See Frederick P. Chary, *The Bulgarian Jews and the Final Solution, 1940–1944* (Pittsburgh: Univ. of Pittsburgh Press, 1972). See also Dawidowicz, *The War Against the Jews*, 388–89.

There were some Germans among those officials who helped Jews. Oliner, *Altruistic Personality*, 110–11, indicates that the behavior of German officials, police, and soldiers toward Jews was not uniform; "good Germans" appear in many rescuer accounts. One "righteous" German official was Eberhard Helmrich, an official in the economic department of the occupation forces in East Galicia (Poland). From early in the occupation Helmrich used all of his authority to sustain Jewish life and even to rescue particular Jews. In Drohobycz, he kept the Jewish hospital supplied with food when most patients in such hospitals were starving to death. In Hyrawka, he ordered underlings to treat Jews decently and to overlook any food taken by Jews. He helped a Jewish woman escape, even hiding her in his own office apartment for two weeks. And he saved other Jewish girls by sending them (under false papers) back to Germany as household help and paying their way. Bauminger, *The Righteous*, 42–44.

A German soldier who helped Jews was Richard Abel. Abel freed five Tunisian Jewish children who were about to be shot for trying to escape Nazi-occupied Tunis. Abel provided the children with food, maps, arms, and directions. "German Soldier Who Saved Jews," *Jewish Observer and Middle East Review* 21, no. 45 (November 10, 1972), 9. Several German and Austrian soldiers were sentenced to death for smuggling weapons and other items to the Jewish resistance at Bialystok. A leading figure in these activities was Otto Busse. Milton, "The Righteous Who Helped Jews," 285. Two German policemen who helped facilitate rescue in Berlin are described in Gross, *The Last Jews in Berlin*, 208–9. Numerous Italian policemen helped rather than hunted Jews. For example, Giovanni Palatucci, chief of police in Fiume, paid for his deeds with death at Dachau. Milton, "The Righteous Who Helped Jews," 284.

97. Bauminger, *The Righteous*, 25ff. Dr. Adelaide Hautval, a French physician imprisoned in Auschwitz for showing sympathy to Jews, was another Gentile who used her relatively privileged position in the camp to take care of sick Jewish women and protect her charges from the gas chambers. She also refused to assist Nazi doctors in their experiments on women. Her story is told in Bejski, "The Righteous Among the Nations," 638–39. An account of an interview with Hautval is Hallam Tennyson, "Protestant Heroine of Auschwitz," *Jewish Digest* 18, no. 3 (December 1972), 50–52.

98. Bauminger, *The Righteous*, 34–37.

99. Some rescuers sought to cling to a more familiar ethic while doing their underground work. For example, Corrie ten Boom's devout sister-in-law, Nollie, as well as her children, refused to lie to the Nazis when asked a direct question about the location of some young men in hiding. Fortunately, the young men were not discovered, but the situation precipitated a bitter argument. *The Hiding Place*, 90–92.

Chapter 5: Many Paths to Righteousness

1. The studies that will receive the most attention here include the following, listed basically in the order in which they appeared: Philip Friedman, "Righteous Gentiles in the Nazi Era," in *Roads to Extinction*, 409–21; *Their Brothers' Keepers*. Friedman, a historian, appears to have been the first scholar to address the question of rescuer motivations. Perry London, "The Rescuers: Motivational Hypotheses about Christians Who Saved Jews from the Nazis," in Jacqueline Macauley and Leonard Berkowitz, eds., *Altruism and Helping Behavior* (New York: Academic Press, 1970), 241–50. A psychologist, London and his associates at the Institute for Righteous Acts (founded by Harold Schulweis) interviewed twenty-seven rescuers and forty-two rescued Jews between 1962 and 1965. This brief but influential article reports the results of the team's never-completed research project. Manfred Wolfson, "Zum Widerstand gegen Hitler: Umriss eines Gruppenporträts deutscher Retter von Juden," in *Tradition und Newbeginn: Internationale Forschungen Deutscher Geschichte im 20. Jahrhundert* 26 (1975), 391–407. Wolfson's research project included seventy Germans who had helped Jews during the Holocaust. Douglas Huneke, "A Study of Christians Who Rescued Jews during the Nazi Era," *Humboldt Journal of Social Relations* 9, no. 1 (Fall/Winter 1981/82), 144–50; Huneke, "The Lessons of Hermann Graebe's Life: The Origins of a Moral Person," in *The Moses of Rovno*, 177–87; Huneke, "Glimpses of Light in a Vast Darkness: A Study of the Moral and Spiritual Development of Nazi Era Rescuers," in *Remembering for the Future*, vol. 1 (New York: Pergamon Press, 1989), 486–93. Before his extensive work on the rescuer Hermann Graebe, Huneke undertook archival research as well as interviews with an undisclosed number of rescuers and rescued Jews. Huneke is a Presbyterian minister working in California. Stanley Coopersmith was a member of the research team at the Institute for Righteous Acts. He did not publish the results of his

research, but his findings are reported in Samuel P. Oliner, "The Need to Recognize the Heroes of the Nazi Era," *Reconstructionist* 48, no. 4 (June 1982), 7–14. Sarah Gordon, *Hitler, Germans, and the "Jewish Question"* (Princeton, N.J.: Princeton Univ. Press, 1984), 210–45. Gordon's project involves an analysis of Gestapo records in the Düsseldorf district concerning 203 Germans who aided Jews, forty-two who were critics of racial persecution, and thirty who were suspected of aiding Jews. In this study she also analyzes the files of 432 Germans who had or were suspected of having had sexual relations with Jews. Frances Henry, *Victims and Neighbors: A Small Town in Germany Remembered* (S. Hadley, Mass.: Bergin and Garvey, 1984); Henry, "Heroes and Helpers in Nazi Germany: Who Aided Jews?" *Humboldt Journal of Social Relations* 13, no. 1–2 (1986), 306–19. Henry, a Canadian anthropologist, studied a Bavarian community in which her grandparents had lived and from which they were deported to their deaths. Her research explores the actions of both rescuers and nonrescuers. Nechama Tec, *When Light Pierced the Darkness*; "Altruism during World War II," in A. Roy Eckardt and Alice Eckardt, editors, *Remembering for the Future*, vol. 1 (New York: Pergamon Press, 1989), 542–49. Tec interviewed thirty-one Polish rescuers and thirty-four rescued Jews, and wove into her account evidence from written accounts involving 565 rescuers. Eva Fogelman, "The Rescuers: A Socio-Psychological Study of Altruistic Behavior during the Nazi Era" (Ph.D. diss., City University of New York, 1987); Fogelman, "Behind Altruistic Behavior under the Nazis," paper presented at the Scholars Roundtable on Altruism under Nazi Terror, Princeton, March 1993. See also Fogelman and Valerie Lewis Wiener, "The Few, the Brave, the Noble," *Psychology Today* 19, no. 8 (August 1985), 60–65. Fogelman, a central figure in rescuer study through her work with the Jewish Foundation for Christian Rescuers (JFCR/ADL) and her own research, interviewed one hundred rescuers and an equal number of rescued Jews. Samuel Oliner and Pearl Oliner, *The Altruistic Personality*; Samuel Oliner, "The Unsung Heroes in Nazi Occupied Europe: The Antidote for Evil," *Nationalities Papers* 12, no. 1 (Spring 1984), 129–36; Pearl Oliner and Samuel Oliner, "Rescuers of Jews during the Holocaust: Justice, Care, and Religion," in A. Roy Eckardt and Alice Eckardt, *Remembering for the Future*, vol. 1 (New York: Pergamon Press, 1989), 506–16. See also several book reviews, listed in the bibliography. The Oliners interviewed 406 rescuers, 126 non-rescuers, and 150 rescued Jews, the largest and most significant rescuer study to date. Samuel Oliner is a sociologist, and Pearl Oliner is an education specialist. Eva Fleischner, "Catholics in France Who Saved Jews during the Holocaust"; Fleischner, "Can the Few Become the Many? Some Catholics in France Who Saved Jews during the Holocaust"; Fleischner, "The Memory of Goodness," in *Remembering for the Future*, vol. 3 (New York: Pergamon Press, 1989), 3159–63. Fleischner is a Roman Catholic professor of religion who interviewed forty-six French Catholic rescuers. Kristen Monroe et al., "Altruism and the Theory of Rational Action"; "John Donne's People: Explaining Differences between Rational Actors and Altruists through Cognitive Frameworks," *Journal of Politics* 53, no. 2 (May 1991), 394–433. Monroe is a political scientist who with a team of researchers interviewed thirteen Gentile rescuers as well as five "heroes" (as identified by the U.S. Carnegie Hero Commission), five philanthropists, five entrepreneurs, and five European nonrescuers of Jews during the Holocaust. Gay Block and Malka Drucker, *Rescuers*. Block, a biographer and children's book writer, and Drucker, a portrait photographer, interviewed (and photographed) 105 rescuers from eleven countries.

Several other studies and reflections offer helpful insight into why rescuers helped Jews. These include Frances Grossman, "A Psychological Study of Gentiles Who Saved the Lives of Jews during the Holocaust," in Israel Charny, ed., *Toward the Understanding and Prevention of Genocide* (Boulder, Co.: Westview Press, 1984), 202–15. Grossman, a New York psychotherapist, studied nine rescuers in depth, some in clinical settings. Research on the activities of the French village of Le Chambon should also be considered. This includes Hallie, *Lest Innocent Blood Be Shed*. Pierre Sauvage, producer and director, *Weapons of the Spirit* (1989); Sauvage, "A Most Persistent Haven: Chambon-Sur-Lignon," *Moment* 8, no. 9 (October 1983), 30–35; Sauvage, "Ten Things I Would Like to Know about Righteous Conduct in Le Chambon and Elsewhere during the Holocaust," in *Humboldt Journal of Social Relations* 13, no. 1–2 (1986), 252–59. Janusz Reykowski, "Cognitive and Motivational Prerequisites of Altruistic Helping: The Study of People Who Rescued Jews during the Holocaust," paper presented at the Scholars Roundtable on Altruism under Nazi Terror, Princeton, March 1993. Ute Klingemann, "The Study of Rescuers of Jews in Berlin: A Progress Report," paper presented to the Eighth Annual Scientific Meeting of the International Society of Political Psychology, Washington, June 1985. Ewa Kurek, "The Role of Polish Nuns in the Rescue of Jews, 1939–1945," paper presented at the Scholars Roundtable on Altruism under Nazi Terror, Princeton, March 1993. Other relevant works include Helen Fein, *Accounting for Genocide*; Bauer, *The Holocaust in Historical Perspective*, ch. 3; Bauer, *A History of the Holocaust*, ch. 12; Lawrence Baron, "Restoring Faith in Humankind," *Sh'ma* 14 (September 7, 1984), 124–28, and Baron, "The Holocaust and Human Decency: A Review of Research on the Rescue of Jews in Nazi Occupied Europe," *Humboldt Journal of Social Relations* 13, no. 1–2 (1986), 237–51; Elsebet Jegstrup, "Spontaneous Action: The Rescue of the Danish Jews from Hannah Arendt's Perspective," *Humboldt Journal of Social Relations* 13, no. 1–2 (1986), 260–84; Manus I. Midlarsky, "Helping during the Holocaust: The Role of Political, Theological, and Socioeconomic Identifications," *Humboldt Journal of Social Relations* 13, no. 1–2 (1986), 285–305; Henry L. Mason, "Testing Human Bonds within Nations: Jews in the Occupied Netherlands," *Political Science Quarterly* 99, no. 2 (Summer 1984), 315–43; Bauminger, *The Righteous*, 10–12; Bejski, "The Righteous among the Nations," 627–47; Milton, "The Righteous Who Helped Jews," 281–87; Robert McAfee Brown, "They Could Do No Other," in Rittner and Myers, eds., *The Courage to Care*, 142–47; Shlomo Breznitz, "The Courage to Care," in *The Courage to Care*, 148–54. Mordecai Paldiel, "Hesed and the Holocaust"; "The Altruism of the Righteous Gentiles," *Holocaust and Genocide Studies* 3, no. 2 (1988), 187–96; Paldiel, interview with author; *The Path of the Righteous* (Hoboken, N.J.: KTAV, 1993). Paldiel, director of the Department of the Righteous at Yad Vashem, offers encyclopedic knowledge of Yad Vashem's rescuer files, a critical reading of rescuer research and theory, and a theological interpretation of the rescuers' altruism.

2. Though in this chapter we will focus on Righteous Gentile research, this literature must be placed in the broader context of interdisciplinary, social scientific research on "altruism." An assessment of the vast altruism literature is beyond the

scope of this book; but I have found it necessary to survey the field during the course of the research, and some of these altruism studies will be cited in this chapter. The term "altruism" itself, which does not commonly appear in Christian ethics, was coined by Auguste Comte in 1851. It has been defined in various ways. One widely used definition has been offered by psychologists Jacqueline Macauley and Leonard Berkowitz: "Behavior carried out to benefit another without anticipation of rewards from external sources." *Altruism and Helping Behavior* (New York: Academic Press, 1970), 3. A fuller definition is provided by John Dovidio: "A special type of helping that involves favorable consequences for the recipient, an intent to help by the benefactor, no obvious external reinforcement, and a motivation directed toward the . . . goal of increasing the other's welfare." "Helping Behavior and Altruism: An Empirical and Conceptual Overview." In *Advances in Experimental Social Psychology*, ed. Leonard Berkowitz (New York: Academic Press, 1984), 366. A third definition is offered by Morton Hunt, who has noted that implicit in most discussion of altruism is some concept of *cost* to the altruist. Thus he offers a revised definition that includes this dimension. Altruism, then, is "behavior carried out to benefit another *at some sacrifice to oneself*, and without, or not primarily because of, the expectation of reward from external sources." *The Compassionate Beast*, p. 21 (emphasis added). The behavior of those classified by Yad Vashem as Righteous Gentiles clearly meets the standard set by any of these definitions. Indeed, most researchers consider the behavior of the Righteous Gentiles an extreme example of altruism, because *(a)* the costs (and potential costs) to these altruists were so high, *(b)* the behavior tended to be not a single deed but continued acts of kindness over months and years, *(c)* the deeds were often performed on behalf of total strangers, some of whom certain rescuers found personally objectionable. Though a Christian ethicist might prefer terms other than altruism to describe rescuer behavior, it will be employed here for convenience.

3. Hunt, *Compassionate Beast*, 109.

4. See Jerome Kagan et al., *Infancy: Its Place in Human Development* (Cambridge: Harvard Univ. Press, 1978); David Rosenhan, "The Natural Socialization of Altruistic Autonomy," in J. Macauley and L. Berkowitz, eds., *Altruism and Helping Behavior*; Carollee Howes and Robert Eldredge, "Responses of Abused, Neglected, and Non-Maltreated Children to the Behaviors of Their Peers," *Journal of Applied Developmental Psychology* 6, no. 2–3, 261–70.

5. Oliner, *Altruistic Personality*, 173 (cf. Table 7.1).

6. Grossman, "A Psychological Study," 214. See also Block and Drucker, *Rescuers*, 9.

7. Coopersmith, in Oliner, "The Need to Recognize the Heroes," 9. London ("The Rescuers," 249) reports that extraordinary family warmth or closeness does *not* show up as a pattern among his sample.

8. Oliner, *Altruistic Personality*, 178–83.

9. Grossman, "A Psychological Study," 212, 214; Fogelman, "The Rescuers," 86.

10. Oliner, *Altruistic Personality*, 182–83. An important study by Martin Hoffmann and Herbert D. Salzstein confirms the significance of the Oliners' finding here. Their research demonstrates that children who are reasoned with begin to

internalize the values the parents are trying to inculcate, while children who are disciplined via physical punishment or the withdrawal of love often perform the desired behavior but do not internalize the values. "Parent Discipline and the Child's Moral Development," *Journal of Personality and Social Psychology* 5, no. 1, 45–57.

11. Dan Olweus et al., eds., *Development of Antisocial and Prosocial Behavior* (New York: Academic Press, 1986); Lizette Peterson, "An Alternative Perspective to Norm-Based Explanations of Modeling and Children's Generosity," *Merrill-Palmer Quarterly* 28, no. 2, 283–90.

12. London, "The Rescuers," 247. But London takes care to argue that rescuers' parents were not *generally* better as role models, only in the area of setting a strong moral example (249).

13. Coopersmith in Oliner, "The Need to Recognize the Heroes," 9, 11.

14. Huneke, "Glimpses of Light in a Vast Darkness," 489; "A Study of Christians Who Rescued Jews," 146.

15. Fogelman, "The Rescuers," 84. See also Block and Drucker, *Rescuers*, 8. Monroe, on the other hand, while finding that most of her sample of rescuers cited a role model, finds that the nonaltruistic control group also cited a role model, and that the norms communicated were virtually the same. "Altruism and the Theory of Rational Action," 111.

16. Ten Boom, *The Hiding Place*, 28, etc. The learning-by-doing pattern is also noted in social psychology. See Ervin Staub, "A Conception of the Determinants and Development of Altruism and Aggression: Motives, the Self, and the Environment," in Carolyn Zahn-Waxler et al., eds., *Altruism and Aggression: Social and Biological Origins* (Cambridge: Cambridge Univ. Press, 1986).

17. Fogelman reports that tolerance was taught to 88 percent of her sample of rescuers. "The Rescuers," 84; Oliner, *Altruistic Personality*, 149–50. See also Block and Drucker, *Rescuers*, 8. On the other hand, Fleischner finds no universal correlation between family attitudes and rescuers' attitudes. Some rescuers, she says, "reacted against their family background," drawing upon other resources. "Can the Few Become the Many?", 242.

18. Oliner, *Altruistic Personality*, 149–51.

19. Ibid., 144.

20. Ibid., 164. Cf. Block and Drucker, *Rescuers*, 9.

21. Ibid., 165.

22. Ibid., 164.

23. Ibid., 292 (Table 6.7).

24. Coopersmith in Oliner, "The Need to Recognize the Heroes," 9; Huneke, "Glimpses of Light in a Vast Darkness," 489–91. Huneke develops the biblical language of "hospitality" nicely as his central motif in this area. Fogelman, "The Rescuers," 84.

25. Coopersmith in Oliner, "The Need to Recognize the Heroes," 9; Grossman, "A Psychological Study," 214; Fogelman, "The Rescuers," 85.

26. Oliner, *Altruistic Personality*, 161–63.

27. Huneke, "Glimpses of Light in a Vast Darkness," 491.

28. Fogelman, "The Rescuers," 209ff.

29. Oliner, *Altruistic Personality*, 181–82.

30. Paldiel, "The Altruism of the Righteous Gentiles," 191.

31. Ibid., 190–91.

32. Wolfson, "Zum Widerstand gegen Hitler," 396.

33. Henry, *Victims and Neighbors*, 104.

34. Gordon, *Hitler, Germans, and the "Jewish Question,"* 222.

35. Fogelman, "The Rescuers," 80–81.

36. Wolfson, "Zum Widerstand gegen Hitler," 396; Gordon, *Hitler, Germans, and the "Jewish Question,"* 220.

37. Henry, *Victims and Neighbors*, 104.

38. Friedman, *Their Brothers' Keepers*, ch. 1; "Righteous Gentiles," 414.

39. Fogelman, "The Rescuers," 200–201.

40. Sauvage, "Ten Questions," 255.

41. Henry, *Victims and Neighbors*, 104; Gordon, *Hitler, Germans, and the "Jewish Question,"* 224–37; Wolfson, "Zum Widerstand gegen Hitler," 399–400; Fogelman, "The Rescuers," 203; Oliner, *Altruistic Personality*, 129.

42. Fogelman, "The Rescuers," 202.

43. Tec, *When Light Pierced the Darkness*, 127–28.

44. Oliner, *Altruistic Personality*, 129. Bejski, on the other hand, finds a disproportionate number of rescuers from the lower classes. "The Righteous Among the Nations," 635.

45. Oliner, *Altruistic Personality*, 159.

46. Tec, *When Light Pierced the Darkness*, 128.

47. Ibid.

48. Ibid., ch. 6.

49. Wolfson, "Zum Widerstand gegen Hitler," 400; Fogelman, "The Rescuers," 202.

50. Tec, *When Light Pierced the Darkness*, 128.

51. Oliner, *Altruistic Personality*, 159–60.

52. Ibid., 289 (Table 6.4).

53. Ibid., 155–57 (cf. Table 6.5, 6.6, 6.7, 290–92).

54. Ibid., 291 (Table 6.6).

55. Sauvage, "Ten Questions," 254. Tec, *When Light Pierced the Darkness*, 145–49; Fleischner, "Catholics in France Who Saved Jews," 51ff. Oliner, *Altruistic Personality*, 156–57.

56. Huneke, "In the Darkness . . . Glimpses of Light: A Study of Nazi-Era Rescuers" (Report to the Oregon Committee for the Humanities: September 1980), 11–20, 25–38. See also the Oliners, discussed below.

57. Hunt, *Compassionate Beast*, 123. Many hundreds of studies have been undertaken to test the effect of disparate situational factors on altruism. Perhaps the most well-known concern is the "bystander effect." See Bibb Latané and John Darley, *The Unresponsive Bystander: Why Doesn't He Help?* (Englewood Cliffs, N.J.: Prentice-Hall, 1970).

58. Oliner, *Altruistic Personality*, 113–23.

59. Ibid., 123–27.

60. Cf. Coopersmith in Oliner, "The Need to Recognize the Heroes," 10–11; Fogelman and Wiener, "The Few, the Brave, the Noble," 65; Oliner, *Altruistic Personality*, 126–27.

61. Oliner, *Altruistic Personality*, 131–32.

62. Ibid., 125.

63. Ibid., 135, 137.

64. Coopersmith makes a similar suggestion in Oliner, "The Need to Recognize the Heroes," 11–12.

65. Oliner, *Altruistic Personality*, 140–41.

66. London, "The Rescuers," 245; Coopersmith in Oliner, "The Need to Recognize the Heroes," 11; Fleischner, "Catholics in France Who Saved Jews," 49–50. Tec, *When Light Pierced the Darkness*, 176. All point to the importance of having been asked to help, and the seeming randomness of this.

67. This definition is culled from what appear to be the working definitions of "personality" in the rescuer literature. Unfortunately, few formal definitions of the term are generally proposed. See Oliner, *Altruistic Personality*, 9–12.

68. See Rasmussen and Birch, *Bible and Ethics in the Christian Life*, 40–41; Richard Bondi, "Character," in *The Westminster Dictionary of Christian Ethics*, James Childress and John Macquarrie, eds. (Philadelphia: Westminster Press, 1986), 82–84; Stanley Hauerwas, *Character and the Christian Life* (San Antonio: Trinity Univ. Press, 1975); Alaisdair C. MacIntyre, *After Virtue*, 2d ed. (Notre Dame: Univ. of Notre Dame Press, 1984).

69. London, "The Rescuers," 245.

70. Huneke, "Glimpses of Light in a Vast Darkness," 489.

71. Fogelman, "The Rescuers," 212.

72. Oliner, *Altruistic Personality*, 184. Block and Drucker do find that some of their rescuers were particularly adventurous people. *The Rescuers*, 10.

73. London, "The Rescuers," 247–48.

74. Huneke, "A Study of Christians Who Rescued Jews," 146; "Glimpses of Light in a Vast Darkness," 489–90.

75. Tec, *When Light Pierced the Darkness*, 154.

76. Fogelman, "The Rescuers," 212.

77. Oliner, *Altruistic Personality*, 176, 306 (Table 7.8). Monroe, "Altruism and the Theory of Rational Action," 116, finds a mix of loners and socially well-integrated rescuers.

78. Paldiel, "The Altruism of the Righteous Gentiles," 191.

79. Tec, *When Light Pierced the Darkness*, 154–60. Tec also appears to have been guilty of suggesting to survivors that rescuers might have been "individualists," thus stimulating several of them to a retrospective interpretation conforming to her theory (158).

80. See Bauer, *A History of the Holocaust*, 286, *The Holocaust in Historical Perspective*, 62–63; Sauvage, "Ten Questions," 255–56; Hallie, *Lest Innocent Blood Be Shed*, 25; Milton, "The Righteous Who Helped Jews," 283–84. There is too much evidence for the importance of various kinds of social marginality to dismiss it entirely. Le Chambon and other evidence suggest the power of a cultivated "dangerous memory" of persecution and oppression, as well as the particular skills that are nurtured in communities that have learned the ways of resistance. See Sharon Welch, *Communities of Resistance and Solidarity* (Maryknoll, N.Y.: Orbis Books, 1985), ch. 3, and discussion here in ch. 6.

81. Oliner, *Altruistic Personality*, 173.

82. Ibid., 174. This is a more narrow finding than is common in social psychological research on the relationship between empathy and altruism. See Ervin Staub, *Positive Social Behavior and Morality*, vol. 1; *Social and Personal Influences* (New York: Academic Press, 1978), 54–55; Martin Hoffman, "Development of Prosocial Motivation: Empathy and Guilt," in Nancy Eisenberg, ed., *The Development of Prosocial Behavior* (New York: Academic Press, 1982); Nancy Eisenberg and Paul Miller, "The Relation of Empathy to Prosocial and Related Behaviors," *Psychological Bulletin* 101, 91–119. Huneke, "Glimpses of Light in a Vast Darkness," 490, describes his sample as having "sophisticated empathic imaginations." Empathy will be considered again in a later section.

83. Oliner, *Altruistic Personality*, 174.

84. Huneke, "Glimpses of Light in a Vast Darkness," 492; Tec, *When Light Pierced the Darkness*, 164–67; Monroe, "Altruism and the Theory of Rational Action," 112.

85. Oliner, *Altruistic Personality*, 327 (Table 9.3).

86. See Sauvage, "Ten Questions," 256–57; Monroe, "Altruism and the Theory of Rational Action," 121–22; Tec, *When Light Pierced the Darkness*, 167ff; McAfee Brown, "They Could Do No Other," 143–44; Block and Drucker, *Rescuers*, 9.

87. Coopersmith in Oliner, "The Need to Recognize the Heroes," 9–10; Huneke, "Glimpses of Light in a Vast Darkness," 490; Grossman, "A Psychological Study of Gentiles Who Saved Jews," 206–7; Fogelman, "The Rescuers," 87; Tec, *When Light Pierced the Darkness*, 160–64; Block and Drucker, *Rescuers*, 10. London does not confirm this finding—"The Rescuers," 249. The Oliners (*Altruistic Personality*, 177–78) find a strong sense of "personal efficacy" and "internal locus of control," but not self-esteem or independence. These distinctions may be too fine. Altruism researchers generally find a relation between high self-esteem and altruism. See Staub, "A Conception of the Determinants and Development of Altruism and Aggression," in Zahn-Waxler, *Altruism and Aggression*, 144–47.

88. Oliner, *Altruistic Personality*, 177.

89. Cf. London, "The Rescuers," 244; Hunt, *The Compassionate Beast*, 96ff; Robert E. Goodin, "Do Motives Matter?", *Canadian Journal of Philosophy* 19, no. 5 (September 1989), 405ff.

90. Bauminger, *The Righteous*, 11; Bejski, "The Righteous Among the Nations," 635; Friedman, "Righteous Gentiles," 411; Milton, "The Righteous Who Helped Jews," 283; Coopersmith in Oliner, "The Need to Recognize the Heroes," 10; Huneke, "Glimpses of Light in a Vast Darkness," 488–89; Grossman, "A Psychological Study," 215; Henry, *Victims and Neighbors*, 105–6; Fogelman, "The Rescuers," 146–61; Tec, *When Light Pierced the Darkness*, ch. 8; Fleischner, "Catholics in France Who Saved Jews," 50–51; Oliner, *Altruistic Personality*, 169; Monroe, "Altruism and the Theory of Rational Action," 116; Paldiel, "Hesed and the Holocaust," 92; Block and Drucker, *Rescuers*, 8.

91. Several researchers point to the motivating power of a philo-Semitic ideology among some rescuers. Because this was almost always theologically grounded, it will be discussed in the next chapter.

92. Oliner, *Altruistic Personality*, 275 (Table 5.1).

93. Ibid., 114–15; Grossman finds a similar pattern in "A Psychological Study," 215.

94. Tec, *When Light Pierced the Darkness*, 129–30.

95. Oliner, *Altruistic Personality*, 304.

96. Ibid., 304.

97. Ibid., 169.

98. Tec, *When Light Pierced the Darkness*, 132.

99. Fogelman, "The Rescuers," 147.

100. Paldiel, "Hesed and the Holocaust," 92.

101. The concept of partnership has not been well developed in Christian ethics. Letty Russell, in *The Future of Partnership* (Philadelphia: Westminster Press, 1979), demonstrates the value of partnership as a moral paradigm. She describes partnership as including "*commitment* that involves responsibility, vulnerability, equality, and trust among persons or groups who share a variety of gifts or resources; *common struggle* and work involving risk, continuing growth, and hopefulness in moving toward a goal transcending the group itself; *contextuality* in interacting with a wider community of persons, social structures, values, and beliefs that may provide support, correctives, or negative feedback" (18). Defined in this way, the concept of partnership nicely describes the moral situation characteristic of most rescue situations under discussion here. In particular, it is helpful in noting the two-sidedness of the rescuer/rescued relationship, the joint effort and pooling of resources, the terribly risky common goal being pursued—mutual survival despite the capital offense of attempting to save Jewish life—and the ferociously negative context in which these partnerships attempted to carry out their work.

102. Oliner, *Altruistic Personality*, 170.

103. Coopersmith in Oliner, "The Need to Recognize," 10; Oliner, *Altruistic Personality*, 136.

104. Baron, "Restoring Faith in Humankind," 127–28.

105. Crossan, "The Life of a Mediterreanean Jewish Peasant," *Christian Century* 108, no. 37 (December 18–25, 1991), 1194ff.

106. See, for example, Friedman, "Righteous Gentiles," 411; *Their Brothers' Keepers*, 86, 92; Henry, "Heroes and Helpers in Nazi Germany," 316.

107. See Gregory Baum, *Compassion and Solidarity* (New York: Paulist, 1990): "It is no exaggeration to say that . . . the solidarity of Christians [has been] confined to Christians" (13).

108. Friedman, "Righteous Gentiles," 411; M. Midlarsky, "Helping during the Holocaust," 291; Milton, "The Righteous Who Helped Jews," 283.

109. Bauer, *A History of the Holocaust*, 282.

110. M. Midlarsky, "Helping during the Holocaust," 291.

111. Friedman, "Righteous Gentiles," 411; Baron, "The Holocaust and Human Decency," 244; Tec, *When Light Pierced the Darkness*, 119–28.

112. London, "The Rescuers," 244; Paldiel, "Hesed and the Holocaust," 92. He calls this "induced altruism." Conformity as a motive for altruism has been explored in social psychology. See Janusz Reykowski, "Origin of Prosocial Motivation: Heterogeneity of Personality Development," in *Studia Psychologica* 22, no. 2, 91–106. This evidence counters or at least forces greater nuancing of the claim

that rescuers tended to be independent-minded and self-reliant. See Paldiel, "The Altruism of the Righteous Gentiles," 190.

113. Oliner, *Altruistic Personality*, 199.

114. See the criticism offered by James Fowler in his review essay, "The Psychology of Altruism," *First Things* 4 (June/July 1990), 48–49.

115. Huneke, "Glimpses of Light in a Vast Darkness," 488. See also McAfee Brown, "They Could Do No Other," 144–45.

116. Fein, *Accounting for Genocide*, 77; Milton, "The Righteous Who Helped Jews," 283; cf. Bejski, "The Righteous Among the Nations": "The dangers involved in helping Jews were in inverse proportion to the number of people in each country who were willing to do so" (634).

117. Bauminger, *The Righteous*, 11.

118. Fleischner, "Catholics in France Who Saved Jews," 52; cf. Grossman, "A Psychological Study," 214.

119. For both, see Fleischner, "Catholics in France Who Saved Jews," 52–53. McAfee Brown speaks of the importance of role models. "They Could Do No Other," 145–46.

120. Oliner, *Altruistic Personality*, 93.

121. See Fowler, "The Psychology of Altruism," 48–49.

122. In contrast, Monroe finds no evidence that group support was a significant factor for her sample of rescuers. "Altruism and the Theory of Rational Action," 112–13. However, her sample is so small as to limit its value considerably.

123. The development of Christian communities of this quality and character has begun to occupy considerable attention in Christian ethics. This has occurred across the theological and political spectrum. Consider Stanley Hauerwas, *A Community of Character*; Rasmussen and Birch, *Bible and Ethics in the Christian Life*; Sharon Welch, *Communities of Resistance and Solidarity*; Rosemary Radford Ruether, "Basic Communities: Renewal at the Roots," *Christianity and Crisis* 41 (September 21, 1981); Harvey Cox, *Religion in the Secular City* (New York: Touchstone, 1984); Alvero Barreiro, *Basic Ecclesial Communities* (Maryknoll, N.Y.: Orbis, 1982), as well as the entire literature emerging from the base Christian communities of Latin America and elsewhere.

124. Bejski, "The Righteous Among the Nations," 635; Milton, "The Righteous Who Helped Jews," 284; Friedman, *Their Brothers' Keepers*, 60ff; Huneke labels this category "subversive rescues." "Glimpses of Light in a Vast Darkness," 488; Henry, "Heroes and Helpers," 316; Fogelman, "The Rescuers," 162ff; Tec, *When Light Pierced the Darkness*, 120; Fleischner, "Catholics in France Who Saved Jews," 50; Oliner, *Altruistic Personality*, 144–49, 157–60; Paldiel, "Hesed and the Holocaust," 92; Block and Drucker, *Rescuers*, 8–9. In contrast, Monroe finds no evidence of this—"Altruism and the Theory of Rational Action," 112.

125. Oliner, *Altruistic Personality*, 149.

126. Friedman, *Their Brothers' Keepers*, 68 (Belgium), 74 (Italy), 146 (Finland), 149ff. (Denmark); Fein, *Accounting for Genocide*, 70; E. Jegstrup, "Spontaneous Action: The Rescue of the Danish Jews," 267; Bauer, *A History of the Holocaust*, 294–95.

127. Fein, *Accounting for Genocide*, 33; Jegstrup, "Spontaneous Action: The Rescue of the Danish Jews," 262ff. Mason points out, however, that the Nazis

succeeded in destroying the Dutch sense of solidarity with their Jewish fellow citizens, even though pre-war ties had been close. See "Testing Human Bonds Within Nations."

128. Friedman, *Their Brothers' Keepers*, 137ff (Lithuania). One German who resisted the Nazis on patriotic grounds was Dietrich Bonhoeffer. See Larry Rasmussen, *Dietrich Bonhoeffer—His Significance for North Americans* (Minneapolis: Fortress Press, 1990), ch. 2.

129. Oliner, *Altruistic Personality*, 157.

130. Tec, *When Light Pierced the Darkness*, 120; Fogelman, "The Rescuers," 162–71.

131. Oliner, *Altruistic Personality*, 159.

132. Bauminger, *The Righteous*, 11; Baron, "The Holocaust and Human Decency," 244; Friedman, "Righteous Gentiles," 418; *Their Brothers' Keepers*, 126. Tec offers a fairly extensive discussion of leftist rescue activities in Poland. See *When Light Pierced the Darkness*, 120–27.

133. See Welch, *Communities of Resistance and Solidarity* and *A Feminist Ethic of Risk* (Minneapolis: Fortress Press, 1989); Gregory Baum, *Compassion and Solidarity*; Johann B. Metz, *Faith in History and Society* (New York: Seabury Press, 1980).

134. Tec, *When Light Pierced the Darkness*, 145.

135. Fogelman, "The Rescuers," 132.

136. Oliner, *Altruistic Personality*, 155.

137. Block and Drucker, *Rescuers*, 8.

138. This correlates in a striking manner with the work of Karen Lebacqz, who grounds her approach to justice in the experience of injustice. *Justice in an Unjust World* (Minneapolis: Augsburg, 1987), Part 1.

139. Oliner, *Altruistic Personality*, 163–67.

140. The Oliners group 19 percent of their sample here. *Altruistic Personality*, 287 (Table 6.2). Fogelman's label is "ideological-moral rescuers," and she finds that 14 percent of her sample fit under that rubric. "The Rescuers," 111ff. See also Block and Drucker, *Rescuers*, 9.

141. This quote is taken from Susan B. Thistlewaite and Toinette M. Eugene, "A Survey of Contemporary Feminist, Womanist, and Mujerista Theologies," in Eldon Jay Epp, ed., *Critical Review of Books in Religion 1991* (Atlanta: Scholars Press, 1991), 1–20.

142. Oliner, *Altruistic Personality*, 168; Carol Gilligan, *In a Different Voice* (Cambridge: Harvard Univ. Press, 1982).

143. See Paul Lauritzen, "Emotions and Religious Ethics," *Journal of Religious Ethics* 16, no. 2 (Fall 1988), 307–24. Lauritzen takes the "constructivist" stance (vs. William James) that emotions are personally and socially constructed and not "a biologically basic and culturally invariant brute experience" (308). Thus he would likely reject my contrasting of emotional responses with cognitive or reasoned moral convictions. See also Beverly Wildung Harrison, "The Power of Anger in the Work of Love," in *Making the Connections* (Boston: Beacon Press, 1985), 3–21.

144. Transcript, *Avenue of the Just*.

145. Mordecai Paldiel offers a rich discussion of the concept of *hesed* (very similar to this cluster of attitudes and actions) as it is articulated in the Hebrew Bible and developed in the rabbinic tradition. See "Hesed and the Holocaust."

146. London points to this difficulty. See "The Rescuers," 244.

Chapter 6: Compelled by Faith

1. Eliezer Berkovits, *Faith After the Holocaust*, 41–42.
2. Quoted by Irving Greenberg, "Cloud of Smoke, Pillar of Fire," 11–12.
3. Tec, *When Light Pierced the Darkness*, 137.
4. Gilbert, *The Holocaust*, 445.
5. Tec, *When Light Pierced the Darkness*, 137.
6. Gilbert, *The Holocaust*, 714.
7. Sauvage, "Ten Things I Would Like to Know," 254.
8. Tec, *When Light Pierced the Darkness*, 148; "A Certain Kind of Christianity" was the key phrase of Nechama Tec's address at the "International Gathering of Children Hidden During World War II," May 26–27, 1991.
9. Baron, "The Holocaust and Human Decency," 244–45, and other articles and addresses; Fein, *Accounting for Genocide*, 114; Mason, "Testing Human Bonds Within Nations," 321; Fleischner, "Can the Few Become the Many?", 239; Donald Dietrich, *Catholic Citizens in the Third Reich: Psycho-Social Principles* (New Brunswick: Transaction Books, 1988), 270–71; Sauvage, "Ten Things I Would Like to Know," 254; Oliner, *Altruistic Personality*, 154–57; Hellman, *Avenue of the Righteous*, 86–91; ten Boom, *The Hiding Place*; Pieter De Jong, "Responses of the Churches in the Netherlands to the Nazi Occupation," in Michael D. Ryan, ed., *Human Responses to the Holocaust* (New York: Edwin Mellen Press, 1981), 121–41; Andre Stein, *Quiet Heroes* (New York: New York Univ. Press, 1988); Hallie, *Lest Innocent Blood Be Shed*; Paldiel, "The Altruism of the Righteous Gentiles," 191; Block and Drucker, *Rescuers*, 8.
10. Fleischner, "Can the Few Become the Many?", 239. Emphasis added.
11. Ibid., 239–40.
12. Quoted in Fein, *Accounting for Genocide*, 114.
13. De Jong, "Responses of the Churches in the Netherlands," 125.
14. Dietrich, *Catholic Citizens*, 270–71.
15. For the rescue efforts of the Reformed Christians of Le Chambon, see Hallie, *Lest Innocent Blood Be Shed*. The French Darbyites, members of a fundamentalist group, also receive attention in Hallie, 182ff. Paldiel mentions the Ukrainian Baptists and Hungarian Methodists in "The Altruism of the Righteous Gentiles," 191. On Ukrainian and Lithuanian Baptists, see also Bauer, *Holocaust in Historical Perspective*, 61–62. The philo-Semitism of the German Plymouth Brethren was brought to my attention by Erich Geldbach, personal conversation, October 1992. Interestingly, John Weidner, a well-known Seventh Day Adventist rescuer, also acted in part on this basis. See Block and Drucker, *Rescuers*, 8.
16. Oliner, *Altruistic Personality*, 154–55, 157.
17. Ten Boom, *The Hiding Place*, throughout. I recognize that this book is not unimpeachable as a primary historical source; but I still believe that its rendering of the nature of the religious faith of Corrie ten Boom and her family can generally be trusted. See Yaakov Ariel, "Jewish Suffering and Christian Salvation: The Evangelical-Fundamentalist Holocaust Memoirs," *Holocaust and Genocide Studies* 6, no. 1

(1991), 63–78. Compare Lawrence Baron, "Evangelical Converts, Corrie ten Boom, and the Holocaust," *Holocaust and Genocide Studies* 7, no. 1 (Spring 1993), 143–48.

18. *The Hiding Place*, 69.

19. Ibid., 74.

20. Ibid., 78.

21. See Stein, *Quiet Heroes*, 39–40; Hallie, *Lest Innocent Blood Be Shed*, 183.

22. John Calvin, *Commentary on Ezekiel* 16:61, quoted in M. Eugene Osterhaven, "Calvin on the Covenant," in Donald K. McKim, ed., *Readings in Calvin's Theology* (Grand Rapids: Baker Book House, 1984), 104.

23. Lawrence Baron first noted this in "Holocaust and Human Decency," 244. See also I. John Hesselink, "Christ, the Law, and the Christian: An Unexplored Aspect of the Third Use of the Law in Calvin's Theology," in McKim, *Readings in Calvin's Theology*, 179.

24. John Calvin, *Institutes of the Christian Religion*, 2.7.13.

25. One of the major Christian ethics textbooks of the past decade or so is *Mere Morality* by Lewis Smedes (Grand Rapids: Eerdmans, 1983). This book, written in the Reformed tradition, surveys Christian ethics by reflecting on the Decalogue. Smedes assumes the continuing validity of the Decalogue for Christians.

26. See Ruether, *Faith and Fratricide*, ch. 3; Littell, *The Crucifixion of the Jews*, ch. 2.

27. Osterhaven, "Calvin on the Covenant," in McKim, *Readings in Calvin's Theology*, 92–93.

28. Rubenstein, *After Auschwitz*, 56–58.

29. Ibid., 72.

30. Hallie, *Lest Innocent Blood Be Shed*; Sauvage, *Weapons of the Spirit*, "Ten Things I Would Like to Know," 255–57; Pamela Oline, "Rescuing the Hidden Story," *Books and Religion* 18, no. 2 (Summer 1991), 4–7, 11. While this section frequently will mention the well-documented rescue efforts in the French village of Le Chambon, Oline argues that rescue was occurring in some seventeen villages of the Plateau Vivarais-Lignon (not just in one of them, Le Chambon), and that French Protestants in the nearby but distinct Cévennes region were also undertaking significant rescue activities during the war. The activities of Catholic rescuers in the region also have been underreported. For these reasons, the famous rescue in Le Chambon needs to be placed into broader perspective. To do so by no means diminishes the importance of the events there. See also Philippe Joutard et al., eds., *Cévennes: Terre de Réfuge, 1940–1944* (Paris: Presses du Languedoc, 1990).

31. Bauer, *Holocaust in Historical Perspective*, 61–62.

32. Hallie, *Lest Innocent Blood Be Shed*, 97–98. Cf. G. A. Rothrock, *The Huguenots* (Chicago: Nelson Hall, 1979).

33. Hallie, *Lest Innocent Blood Be Shed*, 25–26.

34. Sauvage, *Weapons of the Spirit*.

35. Oline, "Rescuing the Hidden Story," 11. Another example of the Jewish plight being seen as paradigmatic of one's own is found in Hallam Tennyson, "Protestant Heroine of Auschwitz," 52.

36. Hallie, *Lest Innocent Blood Be Shed*, 54–55; Oline, "Rescuing the Hidden Story," 6.

37. Sauvage, "Ten Things I Would Like to Know," 254.

38. Oline, "Rescuing the Hidden Story," 6; Hallie, *Lest Innocent Blood Be Shed*, 182–83.

39. Hallie, *Lest Innocent Blood Be Shed*, 101.

40. Oline, "Rescuing the Hidden Story," 7; Fogelman, "The Rescuers," 135; ten Boom, *The Hiding Place*, 131; De Jong, "The Responses of the Churches in the Netherlands," 122, 133; Friedman, *Their Brothers' Keepers*, 71, 98–99; Fein, *Accounting for Genocide*, 114; Dietrich, *Catholic Citizens*, 275; Fleischner, "Can the Few Become the Many?", 238; F. G. Grossman, "A Psychological Study of Gentiles Who Saved the Lives of Jews during the Holocaust," 205; Hallie, *Lest Innocent Blood Be Shed*, 96–97, 101, 170–71; Ramati, *The Assisi Underground*, 56; Jegstrup, "Spontaneous Action: The Rescue of the Danish Jews from Hannah Arendt's Perspective," 266; James Patrick Kelley, "The Best of the German Gentiles: Dietrich Bonhoeffer and the Rights of Jews in Hitler's Germany," in A. Roy Eckardt and Alice Eckardt, eds., *Remembering for the Future*, vol. 1, 83; Allan, "The Priest Who Came to the Bar Mitzvah," 21.

41. Oline, "Rescuing the Hidden Story," 7; Rothrock, *The Huguenots*, 177.

42. Hallie, *Lest Innocent Blood Be Shed*, 167.

43. Ibid., 172.

44. Ibid.

45. Gross, *The Last Jews in Berlin*, 54ff., 100–101; Kelley, "Best of the German Gentiles," 83; Friedman, *Their Brothers' Keepers*, 92ff; Dietrich, *Catholic Citizens*, 268ff., on Catholic resistance; Chester L. Hunt, "A Critical Evaluation of the Resistance of German Protestantism to the Holocaust," in A. Roy Eckardt and Alice Eckardt, eds., *Remembering for the Future*, vol. 1, 248; transcript of *Avenue of the Just*, 8; Fleischner, "Catholics in France Who Saved Jews during the Holocaust," 52; De Jong, "Responses of the Churches in the Netherlands," 123ff.; Mason, "Testing Human Bonds within Nations," p. 321; Dietrich Bonhoeffer, *Ethics* (New York: Collier Books, 1986).

46. I am indebted to Charles C. West of Princeton Theological Seminary for this insight. Unpublished conference paper, March 1993.

47. The text of the Barmen Declaration is readily available. Here the source is Hubert G. Locke, ed., *The Church Confronts the Nazis: Barmen Then and Now* (Lewiston, N.Y.: Edwin Mellen Press, 1984), 19–25.

48. Eberhard Bethge, "Troubled Self-Interpretation and Uncertain Reception in the Church Struggle," in Franklin H. Littell and Hubert G. Locke, eds., *The German Church Struggle and the Holocaust* (Detroit: Wayne State Univ. Press, 1974), 167, reports that Barmen's main drafter, Karl Barth, came to regret this omission deeply.

49. Kelley, "Best of the German Gentiles." See esp. Bonhoeffer, *Ethics*, in which theological analysis of Nazism, the war, Germany's political and moral crisis, and so on, permeate the entire work.

50. Bonhoeffer, "The Church Facing the Jewish Question," quoted and discussed in Kelley, "Best of the German Gentiles," 84–86.

51. Ibid.

52. For a similar view of this controversial matter, see Kelley, "Best of the German Gentiles," 88–89.

53. De Jong, "Responses of the Churches in the Netherlands," 123.

54. Baron, "The Holocaust and Human Decency," 245.

55. De Jong, "Responses of the Churches in the Netherlands," 124–25.

56. Ibid., 123.

57. Ibid., 140–41. For a fuller discussion of Miskotte, see P. De Jong, "Miskotte's Timely Perspective of the Religious Dimension of the Nazi-Ideology," in *The Netherlands and Nazi Genocide*, ed. G. Jan Colijn and Marcia Sachs Littell (Lewiston, N.Y.: Edwin Mellen Press, 1992), 31–52.

58. Dietrich, *Catholic Citizens*, 259.

59. Quoted in Fleischner, "Can the Few Become the Many?", 234.

60. Quoted in Friedman, *Their Brothers' Keepers*, 99.

61. Quoted in Stein, *Quiet Heroes*, 184.

62. Oliner, *Altruistic Personality*, 167.

63. Quoted in Tec, *When Light Pierced the Darkness*, 147.

64. De Jong, "Responses of the Churches in the Netherlands," 124–25.

65. Quoted in Hunt, "A Critical Evaluation of the Resistance of German Protestantism," 249.

66. Quoted in Fein, *Accounting for Genocide*, 117.

67. Hallie, *Lest Innocent Blood Be Shed*, 103; Kelley, "Best of the German Gentiles," 86; Ramati, *The Assisi Underground*, 56.

68. Fein, *Accounting for Genocide*, 116.

69. Quoted in Hallie, *Lest Innocent Blood Be Shed*, 187.

70. Quoted in Dietrich, *Catholic Citizens*, 226.

71. Ibid.

72. Quoted in Friedman, *Their Brothers' Keepers*, 94, and Dietrich, *Catholic Citizens*, 269.

73. Fogelman, "The Rescuers," 138.

74. Hallie, *Lest Innocent Blood Be Shed*, 145.

75. Ibid., 10.

76. Ibid., 34.

77. Ibid., 69.

78. Paldiel, "Hesed and the Holocaust," 104–5. Emphasis added.

79. For a similar listing of key biblical texts, see Huneke, "Glimpses of Light in a Vast Darkness," 490.

80. Fogelman, "The Rescuers," 133.

81. Hallie, *Lest Innocent Blood Be Shed*, 170.

82. Ibid., 180.

83. Paldiel, "Hesed and the Holocaust," 104.

84. Hunt, "A Critical Evaluation of the Resistance of German Protestantism," 249.

85. Quoted in Dietrich, *Catholic Citizens*, 269.

86. Huneke, *The Moses of Rovno*, 179; Hallie, *Lest Innocent Blood Be Shed*, 101, 180; Oliner, *Altruistic Personality*, 207; Stein, *Quiet Heroes*, 187; Sauvage, "A Most Persistent Haven: Chambon-sur-Lignon," 31; Friedman, *Their Brothers' Keepers*, 97.

87. Huneke, *The Moses of Rovno*, 179.

88. Quoted in Tec, *When Light Pierced the Darkness*, 108.

89. Stein, *Quiet Heroes*, 65. On Pieter and Joyce Miedema, see also Block and Drucker, *Rescuers*, 68–71.

90. Tec, *When Light Pierced the Darkness*, 108.

91. Paldiel, "Hesed and the Holocaust," 105.

92. Stein, *Quiet Heroes*, 94–95.

93. Oliner, *Altruistic Personality*, 169.

94. Allan, "The Priest Who Came to the Bar Mitzvah," 21.

95. Hellman, *Avenue of the Righteous*, 174; cf. Tec, *When Light Pierced the Darkness*, 146.

96. Oliner, *Altruistic Personality*, 207.

97. Ibid., 169.

98. Ezratty, "The Consul Who Disobeyed," 55; *Avenue of the Just*, transcript; Fogelman and Wiener, "The Few, the Brave, the Noble," 63; Fleischner, "Catholics in France Who Saved Jews," 51; Fogelman, "The Rescuers," 132ff; Friedman, *Their Brothers' Keepers*, 54; Perry London, "The Rescuers," 248; Stein, *Quiet Heroes*, 19–20, 144, 181.

99. Fogelman, "The Rescuers," 135.

100. Tec, *When Light Pierced the Darkness*, 104.

101. Stein, *Quiet Heroes*, 20.

102. Oliner, *Altruistic Personality*, 207. See also Block and Drucker, *Rescuers*, 10.

103. Stein, *Quiet Heroes*, 198.

104. See Friedman, *Their Brothers' Keepers*, 93, 98; Dietrich, *Catholic Citizens*, 280–81.

105. Gross, *The Last Jews in Berlin*, 246.

106. Ten Boom, *The Hiding Place*, 123.

107. Tec, *When Light Pierced the Darkness*, 145.

108. Quoted in Hallie, *Lest Innocent Blood Be Shed*, 173.

109. Fogelman, "The Rescuers," 133. The text is Psalm 91:1-2, 9-10.

110. Gilbert, *The Holocaust*, 492–93.

111. Quoted in Dietrich, *Catholic Citizens*, 229.

112. Hallie, *Lest Innocent Blood Be Shed*, 110.

113. Stein, *Quiet Heroes*, 93.

114. Hallie, *Lest Innocent Blood Be Shed*, 109–10; Fleischner, "Catholics in France Who Saved Jews," 53; Stein, *Quiet Heroes*, 184.

115. Hallie, *Lest Innocent Blood Be Shed*, 109–10.

116. Stein, *Quiet Heroes*, 40.

117. Fleischner, "Can the Few Become the Many?", 237.

118. Stein, *Quiet Heroes*, 144.

119. Ibid., 92. See Littell, *The Crucifixion of the Jews*.

120. Tec, *When Light Pierced the Darkness*, 111.

121. Friedman, "Righteous Gentiles in the Nazi Era," 419–20.

Chapter 7: The Quest for Righteousness

1. Schulweis, "Remembering the Rescuers," 1126.

2. Michael Berenbaum, "The Nativization of the Holocaust," *Judaism* 35, no. 4 (Fall 1986), 450.

3. Schulweis, "Remembering the Rescuers," 1126.

4. Ibid., 1128.

5. See Baron, "Restoring Faith in Humankind," 124ff.

6. "Righteous of the Nations," *EJ* 12, 184.

7. The term *hasidei* also can be translated "pious," as Mordecai Paldiel argues. "Hesed and the Holocaust," 93ff. Both meanings—"pious" and "righteous"—help to communicate the rich meaning of the term *hasid* in Jewish tradition. The *hasidim* are most commonly seen as people who transcend conventional moral standards on the basis of a profound piety and love for God. Cf. "Hasidim," *EJ* 7, 1383–88. The discussion herein will focus on the righteousness rather than the piety of the *hasid*.

8. David Novak, *The Image of the Non-Jew in Judaism* (New York: Edwin Mellen Press, 1983), ch. 1. Cf. "*Hasidei Ummot Ha-Olam,*" *EJ* 7, 1383; "Gentile," *EJ* 7, 410–14; "Noachide Laws," *EJ* 12, 1189–91; Chaim Clorfene and Yakov Rogalsky, *The Path of the Righteous Gentile* (Southfield, Mich.: Targum Press, 1987).

9. "Noachide Laws," *EJ* 12, 1189–91; Novak, *Image of the Non-Jew in Judaism*, 294.

10. Each of these laws has been the subject of considerable rabbinic (and other) discussion through the centuries. See Novak, *Image of the Non-Jew in Judaism*, chs. 2–8; Clorfene and Rogalsky, *Path of the Righteous Gentile*, chs. 5–11.

11. "Hasidei Ummot Ha-Olam," *EJ* 7, 1383; "Noachide Laws," *EJ* 12, 1189. Novak, *Image of the Non-Jew in Judaism*, discusses the difficult issue of whether Maimonides further required that righteous non-Jews accept the Noachide laws on the authority of revelation. Most interpreters read Maimonides in this way, but Novak points to a crucial textual problem and other writings of Maimonides to cast doubt on this view. See 277, 303. For the opposite view, see "Noachide Laws," *EJ* 12, 1191.

12. "Hasidei Ummot Ha-Olam," *EJ* 7, 1383, citing the Zohar text Exodus 268a.

13. Paldiel, "Hesed and the Holocaust," 93–98; cf. "Hasidim," *EJ* 7, 1383–88; cf. "Righteousness," *EJ* 14, 180–84.

14. "Righteousness," *EJ* 14, 180.

15. Mechilta 38b, quoted in Solomon Schechter, *Aspects of Rabbinic Theology* (New York: Schocken Books, [1909] 1961), 62.

16. Mechilta 62a, 66b, quoted in Schechter, *Aspects of Rabbinic Theology*, 131–32. See also Novak, *Image of the Non-Jew in Judaism*, 257–58.

17. Schechter, *Aspects of Rabbinic Theology*, 132; "Gentile," *EJ* 7, 411, cites Avodah Zarah 2b, Tanh. B, Deut. 54.

18. Schechter, *Aspects of Rabbinic Theology*, 132.

19. Ibid., 58.

20. Ibid., 106, quoting T.K. 86b.

21. Akedat Yizhak, ch. 60, quoted in "Hasidei Ummot Ha-Olam," *EJ* 7, 1383.

22. Eliyahu Sutah 20, quoted in Leo Trepp, *Judaism: Development and Life*, 3d ed. (Belmont, Calif.: Wadsworth Publishing, 1982), 240.

23. Yad Shemittah 13:13, quoted in "Hasidei Ummot Ha-Olam," *EJ* 7, 1383.

24. Tosefta Sanhedrin 13:2, quoted in Trepp, *Judaism*, 159.

25. Ibid., 240, quoting Tanna debe Eliyahu 207.

26. "Hasidei Ummot Ha-Olam," *EJ* 7, 1383. As noted above, there is disagreement on whether Maimonides also required an assent to the Noachide Laws on the grounds of divine revelation.

27. Yoma 38b, PdRE, 25, cited in "Zaddik," *EJ* 16, 911.

28. Yoma 38b, discussed in Schechter, *Aspects of Rabbinic Theology*, 89.

29. "Lamed Vav Zaddikim," *EJ* 10, 1367–68.

30. See Hellman, *The Avenue of the Righteous*, xvii; Moshe Bejski, "Examples of Heroism," in *The Courage to Care*, 128.

31. The distinction between not doing harm and actively doing good is also an important one in moral philosophy. The corresponding technical terms are "nonmaleficence" and "beneficence." See Tom L. Beauchamp and James F. Childress, *Principles of Biomedical Ethics*, 2d ed. (New York: Oxford Univ. Press, 1983), chs. 4–5.

32. Schulweis, "Remembering the Rescuers," 1128.

33. Paul Breines, *Tough Jews* (New York: Basic Books, 1990), 42–44.

34. One major reason this terminological confusion occurs in rabbinic literature is because textual alterations were required due to the vigilance of Christian censors. See "Gentile," *EJ* 7, 411.

35. Neshamit, "Rescue in Lithuania during the Nazi Occupation," 330.

36. Gilbert, *The Holocaust*, 64.

37. Quoted in ibid., 502–3.

38. Quoted in Redlich, "Metropolitan Andrei Sheptyts'kyi, Ukrainians and Jews during and after the Holocaust," 46.

39. Quoted in Levin, "On the Relations between the Baltic Peoples and Their Jewish Neighbors," 56.

40. Birch and Rasmussen, *Bible and Ethics in the Christian Life*, ch. 5.

41. My thinking here is influenced by Reinhold Niebuhr, who emphasized strongly both the possibilities and the limits of human moral resources and the need for a just political order that through coercion hinders the worst instincts of human beings. See *Moral Man and Immoral Society* (New York: Charles Scribner's, 1932), esp. ch. 3. One thinks also of Martin Luther, who recognized both the possibility of tremendous Christian moral freedom and yet the need for coercive state power to prevent anarchy, lawlessness, and injustice. See, for example, "Secular Authority: To What Extent It Should Be Obeyed," in John Dillenberger, ed., *Martin Luther: Selections from His Writings* (Garden City: Anchor, 1961).

42. This claim assumes that the churches have an important role to play in nurturing a healthy public moral order, and that such a role is both a legitimate dimension of Christian fidelity and a contribution that the society legitimately can ask the churches to make. Both church and society are enriched as a result. One key work that takes this position is Richard John Neuhaus, *The Naked Public Square*, 2d ed. (Grand Rapids: Eerdmans, 1984).

43. Lichten, Foreword, in Iranek-Osmecki, *He Who Saves One Life*, x.

44. Interview with Felix Zanman in "Thy Brother's Keepers," "60 Minutes" segment, 1991.

45. Gene Outka, *Agape: An Ethical Analysis* (New Haven: Yale Univ. Press, 1972), 294. Another important discussion of this cluster of issues is found in Margaret Farley, *Personal Commitments* (New York: HarperCollins, 1986), 103–8.

46. J. O. Ormson, "Saints and Heroes," in A. I. Melden, ed., *Essays in Moral Philosophy* (Seattle: Univ. of Washington Press, 1958). Quoted in Outka, *Agape*, 294.

47. Outka, *Agape*, 294.

48. Poul Borchsenius, "The Rescue of the Danish Jews," 7. Emphasis added.

49. Willy Brandt, Foreword, in Henry, *Victims and Neighbors*, vii. Emphasis added.

50. Daniel Carpi, "The Rescue of Jews in the Italian Zone of Occupied Croatia," 504.

51. "Righteousness," *EJ* 14, 181, citing RH16b.

52. The subtleties of the concept cannot be addressed here. See Schechter, *Aspects of Rabbinic Theology*, 242–92.

53. Ibid., citing Ber. 61b.

54. See Victor Furnish, *Theology and Ethics in Paul* (Nashville: Abingdon, 1968); Robin Scroggs, *Paul for a New Day* (Philadelphia: Fortress Press, 1977), ch. 4; J. Christiaan Beker, *Paul: The Triumph of God in Life and Thought* (Philadelphia: Fortress Press, 1980).

55. Eva Fleischner, "Can the Few Become the Many?", 244.

56. Tec, *When Light Pierced the Darkness*, 145; Fogelman, "The Rescuers," 132; Oliner, *Altruistic Personality*, 155; Block and Drucker, *Rescuers*, 8.

57. Fleischner, "Catholics in France Who Saved Jews during the Holocaust," 54.

58. Richard John Neuhaus, "The Chain of Concern," *The World & I* (July 1988), 380–81.

59. Tec, *When Light Pierced the Darkness*, 146.

60. This is a tendency among some of those Christians inclined towards a radical separatism from the "world." For a classic discussion of this form of Christian life and thought, see H. Richard Niebuhr, *Christ and Culture* (New York: Harper and Row, 1951), ch. 2.

61. Much writing in Christian ethics seems to assume either that *(a)* Christian involvement in other commitments, communities, and stories is relatively insignificant to the Christian or that *(b)* such involvements *should be* relatively insignificant to the Christian. This study of the rescuers as well as general observations of church life lead me to believe that (a) is not normally true, and that (b) is a problematic normative stance. I am arguing instead that the church not only should tolerate the presence of these competing communities and commitments but also should welcome their presence, as long as they can be related with integrity to Christian faith. The church should do so in recognition of its own moral limits and weakness as well as the moral resources available to these other communities.

62. See Hauerwas, *Community of Character*; *The Peaceable Kingdom* (Notre Dame: Univ. of Notre Dame Press, 1983), esp. ch. 3; *Character and the Christian Life*; MacIntyre, *After Virtue*; Birch and Rasmussen, *Bible and Ethics in the Christian Life*, esp. chs. 4 and 5; Gilbert Meilander, *The Theory and Practice of Virtue* (Notre Dame: Univ. of Notre Dame Press, 1984).

63. Sauvage, interview with Moyers, PBS, 1989.

64. See John Howard Yoder, *The Politics of Jesus* (Grand Rapids: Eerdmans, 1972), esp. ch. 7; Marcus Borg, *Jesus: A New Vision* (San Francisco: Harper and Row,

1987); Walter Brueggemann, *The Prophetic Imagination* (Philadelphia: Fortress, 1978); C. H. Dodd, *The Founder of Christianity* (New York: Macmillan, 1970); Donald Goergen, *The Mission and Ministry of Jesus* (Wilmington: Michael Glazier, 1986); Juan Luis Segundo, *The Historical Jesus of the Synoptics* (Maryknoll, N.Y.: Orbis Books, 1985).

65. Kenneth Leech, *Soul Friend* (New York: HarperCollins, 1992); *The Eye of the Storm* (New York: HarperCollins, 1992); Richard Foster, *Celebration of Discipline* (New York: HarperSanFrancisco, 1978); Morton Kelsey, *The Other Side of Silence* (New York: Paulist, 1976); Marsha Sinetar, *Ordinary People as Monks and Mystics* (New York: Paulist, 1986); Howard Rice, *Reformed Spirituality* (Louisville: Westminster/ John Knox, 1991).

66. Leech, *The Eye of the Storm*.

67. For discussion of the reading of the Bible in Christian ethics and in communities of faith, see Birch and Rasmussen, *Bible and Ethics in the Christian Life*; Stephen E. Fowl and L. Gregory Jones, *Reading in Communion* (Grand Rapids: Eerdmans, 1991); Thomas W. Ogletree, *The Use of the Bible in Christian Ethics* (Philadelphia: Fortress, 1983); C. Freeman Sleeper, *The Bible and the Moral Life* (Louisville: Westminster/John Knox, 1992); Elisabeth Schüssler Fiorenza, *Bread Not Stone* (Boston: Beacon Press, 1984).

68. My polemic here is against no single ethicist. It is based on the observation that there exist dozens upon dozens of proposals for how to describe the normative moral center of the Christian faith. Occasionally, those offering such proposals leave the impression that their construal of this normative center is superior to other proposals. It is my contention that moral goodness is indeed best imaged as a kaleidoscope. Different theorists capture different aspects of the moral kaleidoscope; often, the particular contexts or life experiences of moral theorists are quite important in determining which aspect of the kaleidoscope will be named and developed. Notable differences do exist between an ethic of rights and an ethic of care, for example. These differences are worth considering. But one who has seen that both contributed to goodness during the Holocaust loses patience with overly strident claims to the superiority of any single moral paradigm or path.

69. Friedlander, *Pius XII and the Third Reich: A Documentation*; Lewy, *The Roman Catholic Church and the Third Reich*; Morley, *Vatican Diplomacy and the Jews during the Holocaust 1939–1943*.

70. Bauer, *Holocaust in Historical Perspective*, 75.

71. See Robert P. Ericksen, *Theologians under Hitler* (New Haven: Yale Univ. Press, 1985).

Bibliography

Abramowicz, Dina. "Anna Simaite, Lifeline to the Ghetto." *Keeping Posted* 24, no. 2 (October 1978): 15–18.

Adorno, Theodor W., et al. *The Authoritarian Personality*. New York: Norton, 1950.

Agar, Herbert. "Christians Who Dared Death to Save Jews." *Jewish Digest* 6, no. 8 (May 1961): 17–20.

Ainsztein, Reuben. "The Jews of Poland Need Not Have Died." *Midstream* (Autumn 1958): 2–4, 101–3.

——. *Jewish Resistance in Nazi-Occupied Eastern Europe*. New York: Barnes and Noble, 1974.

Aleichem, Sholom. *In the Storm*. Translated by Aliza Shevrin. New York: New American Library, [1917] 1984.

Allan, Alfred K. "The Priest Who Came to the Bar Mitzvah." *Reconstructionist* 34, no. 19 (January 31, 1969): 20–24.

Allport, Gordon. *The Nature of Prejudice*. Reading, Mass.: Addison-Wesley, 1979.

Anger, Per. *With Raoul Wallenberg in Budapest*. New York: Holocaust Library, 1981.

Appleman-Jurman, Alicia. *Alicia: My Story*. New York: Bantam Books, 1988.

Arad, Yitzhak. "Jewish Family Camps in the Forest: An Original Means of Rescue." In *Rescue Attempts during the Holocaust*, edited by Yisrael Gutman and Efraim Zuroff, 333–39. Jerusalem: Yad Vashem, 1974.

Arad, Yitzhak, et al. *Documents on the Holocaust*. Jerusalem: Yad Vashem, 1981.

Arendt, Hannah. *Antisemitism*. New York: Harcourt, Brace, and World, 1968.

——. *Eichmann in Jerusalem*. New York: Penguin, 1977.

Ariel, Joseph. "French-Jewish Resistance to the Nazis." *Judaism* 18, no. 3 (Summer 1969): 299–312.

Ariel, Yaakov. "Jewish Suffering and Christian Salvation: The Evangelical-Fundamentalist Holocaust Memoirs." *Holocaust and Genocide Studies* 6, no. 1 (1991): 63–78.

Avenue of the Just. Full text of film produced and directed by Samuel Elfert. Anti-Defamation League of B'nai B'rith, 1979.

Avni, Haim. "The Zionist Underground in Holland and France and the Escape to Spain." In *Rescue Attempts during the Holocaust*, edited by Yisrael Gutman and Efraim Zuroff, 555–90. Jerusalem: Yad Vashem, 1974.

Baron, Lawrence. "Evangelical Converts, Corrie ten Boom, and the Holocaust: A Response to Yaakov Ariel." *Holocaust and Genocide Studies* 7, no. 1 (Spring 1993): 143–48.

———. "The Historical Context of Rescue." Chap. 2 in Samuel P. Oliner and Pearl M. Oliner, *The Altruistic Personality*. New York: Free Press, 1988.

———. "The Holocaust and Human Decency: A Review of Research on the Rescue of Jews in Nazi Occupied Europe." *Humboldt Journal of Social Relations* 13, nos. 1–2 (1986): 237–51.

———. "Interview with Marion P. Pritchard." *Sh'ma* 14 (April 27, 1984): 97.

———. "The Moral Minority: Psycho-Social Research on the Righteous Gentiles." Paper presented at the 20th Annual Scholars' Conference on the Holocaust and the Churches, March 1990.

———. "Restoring Faith in Humankind." *S'hma* 14 (September 7, 1984): 124–28.

Barreiro, Alvero. *Basic Ecclesial Communities.* Maryknoll, N.Y.: Orbis Books, 1982.

Bartoszewski, Wladyslaw. *The Blood Shed Unites Us.* Warsaw: Interpress Publishers, 1970.

Bartoszewski, Wladyslaw, and Zofia Lewinowna. *The Samaritans: Heroes of the Holocaust.* New York: Twyne Publishers, 1970.

Bauer, Yehuda. *A History of the Holocaust.* New York: Franklin Watts, 1982.

———. *The Holocaust in Historical Perspective.* Seattle: Univ. of Washington Press, 1978.

Baum, Gregory. *Compassion and Solidarity.* New York: Paulist Press, 1990.

———. *Is the New Testament Anti-Semitic?* New York: Paulist Press, 1965.

Bauminger, Arieh L. *The Righteous.* 3d ed. Jerusalem: Yad Vashem, 1983.

Beauchamp, Tom L., and James F. Childress. *Principles of Biomedical Ethics.* 2d ed. New York: Oxford Univ. Press, 1983.

Beck, Norman A. *Mature Christianity.* Cranbury, N.J.: Associated University Presses, 1985.

Bedein, David. "The Righteous of Haut-Biol." *Israel Scene* 6, no. 15 (December 1985): 20–21.

Bedrossyan, Mark D. *The First Genocide of the 20th Century.* Manasquan Park, N.J.: Voskedar Publishing, 1983.

Bejski, Moshe. "Examples of Heroism." In *The Courage to Care*, edited by Carol Rittner and Sondra Myers, 126–33. New York: New York Univ. Press, 1986.

———. "The Righteous Among the Nations and Their Part in the Rescue of Jews." In *Rescue Attempts during the Holocaust*, edited by Yisrael Gutman and Efraim Zuroff, 627–47. Jerusalem: Yad Vashem, 1974.

Beker, J. Christiaan. *Paul: The Triumph of God in Life and Thought*. Philadelphia: Fortress Press, 1980.

Berenbaum, Michael. "The Nativization of the Holocaust." *Judaism* 35, no. 4 (Fall 1986): 447–57.

Berenbaum, Michael, ed. *A Mosaic of Victims*. New York: New York Univ. Press, 1990.

Berenstein, Tatiana, and Adam Rutkowski. *Assistance to the Jews in Poland*. Warsaw: Polonia Foreign Language Publishing House, 1963.

Berkovits, Eliezer. *Faith after the Holocaust*. New York: KTAV, 1973.

Bertelsen, Aage. *October '43*. New York: Putnam, 1954.

Bethge, Eberhard. "Troubled Self-Interpretation and Uncertain Reception in the Church Struggle." In *The German Church Struggle and the Holocaust*, edited by Franklin H. Littell and Hubert G. Locke, 167–84. San Francisco: Edwin Mellen Press, 1974.

Bialik, Chaim Nahman. "In the City of Slaughter (1904)." Translated by A. M. Klein. In *The Literature of Destruction*, edited by David G. Roskies, 160–68. Philadelphia: Jewish Publication Society, 1989.

Bierman, John. *Righteous Gentile: The Story of Raoul Wallenberg*. New York: Viking Press, 1981.

Birch, Bruce C., and Larry L. Rasmussen. *Bible and Ethics in the Christian Life*. Rev. and exp. 2d ed. Minneapolis: Augsburg, 1989.

Block, Gay, and Malka Drucker. *Rescuers: Portraits of Moral Courage in the Holocaust*. New York: Holmes and Meier, 1992.

Boehm, Eric. *We Survived*. New Haven: Yale Univ. Press, 1949.

Bondi, Richard. "The Elements of Character." *Journal of Religious Ethics* 12 (1984): 201–18.

Bonhoeffer, Dietrich. *Ethics*. New York: Collier Books, 1986.

Borchsenius, Poul. "The Rescue of the Danish Jews." *Jewish Spectator* 34, no. 6 (June 1969): 7–10.

Borg, Marcus. *Jesus: A New Vision*. San Francisco: Harper and Row, 1987.

Bowman, Stephen. "Jews in Wartime Greece." *Jewish Social Studies* 48, no. 1 (Winter 1986): 45–62.

Brandt, Willy. Foreword to Frances Henry, *Victims and Neighbors*. S. Hadley, Mass.: Bergin and Garvey, 1983.

Breines, Paul. *Tough Jews*. New York: Basic Books, 1990.

Breznitz, Shlomo. "The Courage to Care." In *The Courage to Care*, edited by Carol Rittner and Sondra Myers, 148–54. New York: New York Univ. Press, 1986.

Briskin, Mae. "Rescue Italian Style." *Jewish Monthly* (May 1986): 20–25.

Brown, Robert McAfee. "The Holocaust: Crisis of Indifference." *Conservative Judaism* 31, no. 1–2 (Fall 1976/Winter 1977): 16–20.

————. "They Could Do No Other." In *The Courage to Care*, edited by Carol Rittner and Sondra Myers, 142–47. New York: New York Univ. Press, 1986.

Browning, Christopher R. "The Decision Concerning the Final Solution." In *Unanswered Questions: Nazi Germany and the Genocide of the Jews*, edited by Francois Furet, 96–118. New York: Schocken Books, 1989.

————. "Nazi Ghettoization Policy: 'Attritionists' vs. 'Productionists.' " Paper presented at the German Studies Association Conference, Albuquerque, N.M., September 1986.

————. *Ordinary Men*. New York: HarperCollins, 1992.

Brueggemann, Walter. *The Prophetic Imagination*. Philadelphia: Fortress Press, 1978.

Calvin, John. *Institutes of the Christian Religion*. Edited by John T. McNeill, translated by Ford Lewis Battles. Philadelphia: Westminster Press, [1559] 1960.

Cargas, Harry James. *A Christian Response to the Holocaust*. New York: Stonehenge Books, 1982.

————. *When God and Man Failed*. New York: Macmillan, 1981.

Carpi, Daniel. "The Rescue of Jews in the Italian Zone of Occupied Croatia." In *Rescue Attempts during the Holocaust*, edited by Yisrael Gutman and Efraim Zuroff, 465–507. Jerusalem: Yad Vashem, 1974.

Chambers, Mortimer, et al. *The Western Experience*. 3d ed. New York: Knopf, 1983.

Charmandarien, Mamikon. "Unforgettable Days." *Conservative Judaism* 28, no. 3 (Spring 1974): 49–56.

Chary, Frederick P. *The Bulgarian Jews and the Final Solution, 1940–1944*. Pittsburgh: Univ. of Pittsburgh Press, 1972.

Cholawski, Shalom. *Soldiers from the Ghetto*. San Diego: A. S. Barnes, 1980.

Clorfene, Chaim, and Yakov Rogalsky. *The Path of the Righteous Gentile*. Southfield, Mich.: Targum Press, 1987.

Colijn, G. Jan, and Marcia Sachs Littell, eds. *The Netherlands and Nazi Genocide*. Lewiston, N.Y.: Edwin Mellen Press, 1992.

Conn, Walter E. "Passionate Commitment: The Dynamics of Affective Conversion." *Cross Currents* 34 (Fall 1984): 329–36.

Conquest, Robert. "First the Slaughter, Then the Lie." Review of *Katyn* by Allen Paul. *New York Times Book Review*, September 1, 1991, 11–13.

————. *The Great Terror: A Reassessment*. New York: Oxford Univ. Press, 1990.

————. *The Harvest of Sorrow*. New York: Oxford Univ. Press, 1986.

The Courage to Care. Produced and directed by Robert Gardner. United Way, 1986.

Cox, Harvey. *Religion in the Secular City*. New York: Touchstone, 1984.

Crossan, John Dominic. "The Life of a Mediterreanean Jewish Peasant." *Christian Century* 108, no. 37 (December 18–25, 1991): 1194–1200.

Curran, Charles E., and Richard McCormick, eds. *Readings in Moral Theology, No. 1: Moral Norms and Catholic Tradition*. New York: Paulist Press, 1979.

Daum, Annette, and Eugene Fisher, eds. "Confronting Our Histories Past and Present." Part 3 of *The Challenge of Shalom for Catholics and Jews*. New York: United American Hebrew Congregations and the National Conference of Catholic Bishops, 1985.

Davies, Alan. *Antisemitism and the Christian Mind*. New York: Seabury Press, 1969.

Davies, Alan T., ed. *Antisemitism and the Foundations of Christianity*. New York: Paulist Press, 1979.

Dawidowicz, Lucy S. *From That Place and Time*. New York: Norton, 1989.

————. *The War Against the Jews, 1933–1945*. New York: Bantam Books, 1975.

De Jong, Pieter. "Responses of the Churches in the Netherlands to the Nazi Occupation." In *Human Responses to the Holocaust*, edited by Michael D. Ryan, 121–41. New York: Edwin Mellen Press, 1981.

Des Pres, Terrence. *The Survivor*. New York: Oxford Univ. Press, 1976

Dietrich, Donald J. *Catholic Citizens in the Third Reich: Psycho-Social Principles*. New Brunswick, N.J.: Transaction Books, 1988.

Dobroszycki, Lucjan, ed. *The Chronicle of the Lodz Ghetto, 1941–1944*. New Haven: Yale Univ. Press, 1984.

Dodd, C. H. *The Founder of Christianity*. New York: Macmillan, 1970.

Donat, Alexander. *The Holocaust Kingdom: A Memoir*. New York: Holt, Rinehart, 1965.

Dovidio, John. "Helping Behavior and Altruism: An Empirical and Conceptual Overview." In *Advances in Experimental Social Psychology*, edited by Leonard Berkowitz. New York: Academic Press, 1984.

Eckardt, A. Roy. "Contemporary Christian Theology and a Protestant Witness for the *Shoah*." *Union Seminary Quarterly Review* 38, no. 2 (Spring 1983): 139–45.

———. *Elder and Younger Brothers*. New York: Scribner, 1967.

———. *Your People, My People*. New York: Quadrangle, 1974.

Eckardt, A. Roy, and Alice Eckardt. *Long Night's Journey into Day*. Detroit: Wayne State Univ. Press, 1982.

Eckardt, A. Roy, and Alice Eckardt, eds. *Remembering for the Future: Jews and Christians during and after the Holocaust*. Oxford: Pergamon Press, 1989.

Eichel, Mietek. "Warsaw and After." In *The Root and the Bough*, edited by Leo W. Schwarz, 284–93. New York: Rinehart and Co., 1949.

Eisenberg, Nancy, and Paul Miller. "The Relation of Empathy to Prosocial and Related Behaviors." *Psychological Bulletin* 101: 91–119.

Eliach, Yaffa. *Hasidic Tales of the Holocaust*. New York: Vintage Books, 1982.

Ellis, Marc H. *Beyond Innocence and Redemption*. New York: Harper and Row, 1990.

———. *Toward a Jewish Theology of Liberation*. Maryknoll, N.Y.: Orbis Books, 1987.

Encyclopedia of the Holocaust. Vol. 3: "Pius XII," "Righteous Among the Nations." New York: Macmillan, 1990.

Encyclopedia Judaica. Vol. 7: "Gentile," "Hasidei Ummot Ha-Olam," "Hasidim." Vol. 10: "Lamed Vav Zaddikim." Vol. 12: "Noachide Laws." Vol. 14: "Righteous of the Nations," "Righteousness." Vol. 16: "Zaddik." Jerusalem: Keter Publishing House, 1972.

Engelmann, Bernt. *In Hitler's Germany*. New York: Schocken Books, 1986.

Ericksen, Robert P. *Theologians under Hitler*. New Haven: Yale Univ. Press, 1985.

Etzioni, Amitai. "The Banality of Altruism." *The World & I* (July 1988): 388–92.

Evison, Ian S. Review of *The Altruistic Personality* by Samuel P. Oliner and Pearl M. Oliner. *Social Service Review* 64 (March 1990): 160–62.

Ezratty, Harry. "The Consul Who Disobeyed: A Christian Who Sacrificed His Career to Save Jewish Lives." *Jewish Digest* 13, no. 12 (September 1968): 54–56.

Fabre, Emil C., ed. *God's Underground*. St. Louis: Bethany Press, 1970.

Fackenheim, Emil. *The Jewish Return into History*. New York: Schocken Books, 1978.

———. "The Nazi Holocaust as a Persisting Trauma for the Non-Jewish Mind." *Journal of the History of Ideas* 36, no. 2 (April–May 1975): 369–76.

Farley, Margaret. *Personal Commitments*. New York: HarperCollins, 1986.

Fasching, Darrell J. *Narrative Theology after Auschwitz*. Minneapolis: Fortress Press, 1992.

Feigenbaum, M. J. "Life in a Bunker." In *The Root and the Bough*, edited by Leo W. Schwarz, 142–54. New York: Rinehart and Co., 1949.

Fein, Helen. *Accounting for Genocide*. New York: Free Press, 1979.

Fersen-Osten, Renee. *Don't They Know the World Stopped Breathing?* New York: Shapolsky Publishers, 1991.

Fest, Joachim C. *Hitler*. New York: Vintage Books, 1975.

Fisher, David James. Review of *Weapons of the Spirit* by Pierre Sauvage. *The American Historical Review* 95, no. 4 (October 1990): 1136–37.

Fisher, Eugene. "Faith in Humankind: Rescuers of Jews during the Holocaust." *Journal of Ecumenical Studies* 21 (Summer 1984): 636–37.

Flannery, Edward. *The Anguish of the Jews*. New York: Macmillan, 1964.

Fleischner, Eva. "Can the Few Become the Many? Some Catholics in France Who Saved Jews during the Holocaust." In *Remembering for the Future*, edited by A. Roy Eckardt and Alice Eckardt, vol. 1, 233–47. Oxford: Pergamon Press, 1989.

———. "Catholics in France Who Saved Jews during the Holocaust." *Journal of Philosophy and Theology* 3 (Fall 1988): 45–56.

———. "The Memory of Goodness." In *Remembering for the Future*, edited by A. Roy Eckardt and Alice Eckardt, vol. 3, 3159–63. New York: Pergamon Press, 1989.

Fleischner, Eva, ed. *Auschwitz: Beginning of a New Era?* New York: KTAV, 1977.

Flender, Harold. *Rescue in Denmark*. New York: Simon and Schuster, 1963.

Fletcher, Joseph. *Situation Ethics*. Philadelphia: Westminster Press, 1966.

Fogelman, Eva. "The Rescuers: A Socio-Psychological Study of Altruistic Behavior during the Nazi Era." Ph.D. diss., City University of New York, 1987.

Fogelman, Eva, and Valerie Lewis Wiener. "The Few, the Brave, the Noble." *Psychology Today* 19, no. 8 (August 1985): 60–65.

Foster, Richard. *Celebration of Discipline*. New York: HarperSanFrancisco, 1978.

Fowl, Stephen E., and L. Gregory Jones. *Reading in Communion*. Grand Rapids: Eerdmans, 1991.

Fowler, James W. "The Psychology of Altruism." *First Things* 4 (1990): 43–49.

Frank, Anne. *The Diary of a Young Girl*. New York: Washington Square Press, [1947] 1967.

Freuchen, Peter. *Vagrant Viking*. New York: 1953.

Friedlander, Saul. *Pius XII and the Third Reich*. New York: Alfred A. Knopf, 1966.

Friedman, Philip. "Jewish Resistance to Nazism." In *Anthology of Holocaust Literature*, edited by Jacob Glatstein, 275–90. New York: Jewish Publication Society, 1969.

———. *Martyrs and Fighters*. New York: Lancer Books, 1954.

———. *Roads to Extinction*. Edited by Ada June Friedman. New York: Jewish Publication Society, [1955] 1980.

———. *Their Brothers' Keepers*. New York: Holocaust Library, [1957] 1978.

Friedman, Thomas. *From Beirut to Jerusalem*. New York: Anchor Books, 1990.

Furet, Francois. *Unanswered Questions: Nazi Germany and the Genocide of the Jews.* New York: Schocken Books, 1989.

Furnish, Victor. *Theology and Ethics in Paul.* Nashville: Abingdon Press, 1968.

Gager, John. *The Origins of Antisemitism: Attitudes Towards Judaism in Pagan and Christian Antiquity.* New York: Oxford Univ. Press, 1985.

Garfinkel, Perry. "The Human Face of Altruism." *The World & I* (July 1988): 383–87.

Gaylin, Robert. *In the Service of Their Country.* New York: Viking Press, 1970.

"German Soldier Who Saved Jews." *Jewish Observer and Middle East Review* 21, no. 45 (November 10, 1972): 9.

"German Who Saved Danish Jewry." *Israel Digest* 14, no. 8 (April 18, 1971): 5.

Gies, Miep. *Anne Frank Remembered: The Story of the Woman Who Helped to Hide the Frank Family.* New York: Simon and Schuster, 1987.

Gilbert, Martin. *Atlas of the Holocaust.* Rev. and exp. edition. New York: Morrow and Co., 1993.

_____. *The Holocaust.* New York: Henry Holt and Co., 1985.

Gilligan, Carol. *In a Different Voice.* Cambridge: Harvard Univ. Press, 1982.

Gitelman, Zvi. "History, Memory, and Politics: The Holocaust in the Soviet Union." *Holocaust and Genocide Studies* 5, no. 1 (1990): 23–38.

Glatstein, Jacob, et al., eds. *Anthology of Holocaust Literature.* New York: Jewish Publication Society, 1969.

Goergen, Donald. *The Mission and Ministry of Jesus.* Wilmington: Michael Glazier, 1986.

Goldberg, Michael. *Jews and Christians: Getting Our Stories Straight.* Nashville: Abingdon Press, 1985.

Goldberger, Leo. *The Rescue of the Danish Jews.* New York: New York Univ. Press, 1987.

Goldstein, Bernard. *The Stars Bear Witness.* New York: Viking Press, 1949.

_____. "Girding Our Strength." In *The Root and the Bough*, edited by Leo W. Schwarz, 16–43. New York: Rinehart and Co., 1949.

Goodin, Robert E. "Do Motives Matter?" *Canadian Journal of Philosophy* 19, no. 5 (September 1989): 405–20.

Gordon, Sarah. *Hitler, Germans, and the "Jewish Question."* Princeton, N.J.: Princeton Univ. Press, 1984.

Gotfryd, Bernard. *Anton the Dove Fancier and Other Tales of the Holocaust.* New York: Washington Square Press, 1990.

Gray, Martin, with Max Gallo. *For Those I Loved.* Boston: Little, Brown, and Co., 1971.

Greenberg, Irving. "Cloud of Smoke, Pillar of Fire." In *Auschwitz: Beginning of a New Era?* Edited by Eva Fleischner. New York: KTAV, 1977.

_____. "The Ethics of Jewish Power." New York: CLAL, 1988.

_____. "The Third Era of Jewish History: Power and Politics." New York: CLAL, 1980.

_____. "The Third Great Cycle of Jewish History." New York: CLAL, 1981.

_____. "Voluntary Covenant." New York: CLAL, 1982.

Gross, Leonard. *The Last Jews in Berlin.* New York: Touchstone, 1982.

Grossman, Frances G. "A Psychological Study of Gentiles Who Saved the Lives of Jews during the Holocaust." In *Toward the Understanding and Prevention of Genocide*, edited by Israel Charny, 202–15. Boulder, Colo.: Westview Press, 1984.

Grynberg, Henryk. *Childhood of Shadows*. London: Vallentine, Mitchell, 1969.

Gutman, Yisrael. "The Attitude of the Poles to the Mass Deportations of Jews from the Warsaw Ghetto in the Summer of 1942." In *Rescue Attempts during the Holocaust*, edited by Yisrael Gutman and Efraim Zuroff, 399–434. Jerusalem: Yad Vashem, 1974.

Gutman, Yisrael, and Efraim Zuroff, eds. *Rescue Attempts during the Holocaust*. Jerusalem: Yad Vashem, 1974.

Haas, Peter J. *Morality after Auschwitz*. Philadelphia: Fortress Press, 1988.

Haesler, Alfred. *The Lifeboat Is Full: Switzerland and the Refugees, 1933–1945*. New York: Funk and Wagnalls, 1969.

Hallie, Philip. *Lest Innocent Blood Be Shed*. New York: Harper and Row, 1979.

Halperin, Michael. "He Who Saves One Life." *Moment* 6, no. 7 (July/August 1981): 37-41.

Harrelson, Walter, and Randall M. Falk. *Jews and Christians: A Troubled Family*. Nashville: Abingdon Press, 1990.

Harrison, Beverly Wildung. "The Power of Anger in the Work of Love." In *Making the Connections*, 3–21. Boston: Beacon Press, 1985.

Hauerwas, Stanley. *Character and the Christian Life*. San Antonio: Trinity Univ. Press, 1985.

———. *A Community of Character*. Notre Dame: Univ. of Notre Dame Press, 1981.

———. *The Peaceable Kingdom*. Notre Dame: Univ. of Notre Dame Press, 1983.

———. "Remembering as a Moral Task: The Challenge of the Holocaust." Chap. 4 in *Against the Nations*. San Francisco: Harper and Row, 1985.

Hay, Malcolm. *Europe and the Jews*. Boston: Beacon Press, 1960.

Heard, Raymond. "He Cheated the Nazis of 50 Lives." *Jewish Digest* 14, no. 9 (June 1969): 49–51.

Hellman, Peter. *Avenue of the Righteous*. New York: Atheneum Publishers, 1980.

Henry, Frances. "Heroes and Helpers in Nazi Germany: Who Aided Jews?" *Humboldt Journal of Social Relations* 13, no. 1–2 (1986): 306–19.

———. *Victims and Neighbors: A Small Town in Germany Remembered*. S. Hadley, Mass.: Bergin and Garvey, 1984.

Hertzberg, Arthur. *The French Enlightenment and the Jews: The Origins of Modern Anti-Semitism*. New York: Columbia Univ. Press, 1968.

Herzer, Ivo. "How Italians Rescued Jews." *Midstream* 29, no. 6 (June/July 1983): 35–38.

Hesselink, I. John. "Christ, the Law, and the Christian: An Unexplored Aspect of the Third Use of the Law in Calvin's Theology." In *Readings in Calvin's Theology*, edited by Donald K. McKim, 179–91. Grand Rapids: Baker Book House, 1984.

Hilberg, Raul. *The Destruction of the European Jews*. 3 vols., rev. ed. New York: Holmes and Meier, 1985.

———. *Perpetrators Victims Bystanders*. New York: HarperCollins, 1992.

Hillesum, Etty. *An Interrupted Life: The Diaries of Etty Hillesum, 1941–1943*. New York: Pantheon Books, 1983.

Hitler, Adolf. *Mein Kampf*. Boston: Houghton Mifflin, [1925] 1971.

Hoffman, Martin. "Development of Prosocial Motivation: Empathy and Guilt." In *The Development of Prosocial Behavior*. Edited by Nancy Eisenberg. New York: Academic Press, 1982.

Hoffmann, Martin, and Herbert D. Salzstein. "Parent Discipline and the Child's Moral Development." *Journal of Personality and Social Psychology* 5, no. 1: 45–57.

Hoffmann, Peter. *The History of the German Resistance, 1933–1945*. Cambridge, Mass.: MIT Press, 1977.

Höhne, Heinz. *The Order of the Death's Head*. New York: Ballantine Books, 1969.

"Holocaust Heroes Honored." Unsigned. *Christian Century* 101 (October 17, 1984): 952.

Horbach, Michael. *Out of the Night*. New York: Frederick Fell, 1967.

Höss, Rudolf. *Commandant of Auschwitz*. Translated by Constantine Fitzgibbon. London: Pan Books, 1974.

Howes, Carollee, and Robert Eldredge. "Responses of Abused, Neglected, and Non-Maltreated Children to the Behaviors of Their Peers." *Journal of Applied Developmental Psychology* 6, no. 2–3: 261–70.

Hsia, R. Po-Chia. *The Myth of Ritual Murder*. New Haven, Conn.: Yale Univ. Press, 1988.

Huneke, Douglas. "In the Darkness . . . Glimpses of Light: A Study of Nazi-Era Rescuers." A Report to the Oregon Committee for the Humanities, September 1980.

_____. "Glimpses of Light in a Vast Darkness: A Study of the Moral and Spiritual Development of Nazi Era Rescuers." In *Remembering for the Future*, edited by A. Roy Eckardt and Alice Eckardt, vol. 1, 486–93. New York: Pergamon Press, 1989.

_____. "The Lessons of Hermann Graebe's Life: The Origins of a Moral Person." In *The Moses of Rovno*, 177–87. New York: Dodd Mead, 1985.

_____. *The Moses of Rovno*. New York: Dodd Mead, 1985.

_____. "A Study of Christians Who Rescued Jews during the Nazi Era." *Humboldt Journal of Social Relations* 9, no. 1 (Fall/Winter 1981/82): 144–50.

Hunt, Chester L. "A Critical Evaluation of the Resistance of German Protestantism to the Holocaust." In *Remembering for the Future*, edited by A. Roy Eckardt and Alice Eckardt, 241–53. New York: Pergamon Press, 1989.

Hunt, Morton. *The Compassionate Beast*. New York: William Morrow & Co., 1990.

Huttenbach, Henry. "The Emigration of Jews from Worms (November 1938–October 1941): Hopes and Plans." In *Rescue Attempts during the Holocaust*, edited by Yisrael Gutman and Efraim Zuroff, 266–88. Jerusalem: Yad Vashem, 1974.

Ingber, Abraham, trans. "The Rescue of Fania Paszht." *Moment* 11, no. 5 (May 1986): 48–49.

Iranek-Osmecki, Kazimierz. *He Who Saves One Life*. New York: Crown Publishers, 1971.

Isaac, Jules. *The Teaching of Contempt: Christian Roots of Anti-Semitism*. Edited by Claire Huchet-Bishop and translated by Helen Weaver. New York: Holt, Rinehart, and Winston, 1964.

Jegstrup, Elsebet. "Spontaneous Action: The Rescue of the Danish Jews from Hannah Arendt's Perspective." *Humboldt Journal of Social Relations* 13, no. 1–2 (1986): 260–84.

Joutard, Philippe, ed. *Cévennes: Terre de Réfuge, 1940–1944.* Paris: Presses de Languedoc, 1990.

Kagan, Jerome, et al. *Infancy: Its Place in Human Development.* Cambridge: Harvard Univ. Press, 1978.

Kammer, Feiga. "Winter in the Forest." In *Anthology of Holocaust Literature,* edited by Jacob Glatstein, 155–57. New York: Jewish Publication Society, 1969.

Kanabus, Felix. "Address at the J.N.F." In *Anthology of Holocaust Literature,* edited by Jacob Glatstein, 392–95. New York: Jewish Publication Society, 1969.

Kaplan, Chaim. *Scroll of Agony.* New York: Macmillan, 1965.

Katz, Jacob. *From Prejudice to Destruction: Anti-Semitism, 1700–1933.* Cambridge, Mass.: Harvard Univ. Press, 1980.

Ka-Tzetnik 135633. *Shivitti: A Vision.* San Francisco: Harper and Row, 1989.

Kelley, James Patrick. "The Best of the German Gentiles: Dietrich Bonhoeffer and the Rights of Jews in Hitler's Germany." In *Remembering for the Future,* edited by A. Roy Eckardt and Alice Eckardt, vol. 1, 80–92. New York: Pergamon Press, 1989.

Kelsey, Morton. *The Other Side of Silence.* New York: Paulist Press, 1976.

Keneally, Thomas. *Schindler's List.* New York: Penguin Books, 1983.

Kermish, Joseph. "The Activities of the Council for Aid to Jews (Zegota) in Occupied Poland." In *Rescue Attempts during the Holocaust,* edited by Yisrael Gutman and Efraim Zuroff, 367–98. Jerusalem: Yad Vashem, 1974.

Klee, Ernst, et al. *"The Good Old Days."* New York: Free Press, 1991.

Klingemann, Ute. "The Study of Rescuers of Jews in Berlin: A Progress Report." Paper presented at the Scholars Roundtable on Altruism under Nazi Terror, Princeton, March 1993.

Kogan, Shlomo. "The Long Road." In *The Root and the Bough,* edited by Leo W. Schwarz, 100–111. New York: Rinehart and Co., 1949.

Kogon, Eugen. *The Theory and Practice of Hell.* New York: Berkley Books, 1950.

Köhn, Alfie. "Evidence for a Moral Tradition." Review of *The Altruistic Personality* by Samuel P. Oliner and Pearl M. Oliner. *Psychology Today* 23 (Jan./Feb. 1989): 72–73.

Kolbik, Steven. *The Stones Cry Out: Sweden's Response to the Persecution of the Jews.* New York: Holocaust Library, 1988.

Krakowski, Shmuel. *The War of the Doomed: Jewish Armed Resistance in Poland, 1942–1944.* New York: Holmes and Meier, 1984.

Krakowski, Shmuel, and Yisrael Gutman. *Poles and Jews between the Wars.* New York: Schocken Books, 1986.

Kranzler, David. "How 18,000 Jews Survived the Holocaust While Europe Burned." *Jewish Life,* vol. 1 (new series) (1975): 29-39.

Kren, George M., and Leon Rappoport. *The Holocaust and the Crisis of Human Behavior.* New York: Holmes and Meier, 1980.

Kulka, Otto D. "Major Trends and Tendencies in German Historiography on National Socialism and the 'Jewish Question' (1924–1984)." *Leo Baeck Institute Year Book* 30 (1985): 234.

Kuper, Jack. *Child of the Holocaust*. New York: New American Library, 1967.

Kuper, Leo P. *Genocide*. New Haven: Yale Univ. Press, 1981.

———. "The Turkish Genocide of Armenians." In *The Armenian Genocide in Perspective*, edited by Richard P. Hovannisian, 43–59. New Brunswick, N.J.: Transaction Books, 1988.

Kurek, Ewa. "The Role of Polish Nuns in the Rescue of Jews, 1939–1945." Paper presented at the Scholars Roundtable on Altruism under Nazi Terror, Princeton, March 1993.

Lapomarda, Vincent A. *The Jesuits and the Third Reich*. Lewiston, N.Y.: Edwin Mellen Press, 1989.

Latané, Bibb, and John Darley. *The Unresponsive Bystander: Why Doesn't He Help?* Englewood Cliffs, N.J.: Prentice-Hall, 1970.

Latour, Anny. *The Jewish Resistance in France (1940–1944)*. Translated by Irene R. Ilton. New York: Holocaust Library, 1981.

Lauritzen, Paul. "Emotions and Religious Ethics." *Journal of Religious Ethics* 16, no. 2 (Fall 1988): 307–24.

Le Boucher, Fernande. *The Incredible Mission of Father Benoit*. Translated by J. F. Bernard. Garden City, N.Y.: Doubleday, 1969.

Lebacqz, Karen. *Justice in an Unjust World*. Minneapolis: Augsburg, 1987.

Leech, Kenneth. *The Eye of the Storm*. New York: HarperCollins, 1992.

———. *Soul Friend*. New York: HarperCollins, 1980.

Leuner, H. D. *When Compassion Was a Crime*. London: Oswald Wolf, 1966.

Levi, Primo. *Survival in Auschwitz*. New York: Collier Books, 1961.

Levin, Dov. "On the Relations between the Baltic Peoples and Their Jewish Neighbors before, during, and after World War II." *Holocaust and Genocide Studies* 5, no. 1 (1990): 53–66.

Levy, Claude, and Paul Tillard. *Betrayal at the Vel d'Hiv*. New York: Hill and Wang, 1969.

Lewis, Kevin. "The Auschwitz Museum and the Clash of Memories." *Christian Century* 108, no. 3 (January 23, 1991): 75–77.

Lewy, Guenther. *The Roman Catholic Church and the Third Reich*. New York: McGraw-Hill, 1964.

Lichten, Joseph. Foreword to *He Who Saves One Life*, by Kazimierz Iranek-Osmecki. New York: Crown Books, 1971.

Lifton, Robert Jay. *The Nazi Doctors*. New York: Basic Books, 1986.

Lincoln, Bruce. *Red Victory*. New York: Touchstone, 1989.

Littell, Franklin. *The Crucifixion of the Jews*. Macon, Ga.: Mercer Univ. Press, 1975.

Littell, Franklin, and Hubert G. Locke, eds. *The German Church Struggle and the Holocaust*. Detroit: Wayne State Univ. Press, 1974.

Littell, Marcia, ed. *The Holocaust, Forty Years After*. Lewiston, N.Y.: Edwin Mellen Press, 1989.

Locke, Hubert G., ed. *The Church Confronts the Nazis: Barmen Then and Now*. Lewiston, N.Y.: Edwin Mellen Press, 1984.

London, Perry. "The Rescuers: Motivational Hypotheses about Christians Who Saved Jews from the Nazis." In *Altruism and Helping Behavior*, edited by Jacqueline Macauley and Leonard Berkowitz, 241–50. New York: Academic Press, 1970.

Lukas, Richard C. *The Forgotten Holocaust: The Poles under German Occupation, 1939– 1944*. Lexington, Ky.: Univ. of Kentucky Press, 1986.

Luther, Martin. "Secular Authority: To What Extent It Should Be Obeyed." In *Martin Luther: Selections from His Writings*. Edited by John Dillenberger. Garden City: Anchor, 1961.

Lynne, Edward. "Brave Lady from Holland." *Jewish Observer and Middle East Review* 16, no. 16 (April 21, 1967): 9.

———. "Heroine from Holland." *Jewish Digest* 13 (December 1967): 39–40.

Macauley, Jacqueline, and Leonard Berkowitz, eds. *Altruism and Helping Behavior*. New York: Academic Press, 1970.

MacIntyre, Alasdair C. *After Virtue*. 2d ed. Notre Dame: Univ. of Notre Dame Press, 1984.

Margaliot, Abraham. "The Problem of the Rescue of German Jewry during the Years 1933–1939." In *Rescue Attempts during the Holocaust*, edited by Yisrael Gutman and Efraim Zuroff, 247–65. Jerusalem: Yad Vashem, 1974.

Marks, Jane. "The Hidden Children." *New York* (February 25, 1991): 39–45.

———. *The Hidden Children*. New York: Fawcett Columbine, 1993.

Marrus, Michael. *The Holocaust in History*. New York: New American Library, 1987.

Marrus, Michael R., and Robert O. Paxton. *Vichy France and the Jews*. New York: Schocken Books, 1983.

Mason, Henry L. "Testing Human Bonds within Nations: Jews in the Occupied Netherlands." *Political Science Quarterly* 99, no. 2 (Summer 1984): 315–43.

Mayer, Arno J. *Why Did the Heavens Not Darken?* New York: Pantheon Books, 1990.

McKim, Donald K., ed. *Readings in Calvin's Theology*. Grand Rapids: Baker Book House, 1984.

Meilander, Gilbert. *The Theory and Practice of Virtue*. Notre Dame: Univ. of Notre Dame Press, 1984.

Metz, Johann B. *Faith in History and Society*. New York: Seabury Press, 1980.

Midlarsky, Manus I. "Helping during the Holocaust: The Role of Political, Theological and Socioeconomic Identifications." *Humboldt Journal of Social Relations* 13, no. 1–2 (1985/86): 285–305.

Miller, Judith. *One by One by One*. New York: Simon and Schuster, 1990.

Milton, Sybil. "The Righteous Who Helped Jews." In *Genocide: Critical Issues of the Holocaust*, edited by A. Grobman and D. Landes, 282–87. Los Angeles: Simon Wiesenthal Center, 1983.

Minco, Marga. *Bitter Herbs*. New York: Oxford Univ. Press, 1960.

"A *Moment* Interview with Marion Pritchard." *Moment* 9, no. 1 (December 1983): 26–31.

Monroe, Kristen R. "John Donne's People: Explaining Differences between Rational Actors and Altruists through Cognitive Frameworks." *Journal of Politics* 53, no. 2 (May 1991): 394–433.

Monroe, Kristen R., et al. "Altruism and the Theory of Rational Action: Rescuers of Jews in Nazi Europe." *Ethics* 101 (October 1990): 103–22.

Morley, John F. *Vatican Diplomacy and the Jews during the Holocaust, 1939–1943.* New York: KTAV, 1980.

Mosse, George. *Toward the Final Solution: A History of European Racism.* Madison: Univ. of Wisconsin Press, 1978.

Nalkowska, Sofia. "At the Railroad Tracks." In *Anthology of Holocaust Literature,* edited by Jacob Glatstein, 361–63. New York: Jewish Publication Society, 1969.

Neal, Marie Augusta. "The Future of Altruism." *Cross Currents* 36 (Winter 1986/87): 418–35.

Neshamit, Sarah. "Rescue in Lithuania during the Nazi Occupation (June 1941– August 1944)." In *Rescue Attempts during the Holocaust,* edited by Yisrael Gutman and Efraim Zuroff, 289–332. Jerusalem: Yad Vashem, 1974.

Neuhaus, Richard John. "The Chain of Concern." *The World & I* (July 1988): 374–82.

———. *The Naked Public Square.* 2d ed. Grand Rapids: Eerdmans, 1984.

Niebuhr, Reinhold. *Moral Man and Immoral Society.* New York: Charles Scribner's Sons, 1932.

Niebuhr, H. Richard. *Christ and Culture.* New York: Harper and Row, 1951.

Noakes, J., and G. Pridham, eds. *Nazism: A History in Documents and Eyewitness Accounts, 1919–1945.* 2 vols. New York: Schocken Books, 1990.

Novak, David. *The Image of the Non-Jew in Judaism.* New York: Edwin Mellen Press, 1983.

———. "A Jewish Theological Understanding of Christianity in Our Time." *First Things* 9 (January 1991): 26–33.

Nuit et Brouillard ("Night and Fog"). Produced by Alain Resnais. 1955.

Nussbaum, Rudi H. Review of *The Altruistic Personality* by Samuel P. Oliner and Pearl M. Oliner. *International Journal of American Sociology* 30, no. 3–4 (1989): 274–77.

Ochs, Abraham. "The Dark Clouds." In *Alliance for Murder,* edited by B. F. Sabrin, 20–35. New York: Sarpedon Pubs., 1991.

Ofer, Dalia. "The Activities of the Jewish Agency Delegation in Istanbul in 1943." In *Rescue Attempts during the Holocaust,* edited by Yisrael Gutman and Efraim Zuroff, 435–50. Jerusalem: Yad Vashem, 1974.

Ogletree, Thomas W. *The Use of the Bible in Christian Ethics.* Philadelphia: Fortress Press, 1983.

Oline, Pamela. "Rescuing the Hidden Story." *Books and Religion* 18, no. 2 (Summer 1991): 4–7, 11.

Oliner, Pearl M., and Samuel P. Oliner. "Rescuers of Jews during the Holocaust: Justice, Care, and Religion." In *Remembering for the Future,* edited by A. Roy Eckardt and Alice Eckardt, vol. 1, 506–16. New York: Pergamon Press, 1989.

Oliner, Samuel P. "The Need to Recognize the Heroes of the Nazi Era." *Reconstructionist* 48, no. 4 (June 1982): 7–14.

———. "In Praise of Righteous Gentiles." *Jewish Digest* 28 (October 1982): 27–32.

———. *Restless Memories: Recollections of the Holocaust Years.* Berkeley: Judah Magnes Memorial Museum, 1986.

———. "The Unsung Heroes in Nazi-Occupied Europe: The Antidote for Evil." *Nationalities Papers* 12, no. 1 (Spring 1984): 129–36.

Oliner, Samuel P., and Pearl M. Oliner. *The Altruistic Personality: Rescuers of Jews in Nazi Europe*. New York: Free Press, 1988.

Olweus, Dan, et al., eds. *Development of Antisocial and Prosocial Behavior*. New York: Academic Press, 1986.

Oral History Project, Stockton State University, N.J. Testimonies of R. Weiss, R. Haas, Z. Gurland.

Orenstein, Henry. *I Shall Live*. New York: Simon and Schuster, 1987.

Osterhaven, M. Eugene. "Calvin on the Covenant." In *Readings in Calvin's Theology*, edited by Donald K. McKim, 89–106. Grand Rapids: Baker Book House, 1984.

Outka, Gene. *Agape: An Ethical Analysis*. New Haven: Yale Univ. Press, 1972.

Paldiel, Mordecai. "The Altruism of the Righteous Gentiles." *Holocaust and Genocide Studies* 3, no. 2 (1988): 187–96.

———. "Hesed and the Holocaust." *Journal of Ecumenical Studies* 23, no. 1 (Winter 1986): 90–106.

———. Interview with author, December 1991.

———. *The Path of the Righteous*. Hoboken: KTAV, 1993.

Papanek, Ernst, and Edward Linn. *Out of the Fire*. New York: Morrow, 1975.

Parkes, James. *The Conflict of the Church and the Synagogue*. New York: Atheneum, 1969.

Paulowicz, Sala, with Kevin Klose. "The Wache." In *Anthology of Holocaust Literature*, edited by Jacob Glatstein, 206–15. New York: Jewish Publication Society, 1969.

Pawlikowski, John. *Christ in the Light of the Christian-Jewish Dialogue*. New York: Paulist Press, 1982.

———. *Jesus and the Theology of Israel*. Wilmington: Michael Glazier, 1989.

———. *Sinai and Calvary*. Beverly Hills: Benziger, 1976.

Peterson, Lizette. "An Alternative Perspective to Norm-Based Explanations of Modeling and Children's Generosity." *Merrill-Palmer Quarterly* 28, no. 2: 283–90.

Pinchewski, Rosa. "Rosa's Journey." In *The Root and the Bough*, edited by Leo W. Schwarz, 297–99. New York: Rinehart and Co., 1949.

Poliakov, Leon. *Harvest of Hate*. New York: Holocaust Library, [1951] 1979.

———. *History of Anti-Semitism*. 4 vols. New York: Viking Press, Vanguard Press, 1965–1986.

Poliakov, Leon, and Jacques Sabille. *Jews under the Italian Occupation*. New York: Howard Fertig, 1983.

Prager, Dennis, and Joseph Telushkin. *Why the Jews?* New York: Simon and Schuster, 1983.

Presser, Jacob. *The Destruction of the Dutch Jews*. New York: E. P. Dutton and Co., 1969.

Pritchard, Marion P. "It came to pass in those days . . ." *Sh'ma* 14 (April 27, 1984): 97–102.

Ramati, Alexander. *The Assisi Underground*. New York: Stein and Day, 1978.

Rasmussen, Larry L. *Dietrich Bonhoeffer: His Significance for North Americans*. Minneapolis: Fortress Press, 1990.

Rausch, David A. *A Legacy of Hatred*. 2d ed. Baker, 1991.

Ravel, Aviva. "My Sister's Keeper." *Jewish Digest* 18, no. 1 (October 1972): 35–42.

Rawls, John. *A Theory of Justice*. Cambridge: Harvard Univ. Press, 1971.

Redlich, Shimon. "Metropolitan Andrei Sheptyts'kyi, Ukrainians and Jews during and after the Holocaust." *Holocaust and Genocide Studies* 5, no. 1 (1990): 39–51.

Reykowski, Janusz. "Origin of Prosocial Motivation: Heterogeneity of Personality Development." *Studia Psychologica* 22, no. 2: 91–106.

———. "Cognitive and Motivational Prerequisites of Altruistic Helping: The Study of People Who Rescued Jews during the Holocaust." Paper presented at the Scholars Roundtable on Altruism under Nazi Terror, Princeton, March 1993.

Rice, Howard. *Reformed Spirituality*. Louisville: Westminster/John Knox, 1991.

Rigby, Paul, and Paul O'Grady. "Agape and Altruism: Debates in Theology and Social Psychology." *Journal of the American Academy of Religion* 57, no. 4 (Winter 1989): 719–38.

Ringelblum, Emmanuel. *Notes from the Warsaw Ghetto*. New York: Schocken Books, 1974.

———. *Polish-Jewish Relations during the Second World War*. Jerusalem: Yad Vashem, 1974.

Rittner, Carol, and Sondra Myers, eds. *The Courage to Care: Rescuers of Jews during the Holocaust*. New York: New York Univ. Press, 1986.

Rosenberg, Alan, and Gerald E. Myers, eds. *Echoes from the Holocaust*. Philadelphia: Temple Univ. Press, 1988.

Rosenhan, David. "The Natural Socialization of Altruistic Autonomy." In *Altruism and Helping Behavior*. Edited by J. Macauley and L. Berkowitz. New York: Academic Press, 1970.

Roskies, David G., ed. *The Literature of Destruction*. New York: Jewish Publication Society, 1989.

Rothrock, G. A. *The Huguenots*. Chicago: Nelson Hall, 1979.

Rubenstein, Richard. *After Auschwitz*. Indianapolis: Bobbs-Merrill, 1966.

Rubenstein, Richard, and John K. Roth. *Approaches to Auschwitz*. Atlanta: John Knox Press, 1987.

Ruether, Rosemary Radford. "Basic Communities: Renewal at the Roots." *Christianity and Crisis* 41 (September 21, 1981).

———. *Faith and Fratricide*. Minneapolis: Seabury Press, 1974.

Russell, Letty M. *The Future of Partnership*. Philadelphia: Westminster Press, 1979.

Ruttenberg, Katherine M. "A Righteous Gentile." *Jewish Spectator* 48, no. 2 (Summer 1983): 60–61.

Ryan, Michael. "A Simple Deed with Awesome Power." *Parade* (August 19, 1990), 4–7.

Ryan, Michael D., ed. *Human Responses to the Holocaust*. New York: Edwin Mellen Press, 1981.

Sabini, John, and Maury Silver. *Moralities of Everyday Life*. New York: Oxford Univ. Press, 1982.

Sabrin, B. F., ed. *Alliance for Murder*. New York: Sarpedon Pubs., 1991.

Salisbury, Harrison E. *The 900 Days: The Siege of Leningrad*. New York: Da Capo Press, 1990.

Sartre, Jean-Paul. *Anti-Semite and Jew.* New York: Schocken Books, 1948.

Sauvage, Pierre. Interview with Bill Moyers. Public Broadcasting System, 1989.

————. "A Most Persistent Haven: Le Chambon-Sur-Lignon." *Moment* 8, no. 9 (October 1983): 30–35.

————. "Ten Things I Would Like to Know about Righteous Conduct in Le Chambon and Elsewhere during the Holocaust." *Humboldt Journal of Social Relations* 13, no. 1–2 (1986): 252–59.

Schechter, Solomon. *Aspects of Rabbinic Theology.* New York: Schocken Books, [1909] 1961.

Schell, Jonathan. *The Fate of the Earth.* New York: Avon Books, 1982.

Schmidt, Maria. "Margit Slachta's Activities in Support of Slovakian Jewry 1942–1943." *Holocaust and Genocide Studies* 5, no. 1 (1990): 67–72.

Schott, Francis H. "Kristallnacht in Solingen." *The New York Times,* November 9, 1988.

Schulweis, Harold M. "The Bias Against Man." *Jewish Educator* 34, no. 1 (Fall 1963): 6–14.

————. Foreword to *The Altruistic Personality* by Samuel P. Oliner and Pearl M. Oliner. New York: Free Press, 1988.

————. "In Praise of Good People." *Jewish Spectator* 48, no. 1 (Spring 1983): 16–18.

————. "Remember the Righteous Redeemers." *Jewish Digest* 9, no. 1 (October 1963): 65–69.

————. "Remembering the Rescuers: The Post-Holocaust Agenda." *Christian Century* 105 (December 7, 1988): 1126–28.

————. "They Were Our Brothers' Keepers." *Moment* 11, no. 5 (May 1986): 47–50.

Schüssler Fiorenza, Elisabeth. *Bread Not Stone.* Boston: Beacon Press, 1984.

Schwarz, Irene. "The Small Still Voice." In *The Root and the Bough,* edited by Leo W. Schwarz, 189–200. New York: Rinehart and Co., 1949.

Schwarz, Leo W., ed. *The Root and the Bough.* New York: Rinehart and Co., 1949.

Scroggs, Robin. *Paul for a New Day.* Philadelphia: Fortress Press, 1977.

Segundo, Juan Luis. *The Historical Jesus of the Synoptics.* Maryknoll, N.Y.: Orbis Books, 1985.

Sereny, Gitta. *Into That Darkness.* New York: Vintage Books, 1974.

Sijes, B. A. "Several Observations concerning the Position of Jews in Occupied Holland during World War II." In *Rescue Attempts during the Holocaust,* edited by Yisrael Gutman and Efraim Zuroff, 527–53. Jerusalem: Yad Vashem, 1974.

Sinetar, Marsha. *Ordinary People as Monks and Mystics.* New York: Paulist Press, 1986.

Sivard, Ruth Leger. *World Military and Social Expenditures 1986.* Washington: World Priorities, 1986.

Sleeper, C. Freeman. *The Bible and the Moral Life.* Louisville: Westminster/John Knox, 1992.

Smedes, Lewis. *Mere Morality.* Grand Rapids: Eerdmans, 1983.

Sommerhausen, Anna. *Written in Darkness.* New York: 1946.

Staub, Ervin. "A Conception of the Determinants and Development of Altruism and Aggression: Motives, the Self, and the Environment." In *Altruism and Aggression: Social and Biological Origins.* Edited by Carolyn Zahn-Waxler et al. Cambridge: Cambridge Univ. Press, 1986.

———. *Positive Social Behavior and Morality.* New York: Academic Press, 1978.

———. "The Roots of Altruism and Heroic Rescue." *The World & I* (July 1988): 393–401.

Stein, Andre. *Quiet Heroes.* New York: New York Univ. Press, 1988.

Steinberg, Lucien. "Jewish Rescue Activities in Belgium and France." In *Rescue Attempts during the Holocaust,* edited by Yisrael Gutman and Efraim Zuroff, 603–26. Jerusalem: Yad Vashem, 1974.

———. *Not as a Lamb: The Jews Against Hitler.* Translated by M. Hunter. Farnborough, England: Saxon House, 1974.

Steinfels, Margaret O'Brien. "On the Outskirts of Auschwitz." Review of *The Convent at Auschwitz* by Wladyslaw T. Bartoszewski. *New York Times Book Review,* September 8, 1991: 15.

Stern, Fritz. *The Politics of Cultural Despair.* Berkeley: Univ. of California Press, 1961.

Suhl, Yuri. *They Fought Back: The Story of the Jewish Resistance in Nazi Europe.* New York: Schocken Books, 1975.

Syrkin, Marie. *Blessed Is the Match: The Story of Jewish Resistance.* New York: Jewish Publication Society, 1976.

Szwager, Adina Blady. *I Remember Nothing More.* New York: Pantheon Books, 1991.

Tal, Uriel. *Christians and Jews in Germany: Religion, Politics, and Ideology in the Second Reich, 1870–1914.* Ithaca: Cornell Univ. Press, 1975.

Tec, Nechama. "Altruism during World War II." In *Remembering for the Future,* edited by A. Roy Eckhardt and Alice Eckhardt, vol. 1, 542–49. New York: Pergamon Press, 1989.

———. *Dry Tears: The Story of a Lost Childhood.* New York: Oxford Univ. Press, 1984.

———. *When Light Pierced the Darkness.* New York: Oxford Univ. Press, 1986.

ten Boom, Corrie. *The Hiding Place.* New York: Bantam Books, 1971.

———. "Learning to Forgive." *Jewish Digest* 21, no. 3 (December 1975): 28–29.

———. *A Tramp for the Lord.* New York: Jove Books, 1974.

Tenenbaum, Joseph. *In Search of a Lost People.* New York: The Beechhurst Press, 1948.

Tennyson, Hallam. "Protestant Heroine of Auschwitz." *Jewish Digest* 18, no. 3 (December 1972): 50–52.

Thistlewaite, Susan B., and Toinette M. Eugene. "A Survey of Contemporary Feminist, Womanist, and Mujerista Theologies." In *Critical Review of Books in Religion 1991,* edited by Eldon Jay Epp, 1–20. Atlanta: Scholars Press, 1991.

"Thy Brother's Keeper." Produced by Suzanne St. Pierre. "60 Minutes," CBS, 1990.

Tillich, Paul. *The Courage to Be.* New Haven: Yale Univ. Press, 1952.

Trepp, Leo. *Judaism: Development and Life.* 3d ed. Belmont, Calif.: Wadsworth Publishing, 1982.

Trocmé, André. "The Law Itself Was a Lie." *Fellowship* (January 1955): 4.

———. *Jesus and the Nonviolent Revolution.* Scottdale, Pa.: Herald Press, 1973.

Tugend, Tom. "Coping with Goodness." *Hadassah* (November 1990): 18–21.

Ungar, Bela. "Surviving in Nazi Hungary." *Jewish Spectator* 34, no. 6 (June 1969): 15–18.

Vago, Bela, and George L. Mosse, eds. *Jews and Non-Jews in Eastern Europe, 1918–1945.* New York: Halsted Press, 1974.

Van Buren, Paul M. *A Theology of the Jewish-Christian Reality.* 3 vols. New York: Harper and Row, 1980–1988.

Van Ness, Peter. "To Hear the Cries: Thoughts on Philosophy, Theology and Suffering." Unpublished paper.

Vinay, Tullio. "On the Side of the Oppressed." *Ecumenical Review* 35, no. 1 (Winter 1983): 97.

Waagenar, Sam. *The Pope's Jews.* LaSalle, Ill.: Alcove Press, 1974.

Warmbrunn, Werner. *The Dutch under German Occupation, 1940–1945.* Palo Alto, Calif.: Stanford Univ. Press, 1963.

Weapons of the Spirit. Produced and directed by Pierre Sauvage. 1989.

Weinberg, Werner. "A Dutch Couple." *Christian Century* 100 (June 22–29, 1983): 611–15.

Weiss-Rosmarin, Trude. "Heroism and Martyrdom." *Jewish Spectator* 38, no. 3 (March 1973): 2–4.

Welch, Sharon D. *Communities of Resistance and Solidarity.* Maryknoll, N.Y.: Orbis Books, 1985.

———. *A Feminist Ethic of Risk.* Minneapolis: Fortress Press, 1989.

Wells, Leon. *The Janowska Road.* New York: Macmillan, 1963.

Wiener, Valerie L. "Why Righteous Gentiles Risked Their Lives to Save Jews." *Jewish Monthly* 99 (January 1985): 16–19.

Wiesel, Elie. *Night.* New York: Bantam Books, [1958] 1982.

Willis, Robert E. "What Are Christians Saying to Jews? An Analysis of Some Recent Statements from Church Bodies." In *The Netherlands and Nazi Genocide,* edited by G. Jan Colijn and Marcia S. Littell, 337–54. Lewiston, N.Y.: Edwin Mellen Press, 1992.

Wilson, Edward O. "Altruism." *Harvard Magazine* (November–December 1978): 27.

Wistrich, Robert S. *Antisemitism: The Longest Hatred.* New York: Pantheon Books, 1991.

Wolf, Jacqueline. *"Take Care of Josette": A Memoir in Defense of Occupied France.* New York: Franklin Watts, 1981.

Wolfson, Manfred. "Zum Widerstand gegen Hitler: Umriss eines Gruppenporträts deutscher Retter von Juden." *Tradition und Newbeginn: Internationale Forschungen Deutscher Geschichte im 20. Jahrhundert* 26 (1975): 391–407.

"Women's Resistance to Gestapo to Be Commemorated in Stone." *The Week in Germany* (March 13, 1992): 7.

Wyman, David. *The Abandonment of the Jews.* New York: Pantheon, 1984.

Yahil, Leni. *The Holocaust.* New York: Oxford Univ. Press, 1990.

———. *The Rescue of Danish Jewry, Test of a Democracy.* Translated by Morris Gradel. New York: Jewish Publication Society of America, 1969.

Yoder, John Howard. *The Politics of Jesus.* Grand Rapids: Eerdmans, 1972.

Zahn, Gordon. "Catholic Resistance? A Yes and a No." In *The German Church Struggle and the Holocaust*, edited by Franklin H. Littell and Hubert G. Locke, 203–37. Detroit: Wayne State Univ. Press, 1974.

Zamoyska-Panek, Christine. *Have You Forgotten?* New York: Doubleday, 1989.

Zerner, Ruth. "Holocaust: A Past That Is Also Present." *Journal of Ecumenical Studies* 16 (Summer 1979): 518–24.

Zuccotti, Susan. *The Holocaust, the French, and the Jews.* New York: Basic Books, 1993.

_____. *The Italians and the Holocaust.* New York: Basic Books, 1988.

Index of Biblical References

OLD TESTAMENT

Genesis
1:27   133
2:7   133
2:16   151
4:8-10   140
9:4   151
18:22-33   153
19:24   153

Exodus
2:1-10   45
20:13   145
22:21-24   128

Numbers
35:9-29   145

Deuteronomy
7:7   153
19:1-13   145
30:19   3

Joshua
20:1-9   145

1 Samuel
2:8   154

Psalms
91   144

Isaiah
65:25   12
45:22-23   152
26:2   153

Jeremiah
10:7   152
32:27   152

Malachi
1:11   153

NEW TESTAMENT

Matthew
2:16   146
6:10   12
7:12   139
22:34-40   137-8, 172
25:31-46   138-9
26:14-16   145

28:19-20   174

Luke
10:7   147
10:25-37   136-7

Romans
13   127

2 Corinthians
10:4   136

Galatians
3:28   134
5:5   164
5:22   164

Ephesians
5:22   174
6:10-17   136

Philippians
2:10-11   152

James
1:18   174

1 Peter
2:9   174

Revelation
13   128
20:4   174

Index of Modern Authors

Abramowicz, D., 206 n.90
Adorno, T., 182 n.45
Aleichem, S., 60
Allan, A., 201 n.53, 224 n.94
Allport, G., 183 n.45
Altus, A., 27
Arad, Y., 191 n.43
Arendt, H., 182 n.45, 183 n.46
Ariel, J., 194 n.7
Ariel, Y., 220 n.17
Avni, H., 74, 199 n.36

Baron, L., ix, 107, 130, 190 n.16, 56, 193 n.2, 209 n.1, 217 n.111, 219 n.132, 220 nn.9, 17; 221 n.23, 225 n.5
Barreiro, A., 218 n.123
Bartoszewski, W., 189 n.5, 194 n.7
Bauer, Y., 108, 125, 173, 178 nn.14, 15; 179 n.18, 180 n.22, 186 n.52, 187 nn.70, 82; 188 nn.86, 96; 190 n.16, 207 n.95, 209 n.1, 215 n.80, 218 n.126, 220 n.15
Baum, G., 182 n.45, 217 n.107, 219 n.133
Bauminger, A., 198 nn.30, 32, 34; 202 nn.57, 58, 205 n.82, 206 n.90, 207 nn.93-95, 208 nn.96, 97; 209 nn.98, 1; 216 n.90, 218 n.117, 219 n.132
Beauchamp. T., 226 n.31
Bedein, D., 203 n.69
Bedrossyan, M., 178 n.6

Bejski, M., 199 nn.35, 37; 203 n.69, 207 n.95, 208 n.97, 209 n.1, 214 n.44, 216 n.90, 218 nn.116, 124
Beker, C., 227 n.54
Berenbaum, M., 188 n.98, 224 n.2
Berkovits, E., 117, 182 n.44, 209 n.1
Bertelsen., A., 198 n.34
Bethge, E., 222 n.48
Bialik, C., 45
Bierman, J., 207 n.94
Birch, B., 182 n.42, 183 n.46, 191 n.54, 215 n.68, 218 n.123, 226 n.40, 227 n.62, 228 n.67
Block G., 112, 115, 164, 185 n.44, 205 nn.70, 87; 209 n.1, 213 nn.17, 20; 216 nn.86-87, 90; 218 n.124, 219 n.140, 220 nn.9, 15; 224 n.102
Bondi, R., 215 n.68
Bonhoeffer, D., 130, 173, 219 n.128, 222 nn.40, 45
Borchsenius, P., 161-62, 198 n.34,
Borg, M., 227 n.64
Bowman, S., 197 n.23, 205 n.82
Brandt, W., 161, 227 n.49
Breines, P., 226 n.33
Breznitz, S., 209 n.1
Brown, R. M., 209 n.1, 216 n.86, 218 nn.115, 119

Browning, C., 28, 183 n.46, 187 n.75, 190 n.23
Brueggemann, W., 227 n.64

Calvin, J., 122-25
Camus, A., 162
Carpi, D., 162, 197 n.24
Cargas, H., 182 n.44
Chambers, M., 177 n.5
Chary, F., 208 n.96
Childress, J., 215 n.68, 226 n.31
Clorfene, C., 225 nn.8, 10
Colijn, G., 223 n.57
Comte, A., 211 n.2
Conquest, R., 178 nn.8-9; 189 n.4, 190 n.20
Coopersmith, S., 93-95, 209 n.1, 214 n.60, 215 n.66, 216 nn.87, 90; 217 n.103
Cox, H., 218 n.123
Crossan, J. D., 107

Dobroszycki, 185 n.43
Darley, J., 214 n.57
Davies, A., 178 n.45
Dawidowicz, L., 25, 178 n.15, 183 nn.46, 5, 6; 184 nn.8, 10; 184 nn.14, 18, 22, 30, 31; 185 nn.35, 37, 188, 43, 47; 186 nn.51, 52, 60; 187 nn.67, 68, 70, 85; 188 nn.86, 96; 193 n.5, 199 n.40, 208 n.96
DeJong, P., 131, 220 nn.9, 13; 222 nn.45, 53; 223 n.64
Dietrich, D., 120, 220 n.9, 222 nn.40, 45; 223 nn.70, 71, 72, 85; 224 nn.104, 111
Dodd, C. H., 227 n.64
Donat, A., 185 n.43, 188 nn.105, 106
Dovidio, J., 211 n.2
Drucker, M., 112, 115, 164, 185 n.44, 204 n.70, 205 n.87, 209 n.1, 213 nn.17, 20; 216 nn.86, 87, 90; 218 n.124, 219 n.140, 220 nn.9, 15, 224 n.102
Dworzecki, M., 195 n.9

Eckardt, A., 182 nn.44, 45; 209 n.1, 222 n.45
Eckardt, A. R., 182 nn.44, 45; 209 n.1, 222 n.45
Eichel, M., 59
Eisenberg, N., 215 n.82
Eldredge, R., 212 n.4
Eliach, Y., 192 n.70
Epp, E. J., 219 n.141
Ericksen, R., 174
Eugene, T., 219 n.141
Ezratty, H., 224 n.98

Fabre, E., 194 n.7

Farley, M., 226 n.45
Fasching, D., 182 n.45
Feigenbaum, M. J., 63
Fein, H., 19, 109, 134, 179 n.21, 187 n.85, 188 n.86, 193 n.2, 209 n.1, 109, 218 nn.126, 127; 220 nn.9, 12; 222 n.40, 134
Fersen-Osten, R., 193 n.1, 197 nn.25, 26; 200 nn.41, 47; 201 n.56, 204 n.71
Fest, J., 183 n.46
Fiorenza, E. S., 228 n.67
Fisher, E., 181 n.33, 197 n.24
Fitzgibbon, C., 183 n.46
Flannery, E., 182 n.45
Fleischner, E., x, 94, 100, 109, 115, 119, 120, 164, 165, 209 n.1, 215 n.66, 216 n.90, 218 n.124, 222 n.45, 223 n.59, 224 nn.114, 117
Flender, H., 198 n.34
Fogelman, E., 98, 103, 106, 111, 112, 115, 144, 163, 164, 209 n.1, 212 n.5, 213 n.28, 214 n.35, 216 nn.87, 90; 218 n.124, 219 n.140, 222 n.40, 223 nn.73, 80; 224 nn.98, 99, 109
Fowl, S., 228 n.67
Fowler, J., 218 nn.114, 121
Frank, A., 81
Freuchen, P., 198 n.34
Friedlander, S., 183 n.47, 228 n.69
Friedman, P., 98, 146, 185 n.48, 187 n.62, 188 nn.86, 103, 107; 189 n.9, 194 n.6, 197 nn.26, 27; 198 nn.30, 32, 34; 200 nn.41, 44; 201 n.55, 202 n. 57, 205 n.86, 206 n.88, 209 n.1, 216 n.90, 217 nn.106, 108, 111; 218 nn.124, 126, 128, 132; 222 nn.40, n.45; 223 nn.60, 72, 86; 224 nn.98, 104
Furet, F., 187 n.75
Furnish, V., 227 n.54

Gager, J., 182 n.45
Gelbach, E., 220 n.15
Gilbert, M., 43, 66, 157, 177 n.2, 178 n.15, 184 n.16, 17, 19, 21, 23, 25; 185 nn.33, 39, 47; 186 nn.56, 58, 59, 60; 187 nn.63, 64, 65, 66, 69, 77, 79; 188 nn.87, 89, 90, 94; 189 nn.5, 10, 13, 14; 190 nn.17, 24, 31, 32, 33, 35; 191 nn.41, 42, 44, 51, 52, 56, 57, 58, 60; 192 nn.63, 64, 71, 74; 196 n.21, 199 n.39, 220 nn.4, 6; 224 n.110
Gilligan., C., 113
Gitelman, Z., 189 n.5
Glatstein, J., 185 n.48, 188 n.103
Goergen, D., 227 n.64
Goldstein, B., 188 n.102
Goodin, R., 216 n.89
Gordon, S., 97, 209 n.1

Greenberg, I., x, 182 n.44
Grobman, A., 194 n.8
Gross, L., 191 n.47, 195 nn.15, 16; 196
    nn.20, 22; 199 n.35, 200 nn.42, 43, 44; 202
    nn.61, 62; 203 n.63, 204 nn.70, 73; 205
    n.80, 208 n.96, 222 n.45, 224 n.105
Grossman, F., 93, 95, 115, 209 n.1, 216
    nn.87, 90; n.118; 222 n.40
Gustafson, J., 155
Gutman, Y., 191 n.43, 193 n.5, 194 n.7, 195
    nn.9, 11; 196 nn.17, 22; 197 n.24, 198 n.28

Haas, P., 183 n.46
Haesler, A., 199 n.37
Hallie, P., 136-37, 144, 194 n.8, 203 n.69,
    220 n.15, 221 nn.21, 30, 36; 126,
    223nn.67, 69, 74, 75, 76, 86; 224 nn.112,
    114, 115
Halperin, M., 203 n.68, 205 nn.85, 87
Harrison, B., 219 n.143
Hauerwas, S., 182 n.43, 215 n.68, 218
    n.123, 227 n.62
Hay, M., 182 n.45
Hellman, P., 191 nn.47, 60; 195 n.10, 197
    nn.26, 27; 200 nn.41, 44, 45; 201 nn.52,
    53, 54, 55; 202 n.59, 203 n.68, 204 nn.70,
    73; 205 nn.76, 80; 220 n.9, 224 n.95, 226
    n.30
Henry, F., 97, 98, 209 n.1, 216 n.90, 217
    n.106, 218 n.124
Hertzberg, A., 182 n.45
Herzer, I., 197 n.24
Hesselink, I., 221 n.23
Hilberg, R., 55, 61, 179 nn.16, 17; 180
    nn.24, 25, 26; 183 n.46, 183 nn.3, 4; 184
    nn.7, 21, 20; 185 nn.37, 40, 49; 186 n.53,
    187 n.70, 188 nn.86, 96; 189 nn.10, 11;
    190 nn.15, 17, 22, 25, 26, 27, 28
Hoffman, M., 212 n.10, 215 n.82
Höhne, H., 183 n.46
Höss, R., 183 n.46
Hovannisian, R., 178 n.6
Howes, C., 212 n.4
Huneke, D., 94, 95, 103, 109-110, 207 n.92,
    209 n.1, 214 n.56, 216 nn.82, 87, 90; 223
    nn.79, 86, 87
Hunt, M. 179 n.21, 212 n.3, 214 n.57, 222
    n.45, 223 nn.65, 84
Huttenberg, H., 196 n.22

Ilton, I., 194 n.7
Ingber, A., 203 n.68
Iranek-Osmecki, K., 191 nn.43, 60; 192
    nn.63, 68, 75; 194 n.7, 203 n.69, 205

nn.81, 82, 83, 86; 226 n.43
Isaac, J., 119, 182 n.45

Jegstrup, E., 209 n.1, 218 nn.126, 127; 222
    n.40
Jones, G., 228 n.67
Joutard, P., 203 n.69, 226 n.30

Kagan, J., 212 n.4
Kammer, F., 56, 62
Kanabus, F., 201 n.49
Kaplan, C., 29
Katz, J. 182 n.45
Kelley, J. P., 222 nn.45, 49, 50, 52; 223 n.67
Keneally, T., 207 n.95
Kermish, J., 191 n.47, 194 n.7, 200 n.46, 205
    nn.77, 87
Klee, E., 183 n.46
Klose, K., 185 n.48
Klukowski, Z., 157
Kogan, S., 53, 186 n.57
Kolbik, S., 198 n.34
Krakowski, S., 191 n.42
Kranzler, D., 196 n.22
Krausnick, H., 34, 186 n.53
Kulka, O. D., 179 n.20, 180 n.23
Kuper, L., 178 n.6
Kurek, E., 209 n.1

Landes, D., 194 n.8
Latané, B., 214 n.57
Latour, A., 194 n.7
Lauritzen, P., 219 n.143
LeBoucher, F., 198 n.32
Leech, K., 170
Lebacqz, K., 219 n.138
Leuner, H. D., 194 n.8
Levi, P., 185 n.48
Levin, D., 190 nn.17, 37; 206 n.90, 226 n.39
Lewinowna, Z., 194 n.7
Lewy, G., 183 n.47, 228 n.69
Lichten, J., 160, 192 n.75
Lifton, R.J., 179 n.21, 183 n.46, 187 n.81
Lincoln, B., 178 n.7, 190 n.19
Linn, E., 194 n.7
Littell, M. S., 222 n.57, 224 n.119
Littell, F., 182 n.44, 183 n.47, 221 n.26, 222
    n.48
Locke, H., 182 n.44, 183 n.47, 222 nn.46, 48
London, P., 94, 103, 115, 209 n.1, 215 n.66,
    216 nn.87, 89; 217 n.112, 224 n.98
Luther, M., 226 n.41
Lynne, E., 196 n.18

Macauley, J., 209 n.1, 211 nn.2, 212 n.4

MacIntyre, A., 215 n.68, 227 n.62
Macquarrie, J., 215 n.68
Margaliot, A., 196 nn.17, 22
Marrus, M., 2, 34, 43, 178 nn.10, 11, 12, 14; 179 n.20, 183 n.6, 184 nn.8, 10; 185 nn.36, 38, 41; 186 n.53, 187 nn.73, 74; 188 n.95, 188 n.104, 189 n.12, 194 nn.7, 8
Mason, H. L., 209 n.1, 218 n.127, 222 n.45
McKim, D., 221 nn.22, 23, 27
Meilander, G., 227 n.62
Melden, A. I., 227 n.46
Metz, J. B., 219 n.133
Midlarsky, M., 209 n.1, 217 nn.108, 110
Miller, J., 42
Miller, S., 215 n.82
Milton, S., 194 n.8, 208 n.96, 216 n.90, 217 n.108, 218 nn.116, 124
Monroe, K., 110, 115, 179 n.21, 209 n.1, 215 n.77, 216 nn.86, 90
Morley, J., 183 n.47, 228 n.69
Mosse, G., 182 n.45, 184 nn.8, 9
Myers, S., 181 n.33, 207 n.92, 209 n.1

Nalkowska, S., 64, 66
Neal, M.A., 179 n.21, 180 n.23
Neshamit, S., 156, 191, n.60, 205 nn.82, 84; 206 n.90
Neuhaus, R., 165, 226 n.42
Niebuhr, H. R., 227 n.60
Niebuhr, R., 226 n.41
Noakes, J., 183 nn.1, 5; 186 nn.50, 51, 54, 55; 207 n.92
Novak, D., 11, 225 nn.8, 9, 10, 11, 16

Ochs, A., 190 n.29, 192 n.62
Ofer, D., 193 n.3, 197 n.23
Ogletree, T., 228 n.67
Oline, P. 203 n. 69, 221 nn.30, 36
Oliner, P. and Oliner S., 73, 93-96, 98-102, 104, 106-9, 111-113, 115, 121, 126, 133, 140, 142, 163, 164, 169, 179 n.21, 180 n.24, 181 n.40, 189 n.8, 190 n.16, 192 nn.68, 73; 195 nn.12, 14; 200 n.41, 203 nn.68, 69; 205 n.83, 208 n.96, 209 n.1, 215 n.67, 216 nn.85, 87, 88, 90; 218 nn.124, 125; 220 n.9, 223 n.86, 224 n.102
Olweus, D., 213 n.11
Ormson, J. O., 227 n.46
Osterhaven, M. E., 221 nn.22, 27
Outka, G., 161, 226 n.45

Paldiel, M., 104, 107, 115, 119, 138, 179 n.21, 180 n.23, 181 nn.28, 31, 32, 37; 190 n.34, 55, 191 n.47, 192 nn.75, 82; 200 nn.46, 48; 209 n.1, 213 nn.30, 31; 216

n.90, 217 n.112, 218 n.124, 219 n.145, 220 n.15, 223 n.78, 224 n.91, 225 nn.7, 13
Papanek, E., 194 n.7
Parkes, J., 182 n.45
Paul, A., 189 n.4
Paulowicz, S., 185 n.48
Pawlikowski, J., 182 n.45
Paxton, R., 194 nn.7, 8
Peker, M., 191 n.58
Peterson, L., 213 n.11
Pinchewski, R., 55, 56, 60
Pinkus, O., 205 n.82
Poliakov, L., 182 n.45, 184 n.32, 185 n.38, 186 n.54, 189 n.12, 190 n.16, 197 n.24
Pridham, G., 183 nn.1, 5; 186 nn.50, 51, 54, 55; 207 n.92

Ramati, A., 194 n.8, 202 n.57, 222 n.40, 223 n.67
Rasmussen, L., 182 n.42, 183 n.46, 191 n.54, 215 n.68, 218 n.123, 219 n.128, 226 n.40, 227 n.62
Rausch, D., 14
Redlich, S., 190 n.18, 226 n.38
Reykowski, J., 209 n.1, 217 n.112
Rittner, C., 181 n.33, 207 n.92, 209 n.1
Rogalsky, Y., 225 nn.8, 10
Rosenblum, M., 54
Rosenhan., D., 212 n.4
Rubenstein, R., 124, 182 n.44
Ruether, R. R., 182 n.45, 218 n.123, 221 n.26
Russell, L., 217 n.101
Roth, J. K., 182 n.44
Ruttenberg, K., 208 n.96
Ryan, M., 220 n.9

Sabille, J., 197 n.24
Sabini, J., 183 n.46
Sabrin, B. F., 190 nn.21, 37
Salisbury, H., 188 n.99
Salzstein, H., 212 n.10
Sartre, J. P., 182 n.45
Sauvage, P., 100, 119, 127, 168, 209 n.1, 214 n.40, 216 n.86, 221 n.34, 223 n.86
Schechter, S., 225 nn.15, 16, 17, 18, 19, 20; 227 nn.52, 53
Schell, J., 178 n.13
Schott, F., 184 n.26
Schulweis, H., 9, 10, 149, 150, 202 n.57, 206 nn.87, 88; 207 n.92, 226 n.32
Schwarz, I., 188 nn.93, 102; 192 n.72, 206 n.88
Schwarz, L., 188 n.93

Scroggs, R., 227 n.54
Segundo, J. L., 227 n.64
Shyapeltoh, V., 191 n.56
Sijes, B. A., 195 n.11, 204 n.70
Silver, M., 183 n.46
Sivard, R. L., 177 n.5, 178 nn.7, 12
Sleeper, C. F., 228 n.67
Smedes, L., 221 n.25
Somerhausen., A., 194 n.7
Spielberg, S., 207 n.95
Staub, E., 179 n.21, 215 n.82, 216 n.87
Stein, A., 114, 139, 220 n.9, 221 n.21, 223
  nn.61, 86; 224 nn.92, 98, 101, 103, 113,
  116, 118, 119
Steinberg, L., 193 n.3, 194 n.6, 198 n.29,
  204 n.74
Steinfels, M. 189 n.5
Syrkin, M., 198 n.29

Tal, V., 182 n.45
Tec, N., 58, 61, 62, 65, 95, 98, 99-100, 111,
  112, 115, 119, 143-44, 163-64, 189 nn.3, 7;
  191 nn.50, 55; 200 nn.41, 45, 46, 47, 48;
  201 nn.50, 51; 203 n.64, 205 nn.77, 78;
  206 n.88, 207 n.93, 209 n.1, 215 nn.66, 75;
  104, 216 nn.86, 87, 90; 106, 217 n.111, 218
  n.124, 220 nn.3, 5; 223 nn.63, 88; 224
  nn.90, 95, 120; 227 n.59
Ten Boom, C., 143-144, 171, 203 n.67, 204
  n.72, 209 n.99, 213 n.16, 220 n.17, 222
  n.40
Tennyson, H., 221 n.35
Thistlewaite, S., 219 n.141
Trepp, L., 153
Tugend, T., 193 n.4

Ungar, B., 207 n.94

Van Buren, P., 182 n.45

Waagenar, S., 194 n.8
Warmbrunn. W., 194 n.7
Wdowinski, D., 190 n.31
Weinberg, W., 201 n.53
Weiss-Rosmarin, T., 198 n.34
Welch, S., 218 n.123, 219 n.133
West, C., 222 n.46
Wiener, V. L., 224 n.98
Wiesel, E., 193 n.1
Wilhelm, H. H., 34, 186 n.53
Wilson, E. O., 179 n.21
Wistrich, R., 182 n.45
Wolf, J., 195 nn.13, 15; 197 nn.25, 27; 198
  n.28, 200 nn.41, 47; 201 nn.53, 56; 206
  nn.89, 91
Wolfson, M., 97, 98, 209 n.1

Yahil, L., 179 n.17, 183 nn.5, 6; 184 nn.7, 9,
  11, 13, 18, 20; 185 n.42, 186 n.60, 187
  nn.78, 79, 80, 83, 84, 85; 188 nn.86, 91,
  92; 193 n.5, 198 n.34
Yoder, J. H., 227 n.64

Zabecki, F., 190 n.33
Zahn, G., 183 n.47
Zahn-Waxler, 216 n.87
Zamoyska-Panek, C., 189 n.6, 200 n.41
Zuccotti, S., 197 n.24
Zuroff, E., 191 n.43, 193 n.5, 194 n.7, 195
  nn.9, 11, 196 nn.17, 22; 197 n.24, 198
  n.28

Index of Rescuers

Abel, R., 208 n.96

Barraud, G., 137
Bartulovic, D., 202 n.57
Bartulovic, O., 202 n.57
Benoit, M., 74-75
Bertelsen, A., 198 n.34
Binder, A., 88
Bonhoeffer, D., 75, 132, 219 n.128
Borchsenius, P., 161, 162
Borkowska, A., 206 n.88
Bouwma, B., 143
Busse, O., 207 n.95, 208 n.96

Celka, A., 144
Celis, H., 141, 201 n.53
Chaumat, H., 201 nn.52, 53, 54
Christensen, A., 75, 198 n.34
Cohn, M., 197 n.27
Collins, M. 195 n.13
Coward, C., 88-89

Daman-Scaglione, J., 201 n.55
de Graaf, N. H., 131, 133
Donadille, M., 128
Duckwitz, G., 75

Foley, F., 73
Freuchen, P., 198 n.34

Gies, M., 203 n.65

Gotautas, B., 204 n.75
Graebe, H., 138, 207 n.92, 209 n.1
Grueninger, P., 75

Hautval, A., 208 n.97
Hedenqvist, G., 73
Helmrich, E., 208 n.96
Horska, H., 143

Jaromirska, L., 141, 201 nn.52, 53; 205 n.76
Jauch, F., 143
Jerneitzig, R., 195 n.15

Kmita, K., 84
Kmita, M., 84
Kossak-Szczucka, Z., 138-39, 140
Kutorgiene, H., 158

Laporterie, R., 74
Le Boucher, F., 198 n.32
Lichtenberg, B., 138
Luckner, G., 194 n.8

Macineviciene, A., 205 n.84
Macineviciene, M., 205 n.84
Madritsch, J., 87
Maltzan, M., 204 n.70
Mendes, A., 76
Miedema, P., 139, 140, 145, 146
Misiuna, W., 87
Miskotte, K. H., 131-2

Mother Maria (E. Skobtsova), 89, 202 n.57

Palatucci, G., 208 n.96
Perlasca, G., 207 n.94
Peshev, D., 208 n.96
Popovici, T., 208 n.96
Preysing, C., 135
Pritchard, M., 83, 195 nn.10, 11; 200 n.40, 201 n.54
Pulholsky, A., 160

Reviczky, I., 88
Ros, L., 202 n.60
Roslan, A., 114, 203 n.68, 205 nn.85, 87
Roslan, M., 205 n.87

Sagan, J., 136, 140
Saliège, J-G., 134-35
Sarna, L., 165
Schindler, O., 207 n.95

Simaite, O., 85-86, 150
Skobtsova, E. (see Mother Maria)
Sletten, I., 198 n.34
Socha, L., 118
Soroka, T., 138

Ten Boom, C., 64, 81, 121-122, 143-44, 209 n.99
Théas, P-M., 132
Theis, E., 137
Trocmé, A., 127-28, 135-37, 144, 145-46

Wallenberg, R., 42, 150, 207 n.94
Weidner, J., 220 n.15
Westerweel, J., 74, 202 n.58
Westerweel, W., 202 n.58
Wijsmuller-Meyer, G., 196 n.18
Wirkus, J., 202 n.59
Wirkus, K., 202 n.59